ECONOMICS AS AN
ART OF THOUGHT

G. L. S. Shackle, FBA (1903–1992) was one of the leading economic philosophers of the twentieth century, who made major contributions to the theory of choice under uncertainty, to economic method and the history of economic thought, and to monetary and macroeconomic theory. His work became legendary not only for the purity of its subjectivist thought but also for the literary quality of his numerous books and articles. As the chapters in this volume make clear, he has been a major influence to economists of the Austrian, behavioural and Post Keynesian schools of economics, as well as linking with aspects of institutionalist economics and hermeneutic method.

The volume was originally conceived by Stephan Boehm, Stephen Frowen and John Pheby as a ninetieth birthday present for Professor Shackle. Sadly, he died before reaching this age and initial versions of some of the chapters were instead presented at a conference to celebrate his life and work, held in Aldeburgh in 1992.

Since Shackle's death interest in his work has continued to grow, sometimes in new directions. Shackle's extensive writings and correspondence have recently been made available, revealing not only how he worked and developed his ideas, but also the remarkable extent to which he was a man of letters.

In bringing the volume to the publication stage, Peter Earl and Stephen Frowen have sought where possible to ensure that the original chapters are placed in the context of the latest literature. They have also incorporated several brand new chapters that relate his work to complexity theory and management accounting, and present a fascinating journey into the Shackle archive.

Peter E. Earl is Professor of Economics at Lincoln University, Canterbury, New Zealand. **Stephen F. Frowen**, formerly Bundesbank Professor at the Free University of Berlin, is Honorary Research Fellow in the Department of Economics, University College London.

Professor G.L.S. Shackle, FBA
14 July 1903–3 March 1992
Photograph by Ramsey and Muspratt, Cambridge, 1949

ECONOMICS AS AN ART OF THOUGHT

Essays in memory of G. L. S. Shackle

Edited by

Peter E. Earl and Stephen F. Frowen

London and New York

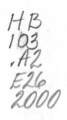
First published 2000
by Routledge
11 New Fetter Lane, London EC4P 4EE

Simultaneously published in the USA and Canada
by Routledge
9 West 35th Street, New York, NY 10001

Routledge is an imprint of the Taylor & Francis Group

Typeset in Garamond by Peter E. Earl
Printed and bound in Great Britain by
St Edmundsbury Press, Bury St Edmunds, Suffolk

British Library Cataloguing in Publication Data
A catalogue record for this book is available from the British Library

Library of Congress Cataloging in Publication Data
Economics as an art of thought : essays in memory of G. L. S. Shackle /
[edited by] Peter E. Earl and Stephen F. Frowen.
p.   cm.
Includes bibliographical references and index.
1. Economics–Great Britain–History–20th century.
2. Economics–Methodology–History–20th century.
3. Keynsian economics. 4. Shackle, G. L. S. (George Lennox Sharman), 1903–
II. Frowen, Stephen F. III. Earl, Peter E.
HB103.A2 E26 2000   99-059596
330–dc21

ISBN 0–415–10162–X

FOR CATHERINE SHACKLE
WITH GREAT ADMIRATION

CONTENTS

CONTENTS

FIGURES

CONTRIBUTORS

Moacir dos Anjos, Jr, Senior Researcher, Fundação Joaquim Nabucco, Insituto de Cultura, Rua Henrique Dia, 609, 52010-100 Recife – PE, Brazil.

Kathleen Cann, Manuscripts Department, Cambridge University Library, West Road, Cambridge, CB3 9DR, UK.

Victoria Chick, Professor of Economics, Department of Economics, University College London, Gower Street, London, WC1E 6BT, UK.

Kenneth C. Cleaver, Lecturer in Economics and Accounting, Department of Economics and Accounting, University of Liverpool, Eleanor Rathbone Building, Bedford Street South, Liverpool, L69 7ZA, UK.

Peter E. Earl, Professor of Economics, Commerce Division, P.O. Box 84, Lincoln University, Canterbury, New Zealand. This volume was completed while he was Visiting Professor, Department of Economics, University of Queensland, St Lucia, Queensland 4072, Australia.

Stephen F. Frowen, formerly Bundesbank Professor at the Free University of Berlin, is Honorary Research Fellow in the Department of Economics, University College London, Gower Street, London, WC1E 6BT, UK. He is also Senior Research Associate, Von Huegel Institute, St. Edmund's College Cambridge, and External Professorial Research Associate, Institute for German Studies, University of Birmingham.

CONTRIBUTORS

G. C. Harcourt, Professor Emeritus, University of Adelaide, Emeritus Reader in the History of Economic Theory, University of Cambridge, Emeritus Fellow, Jesus College, Cambridge, CB5 8BL, UK.

Shaun P. Hargreaves Heap, Senior Lecturer in Economics, School of Economic and Social Studies, University of East Anglia, Norwich NR4 7TJ, UK.

Geoffrey M. Hodgson, Research Professor, The Business School, University of Hertfordshire, Mangrove Road, Hertford, Hertfordshire SG13 8QF, UK.

Donald W. Katzner, Professor of Economics, University of Massachusetts/Amherst, Amherst, MA 01003, USA.

J. A. Kregel, Professor of Economics, Dipartimento di Scienze Economiche, Università di Bologna, Strada Maggiore, 45, Bologna, Italy. He is also a consultant to the United Nations.

Stephen C. Littlechild, Honorary Professor, Department of Industrial Economics and Business Studies, University of Birmingham, P.O. Box 363, Birmingham, BT15 2TT, UK.

Brian J. Loasby, Emeritus Professor of Management Economics, Department of Economics, University of Stirling, Stirling, FK9 4LA, Scotland, UK.

Stephen D. Parsons, Principal Lecturer, Department of Economics and Social Sciences, De Montfort University, Hammerwood Gate, Kents Hill, Milton Keynes MK7 6HP, UK.

Jason Potts, Lecturer in Economics, Department of Economics, University of Queensland, St Lucia, Queensland 4072, Australia.

Jochen Runde, Lecturer in Economics, Judge Institute of Management Studies, Trumpington Street, Cambridge CB2 1AG, UK.

Claudio Sardoni, Professor of Economics (professore associato), Dipartimento di Scienze Economiche, Università degli Studî di Roma 'La Sapienza', Via Cesalpino 12 –00161, Rome, Italy.

Ian Steedman, Research Professor in Economics, Department of Economics, Manchester Metropolitan University, Tylecote Building, Cavendish Street, Manchester M15 6BG, UK.

INTRODUCTION

Peter E. Earl and Stephen F. Frowen

1 G. L. S. SHACKLE: HIS LIFE AND WORK

'George Lennox Sharman Shackle, 1903–1992, Economist Philosopher Writer.' Thus reads the inscription on his tombstone in the churchyard of the Parish Church of St. Peter and St. Paul in Aldeburgh, Suffolk. Together with his own prayer on the tombstone

> O Lord I beseech Thee
> Shape my thought to beauty[1]

one gets some feeling of the outstanding person and wide-ranging scholar that George Shackle was. A man of both tremendous depth and sound knowledge, a fundamental thinker in his chosen fields, yet always ready to acknowledge and praise even the smallest achievements of others.

George Shackle was born on 14 July 1903 and educated at the Perse School, Cambridge. His intellectual Cambridge family was of modest means — his father Robert Walker Shackle, a mathematician, successfully coached John Maynard Keynes for a scholarship at Eton — and lacked the funds at the time for their son's university education. He therefore started his working life as a humble bank clerk at the age of seventeen to be followed by ten years as a schoolmaster. During that time he took his external B.A. (London) degree. It was in 1931 when he received the 'sealed orders' for his career by reading Keynes's *A Treatise on Money* and *Prices and Production* by Friedrich A. von Hayek. 'In these books', he stated, 'I embarked on a thrilling voyage' (Shackle 1983: 231).

At this time, as an outsider, he published an article in a London School of Economics student magazine. The paper startled the 'natives' at the L.S.E. to such an extent that the Registrar wrote to Shackle with the suggestion to apply for a Leverhulme Research Scholarship, which under normal circumstances should have gone to an internal L.S.E. student.[2]

The application was successful and the Leverhulme Research Scholarship enabled him to read for a Ph.D. at the L.S.E. He was expected to start at the beginning of the Autumn Term 1934, but not wanting to let his employer down, he did not arrive there until 1 January 1935. George Shackle's After-Dinner-Speech at the 1984 conference in his honour contains a fascinating account of his L.S.E. experience and of a joint seminar at Cambridge in 1935, for research students at the L.S.E. and some from Oxford, when Joan Robinson and Richard Kahn discussed with them the theme of Keynes's *General Theory*.[3] It was this experience which, with the understanding approval of Hayek — his supervisor — made him change the subject of his research 'to translate', as he said, 'the *General Theory* into Myrdalian lines' (Shackle 1990: 194). He was granted his Ph.D. in 1937 and the thesis was published in 1938 entitled *Expectations, Investments and Income.*.

In 1937 George Shackle went to New College Oxford and took a D.Phil. in 1940 while working at the Oxford University Institute of Statistics. After a short spell at the University of St. Andrews in 1939, he spent the war years at the Admiralty and Cabinet Office in Sir Winston Churchill's Statistical Branch, joining the Economic Section of the Cabinet Secretariat in 1945 It was in 1950 by the time he returned to academic life, as Reader in Economic Theory at the University of Leeds. The Brunner Professorship of Economic Science in the University of Liverpool he held from 1951 until his retirement in 1969 when he became Professor Emeritus.

But 'retirement' to George simply meant having more time for writing. And, indeed, his published work even since his retirement has been phenomenal, except for a few years during the second half of the 1970s when his first wife Susan was suffering from a prolonged illness finally leading to her death in April 1978. In a letter to Stephen Frowen, dated 19 January 1979, he wrote: 'All this turmoil has left me rather drained of strength for the ordinary obligations of life', but also talked of 'a new source of serenety and hope which has again given my life some sense of purpose'[4] The source of serenity and hope was Catherine, George's second wife. They were married at the end of January 1979. In his letter to Stephen Frowen of 19 June 1979, in which he mentions his marriage, he adds: 'During my lonely time last summer, I tried to work, but found it fruitless. I am now very well cared for and have made what I hope will be a fresh start at some writing.[5] The essays he then wrote, published as *Business, Time and Thought* reveal his usual and in some cases quite exceptional brilliance and insight — a scholar looking back and pondering, as one of us has elsewhere noted, 'on the basic problems of our subject in general terms' (Earl 1993: 260). How eternally grateful we should be to Catherine Shackle, without whose care and encouragement George would have been deprived of the strength needed to produce this work at his age. Despite his failing eyesight, he was still reviewing books, which had to be read to him, during the last year or two of his life. And even on his deathbed, a few days before he died, his mind was alert, and pressing Stephen Frowen's hand he said: 'Stephen, I must get better, there is still so much I want to do.'

The history of the present volume goes back to the six months preceding George Shackle's death on 3 March 1992, caused by complications following a fall in the early Autumn of 1991 in which he broke a femur. Around this time, Stephan Boehm was in the process of sending out invitations, on behalf of himself, Stephen Frowen and John Pheby, for contributions to be specifically written for a *Festschrift* to mark George's ninetieth birthday. At that stage, no title had been settled upon for the book and many potential contributors, who responded swiftly and with enthusiasm, were unaware that George's health had taken a turn for the worse.

When Stephen Frowen visited George at Ipswich Hospital, together with George's wife Catherine, George expressed his regret never again to be able to attend any of the Malvern Political Economy Conferences,[6] which he enjoyed and where he felt happy in the company of colleagues he appreciated and who loved and admired him. Stephen Frowen responded immediately by saying that if he should really feel unable to travel to Malvern, then the Malvern Conference would come to him and would be held in Aldeburgh. George beamed at this possibility and asked Catherine and Stephen to leave him alone for a little while to think of a suitable topic. When they returned he had written on a little piece of paper the title 'Economics as an Art of Thought'.

This then became the subject of a Malvern Conference in Aldeburgh intended to be a celebration of his ninetieth birthday in 1993. Sadly, George died not long before reaching this age, but the conference was held nevertheless in his memory, coinciding with a Memorial Service at the Aldeburgh Parish Church in September 1992, to celebrate his life and work.[7] Initial versions of some of the chapters below were originally presented at this conference. Thus the book originally envisaged as a *Festschrift* was to become in part a volume of conference proceedings under the editorship of Stephan Boehm, Stephen Frowen and John Pheby. Unfortunately, a number of factors prevented Stephan Boehm from completing his task. The two editors of the present volume took over the project at the beginning of 1999, starting more or less from scratch.

The chapters presented here attempt to project, apply and where possible develop further the ideas which George Shackle has expounded in his own books, his numerous journal articles and contributions to collected volumes. Where possible, we have sought to ensure that original chapters have been placed in the context of the latest literature. We have also incorporated several brand new chapters that relate his work to complexity theory and to management accounting and provide a fascinating journey into the Shackle archive at Cambridge University Library. It is an attempt, we hope, George Shackle would have welcomed. By coincidence, the book's belated time 'in press' overlaps with the ninetieth birthday of Catherine Shackle, and it is of course to Catherine that we are delighted to dedicate it.

2 THE ESSENCE OF SHACKLE'S THOUGHT

In editing the present volume we have tried to follow guidelines recommended by George Shackle for the 1984 Shackle Conference. The earlier conference focused on what Stephen Frowen, then working at the University of Surrey, encapsulated as Shackle's efforts to make 'a theory of business as essentially an imaginative process',[8] When he wrote to Shackle propounding the idea, Shackle replied (10 November 1982) with the suggestion that, 'To do its proper job, it [the conference] should of course include a variety of potential creative critics', adding in his modest way, 'if there are people who would think such a task worthwhile'. He continued that 'in order to be fertile, the discussion should bear on certain questions where I have most radically discarded the received notions of the purpose, style of thought, and conceptual tools of a theory of business decision'.[9]

In the same letter, Shackle set out the ideas he should specially like critics to regard as the essence of his scheme as follows:

1 The right word is not uncertainty but *Unknowledge*. We know a little about the texture of the material, but nothing about how history will cut the garment.

2 Knowledge of the texture can perhaps tell us what can be made to seem possible by specified use of specified resources, on condition of exposing us to what misfortune. The right question for the enterprise-investor to ask is: *At best*, and *at worst*, what *can* the sequel be if I do this, or this?

3 If, in the elemental sense, history is made by human decisions (that is to say, if a decision can be in some respects an uncaused cause) the sequels of specified action will be in principle (and not merely in practice) *unlistable*.

4 If so, the claim of any hypothetical sequel to be taken seriously, its *epistemic standing*, cannot be appropriately expressed as a *share of certainty*, for this share will be affected by the number of rival hypotheses, which number (we are assuming) can increase without limit. We therefore cannot say that any given list of them is complete, nor that it is completeable. Instead, my scheme requires imagined sequels to be judged possible or not possible. Then by taking *disbelief* instead of belief, as the expression of epistemic standing, we express perfect (subjective) possibility as *zero disbelief*. This is a non-distributive variable and enables the highest level of epistemic standing to be assigned to each of an unlimited number of hypotheses.

5 *Disbelief* can be given an emotional interpretation (a meaning in terms of feeling, so as to be deemed capable of different intensities) and thus made quantifiable, by identifying it with potential surprise. If we wish, we can then refine in some sense the notion of 'best' and 'worst' imagined sequels amongst those deemed *possible*, by referring instead to the best and worst *not too difficult* to envisage as coming true.

(Shackle: letter to Stephen Frowen, 10 November 1982,
emphasis in the original)

George Shackle further elaborated on his main interests in another letter to Stephen Frowen at a time when the latter was engaged in editing the collection of Shackle's essays *Business, Time and Thought*, published in 1988. It reads as follows:

> Mr. Farmiloe [Macmillan Publishing Director] dislikes Time and Thought [in the book title] because it suggests philosophy. It is the philosophical aspect of economics that I have always been mainly interested in. My books are concerned with philosophical problems: with 'epistemics', especially with the inescapable need to decide in the face of *un*knowledge. Economics is as wholly entangled with time as history itself is...
>
> These essays are not about cut-and-dried simplified 'models' but about the mutual forming of thought and event, linked by the middle term of action, enterprise. This has always been my slant on economics, and it is known to be...
>
> I have a title, which would bring the philosophical problems right into the market place: Business, Time and Thought.
>
> 'Business' describes our field better than economics, a word fudged up from two Greek ones. You yourself Stephen have spoken of the 'theory of business'. That suggests a rather detailed technical concern. I do not claim to discuss as wide and complex a field as 'that': only the business of business-decision.
>
> (Shackle: letter to Stephen Frowen, 2 August 1985)[10]

This volume contains much of what George Shackle would surely have liked to be covered on these lines. We have tried to ensure that the discussion at least in part bears on certain questions where Shackle has most radically discarded the received notions of the purpose, style of thought, and conceptual tools of a theory of business decision.

3 THE CHAPTERS IN THIS VOLUME

The book begins with a pair of chapters focused on two fundamental and related problems raised by Shackle's work: how can decision makers construct some kind of foundation for their choices; and how can university teachers of economics avoid creating panic among their students if they try to teach that not only is the business environment uncertain but also that it has been far from clear to the academic community how to make sense of what goes on in business. In Chapter 1 Brian Loasby explores the question 'How do we know?' both in terms of the problem that we cannot know anything for sure — even the rules of a game we find ourselves playing — and the methods we use to get by in the face of this problem. He discusses the role of economic organization in enabling the system to generate a greater volume of knowledge despite the bounded rationality of individuals, and hence permit the system to evolve and progress. Loasby pays particular attention to the role of shared conjectures, as in a corporate culture, as devices for reducing transaction costs, and views learning as a consequence of encountering situations in which conjectures are falsified.

In Chapter 2, Peter Earl examines barriers to multi-paradigm, open-ended undergraduate teaching of the kind advocated by Shackle. Whereas these barriers are normally seen as including faculty politics and difficulties in finding suitable texts, as well as the practical difficulties of 'cramming a quart into a pint pot', the focus of his chapter is on the hurdle posed the expectations of students and the learning strategies that are associated with these expectations. He draws heavily upon research by Harvard educationalist William G. Perry, Jr, which suggests that cognitive development passes through a multi-stage process beginning with dualism and ending up with relativism. Non-deterministic teaching of economics may run into severe difficulties if students have not reached the relativism stage. But lecturers need not take the state of cognitive development of their students as given: instead, they may use their teaching style to help students towards a relativistic way of thinking. Strategies for doing this are discussed in the chapter.

The next two chapters examine the relationship between Shackle's world-view and two non-mainstream economics research programmes. In Chapter 3, Geoff Hodgson sets out to show what Shackle's work and that of the institutionalists can offer each other. He begins by demonstrating that they have a great deal in common in their reasons for rejecting neoclassical theory. Further analysis reveals that their perspectives differ on the nature of human agency, even though they both place it at the centre of their work. Hodgson suggests that modern chaos theory may provide a means of reconciling the views of institutionalists on determinacy with Shackle's vigorously non-deterministic stance. Finally, Hodgson argues that, by recasting human agency in terms of both the imagination (from Shackle) and habits and routines (form the institutionalists), we can end up with a view of economics that is less susceptible than that of Shackle to charges that it is nihilistic.

In Chapter 4 Geoff Harcourt and Claudio Sardoni explore the influence of Shackle on Post Keynesian economics, beginning with the area of expectations and investment. Shackle's emphasis on the potential volatility of expectations made him much more uncomfortable than many Post Keynesians with the notion of aggregate demand management, whilst sharing their doubts about the usefulness of much general equilibrium theorizing. Harcourt and Sardoni argue that there was much more to Shackle's views here than the idea that movements in schedules are more important than movements along them, having more to do with the difficulties he saw in attempts to reconciling mathematics with history. They suggest that contrasts between the approach to time adopted by Shackle and other Post Keynesians such as Kalecki might be understood in the terms of differences between the importance accorded to financial capital (on which Shackle focused) and industrial capital. Having begun their analysis by likening Shackle's influence on Post Keynesianism to that of Hicks on neoclassical economics, Harcourt and Sardoni move towards their conclusion by examining the relationship between Shackle and Hicks as the latter increasingly recognized the limitations of equilibrium economics and moved closer to the Post Keynesians.

Ian Steedman examines in Chapter 5 some of the diverse ways in which economists use the term 'rationality' in their writings. He begins by examining the textbook consumer behaviour literature in which the term is portrayed mainly as a technical one concerned with consistency of behaviour as seen from the standpoint of a theoretical framework that seeks to rationalize what is observed rather than make predictions: choice is rational if it can be rationalized by the theory. Steedman then moves on to review literature, including, of course, Shackle's work, that is critical of this approach to 'rational' choice. Steedman is particularly concerned to highlight the fact that behaviour can be inconsistent with what mainstream theorists expect or approve of and yet still be based on reasons and a personal reading of one's own predicament, rather than being symptomatic of a lack of any underlying logic. From the Austrian perspective, as Steedman shows in the final part of his chapter, all behaviour comes to be seen as rational: though we may not presume to know what motivates an individual or how an individual works out what to do to meet a set of goals, human action in general at least seems purposive. The task of the economist is then to form a clearer picture of factors that comprise human predicaments, rather than abstracting from them, and to acquire a broader understanding of the kinds of reasons that underlie the diverse choices that people make, rather than force-fitting everyone into conformity with a particular view of rationality.

Steedman's review provides a very useful overture for the next two chapter, which also focus on rationality, reasoning and the subjectivist way of doing economics. In Chapter 6, Stephen Parsons explores the relationship between Shackle's perspective and the Cartesian view of the nature of existence and knowledge. For Shackle, choice entails using one's free will, rather than the mere application of reason. Thus in contrast to the view of mainstream economists, knowledge of a chooser's circumstances coupled with the application of reason may not be sufficient to enable choice to be predicted — creativity may intervene and the individual's interpretation of his or her circumstances may differ from that of the analyst. When we identify causal relationships we do so not merely by applying reason but also via our imagination. Parsons emphasizes that to incorporate the unfolding of future time into thoughts seems to require considerable cognitive capacity given the huge range of things that, in principle, we might do (the more so, the less constrained we are by our budgets). However, he suggests that Shackle places too great a burden on this: what we can imagine doing is bounded not merely by cognitive capacity but by our views of what makes us the people we are, by our self-understanding. There are many things a person simply would not imagine doing, but these differ across individuals. Because we have an idea of the sorts of people we are, our ranges of conceivable choice are much reduced. Because we have an idea of how people with whom we interact see themselves, we can predict their behaviour within relatively restricted bounds, which makes our own decisions even easier. The identities/ personalities of economic actors are thus, in an important sense, institutional features.

In Chapter 7, Shaun Hargreaves Heap takes the analysis further from the Enlightenment towards Postmodern methodology. He suggests that George Shackle may have been the foremost exponent of hermeneutics in economics during the twentieth century and then focuses on the question 'How far can you go with hermeneutics?' — in other words, if one takes a subjectivist position and emphasizes the role of free will in choice, how much further does that take the economist than an analysis which ignores the internal point of view and does not seek to understand what people think they are doing as they try to cope with the ordinary business of everyday life? Potential gains are explored in the areas of methodology, the appreciation of institutions in economic life, and normative decision making.

Chapter 7 ends by commenting on the relevance of a hermeneutic approach if one is trying to avoid the kinds of outcomes that have been evident when mainstream economic thinking has been used as a basis for policy designs in Eastern Europe and the former Soviet Union. The economics of transition are then examined at greater length in Chapter 8 by Jan Kregel. In searching for causes of the 'missing output' in these economies, Kregel focuses on the failure of policy makers to appreciate the significance of existing organizational capital, in particular the creative capabilities that had been developed to cope with the deficiencies of the former regime and which were often made obsolete or otherwise destroyed by privatization policies. Kregel suggests that a Shacklean perspective on the role for government sees it in promoting imaginative thinking about economic problems, not in direct interference. Rather than constraining action, government agencies can more usefully serve by helping to bring about environments in which creative entrepreneurs are not fearful of the scale of the potential losses and can see opportunities for high rewards.

Though it links with material on chaos theory in Chapter 2, Jason Pott's contribution to this volume seems more appropriately located as Chapter 9, as a bold bridge between Jan Kregel's case study and subsequent chapters on decision making under uncertainty. An underlying message of Kregel's work is that the success of a transition to market economy depends on the imaginative vision applied to the problem of reconfiguring the structural combinations of existing resources. Potts explores the workings of the imagination in a combinatorial manner, bringing together Shackle's work on expectations and recent thinking in General Systems Theory. He suggests that the mathematics of Graph Theory provides a ready framework for formalizing this perspective. The systems view presented by Potts works at a variety of levels: expectations are formed by making new combinations of existing thought-elements, and individual decision makers' actions are interwoven in ways that they may seek to manage. The trouble is, according to Potts, that attempts to resolve uncertainty on the part of an individual cause uncertainties for others in the system: uncertainty can only be reduced so far. Moreover, the more connections that are built into a system, the more dynamically unstable — the more kaleidic, in Shackle's terms — it becomes. These phenomena are obscured by traditional analysis, which abstracts from the connective structure of the economic system via a focus on a 'representative agent'.

In Chapter 10 Jochen Runde examines Shackle's extensive critiques of the use of probability concepts in economics. He begins with a sketch of the components that Shackle regarded as fundamental to the theory of choice under uncertainty and a brief review of the standard expected utility model, before moving on to present and assess Shackle's views on the frequency interpretation and the subjective and logical interpretations of probability. Runde argues that while the expected utility model and some subsequent theoretical developments are resistant to Shackle's criticisms, his most important one — directed at the assumption that decision-makers know the complete set of events to which probabilities are to be assigned — is as pertinent as ever. Finally, he draws some parallels between the thinking of Shackle and Keynes on the nature of uncertainty and degrees of belief.

Chapters 11 and 12 extend the analysis of choice under uncertainty into the realm of monetary theory. In Chapter 11 Moacir dos Anjos, Jr and Victoria Chick examine the nature of liquidity, a concept as slippery as its name suggests. They argue that though there have been many attempts to arrive at some description of how an agent might act in an environment of uncertainty, these have largely involved bringing the classical theory of probability to bear on the question. This has been done despite difficulties inherent in the theory, in particular its assumption of stability in the underlying environment, precisely the conditions in which the need for liquidity is at a minimum. By contrast, the case for bringing radical uncertainty into the picture is evident in the roller-coaster experience of a country such as Brazil (an episode from which they use as a case study). Accordingly, they employ Shackle's decision making framework to evaluating liquidity. They demonstrate how Shackle's analysis can produce, from a more general standpoint, the famous figure from Tobin's subsequent model of liquidity preference and that a Shacklean approach allows a unified treatment of the whole spectrum of liquidity.

In Chapter 12, Donald Katzner examines the theoretical foundations of the demand for money as a medium of exchange and store of value. His chapter is divided into two main sections. First, he critically surveys the orthodox literature that seeks to explain the demand for money primarily with reference to the transaction costs of using futures markets or in terms of overlapping generations models. These models rely upon the typical general equilibrium assumption that individuals are fully informed planners who know all that might happen in the future and have an idea of the probabilities of particular events occurring at particular points in time. He then explores the demand for money in an uncertain world in terms of a formal analysis based on the work of both George Shackle and Douglas Vickers, that focuses on the realities of human ignorance and historical time.

The theme of decision-making under uncertainty also dominates Chapter 13 but here Kenneth Cleaver's focus is on capital budgeting and investment decisions, with particular reference to the insights that management accountants might derive from studying Shackle's work. Cleaver highlights the sharp contrast between what is taught in normative investment analysis and the repeated finding in empirical studies that managers use payback-period decision criteria, with time horizons of only a few years, as a basis for choice. The practical use of such decision criteria is fully consistent with Shackle's emphasis on the problem of radical uncertainty as something that should be central to theoretical analysis. Cleaver concludes his chapter by exploring how management accounting perspectives might be modified if they were informed by Shackle's vision of the business predicament.

The final pair of chapters concern the Shackle archive in Cambridge University Library and their contents have many surprises in store, even for those who believe themselves well acquainted with Shackle's life and work. In Chapter 14 Stephen Littlechild presents a taste of the kind of experience that may entertain, fascinate and enlighten those who visit this extraordinary collection. He begins by presenting an overview of the books, papers and letters of which it is comprised and then concentrates on showing how George Shackle worked as a scholar. Littlechild then moves on to reveal Shackle's views on topics such as the roles of mathematics and psychology in economics. This chapter ends with a moving account of Shackle's final months.

INTRODUCTION

Littlechild's chapter deserves serious attention from anyone interested in the changing nature of scholarship. George was not of the modern 'Harvard-system referencing' school of scholars whose prodigious lists of sources are set up to protect their work from assaults of referees and readers and whose papers are nonetheless produced at high speed under pressure of research audits. The Shacklean approach to scholarship entails relatively few sources being used for inspiration and footnoted, but each source is subject to intense scrutiny until it is mastered and its essential messages distilled.

Shackle might have read more in this painstaking fashion, and might himself have further explored pathways considered elsewhere in this volume had he not also been a truly remarkable man of letter-writing. Stephen Littlechild gives a taste of the astonishing array of correspondents with whom Shackle shared his thinking and in whose minds he tried to plant the seeds of further inquiries. Shackle's carefully worded letters, in his instantly recognizable large script, poured forth at a rate that will give today's internet-based scholars pause for thought. That so many famous economists should figure in the collection of letters is testimony to the significance of Shackle's work, since in general (and not surprisingly given the volume of letters to which he had to reply), it was not he who initiated an exchange. The sheer scale becomes clear from Chapter 15, in which Kathleen Cann brings the volume to a close by presenting her extensive catalogue of the Cambridge collection. Taken together, Chapters 14 and 15 should prove invaluable to anyone planning to do further research on George Shackle's life and his imagination.

NOTES

1 The prayer on George Shackle's tombstone is his own taken down by Catherine Shackle during his final illness at Ipswich Hospital.
2 We are grateful to Catherine Shackle for drawing our attention to G. L. S. Shackle's first published paper, which is not listed in any of his bibliographies.
3 This conference in honour of G.L.S. Shackle was held at the University of Surrey in September 1984 and the proceedings were published in 1990 as *Unknowledge and Choice in Economics*.
4 Letter published in Frowen (2000).
5 Letter published in Frowen (2000).

6 The Malvern Political Economy conferences were organized by John Pheby for ten years, beginning in 1987 (see Pressman, ed. 1996). George Shackle's paper 'What did the *General Theory* do?', presented at the first Malvern conference, was published in Pheby, ed. (1989).
7 For the Addresses given at the Memorial Service and further tributes, see *Review of Political Economy* (1993: 263–73).
8 Letter published in Frowen (2000).
9 Letter published in Frowen (2000).
10 Letter published in Frowen (2000).

REFERENCES

Earl, P. E. (1993) 'The economics of G. L. S. Shackle in retrospect and prospect', *Review of Political Economy* 5: 245–61.

Frowen, S. F. (ed.) (1988, *Business, Time and Thought: Selected Papers of G. L. S. Shackle*, London: Macmillan; New York: New York University Press.

—— (ed.) (1990) *Unknowledge and Choice in Economics: Proceedings of a Conference in Honour of G. L. S. Shackle*, London: Macmillan; New York: St. Martin's Press.

—— (ed.) (2000), *Economists in Discussion: The Correspondence Between G .L. S. Shackle and S. F. Frowen, 1951-1992*, London: Macmillan; New York: St. Martin's Press.

Pheby, J. (ed.) (1989) *New Directions in Post Keynesian Economics*, Aldershot: Edward Elgar.

Pressman, S. (ed.) (1996) *Interactions in Political Economy: Malvern After Ten Years*, London: Routledge.

Review of Political Economy (1993) 'Tributes [to G. L. S. Shackle]', *Review of Political Economy*, G. L. S. Shackle Memorial Issue, 5: 263–73.

Shackle, G. L. S. (1938) *Expectations, Investment and Income*, Oxford: Oxford University Press.

—— (1983) 'A student's pilgrimage', *Banca Nazionale del Lavoro Quarterly Review*, no. 145, June: 107-16. Reprinted in Frowen, S. F. (ed.) (1988) *Business, Time and Thought*, London: Macmillan: New York: New York University Press, 230-9.

—— (1990) 'Speech by G. L. S. Shackle at the Conference Dinner of the George Shackle Conference, University of Surrey, Guildford, 7 September 1984', in Frowen, S. F. (ed.) *Unknowledge and Choice in Economics*, London: Macmillan, 192-6.

1

HOW DO WE KNOW?

Brian J. Loasby

1 THE PROBLEM OF KNOWLEDGE

To the question 'How do we *know*?' the answer is simple: we don't. There is no way of demonstrating the truth of any general empirical proposition about the universe, or any part of it, no means of proving that we have the correct theory about anything. We may be able to prove logical propositions, but we can never be certain that they are applicable to any particular phenomenon or situation. And yet there are many branches of science which claim to be increasing our knowledge within their various domains, and many applied sciences which make use of such knowledge with a fair measure of success. So we may ask: how is science possible?

If economics is to be considered a science, then this is a question for economists. But economics is a very special case, since its declared subject-matter is purposeful human action, and action can hardly be purposeful without knowledge. So ideas and assumptions about knowledge are at the heart of economics, as George Shackle insisted; and economists must give some answer to the question: what can people know? In particular, they must take some view about the ability of individuals to interpret the system of which they are part, and about the ways in which that system influences their knowledge. Often this answer emerges only by implication — notably in the routine assumption that the knowledge required to undertake transactions is freely available (Coase 1988a); and when the answer is explicit, as in the assumption that expectations are rational, we are given no credible epistemic justification for that answer. This chapter is shaped as a commentary on the ideas, explicit and implicit, about knowledge in a number of books and papers, and two PhD theses, which I read between May and August of 1992. As presented to the Conference from which this volume has evolved, it was a commentary on current work; the work is still valuable, and the argument presented is, I believe, still valid.

In his survey of game theory in the *Scottish Journal of Political Economy*, Alistair Munro (1992: 340) quotes the philosopher A. J. Ayer:

> A being whose intellect was infinitely powerful would take no interest in logic and mathematics. For he would be able to see at a glance everything that his definitions implied, and, accordingly, could never learn anything from logical inference which he was not fully conscious of already.
>
> (Ayer 1971: 114)

That our interest in logic and mathematics should be a consequence of our bounded rationality suggests that there is something paradoxical about economists' fascination with the logic of fully-informed choice. But the problem goes far beyond the human limitations on absorbing and processing data, on which Herbert Simon's interest has been so productively focused, and which he sometimes seems to suggest are the only — if formidable — obstacles to perfect knowledge. A more extensive treatment of these obstacles is offered in Loasby (1999); here we will mention two. The irremediable difficulty is that not even an infinitely powerful intellect could know that any general empirical proposition was true; as David Hume pointed out, that could not be established without collecting all possible instances of the phenomena to which the proposition referred; and past instances are very often beyond recovery, and future instances always beyond reach.

When we come to situations in which human interdependencies matter, we encounter a second class of difficulties. For two people to understand what is in each other's mind, when that includes an understanding of that understanding, leads to an infinite regress: as Alan Coddington (1975: 154) once observed, 'There can be at most one omniscient being'. Game theorists commonly circumvent this problem by postulating common knowledge, which of course includes the knowledge that the particular game currently being analysed is the one which all participants will play. Adam Smith (1976a) sought partially to circumvent it by his analysis of sympathy, which not only provides some explanation of what knowledge might reasonably be treated as common, but has important — and much neglected - implications for the operation of free markets.

George Shackle (1972: 422) drew attention to the paradox by which the creative imagination of von Neumann and Morgenstern inspired a body of theory which denies the possibility of creative imagination to the agents whose behaviour is to be analyzed. Thus the invention of the theory of games is a refutation of the premises on which that theory is based. Shackle's (1972: 424–5) criticism, it may be noted, is focused not on the highly problematic assumption of a closed set of rules for 'Business, and the General Human Affair', but on the assumption that the players could ever know — still less be sure that they knew — what these rules were. As always, the crucial issue for him was epistemic. There are indeed, Shackle concedes, contests, such as typical board games, in which the rules define a precise set of moves, and a precise sequence of play; but the games of life are not like that. What he might have argued is that there are also many games which are not like that. In cricket, football, or tennis, for example, we find a very limited definition of sequence, and a set of rules which define the boundaries of the decision space; the contents remain to be explored, and in many such games new possibilities are still being discovered or invented.

In these games, as in business, and in the development of an academic discipline, there are surprises, as Shackle often reminded us. But surprises are a threat to the complete specification which formal theory demands — even though the prospect of creating surprises, of discovering something novel, is necessary to maintain a puzzle-solving tradition in normal science (Kuhn 1962, 1970). Some restrictions on the set of permitted actions is necessary for a game — or any other kind of economic analysis — to possess an equilibrium solution, and those restrictions cannot be explained by the analysis which depends on them. Even that is not always sufficient; as Munro points out, sometimes we need restrictions on the definition of rationality itself. That would certainly not surprise Adam Smith.

Game theory cannot possibly offer a complete theory of rational choice, even in the restricted sense of that concept prevalent in economics; nor can any other kind of theory. That is not to say that we should not use theories of rational choice — merely that we should use them, like all theories, with care. What the development of game theory has confirmed is that even if rationality were complete in the sense of Ayer and Simon, nevertheless our knowledge would still be bounded. Although 'it is a tautology that a rational player will defect in a one-shot Prisoners' Dilemma' (Binmore 1999: F212), the definition of

3

any situation as a one-shot prisoners' dilemma is not a tautology but a fallible conjecture. Indeed, the story which is embedded in the name of this game involves interactions between each prisoner and the interrogator, and, implicitly, also with participants in a judicial or quasi-judicial process; these interactions may be crucial to reasoned decisions, but they are not modelled.

If we return to the question of this paper, and change the intonation, so that we ask '*How* do we know?', we shall find that we know by setting bounds to what we seek to know, and ignoring — as game theorists regularly do — what lies beyond. Of course this policy exposes us to the risk that our apparent knowledge will be invalidated by what we have shut out, as an apparently optimal strategy in a game may (as in sport, business and war) be overcome by a move which had been left out of the presumed set of common knowledge; and so it remains true that we never *know*. 'When the compass of potential knowledge as a whole has been split up into superficially convenient sectors, there is no knowing whether each sector has a natural self-sufficiency.... Whatever theory is then devised will exist by sufferance of the things which it has excluded' (Shackle 1972: 353–4). Charles Suckling, whose career was devoted to the management of innovation, identified this proposition as the epistemic key to such management, as it is the key to any use of models. Its absence from standard economic analysis of research and development is a serious deficiency. But no economist ought to be surprised to find that any policy for improving knowledge entails opportunity costs — opportunity cost is, in my view, the central concept in economics. For economics is about choice, and choices are hardly worth studying unless they make a difference: hence the need to compare the benefits envisaged by following the chosen path with the prospects which are necessarily abandoned by not taking the most attractive of the perceived alternatives.

The opportunity costs of any programme for gaining knowledge have important consequences to which economists have given inadequate recognition. As Simon (1992: 21) has observed, 'Any direction you proceed in has a very high *a priori* probability of being wrong; so it is good if other people are exploring in other directions — perhaps one of them will be on the right track.' Simon's observation was primarily directed towards the importance of variety in economics, and is particularly relevant to an academic regime of research assessment: it may also be applied — and will be later — to the economy. In both, 'the tendency to variation is a chief cause of progress' (Marshall 1920: 355), because system diversity reduces the opportunity costs to the system of individual choices of direction. Perfect competition requires the suppression of diversity, and cannot therefore be part of a realistic welfare ideal.

Not only is knowledge necessarily bounded; the bounds are necessarily imprecise. The models that we use are always abstractions from a complex reality and their domain of sufficiency can never be known. Many of our concepts are ambiguous — a point to which I shall return. We are surrounded by uncertainty, in Shackle's sense; not only can we not complete our lists of parameters, we cannot be at all sure about the structures on which we are forced, at least provisionally, to rely. Logical coherence provides no assurance of relevance, or even of empirical validity. The imposition of probability distributions, whether subjective or supposedly objective, on closed sets is a pretence of knowledge. Yet it is this very uncertainty which holds out the prospect of discovery, or favourable surprises, as both Lombardini (1992: 14), in his contribution to a colloquium with Simon, and Lesourne (1992: 9), in his analysis of self-organizing markets, point out. That, of course, is the good news on which Shackle insisted, and which game theory excludes.

It is obviously impossible to predict the content of any discovery without actually making that discovery; therefore, as Simon (1992: 14) points out, 'a theory of technical change [or, we may add, of any kind of new knowledge] must be a theory of processes that bring about change rather than a theory of the specific nature of the changes'. So the question 'How do we know?' may be construed as 'By what processes do we acquire knowledge?', together with its corollary 'What are the influences of the process on the content and quality of the knowledge that is acquired?' We must expect to find substantial path-dependency, both in the development of economics and in the development of every economy: the opportunities that were open both to British economists and the British economy in September 1992, after the forced exit from the ERM, were very different from what they might have been had alternative paths been followed earlier. Organization aids knowledge, as Marshall clearly perceived; and it does so by constraining the flow of information and the possibilities of interpreting it. Any particular scheme of organization therefore excludes many possible kinds of knowledge.

The creation of knowledge is structured by institutions, which include, at one level, academic disciplines, firms and markets, and at a lower level, research programmes within disciplines, culture and strategy within firms, and custom and practice within markets. All these are social institutions, guiding social processes, and these processes are interactive. Relationships within an academic discipline include both collaboration and competition, and many relationships embody a rich mixture. Competition is fundamental, because of scarcity; and collaboration is a response to scarcity which seeks to enlarge the attainable set by maintaining the differing frameworks which are essential to different kinds of knowledge.

But although these institutions are much more important than even many institutional economists recognize, I believe that we need even greater changes in the ways that economists treat the individual. For despite the wide acceptance of methodological individualism as a constraint in our research programmes, nevertheless, as Hahn (1973; 1984: 64) has reminded us, 'traditional equilibrium theory does best when the individual has no importance — he is of measure zero'. But if we wish to study the generation and use of knowledge, then the role of the individual is crucial; and what matters is that some individuals should be different. That entrepreneurship implies differentiation has kept the topic outside modern mainstream economics — it makes the briefest of appearances in Milgrom and Roberts' (1992) magisterial exposition of the economics of organization (which is appraised in Loasby 1995); that Lesourne recognizes the necessity for initiative if orderly markets are to appear is, to my mind, one of the most significant features of his book — even though it is a feature which, because of his neoclassical conditioning, he handles with extreme caution.

Because knowledge is central to economics, economics needs a theory of processes within an institutional framework; perhaps, indeed, that should be the core of economics. (For further discussion see Loasby 1999). With sufficient imagination, one can see how such a core might have developed from parts of the work of Smith, Menger, and Marshall — though one needs much less imagination to see why it did not. Since we now have a very different kind of economics, an obvious question to ask is: 'Should we abandon equilibrium?' My answer (to the disappointment of some of my friends) is still No', for three reasons. First, the use of equilibrium as an organizing principle has, like other organizing principles, benefits as well as costs, and it would, I think, be silly to discard the benefits. It directs attention to the interacting forces at work, and does so in the simplest case, when they are in balance; since the number of different solutions to any equilibrium problem is likely to be far fewer than the number of paths to equilibrium, it helps to focus critical interchange among economists, and thus fosters the growth of some kinds of knowledge; and an understanding of stability and order, as well as being important in its own right, is, in my view, a necessary preliminary to understanding change. I still believe that equilibrium usually provides a good basis to start the analysis of a complex problem, even though it does not often provide a good basis on which to conclude.

Second, the use of this organizing principle by economists provides a splendid, and extremely rich, case study of the ways in which the growth of knowledge is shaped by its organizing principles. Third, the concept of equilibrium, especially as interpreted by Frank Hahn in terms of theories and policies, seems very apt to the study of the factors which preserve or modify a particular institutional structure within which knowledge grows (or sometimes decays). I am encouraged in this belief by the fact that my first attempt (Loasby 1991) to use the concept in this way elicited approval both from Frank Hahn and Alfred Chandler, thus linking high theory and business history in a way to which, if asked, I would have attached a very high level of potential surprise.

2 COGNITION AND INTELLIGENCE

In a book which seeks to examine the formation and modification of preferences, Henry Woo (1992: 83) claims that any theory of human action must take a position on human cognition. By choosing to maximize its logical coherence, consumer theory has incurred a high epistemic cost (p. 117), and its predictions, which are based on consumer optimization, neglect the costs of the optimizing process (p. 169). Coase (1988a) has criticized economists for ignoring the transaction costs of trade; Woo criticizes them for ignoring the costs of individual cognition. In their fascination with the specification of equilibrium, where no further effort to discover and exploit opportunities is required, economists have neglected the means by which equilibrium might be achieved or preserved.

Woo offers a basic economic analysis of cognition by considering the human mind as an artifact of an evolutionary process (See also Hayek 1952). Before the development of consciousness, natural selection favoured brains with good storage, quick retrieval from a distributed memory, and rapid response, rather than extensive processing capacity (p. 77). Images and patterns serve to pre-combine information in a way that can directly trigger action; processing, by contrast, takes time and consumes energy. In an environment of sudden danger and fleeting opportunity, to act without thinking is often the only chance of acting at all. It is not optimal to 'optimize' in any calculable sense. We carry this biological inheritance, in which quick retrieval has priority over the control of what is retrieved, and in which an orderly rearrangement of the contents of our memory is an extremely formidable task. The subsequent development of language and the preservation of language in documents have alleviated, but not removed, the limitations of mental processing.

The construction of a preference ordering which complies with the standard axioms is therefore not a task well-suited to the human brain. Its expected value is well below its cost; and since natural selection operates on populations, expected value seems the appropriate measure here. Partial orderings are constructed in the process of choice; thus the consumer capital which economists represent by preference functions is accumulated during a sequence of choices (Woo 1992: 110–2). That is why conventional preference theory seems to work well for goods which are frequently purchased, and less well for infrequent purchases, in which preferences are not merely revealed but formulated in the process of choice. This consumer capital can be destroyed by rapid change, just as producer capital is destroyed by Schumpeterian innovations: both kinds of capital consist of routines which, in Schumpeter's (1934: 80) words, 'things have had time to hammer ... into men'. That people suddenly removed from the arena of familiar experiences find it very hard even to formulate principles of rational behaviour seems to be well confirmed: we even find an economist in Simon's (1992) book confessing that he would be lost outside his neoclassical conventions (Fornero 1992: 21). The conventions of consumer theory may be adequate predictors within the context in which they are taught to students — repeated purchases in a stable environment; but should we not warn students that they should not be used outside this range without great caution? (For further discussion of consumer choice and the development of consumption skills, see Bianchi 1998.)

Experience is not simply a matter of information, in the conventional sense; what one learns from events depends on the interpretation that is placed upon them. (Just think of the contradictory lessons that have been drawn from the 1992 devaluation of sterling.) When these interpretations are fitted into a more general pattern we can talk, if only loosely, of a theory. Ayer's super-beings, remember, have no need of theories: every case is a singleton. We require a theory of rational choice only because we do not have the knowledge that we would need to behave rationally. Because that is true of all of us, this human limitation actually helps us to predict the behaviour of other people. It is because it is rarely possible for any of us to take into account the fine detail of the situations in which we have to act that we do not need to know the fine detail of other people's situations; it is because other people rely on general principles in deciding what to do that we can usually rely on general principles in predicting their decisions. This insight is due to Heiner (1983), who refers (p. 573) to Adam Smith's (1976a) *Theory of Moral Sentiments*, but does not appear to recognize, as Choi (1993) does, the importance of sympathy in helping each of us to understand the principles that others use. It may help to resolve some of the difficulties in game theory, which I shall not discuss further, and also help to explain the cohesion of organizations and of markets, which will receive some attention.

The emergence of general principles is a major theme of work on artificial intelligence, the principal topic of the thesis by Marengo (1992a and b) and the book by Simon and his co-authors. In standard models of information processing, the information partition is assumed to be given and, though coarse, to be free from error. Marengo is not satisfied with this practice, and constructs models in which people who need to co-ordinate their productive activities develop their own information partitions and corresponding partitions of the action space. This is an implicitly Coasean view of the firm as a device for improving co-ordination in a world of imperfect knowledge. The central idea is that of learning by deciding, a theme which is also explored by Woo (1992). The learning environment for each simulation is provided by repeated manifestations of a particular variant of a co-ordination problem, for which agents develop rules for classifying situations and choosing actions. The rules are generated by chance, and evaluated by the outcome of the decisions to which they lead; the success rate defines the likelihood that they will be evoked on a future occasion. There is no backward induction from anticipated futures; new rules are generated in the neighbourhood of existing rules, some of which they displace. Everyone is boundedly rational, and therefore can never handle more than a fraction of the possible classification systems.

Marengo simulates the development of classification systems for several variants of the co-ordination problem. In the extreme cases of static and randomly fluctuating environments the search for better rules has no benefits, and sometimes incurs substantial costs in avoidable bad decisions: if there is nothing to be learnt, those who don't try to learn do best. When there is knowledge to be gained about systematic changes in the environment, multiple schemes of search are helpful, but when search is useless increasing the number of search parties only makes things worse. Both results reflect the trade-off between static efficiency and the development of capabilities for future use — which have no value within an equilibrium specification, and also the trade-off between the advantages of shared representations in facilitating co-ordination and of diverse representations in promoting innovation. The latter has been noted by Langlois in his analysis of business history (for example, Langlois 1992: 119–22) , and also by Meyerson (1992) in a study of the response of 29 Swedish companies to adverse shocks.

The twin virtues of these models, in my view, is that they embody two fundamental principles which underlie any answer to the question: 'How do we know?' First, there can be no learning, and no choice, without rules which are external to the particular process of learning or choice which is being analyzed. (These rules may themselves be generated in a higher-level learning process, which is governed by higher-level rules). Second, classification systems have a major influence in determining what we can know; our information partitions are located in the space of representations, and what cannot be represented cannot be known — except, sometimes, as a distorted image. Walrasian equilibria, for example, do not readily accommodate either money or involuntary unemployment.

To set against these virtues there is one serious limitation, which is inherent in the technique. In these models of artificial intelligence the people being modelled do not themselves seem to be intelligent. Because the model itself must be fully defined in order to support the computer program on which the simulation depends, it is necessarily the analyst who defines the sample, the set of possible categories and decision-rules on which chance is to operate, and the rules for mutation and selection. So it is not clear whether we should regard these models as highly-simplified representations of human brains, or as creations of the analyst: do they show us how people learn in the kind of situation which is modelled, or how Marengo learnt to model learning? If the latter, we should note that this thesis marks the beginning of his work, which has great potential. (For an application of classification systems to speculative markets, see Marengo and Tordjman 1996.)

It seems to me that the constructors of such models — not excluding Simon — are in danger of a very common kind of arrogance, against which George Kelly (1963) warned his fellow psychologists: the assumption that the analyst, as a scientist, is quite unlike the people being studied, who are, frankly, pretty stupid. This attitude is not uncommon in economics; Lesourne's book is not free from it. Robert Lucas deserves great credit for forcing economists to confront the possibility that the people being studied might actually be quite as clever as the analyst who is studying them. It is a great pity, though easy to understand, that the overwhelming response to Lucas's challenge, inspired by Lucas himself, has been to accept as an organizing principle a concept of rational expectations which is incompatible with our understanding of the process of gaining knowledge. What Lucas, in common with most economists, completely neglects is the role of conjecture: the invention of a principle which will link together previously separate phenomena in a way which goes beyond the inductive procedures of artificial intelligence or a Bayesian convergence on correct models — even though such conjectures are the basis of their own contributions.

Lesourne's models of self-organizing markets offer a multi-personal analogue of artificial intelligence, in which convergent learning may lead to stable states — but not always, because some models do not permit the learning which is needed for stability. Moreover, the acquisition of knowledge is costly, though the costs do not extend, as in Woo's analysis, to cognition. Therefore equilibria are often path-dependent, and false knowledge along the path may have irreversible effects. If a stable outcome is attained it may not be efficient, in the conventional sense that at least one other possible stable outcome of the initial conditions is Pareto superior; but, since trajectories cannot be retraced without incurring additional costs, an inefficient outcome, once attained, may not be open to improvement. Opportunities as well as costs may be sunk. All this accords well with the ideas about knowledge that underlie this paper.

So too does Lesourne's recognition of the value of individual initiative; but his modelling strategy requires this initiative to be exercised only in the ways that are prescribed in the definition of his models. Indeed I was struck by the similarities between Lesourne and Kirzner (1973), which I suspect would be equally disconcerting to both. Both are looking for processes which will lead to successful co-ordination; Lesourne is actually more radical than Kirzner's original formulation in not insisting on success. This leads them both to treat knowledge as the dual of equilibration, and to recognise the importance of having some — but not too many — agents who are alert. Both eschew creativity, which is a threat to stability — as of course, Schumpeter believed. Both exclude Popperian conjectures, though these are implicit in Kirzner's (1992) more recent work.

3 CONJECTURES AND CATEGORIES

In sharp contrast to this category of model is a PhD thesis (Harper 1992), now developed into a book (Harper 1995), in which Kirzner's theory of entrepreneurship is transformed by attributing to the entrepreneur not the first recognition of a new reality but the formation of a Popperian conjecture — indeed the formation of a cluster of conjectures which constitutes a business plan. If the entrepreneur goes ahead these conjectures will be appraised by consumers, resource owners, competitors — both actual and potential, and current and prospective collaborators. This critical appraisal is the fundamental justification for markets (which is itself a conjecture). But 'the testing of plans in the market' (Kirzner 1973: 10) may be very expensive; it is often therefore worthwhile to develop pre-market tests. Instead of discovering a $10 bill already in his hand, the entrepreneur therefore faces the prospect of spending many $10 bills in devising and performing severe Popperian tests on his conjecture, and the core of the thesis was an investigation of what this involved. Harper's theoretical approach may be usefully compared with a screening process developed within ICI, for the explicit purpose of anticipating market tests and thereby replacing expensive market failure with low-cost disposal or successful redesign (Bradbury, Gallagher and Suckling 1973). Redesign in response to discoveries generated by the testing procedure is a notable feature of both the ICI scheme and Harper's study; it is a common characteristic of innovation studies, though not often reflected in economic theory. That entrepreneurship should be analyzed, not as a function, or as a type of personality, or as an event, but as a process, in which discovery is not merely the trigger but part of the content, seems to me at once reasonable and an example of the importance of taxonomy in constraining and enabling the growth of knowledge.

If taxonomy is equivalent to anatomy, then the equivalent to physiology may be cognitive mapping, the theme of an issue of the *Journal of Management Studies* (Eden 1992). Cognitive maps represent both categories and the linkages between them, which together constitute the basic components of a system. Neither categories nor linkages are to be thought of as naturally given; both are imposed by individuals (often subject to outside influences, which may indeed be overwhelming), and the study of group behaviour is illuminated by examining the extent to which models are shared, or the ways in which different models intersect. These intersections should not be assumed to coincide either with organizational interfaces or the structure of problem situations. Cryptic labels provide the glue of the social system; but since the labels are ambiguous, the glue may come unstuck. The focus in these papers is on organizations, but the ideas seem no less applicable to markets, each of which has its own set of institutional arrangements, and may be used to extend game-theoretic analyses to situations (which have many real-world counterparts) in which different players have different conceptions of the game being played. They would enrich Lesourne's analysis of self-organization, though some might be difficult to accommodate within his analytical framework: as always, the way in which we organize knowledge puts limits on the knowledge that we can organize.

Marengo's analysis of organizations omits these considerations. He assumes a common set of rules, codes and languages, all of them well understood, and no disputes over the evaluation of outcomes; the only differences permitted are between the rule systems within sub-units, which are generated by the interaction between local information and the local operation of random mutations. These restrictions on inter-unit divergence are deliberately chosen, and allow Marengo to demonstrate clearly that shared cognitive systems and shared preferences, and the consequent absence of any trace of opportunism, are not sufficient to make co-ordination easy. Since the standard economic analysis of organizations, which is so well deployed by Milgrom and Roberts (1992), is based exclusively on the conflict of incentives, such a demonstration is of crucial value – if it does not continue to be ignored.

However, this high degree of commonality among preferences and decision-procedures does not extend to any shared ideas about the business in which these people are engaged; indeed they begin with no initial conjectures about the environment or about their policy — other than the set of possibilities, which has been conjectured by the analyst and of which they are very imperfectly conscious. Now it is my own conjecture that an organization with no theory of what it is about is unlikely to provide a very useful basis for study. Marengo's firms are seriously under-managed — like almost all firms in economic theory. Lesourne (1992: 6) recognises that firms, and even markets, need a culture: this is not a concept which is popular with economists, but it would have significantly improved the quality of advice given to the formerly planned economies. He does not, however, recognize that firms also need a strategy — not in the sense of a complete set of decision rules for every contingency, but to provide decision premises and decision criteria.

That cognitive maps are both imposed and influential is crisply illustrated by Robert Eisner's (1992) examination of the implications of various plausible ways of measuring the US budget deficit. Simple definitional issues supply a wide range of figures; inflation and employment adjustments open up further possibilities, and the invocation of a public sector balance sheet suggests that a distinction between current and capital expenditure would abolish the perceived problem. (My former colleague Clive Spash commented that the inclusion of environmental costs would, on the contrary, disclose a much greater welfare loss.) But we can go further than Eisner: even the current/capital distinction is not simple. On reading Eisner's paper, my distributed memory presented a statement by Winston Churchill in 1943: 'there is no finer investment for any community than putting milk into babies'. What appears to be consumption may also be investment. Indeed, if we define investment as any action having potential future consequences, then it appears that investment is the wider, and perhaps nearly universal, category. In Woo's formulation, every consumption decision is liable to change the stock of consumer capital — consumers learn by choosing; in Kelly's theory of personality, every event may modify the interpretative framework by which later events are construed; in the framework of Popper and quasi-Popperians, conjectures are fallible and always open to falsification or at least revision. The Greeks, of course, knew this. In the words of Heraclitus, you can't step into the same river twice — to which Cratylus replied, you can't even do it once.

Yet the kind of distinction that is represented by consumption versus investment, or short-run versus long-run, can be very helpful. If there are indeed no discontinuities in nature, as Marshall insisted, then we must impose some if we are to have any hope of understanding nature — as Marshall in fact did in developing his analytical principles, though he failed to impose sufficient discontinuities to enable him to produce his second volume. We should, however, remember that the categories which we use are conjectures too.

At a higher level of organization, we can identify grand strategies of knowledge. Indeed the most interesting grand strategy appears to be the search for patterns, which is reflected in, for example, Adam Smith's (1980) theory of science and Woo's analysis of the economics of cognition. Popper (1969: 49) notes, what experimenters have confirmed, that people look for patterns even where there are none to be found; subjects persist in event-matching when supplied with random data. If one looks at the balance of risks in human evolution, it seems plausible to argue that the perception of false patterns is likely to be less costly than failure to recognize genuine patterns; and pattern recall is more efficient than information processing. Pattern making seems likely to be a good general strategy for increasing knowledge; Einstein's principle that 'God does not play dice' may be a good working rule, even if He sometimes - or even usually — does. Theories are patterns, and the development of theories, like the evolution of species, proceeds through the generation and selection of novel patterns.

We might also pay attention to this principle in seeking to understand behaviour in firms and markets. Raymond Boudon (1992) scolds sociologists for too readily attributing irrationality to people whose mistakes are made 'for good reasons' — because such people assume a pattern that is embedded in a theory which, though fallible, is the best that they have, especially in crucial cases. Among the 'good reasons' particular attention should be given to the co-ordination of decisions which are taken separately, and to the preservation of a coalition which is expected to deliver future benefits. It is partly because an organization — and, one might add, a market — is a collection of routines (Nelson and Winter, 1982), which are sometimes mistakenly applied, that its activities can be tolerably well coordinated.

There is another Popperian grand strategy that may help us to understand how we know: his distinction between the three worlds of physical phenomena, psychological phenomena, and ideas. (Similar distinctions have been offered by others.) The subject matter of conventional economics appears to include elements from World 1 — resources, commodities, and technologies to convert the former into the latter — and from World 2 — preferences and decision algorithms, which also appear to be the domain of artificial intelligence. But economic theory, the concepts on which it relies, and the knowledge which it generates, all belong in World 3. From simple demand curves to the most elaborate models, we are dealing not with natural givens but the products of human imagination. Economic agents, if they are to be treated as humans, must also enter World 3 if they are to accumulate and use knowledge; for it is in World 3 that we develop our understanding of Worlds 1 and 2. Consciously rational behaviour depends on World 3 processes. But although the world of ideas is the arena in which we interpret the physical and psychological worlds, it does not replicate them, for reasons that were set out at the beginning of this chapter: indeed, the relationships between our imaginative conceptions and the other two worlds are the essential problems of both rationality and epistemology. These abstractions need to be interpreted — which allows for ambiguity and argument at cross-purposes; and the sufficiency of any interpretation is always open to question.

There is a further problem. The ideas of World 3, and especially the interactions between them, give rise to their own questions. The concept of equilibrium, for example, suggests questions of existence and uniqueness; the concept of rationality suggests the need for strict internal consistency. Yet the relevance of these issues, in their World 3 formulations, to the problems of the other two worlds is necessarily problematic, and their implications for our knowledge, though often profound, are not necessarily beneficial. Thus Adam Smith's (1976b) problem of achieving social coherence without central direction was tackled by Smith through a combination of jurisprudence, moral sentiments, and the market exchange of benefits — against a background, it should be remembered, of Smith's ideas about knowledge and the use of language. The contemporary economic representation of Smith's problem in World 3 has been designed to fit the requirements of a closed and tractable model — which are World 3 criteria; it is consequently far removed from Smith's conception. Lesourne's fruitful attempt to improve on this representation nevertheless remains firmly in World 3, with no apparent recognition of the dangers of his policy: progress is to be obtained purely by theoretical development, without any need for reference to any other world — or even to any other region of World 3. Marshall and Coase actually visited factories to see how order was achieved: will any other economist follow their example?

Concentration on the internal problems of World 3 can give rise to what Neva Goodwin (1991) has appropriately described as unicorn words: concepts which can be analyzed and manipulated, but which do not correspond to any recognizable phenomena in Worlds 1 or 2. On a bad day it sometimes appears that much of economic theory is concerned with the natural history of unicorns, especially if one stretches the concept from such purely mythical entities as perfect competition, rational expectations and Pareto optimality to include concepts which can only be operationalized (which, for most economists, means represented by manipulable data) in ways which do not correspond to phenomena in the other two worlds: for example, Gross National Product, unemployment, concentration ratio, market, and profit.

Worthy of the special notice which it received from George Shackle is the double shift by which structural uncertainty is replaced by parametric probability, which is then assumed to be necessarily reducible to numbers. Most economists, unlike Keynes (1921), seem to believe that probability is necessarily statistical: if supposedly objective measures are not available, then subjective assessments must be conjured up in order to preserve the economist's unicorn concept of rationality. There are substantial benefits in tractability to be gained by specializing on those phenomena that appear amenable to statistical determination, but to assume that this particular category represents the whole leaves us without a sensible way of dealing with many situations. These include, as Popper has insisted, the appraisal of hypotheses: the numerical probability of the truth of a general empirical hypothesis is a unicorn concept. Moreover, once locked into a probabilistic assessment, the only legitimate response to new evidence is a Bayesian updating of this assessment; there can be no double-loop learning (Argyris and Schon 1978), and no bold conjectures.

4 KNOWLEDGE AND PROGRESS

Human progress depends on the increase of knowledge, and also, because of human limitations, on the ability to use more knowledge than any single person could possibly possess, as Hayek has insisted. To do the latter we need to recognize, with Samuel Johnson (1775), the importance of two kinds of knowledge: direct knowledge of a thing, and knowledge of how to find out. Now if a central planner had complete knowledge — predominantly, we may presume, of the second kind — then a perfect plan might be possible. If it were possible, why should anyone bother with a market system? Decentralization to a market is necessary only when rationality and knowledge are bounded, as Egidi (1992) points out. So the conditions in which markets are needed ensure that they are not perfect, in the conventional economic sense. But when rationality and knowledge are bounded, the acquisition and use of knowledge is costly. It is these costs to which Coase (1937) appeals in seeking to explain why firms exist. Transaction costs are knowledge costs: Ayer's super-beings, whom we met at the outset, experience no transaction costs. If an economy is a knowledge structure, then transaction costs are unavoidable — which is what Coase (1988a) has argued: economic analysis which ignores transactions costs, or invokes them to explain various kinds of failure, is addressing World 3 problems.

A market system is a way of linking specialized activities so that each unit can access the knowledge possessed by others. If knowledge structures were completely decomposable, then nothing else would be required. It would be sufficient to know the capabilities of those with whom we intended to deal, and, as Hayek (1946: 97) has reminded us, it is from the working of the competitive market process that we come to learn what these capabilities are, and therefore from whom 'we can expect to find the most satisfactory solution for whatever particular personal problems we may have to face'. What knowledge is needed to develop such capabilities is a question we would not even need to ask. But as Egidi (1992) reminds us, most of the linkages in a modern economy are found within firms; and Lazonick (1991) has tried to persuade economists that these linkages are what matter for economic performance. (He goes too far in claiming that only these linkages matter.) Decomposability is imperfect, and requires some degree of management: any organizational structure, as Egidi (1992: 167) says, represents a conjecture about a distribution of activities which will allow most sub-problems to be independently solved, if the anticipated cost of finding a solution seems worth while. Different firms may try different schemes of decomposition, which may represent effective adaptations to different circumstances, or simply alternative experiments in the face of common problems which are imperfectly understood (thereby reducing opportunity costs for the system, as noted earlier). But since complete decomposability would leave us with little reason for firms to exist, we must expect that firms will never find a perfect way of distributing their activities, and also that organization structures will generate World 3 problems, supported by data which are artifacts of those structures.

We may go further, as did George Richardson (1972), and recognize that even interdependent activities that are 'closely complementary' may not be best conducted within a single organization; for activities which are closely complementary may nevertheless be very dissimilar, relying on very different ways of organizing knowledge. Such activities cannot be integrated by a pure price system either, for that requires a decomposable structure of knowledge; such integration therefore needs an organized relationship between firms in a market context. There is much more conscious organization, and much more ongoing management, in most markets than one would expect from economic theories of unicorn markets (see Loasby 1998).

In both markets and in firms — and, as Woo has reminded us, within every individual — there are costs of organizing knowledge — transaction costs in Coase's terminology. It is often possible to reduce these costs by making investments in transaction technology, even though some of these activities, like learning by doing, do not take the conventional form of investments. Firms, indeed, may be thought of as clusters of transaction technologies; and so may markets. The creation of such technologies, both within and between firms — what Marshall, who had a deeper understanding of the role of knowledge in economic processes than any of his contemporaries, and almost all his successors, called internal and external organization — takes time, and accumulates sunk costs; we are dealing with time-irreversibility, as Lesourne recognizes. Any change to a new form of organization requires fresh investment, and often a substantial effort at disinvestment, to reorientate individuals and to create new sets of compatible interdependencies. An obvious consequence is the ubiquity of switching costs — a link not explicitly recognized by Paul Klemperer (1992; 1995) who in an otherwise excellent survey attributes such costs exclusively to the search for monopolistic advantage. It is perhaps because of Oliver Williamson's insistence that opportunism is essential to transaction costs that Klemperer assumes switching costs to be similarly avoidable in a world of benevolence. But Williamson is wrong, as Coase (1988b) has stated; and so are the economists whose work Klemperer surveys. They are studying unicorns. Of course, many switching costs, and many transaction costs, are the result of selfish behaviour, but neither could be reduced to zero by perfect altruism. The reference-point is wrong; the analysis is therefore incomplete, and potentially misleading.

What requires more attention is the trade-off between switching costs and the effective organization of knowledge. As Simon (1992: 6) reminds us, joining an organization is a way of simplifying our decision problems, by accepting, for the most part, the problem-definition which the organization provides; and there are mechanisms of identification which make organizations far more coherent, as Simon says, than is acknowledged in conventional economic theory. Transaction costs can be reduced if the transactors use compatible frameworks for interpreting events. Such mechanisms of identification have received some attention — though little of it from economists — under the rubric of corporate culture; and rightly so, for, as noted earlier, culture and strategy are important factors in organizing the growth of knowledge, not least within the economics profession. But they create comparative advantage, if they fit the needs of the situation, at the price of increased costs of switching to other ways of organizing knowledge, as can be seen in many companies. They reduce liquidity, in the non-financial sense. This trade-off is a matter for the attention of chief executives and governing boards. It is also an under-discussed issue of public policy: is it better to encourage flexibility within organizations, or to try to maintain variety between organizations — the equivalent of preserving the gene pool? (For analyses of these issues, with reference to particular industrial contexts, see Langlois 1992, Langlois and Everett 1992, Langlois and Robertson 1992, Langlois and Robertson 1995).

May I end with a reminder that much of this discussion can be applied to academic disciplines? The transactions of learned societies can be conducted at lower cost if the members share a set of conventions about scope and method, and indeed a language in which such transactions are expressed. (Adam Smith (1983), readers will perhaps not be surprised to learn, had something to say about the classificatory function of language). Professional education, in economics as in other fields, creates a framework which facilitates interaction by restricting its scope but thereby increases the costs of switching to other frameworks. Herbert Simon (1992: 7) has some comments on the effect of North American graduate education in economics, on which David Colander and Arjo Klamer (1987) have reported. All knowledge requires conventions, and conventions have consequences. 'How we know' has implications for what we know, and what we do not, perhaps cannot, know as long as we remain within those conventions. It is not only in economics that the obverse of specialised skills is what Lazonick (1991) calls 'trained incapacity'.

The evolutionary process in the natural world relies on birth to provide new forms, by mutation, and death to eliminate the unsuccessful experiments — unsuccessful, that is, within the context of those experiments. (To call this 'survival of the fittest' is not quite accurate, as Marshall (1920: 241-9) duly noted). Human beings are subject to this process. But because human evolution has led to a separation of theory from the organism, humans, as Popper (1972: 261) pointed out, sometimes have the option of letting their ideas die instead of themselves: they can change their representations in World 3 as a means to changing their behaviour in Worlds 1 and 2. This option is not as easy as Popper seems to imply, even when the ideas seem to be leading to disaster; but it is worth investigating the possibilities, their benefits and their costs — for there are always costs, or there would be no economics. How do we go on knowing? By seeking to organise our knowledge within an open system. No one has done more to keep our intellectual systems open than George Shackle.

21

REFERENCES

Argyris, C. and Schon, D. (1978) *Organizational Learning*, Reading, MA: Addison-Wesley.

Ayer, A. J. (1971) *Language, Truth and Logic*, Harmondworth: Penguin.

Bianchi, M. (ed.) (1998) *The Active Consumer*, London: Routledge.

Binmore, K. (1999) 'Review of M. Hollis *Trust within Reason*, Cambridge: Cambridge_University Press, 1998', *Economic Journal* 109, F211-12.

Boudon, R. (1992) 'Subjective rationality and the explanation of social behaviour', in Simon (1992), 123-47.

Bradbury, F. R., Gallagher, W. M., and Suckling, C. W. (1973) 'Qualitative aspects of the Evaluation and control of research and development projects', *R&D Management* 3, 2: 49-57.

Choi, Y. B. (1993) *Paradigms and Conventions: Uncertainty, Decision Making, and Entrepreneurship*, Ann Arbor: University of Michigan Press.

Coase, R. H. (1937) 'The nature of the firm', *Economica* n.s. 4: 386-405.

—— (1988a) ' The firm, the market and the law', in *The Firm the Market and the Law*, Chicago and London: University of Chicago Press, 1-31.

—— (1988b) 'The nature of the firm: influence', *Journal of Law, Economics, and Organization* 4, 1: 33-47.

Coddington, A. (1975) 'Creaking semaphore and beyond', *British Journal for the Philosophy of Science* 26: 151-63.

Colander, D. and Klamer, A. (1987) 'The Making of an Economist', *Journal of Economic Perspectives* 1, 2: 95-111.

Eden, C. (ed.) (1992) 'On the nature of cognitive maps', *Journal of Management Studies* (Special Issue), 29, 3.

Egidi, M. (1992) 'Organizational learning, problem solving and the division of labour', in Simon (1992), 560-95.

Eisner, R. (1992) 'Deficits: which, how much, and so what'? *American Economic Review*, 84, Papers and Proceedings: 295-9.

Fornero, E. (1992) Contribution to colloquium in Simon (1992), 21

Goodwin, N. (1991) *Social Economics: An Alternative Theory: Volume 1, Building Anew on Marshall's Principles*, London and Basingstoke: Macmillan.

Hahn, F. H. (1973; 1984) *On the Notion of Equilibrium in Economics*, Cambridge: Cambridge University Press. Reprinted in *Equilibrium and Macroeconomics*, Oxford: Basil Blackwell.

Harper, D. (1992) 'Entrepreneurship and the market process: an inquiry into the growth of knowledge', Ph.D. thesis, University of Reading.

—— (1995) *Entrepreneurship and the Market Process*, London: Routledge.

Hayek, F. A. (1946) 'The meaning of competition', Stafford Little lecture, Princeton University. Reprinted in F.A. Hayek (1948) *Individualism and Economic Order*, Chicago: University of Chicago Press, 92-106.

—— (1952) *The Sensory Order*, Chicago: University of Chicago Press.

Heiner, R. A. (1983) 'The origin of predictable behavior', *American Economic Review* 75: 560–95.

Johnson, S. (1775) 'Preface', in *A Dictionary of the English Language*, London: W. Strahan for J. and P. Knapton.

Kelly, G. A. (1963) *A Theory of Personality*, New York: W. W. Norton.

Keynes, J. M. (1921) *A Treatise on Probability*, London: Macmillan.

Kirzner, I. M. (1973) *Competition and Entrepreneurship*, Chicago: University of Chicago Press.

—— (1992) *The Meaning of Market Process*, London: Routledge.

Klemperer, P. (1992) 'Competition when consumers have switching costs: an overview', Inaugural Lecture to Annual Conference on Industrial Economics, Madrid.

—— (1995) 'Competition when consumers have switching costs: an overview with applications to industrial organization, macro-economics and international trade', *Review of Economic Studies* 62, 515–39.

Kuhn, T. S. (1962, 1970) *The Structure of Scientific Revolutions*, Chicago: University of Chicago Press.

Langlois, R. N. (1992) 'Transaction cost economics in real time', *Industrial and Corporate Change* 1, 1: 99–127.

—— and Everett, M. J. (1992), 'Complexity, genuine uncertainty, and the economics of organization', *Human Systems Management*, 11, 2; 67–76.

—— and Robertson, P. L. (1992) 'Networks and innovation in a modular system: lessons from the microcomputer and stereo component industries', *Research Policy* 21, 4: 297–313.

—— and —— (1995) *Firms, Markets and Economic Change*, London: Routledge.

Lazonick, W. (1991) *Business Organization and the Myth of the Market Economy*, Cambridge: Cambridge University Press.

Lesourne, J. (1992) *The Economics of Order and Disorder*, Oxford: Clarendon Press.

Loasby, B. J. (1991) *Equilibrium and Evolution*, Manchester: Manchester University Press.

—— (1995) 'Running a business: an appraisal of Economics, Organization and Management by Paul Milgrom and John Roberts', *Industrial and Corporate Change* 4: 471–90.

—— (1998) 'The organization of capabilities', *Journal of Economic Behavior and Organization* 35: 139–60.

—— (1999) *Knowledge, Institutions and Evolution in Economics*, London: Routledge.

Lombardini, S. (1992) Contribution to colloquium in Simon (1992), 12–14.

Marengo, L. (1992a) 'Structure, co-ordination and organizational learning, Ph.D. thesis, University of Sussex.

—— (1992b) 'Co-ordination and organisational learning in the firm', *Journal of Evolutionary Economics* 2: 313–26.

—— and Tordjman, H. (1996) 'Speculation, heterogeneity and learning: a simulation model of exchange rate dynamics', *Kyklos* 49, 3: 407–38.

Marshall, A. (1920) *Principles of Economics*, 8th Edition, London: Macmillan.

Meyerson, E. M. (1992) *The Impact of Ownership Structure and Executive Team Composition On Team Performance: The Resolution of a Leadership Paradox*, Stockholm: IUI.

Milgrom, P. and Roberts, J. (1992) *Economics, Organization and Management*, Englewood Cliffs, NJ: Prentice-Hall.

Munro, A. (1992) 'Developments in game theory', *Scottish Journal of Political Economy*, 39, 3: 337–45

Nelson, R. R. and Winter, S. G. (1982) *An Evolutionary Theory of Economic Change*, Cambridge, MA: Harvard University Press.

Popper K. R. (1969) *Conjectures and Refutations*, 3rd edn, London: Routledge and Kegan Paul.

—— (1972) *Objective Knowledge: An Evolutionary Approach*, Oxford: Clarendon Press.

Richardson, G. B. (1972) 'The organization of industry', *Economic Journal* 82: 883–96.

Shackle, G. L. S. (1972) *Epistemics and Economics*, Cambridge: Cambridge University Press.

Schumpeter, J. A. (1934) *The Theory of Economic Development.* Cambridge, MA: Harvard University Press.

Simon, H. A., with Egidi, M., Marris, R. L. and Viale, R. (1992) *Economics, Bounded Rationality and the Cognitive Revolution*, Aldershot: Edward Elgar.

Smith A. (1976a) *The Theory of Moral Sentiments*, ed. by D. D. Raphael and A. L. Macfie, Oxford: Oxford University Press.

—— (1976b) *An Inquiry into the Nature and Causes of the Wealth of Nations*, ed. R. H. Campbell, A. S. Skinner and W. B. Todd. 2 volumes, Oxford: Oxford University Press.

—— (1980) 'The Principles Which Lead and Direct Philosophical Enquiries: Illustrated by the History of Astronomy', in W. P. D. Wightman (ed.), *Essay on Philosophical Subjects* (1795), Oxford: Oxford University Press.

—— (1983) 'Considerations concerning the first formation of languages', in *Lectures on Rhetoric and Belles Lettres*, ed. J. C. Bryce, Oxford: Oxford University Press.

Woo, H. K. H. (1992) *Cognition, Value and Price*, Ann Arbor, MI: University of Michigan Press.

2

INDETERMINACY IN
THE ECONOMICS CLASSROOM

*Peter E. Earl**

And so to the University course in economics. The first
task of the University teacher of any liberal art is surely to
persuade his students that the most important things he
will put before them are questions and not answers. He is
going to put up for them a scaffolding, and leave them to
build within it. He has to persuade them that they have
not come to the University to learn as it were by heart
things which are already hard-and-fast and cut-and-dried,
but to watch and perhaps help in a process, the driving of
a causeway which will be made gradually firmer by the
traffic of many minds.

(Shackle 1953: 18)

1 INTRODUCTION

The view of the role of the economics lecturer that George Shackle
offered towards the end of his Inaugural Lecture at the University of
Liverpool comes as no surprise to economists familiar with his work.
His writings on the implications of uncertainty for economic analysis
shatter hopes of constructing universal thought schemes and
deterministic models. They point instead towards the creative use of
our imaginations to construct rival scenarios and then debate their
plausibility and implications (Jefferson 1983; Loasby 1990), and to the
study of the stereotypes or drills that people use to cope with the
ordinary business of living (Shackle 1963: 18). However, almost fifty
years after Shackle's inaugural lecture, it is clear that only a minority of
economists are offering the kinds of training that Shackle advocated.

25

What most economics students receive is not a guide to contending perspectives (Barone 1991), which highlights disputed areas, but a thoroughly neoclassical training that focuses on determinate solutions.

This probably reflects factors such as faculty politics, difficulties in finding suitable texts, claims that intellectual standards will inevitably be lowered if attempts are made to 'cram a quart into a pint pot', and a belief that undergraduates simply will not be able to cope with such an approach to teaching. Most academic economists do not try to find out whether all these barriers really exist and are insuperable; they simply take them for granted. This may reflect incentive structures that reward success in publishing in prestigious mainstream journals (see Earl 1983; Colander 1991). Some of the failure to teach non-mainstream modes of thought may reflect a blissful ignorance of the existence of alternatives but insofar as mainstream economists are knowingly failing to alert their classes to schools of thought that are not the 'economics equivalents of the "flat earth society"' (Weintraub 1985: 1118), then serious questions are raised about their academic integrity (see Parvin 1992).

This chapter focuses on how students may be expected to behave if actually presented with a non-deterministic approach to the teaching of economics: in other words, I will be exploring the practical feasibility of Shackle's vision of what might happen in the economics classroom. My interest in this issue was originally triggered by Jefferson's (1983: 146) reports of resistance to scenario planning within the Shell Petroleum Company: many of Shell's managers found it hard to cope with the idea of a system of planning which aimed to highlight uncertainties. Since their normal way of viewing planning was as an activity intended to reduce uncertainty, a scenarios approach seemed to open up risks of error rather than offering scope for them to take responsible choices. If senior managers experienced such difficulties, we might expect similar problems in the economics classroom due to tensions between a non-deterministic approach to teaching economics and the stereotypes used by students to assist their learning. I begin by showing that such fears are indeed well-grounded, but I then consider ways in which university teachers of economics might overcome these difficulties. To do this I call partly on my own, sometimes traumatic experiences as well as on research associated with the work of Harvard educationalist William G. Perry, Jr (1970, 1981, 1985), whose vision of the role of a liberal arts education bears an uncanny resemblance to that expressed by Shackle in his inaugural lecture.

During this chapter, a willingness to make *commitments* to particular ideas will be taken as indicating a high level of intellectual and ethical development. Non-deterministic teaching encourages students to choose for themselves particular ways of sizing up economic problems in the light of (i) their new-found knowledge of commitments made by economists who have gone before them and (ii) criticisms offered by members of rival schools who have thought long and hard about what it going on in their opponents' camps. If students are offered this knowledge they are not merely being given an honest guide to the difficulties that economics presents, they are more likely to become conscious of the core notions that provide the basis for mainstream economics, let alone its rivals. For example, it may take a discussion of the idea of satisficing behaviour to clarify what is involved in constrained optimization, or an outline of 'normal cost' price theory to render transparent the market-clearing philosophy embodied in marginalist approaches to pricing (cf. Lee 1984).

Such an approach to teaching economics does not require that the lecturer maintains a detachment from any particular school of thought in economics. On the contrary, as we shall see, students may benefit from being taught by economists who are candid about the factors that have led them to make particular commitments. So long as lecturers are committed to the idea that it is desirable for students to be exposed to contending perspectives and try to present alternative points of view in ways which 'do unto rival viewpoints as they would like to see the latter's proponents do unto their own', multi-paradigm teaching is compatible with lecturers having made commitments to particular approaches to theorising about particular situations. In fact, an economist who feels particularly attracted to one school of thought may be a particularly exciting teacher of not only its strengths and weaknesses but also of those of its rivals: as Shackle (1967: 295–6) argued, 'Only a theory that one has come to terms with can be taught with zest and conviction; but this deep assessment of a theory implies a consciousness of its weaknesses and possible alternatives, as well as of efficiency and beauty.'

2 PERRY'S SCHEME OF COGNITIVE AND ETHICAL DEVELOPMENT

When students perform poorly their teachers often blame a lack of effort or ability. After interviewing many undergraduates at Harvard, William Perry offered a rather different perspective: the problem may be that the ways in which students are setting about trying to learn may be grossly out of line with the views of learning on which their teachers are building their courses. Perry identified a sequence of different ways of thinking that students tended to pass through in a kind of Pilgrim's Progress towards the sort of way of making sense of the world used by their teachers. Some might be well advanced along this road even by the time they matriculated; others might fail to go far along it even after three or four years of diligent study. It may be summarized as follows:

Level 1: Dualism

The least mature stage in Perry's scheme is a world-view in which students see things in dualistic terms: everything is expected to be either black or white. It is rarely encountered in empirical research (Perry 1981) but is worth outlining to clarify what dualism might entail at the extreme 'Garden of Eden' stage. Dualistic students see themselves rather as empty vessels waiting to be filled with the truth and having a duty to pay attention in lectures, taking down what their teachers say and afterwards memorising it. They expect that, if they work hard, following up every reading instruction and learning the Right Answers, they will be duly rewarded at examination time for demonstrating to their teachers their diligence and grasp of the Truth. They see their teachers as experts who know what is correct and whose role therefore is to present the Truth to them in a way that makes it easy to grasp; this is seen to involve clearly structured lectures and assignments, with the teacher ensuring that the class is under control. Lecturers who are repeatedly interrupted by students asking questions and who cannot always deal with these questions are seen by dualistic students as poor teachers: if these lecturers knew their subjects properly and were able to present the material more clearly they would not be causing such confusion and allowing such interruptions to disrupt the process of transferring the truth from themselves to the students.

Dualistic students have a great deal of trouble seeing the point of class discussions, for they do not see their peers as knowing any more than themselves what needs to be learned. They get very frustrated by abstract learning experiences that do not seem to have clear answers and if asked to work out answers for themselves they aim their efforts largely at finding out what the teachers expect. They believe that better grades follow automatically if they provide more information, for grading is simply a matter of counting up the amount of correct information that they have supplied.

Level 2: Dualism questioned

It is not surprising that extreme Type 1 dualism is rather rarely observed. Sooner or later, students are likely to encounter lecturers who point out differences in opinions in particular areas, who seem to wish to challenge things that are in textbooks, and who seem happy to leave their classes with unresolved problems rather than sets of answers. Students at the second stage are alert to this phenomenon but seek to resolve its apparent contradiction with their dualistic style of thinking by inferring that some Authorities must be right and others wrong. If those that they judge not to be frauds are nonetheless giving them problems rather than answers, they are prone to infer that the Good Authorities expect them to be able to learn from these problems what the right answers are. This cognitive strategy becomes rather difficult to sustain once some of the Good Authorities admit that they do not yet know all the answers and reward highly students whose answers to identical questions differ greatly: if these lecturers are now not to be thought of as frauds, then a non-dualistic way of looking at things is needed to make sense of their behaviour.

Level 3: Multiplicity, but only for the moment?

The initial way of seeing differences in opinion as legitimate rather than as a sign of differences in competence or honesty of teachers is to see them as states of affairs that will eventually be resolved by the experts working out what the Truth is. (When Shackle wrote the words at the end of this chapter's epigraph — referring to 'the driving of a causeway which will be made gradually firmer by the traffic of many minds' — he might be said to have been taking this perspective himself, though with a long-term time horizon.) Though this may at first restore the students' faiths in their teachers, they then start realizing just how many areas are presently disputed, how long some disputes have been raging and how far many disputes seem from resolution. This leads to a puzzle: if supposed experts can keep on arguing amongst themselves and cannot tell their students what the truth is, then why should they be seen as experts in their fields? It now becomes rather difficult to study merely by memorizing facts. Not merely is it unclear what the facts are, students also become worried that they could do poorly if they do not understand how their teachers think. Grading can no longer be seen merely as counting correct pieces of information,. The Type 3 student begins to wonder whether teachers can be trusted to be fair if the latter hold strong opinions on issues about which they set questions.

Level 4: Anything goes?

Once students can no longer judge their teachers as expert authorities on the basis that they know the Truth, they tend to start thinking that there is *no* basis for saying who is an authority, and that their own views might be at least as good as those of their teachers. They grow more confident about challenging what their teachers say and see greater value in class discussions in which they can share with their peers their ideas on how particular issues might be seen. But they also start to see that although everyone may have a right to his or her own opinions, this does not imply that no one can be wrong, for some opinions may be ones whose proponents seem unable to support with facts and reasons. They start seeing that in some courses teachers are rewarding them not for coming up with the Right Answer but on the basis of whether they are able to think about things in particular ways — whether they have mastered particular concepts, rather than whether they have memorized particular facts — and can justify the conclusions that they reach.

Level 5: Relativism

The next discovery is that this style of thinking pays off in other areas of learning and life. Students begin to see that in interacting with other people it helps to try to understand how they are thinking — where they are coming from and what is important to them. They see that their teachers try to do this, too, but that the latter do not treat every point of view as equally valid: what is acceptable depends on the context and the evidence that is available. They begin to realise that their teachers can serve as models of how people can make sense of uncertainties about their beliefs and can help them think critically about their own experiences and ways of making judgments, and the views of others. A teacher comes to be seen as a valuable resource who can provide positive and negative feedback on students' thinking. Negative evaluations come to be seen as opportunities for reframing things rather than as a bad person making judgments about one's personal worth.

Level 6 and beyond:
Tentative commitments to personal viewpoints

The discovery that knowledge is relative and that teachers can be useful aides for becoming able to see strengths and weaknesses of particular ways of thinking does not solve the problem of what the individual student should believe. Individuals at the most advanced levels in Perry's analysis achieve their individuality by opting not simply to copy others but by making commitments following much soul searching — commitments with a capital 'C', exactly of the kind that Shackle (1967) had in mind in the passage quoted at the end of the introduction to this chapter. If people have made mental commitments, they will be prepared to fight wholeheartedly for their values and yet, if operating at Perry's highest levels, they will remain open to change. They will recognize that to make a single commitment does not solve problems: decisions will still need to be taken from time to time about whether existing commitments need to be revised, abandoned or augmented with new ones.

3 CONSEQUENCES OF MISMATCHES BETWEEN STUDENTS' AND LECTURERS' EXPECTATIONS

The minority of lecturers who have tried to teach in a way which emphasises differences in economists' perspectives and the open-ended nature of many economic puzzles can probably remember being surprised by students who seemed so innocent as to believe that textbooks contained the Truth. I have vivid memories of my first encounter with this phenomenon: an overseas student who shared his astonishment with me at the end of a tutorial in which, mindful of Andrews and Brunner (1975: 32), I had criticized the idea that a firm will stay in production so long as it covers at least its average variable costs. The student found it easy to see that this might not be so if the price failed to cover average fixed costs that could be avoided by closing down (for example, rates, rental payments and outlays on overhead staff), and yet he was perplexed that this was not what was said in the textbook.

Though academics may remember such incidents they probably forget that they were once themselves at the 'Garden of Eden' stage in their expectations about the process of learning and the nature of economics. At best they probably remember the process of becoming committed to the kind of economics that they now practise. They will not be trying, as a matter of routine, to look at their courses from the standpoints that their students might be employing.

This is potentially most unfortunate. The work of Perry and his associates leads one to anticipate major problems if a course is presented to a class on the basis that all members are at the same level of development when in fact they are not. As Perry (1985: 16) points out, to teach a class consisting mainly of Level 5 students as if they are still Level 2 learners is probably going to result in boredom and frustration, but at least the Level 5 students will be able to make sense of what their teacher is doing. Things are very different in the reverse case.

Consider an intermediate microeconomics course which is presented as if the class consists of students that are at level 5 and on this basis includes instruction in a range of ways of thinking about topics such as consumer and producer theory, economic organization and choice under uncertainty. Some, perhaps the majority of the class, may actually be Level 2 students. During the course, their obsessive search for the Right Answers will be a barrier to concentrating on how different perspectives on the problem have been constructed, and on the difficulties in choosing between them that allow their continued coexistence. Such students will be most uncomfortable if faced with an examination question such as 'Discuss the extent to which Shackle's "potential surprise" theory of choice under uncertainty represents an advance on the "expected utility" analysis of how people decide which risks to take.' They will have trouble relating to the question if their teacher has not presented the material in a way which aims to demonstrate that Shackle's model completely dominates over the expected utility theory, or vice versa, and they will probably feel that their time has been wasted if they have been shown a model which, after all, turned out to be 'no good'. They are likely to see this sort of question as involving 'trick' wording. To avoid being caught out, they will look around for alternative questions set out in a more transparent manner. If they *do* attempt the question, they will probably construe it as a strangely worded invitation to present expositions of the two theories, or, if they have been taught in a style which praises Shackle's model, they may simply give an exposition of potential surprise analysis. The Level 2 students will expect that their grades will reflect their abilities to avoid technical errors as they present the theories. They will often miss cues provided by their examiner in wording the question, relating to particular philosophical differences (note, in this example, the use of the words 'uncertainty' and 'risk'). Worse still, they will not see that the question can be answered without any systematic outlining of either theory: an effective answer can readily be constructed around various criteria that might be relevant in judging the quality of a theory, such as predictive capabilities, assumptive realism, range of compass, logical consistency, and so on.

When Level 2 students are presented with questions that invite them to 'compare and contrast' particular pairs of theories or problem situations they are again likely to try to look elsewhere for more clear-cut questions; if they cannot do so, then they will tend to answer in terms of paired expositions of the two theories or pairs of lists of features, rather than in an integrative manner that displays critical thinking (Level 3 students may often produce similar types of answers, but will feel rather more at ease with such questions). Level 2 students will feel comfortable with questions that enable them to show that they have memorized successfully various definitions (for example, 'What is an indifference curve?') or set-piece applications of theory (for example, 'Use the indifference curve/budget line framework to show that a benefit in cash is better for poor people than a benefit in kind of equal cost to the government.'); they are much less able to cope well with applying tools in hitherto untried contexts.

Level 2 students are obviously going to run into trouble if their teachers set examinations that require them to display skills in synthesizing ideas, marshal evidence to back up particular conclusions and make personal judgements about which characteristics of a problem area are significant before they decide which theoretical tool might be useful for dealing with the problem. Their problem is not necessarily one involving limited ability to cope with particular technical issues or lines of thinking. If they tackle the questions in 'Level 2 style' they are likely to be penalized simply because they have not even *tried* to do the things that their teachers expected to see them do: their world-views stop them from answering the question.

Such students sometimes become aware, well before their final examinations, that there is a mismatch between their expectations of what will happen during the learning process and those of their teacher. Yet they may have great trouble facing up to the possibility that they should try to change the way they try to learn, rather than their teachers changing the way that they try to teach. For example, I well recall a distraught student who came to see me and said 'Look, I'm a commerce student, I like seeing things down as figures, in black and white; that's why I enjoy accountancy. I work hard and normally do well, but I'm really having trouble with your microeconomics course. I just don't know what I'm expected to be learning from you, it's all grey right now; I can't see where I am supposed to be going with all this fog.' This student was not yet aware that subjective elements could actually cloud issues in accountancy as well as in economics (cf. Buchanan and Thirlby (eds) 1973; Wolnizer 1987). He had no idea that the kind of economics training he was receiving might prepare him for coping with life as an accountant in a world where matters are not either black or white, and he made it clear that he merely was looking for a way of getting by in his microeconomics course whilst he kept applying his cherished Level 2 approach to learning elsewhere in his studies.

Such a reluctance to make a major change of outlook is entirely analogous with the resistance offered by neoclassical economists to suggestions that in some contexts they should embrace satisficing theory and abandon their core idea that *all* choices can be reduced to acts of constrained optimization. They will have applied the neoclassical hard core in many contexts but they will have little experience in using satisficing notions. Until they learn how to think in the alternative style they may risk making a bigger mess of things by trying to embrace it than by continuing to try to fit all decisions into the constrained optimization framework. We are grossly over-optimistic if we expect that Levele 2 students and/or neoclassical economists will jump at the promise of greater insights that will follow if they invest in an alternative, more complicated way of viewing the world. Perry (1985: 16) even suggests they will need to go through something akin to a process of grieving: 'I believe that students will not be able to take a next step until they have come to terms with the losses that inhere in the step just taken.'

Three alternatives to progression to a higher learning level may be observed when a student finds it altogether too daunting to try thinking about the learning process in a new way recommended by a teacher or peers (see Perry 1981; Baxter Magolda and Porterfield 1988). Some students pursue a *temporizing* strategy, avoiding commitment whilst trying to gather mental strength to face up to the challenge of moving on in, say, the next academic year. Others *retreat* from looming complexity (for example, Level 4) to a simpler position (for example, Level 2 dualism). Yet others seek to *escape* from the task of choosing which ideas to embrace because they notice that any commitment to a way of thinking may seem to have inconvenient implications. Escape strategies involve either of two ways of achieving detachment from current challenges: one is dissociation, in other words, letting things drift so that fate determines the outcome; the other is encapsulation, whereby the student plunges into being busy in familiar ways.

Both escape strategies can manifest themselves at a variety of levels. Least alarming to a teacher may be instances of students avoiding commitment in their essays by making no attempt to argue their way towards a conclusion after putting down conflicting views on the topic in question. As an example of how bad dissociation can get on a grand scale, I will explain what happened when I tried teaching price theory in terms of a history of thinking about pricing and competition from Alfred Marshall to contestability theory. My intention had been to demonstrate to the class that economists can spend decade after decade stumbling from one puzzle to another, misunderstanding each other and going round in circles reinventing each other's ideas, with key questions remaining unresolved. I then expected to show the class how, despite the mess, they might begin to feel comfortable with most of the ideas, not simultaneously but in different applied contexts. With hindsight, my strategy amounted to an attempt to lead my class at high speed first on to Perry's Level 3 and then up to Level 5. However, since I was then still oblivious of Perry's work, I had not spent enough time explaining to them what they might experience.

Much to my dismay, lecture attendance soon dropped off

dramatically. The students' representatives informed me that a large part of the class simply 'could not take all the different names contradicting one another' and had 'decided to spend their time concentrating on other courses where it was clearer what was wanted and where they were supposed to be going'. To win back the attention of the class took a major effort in terms of supplying handouts summarizing the individuals' key contributions and demonstrating that many of the prime sources that I had been discussing were actually footnoted in their texts (Marshall, Robinson, Chamberlin, Hall and Hitch, Sweezy, Baumol, and so on). The experience made very clear to me just how desperately my students wanted me to present a bland, finished product to them rather than show them potential building blocks and what use had been made of them; many students simply fled once I started showing them with chapter and verse how their textbook misrepresented or misinterpreted primary contributions. They were unwilling to derive self-confidence from being shown how even famous economists sometimes end up following questionable lines of logic or failing to see the point of what someone else has written.

It is possible to observe signs of thinking below the committed relativism level even among Masters students. If they have not been used to having their opinions and expertise respected by their teachers they appear prone to interpret, for example, an instruction to 'prepare a critical review of' as merely to mean 'prepare a summary of'. Indeed, they often write up their work under the latter heading even though the former is what is written in their course outline. It is not that they cannot be critical if they try but that they still expect the published word to be free of problems. When they read something that does not seem to make sense, they tend to fudge what they write about it on the basis that they are failing to understand it (which certainly *may* be true) rather than criticize it as not making sense for a particular set of reasons (which may well be the case, from particular standpoints).

4 PHASES OF DEVELOPMENT AMONG ACADEMIC ECONOMISTS, TOO?

A non-deterministic approach to teaching economics obviously has major potential to turn out disastrously if presented to an audience that consists largely of dualistic thinkers, for it highlights areas of difficulties rather than presenting the Truth and it invites students to make personal commitments when dealing with problems. I will shortly explore some ways of trying to help students move towards making commitments to relativism; thereby I hope to make it harder for entrenched interests to argue that such courses cannot work at the undergraduate level. But before I do this I think it may be useful to raise and relate to the process of economic discovery a further theme in Perry's work, namely, that in different parts of their lives people may be operating with the aid of different levels of thought. If this is so, it is conceivable that academic economists may implicitly lament the fact that their students are answering questions in a Level 2 manner when the questions were set up in the hope that Level 5 or 6 answers would be offered and yet, in their own work as academics, they may in some areas actually be operating rather as if they are, say, Level 2 or Level 3 thinkers. This being so, an awareness of the Perry progression may enable them to advance intellectually.

One area in which we may expect to see the Perry progression at work is in different strategies that scholars use for coping with critical reactions of referees, for though they may have ceased being students, academics do not cease having to undergo examinations. Suppose the submission of a paper to a journal leads to a pair of opposing referee reports, one quite supportive and the other fairly critical. A relatively inexperienced academic may not be at the stage where the automatic reaction is to try to see how the critical referee may have come to see the paper as he/she did and then look for opportunities in the critical comments for improving the paper so that it will both satisfy the referee and extend its author's own line of thinking. Instead, the inexperienced academic may be prone to take strength from the positive report and dismiss the critical report as coming from someone who has not spent enough time seeing what the paper achieves. The trouble is, such behaviour is not going to be very helpful towards ensuring that the paper is revised in a way which will be acceptable to the presently hostile referee. What will probably be needed is a revision (and an accompanying letter) which shows the author's understanding of how the critical verdict was arrived at and argues the author's case (if it is possible to do so) in a manner which will make sense to the critic and, ultimately, to others who think in much the same way.

In outlining the Perry framework I tended to highlight problems that could arise if students were working at lower levels than their teachers: I did not consider what might happen if, say a Level 5 student sat an examination set by a Level 2 teacher. However, the latter kind of situation is one that may well arise when academic economists are having their work examined by their peers, whether in the process of screening contributions for possible publication or as part of critical discussions within works accepted for publication. (I suspect it is by no means unknown in the teaching context.) A very good illustration of this phenomenon is provided by the contrasting works of Caldwell (1982, 1989) and Dow (1985, 1992).

Caldwell ends his excellent examination of philosophical debates about methodology and the methodological practices of economists by making a commitment to methodological pluralism on the basis that 'the quest for a single, universal, prescriptive scientific methodology is quixotic' (1982: 244) and 'that results obtained within specific research programs which of necessity follow particular methodological precepts are program specific' (1982: 250–1). This sounds very much like Level 5–6 thinking. However, whilst Caldwell believes that it may be helpful if economists are conscious of the diversity of research programmes when they present their work, he stresses that he is only proposing methodological pluralism 'as a program for *methodologists*' (1982: 251, emphasis in original). Dow (1985) likewise argues that economists have much to learn from trying to understand the different methodological perspectives from which arguments are being constructed. But the way in which she encapsulates these differences is striking: she suggests that mainstream neoclassical economists have a dualistic view of the business of doing economics, whereas Post Keynesians embrace a diversity of methods each subordinate to their overall world-view. Dualistic thought is manifest in neoclassical work not merely in terms of tendencies to claim that economics that does not conform to the neoclassical way of doing things is 'not scientific' or is 'economic poetry, not real economics' (the latter dual is one that I have seen Professor Hahn use in respect of authors who write from subjectivist and behavioural standpoints); it is also evident in terms of a concern with, for example, a strict separation between endogeneity and exogeneity (Dow 1985: 119–21), By contrast, the Level 5–6 context-specific style of thinking in Post Keynesian writings is manifest via, for example, their emphasis on the importance of institutions and their attitudes to econometrics (Dow 1985: 75–7).

Caldwell (1989) finds it very difficult to come to terms with the Post

Keynesian methodology. For example, he inquires how Eichner's attempts to build an empirically grounded approach to economics can be embraced by the same scholars who feel drawn to those of Shackle's writings that have raised major questions about the possibility of predicting an undetermined future. As Dow (1992) points out, Caldwell's critique of Post Keynesian thinking is based on duals such as *a priorism*/prediction and prediction/explanation that are not actually part of the context-dependent way in which Post Keynesians think. From the standpoint of Perry's framework, it appears while Caldwell argues in Level 5–6 terms that different areas of inquiry may need different types of methodologies, he uses something more akin to a Level 2 mode when he tries to argue that a particular way of thinking about *economic* issues should not involve the use of a range of related methodologies in a context-dependent way. If one of the most highly regarded economic methodologists of our time can fail to appreciate a key aspect of the Post Keynesian version of committed relativism, then what hope should we have that students will be able to cope with a multi-paradigm text such as Dow's (1985) *Macroeconomic Thought: A Methodological Approach* ?

5 STRATEGIES FOR ASSISTING PROGRESSION TOWARDS COMMITTED RELATIVISM AND BEYOND

In a paper which both advocates a 'contending perspectives' approach to the teaching of economics and makes explicit reference to Perry, Barone (1991: 21–2) suggests that one of the payoffs to this kind of teaching is that students appear to move more rapidly from dualistic towards relativistic modes of thinking. This should not be seen as inconsistent with what I have so far been arguing, namely, that attempts to teach economics in a non-deterministic manner have the potential to result in major teaching disasters on account of mismatches between teachers' and students' expectations and learning strategies. The key thing is how one sets about presenting this kind of learning experience. Before I outline possible strategies, however, I think it is important to note that Barone is misrepresenting the teaching process when he reports (1991: 22) that, via the contending perspectives approach to economics, 'we have moved our students to a more advanced intellectual plane.' As Perry points out,

[W]e cannot push anyone to develop, or 'get them to see' or 'impact' them. The causal metaphors hidden in English verbs give us a distracting vocabulary for pedagogy. The tone is Lockean and provocative of resistance. We *can* provide, we *can* design opportunities. We can create settings in which students who are ready will be more likely to make new kinds of sense.

(Perry 1985: 16, italics in original)

If students have not yet created for themselves views of what learning might involve that are similar to those of their teachers, they will not be able to see what their teachers are getting at when the latter try to explain to them what they hope to see them do in their courses.

I know this only too well from the frustrating experience of trying to teach the transaction cost approach to corporate strategy to second and third year students taking a course in strategic marketing. As assignment deadlines and, later, the final examination came closer I would warn the class that if they were, say, appraising a particular company's strategic choices it would not be adequate to suggest that a particular diversification move involving investment in new activities made sense in terms of synergy links with pre-existing activities, for synergy might be (and often is) traded. Thus I warned that high grades would only be awarded where attempts were made to imagine alternative strategies — alternative ways of using corporate resources, possibly involving different contracting relationships with other firms, and their possible pitfalls. In tutorials the students were often well able to come up with possible alternatives if I asked them to do so directly, and were sometimes quite brilliant at devising opportunistic ploys that it might make sense to worry about;. Yet, if left to their own devices and asked to make a critical appraisal of a case-firm's strategic behaviour and suggest future policies, they would in almost all cases descend to producing answers which amounted to little more than the regurgitation of case material with no sign of individual creative thinking about alternatives. (This, I might add, was barely less than what the instructors' manual accompanying their text seemed to imagine might be involved in a 'model' answer.) In other words, the students had not yet got to the stage at which they *automatically* saw critical thinking as involving a consideration of alternative viewpoints, even though I had repeatedly told them that this was what I expected and even though they could conjure up alternative scenarios if asked directly to do so.

One lesson that we might take from the behaviour of such students is that practice is likely to be needed to ensure that potential for thinking at a higher level is realized. This begs the question of the scale of teaching resources that may be required. If teachers give frequent opportunities for experimentation with writing answers to questions that do not give prompts as to exactly how answers might be constructed, they are likely to spend much more of their time marking essays and being visited by students who demand advice on how to tackle to questions. To liberate time for providing feedback in the sort of detail that will assist students in improving future assignments — in other words, not merely grading the paper and adding a brief comment at the end, but painstakingly going through it rather as if refereeing an article and pointing out precisely where redundant material lies, where alternative viewpoints are being ignored, and where non sequiturs are present — it may be worth adopting the rule that absolutely no consultations are allowed about an assignment prior to the date at which it is handed back in marked form. This rule would need to be communicated with colleagues if it were not a department-/faculty-wide policy, for otherwise students from one course might simply increase their visits to other instructors.

The 'no prior consultations' rule would be likely to come as a shock to many students, particularly Level 2 thinkers, who expect to be 'spoon-fed' by their teachers. However, there might be major benefits from explaining to the class why the rule was felt necessary and the effects it might have — perceptions of the role of teachers and the nature of the learning may be changed by students if they are told that the rule is designed to give tutors more time to spend on giving feedback on students' experimental attempts at using their own ways of thinking in particular contexts. It is a chance to try to convey the message that students' own ways of looking at things are taken seriously and that students are expected to take responsibility for the ideas they commit to paper. The teacher can also emphasize that the rule is aimed at increasing fairness by guarding against rent-seeking behaviour by those students who think nothing of trying to get three or four consultations with an instructor even over a minor assignment. To ensure consistency with the emphasis on the experimental nature of written assignments, it would appear necessary to allow the falsification of expectations not to be catastrophic. One way of encouraging relatively safe experimentation is to inform students that while they might tackle all the suggested assignments, only their best, say, three papers would count towards their coursework grades. Having adopted precisely these strategies and explained their rationale to my class, I have been pleasantly surprised to see how the students have accepted them in the spirit that was intended, and they have started to take feedback on their essays very seriously indeed.

If economics teachers are trying to facilitate the recognition by their students of more advanced patterns of thinking, they can augment the provision of feedback on written work by providing in lectures, as handouts or as library resources, detailed information about how questions might be tackled in ways that would be seen as commendable and on the characteristics of answers that are awarded poor or mediocre marks. This can be done not only for assignments currently being used (after they have been marked and returned to the class) but also for previous examination questions, mock examination questions and assignments from previous years (for examples, see Earl 1995). It would be inappropriate to call such collections of information 'model answers', given that the goal is to encourage students to think for themselves. Ideally, these learning resources could be provided to students as integral parts of their textbooks (as in Earl 1995), in contrast to the prevailing situation whereby they tend to be confined to instructors' manuals designed to accompany particular texts. After all, if teachers are trying to get their students to see them as 'people who have been this way before and can help us to achieve new understandings' rather than as the 'them' who examine 'us', then it is clearly inappropriate for instructors' manuals to exist as resources that are not available to students.

Wherever possible, it seems advisable to try to relate the course materials to students' existing repertoires of experiences for, as both Perry and Shackle often remind us, creative thinking involves a resorting of existing elements. Lecturers can do this not merely by keeping theoretical discussions related to problems of economic indeterminacy that students are likely to be experiencing in their lives and encouraging students to try to relate such experiences to the theoretical material. Teachers should also try to be alert to things that students say which reveal an ability to think at higher levels than they are presently thinking in economics. They should not be downhearted if they discover that their students are, say, Level 2 thinkers in economics but Level 5 thinkers when they argue amongst themselves about the merits of various sporting teams, consumer durables or artistic works, for the latter can be used as metaphors that might be applied to economics.

6 WHEN AND HOW TO BRING INDETERMINACY INTO THE ECONOMICS CLASSROOM

When designing a non-deterministic three year university-level programme in economics it might be tempting to view the first-year course as the vehicle for getting students familiar with basic economic concepts and terms, the second-year course as one which opens students' eyes to the range of competing world-views that exist in economics and areas of unresolved debate, and the third-year course as one which involves an emphasis on students thinking for themselves in a variety applied contexts. In terms of Perry's progression, the temptation is to build the introductory course on the assumption that most students are Level 1 or Level 2 learners, the intermediate course in the hope that students switch over to Level 3 or Type 4 thinking styles, and the advanced course on the expectation that students will be ready to switch to the Level 5 or Level 6 styles of thinking. There are a number of reasons why this could prove an unfortunate strategy.

First, it downplays Perry's message that different students in a typical classroom are likely to be at different stages in their intellectual development. A thoroughly dualistic approach to teaching introductory economics may result in the profession failing to captivate most of those students in a first-year class who are already getting towards relativistic thinking as a result of experiences in other parts of their lives. The work of Perry and his associates suggests that courses may be better designed so that they present opportunities for a range of approaches to learning to seem rewarding. This not only helps to reduce the risk that students will become bored or retreat from involvement in the subject, it also gives opportunities for students to discover that different strategies for coping with learning may be required for coping with different kinds of problems. No one ends up feeling excluded.

Secondly, if introductions to economics are presented in a thoroughly cut-and-dried manner, students will not be finding problems with applying dualistic thinking to economics: they may be scoring highly and perceive no need to try to come up with other views of what is going on. A dualistic introduction to economics would involve no change from the present typical introductory course involving mainly formal lectures to huge classes and 'objective testing' via multiple choice examinations. This seems economical in terms of its resource requirements but it has several disastrous consequences for those who try to introduce contending perspectives at the intermediate level. The conventional introductory style of teaching does nothing to falsify expectations that students bring from their high schools based on years of dualistic training. Even if university were expected to be different from school in some vaguely imagined way, then dualistic teaching is likely to signal to the first-year students that it is, in fact, little more than a continuation of school: minds that were open to change are thereby closed. No signal is given that they ought to be expecting to rethink their views of the nature of the learning process.

All this makes a shift to a relativistic style in the second-year course much more of a shock. Resistance to change in this direction is more likely the more that expectations have been firmed up around the idea of economics as a series of diagrams to be learned according to textbook gospel, and lectures as occasions for copying down overhead transparencies rather than interacting with the lecturer or trying to make sense of a discursive presentation rather as if listening to and taking notes from a radio programme. If students see their role in lectures as consisting mainly of copying material down from a screen rather than *making sense of material* on the spot, we should hardly be surprised that they feel out of their depths when confronted with a lecturer who does not use this mode of delivery or that they do not *build up* an increasingly detailed picture of the subject as the semester goes by and instead try to 'learn' the material in the last few weeks or days before the final examination. Dualistic teaching does nothing to demolish the idea that economics is nothing more than a set of tools that can be stored in student folders until needed.

It is not merely these deductions that lead me to advocate an early sowing of seeds of doubt amongst fledgling economists. My experience has been that it is easier to win a first-year class than a second-year class over to the idea of economics as a non-deterministic subject. First-year students did not panic at the idea of neoclassical, institutionalist and Marxian economists having different things to say about burning issues of the day when I taught an elective course on Australian Political Economy in this style; my experience was very similar to that reported by Barone (1991). Yet each time I have taken over a dualistic second-year sequel to a dualistic first-year core unit and tried to reshape it along non-deterministic lines I have found myself dealing with conspicuous student resistance and a desire on the part of students for me to convert everything to diagrams that they could learn. Deterministic first-year teaching in terms of a multitude of diagrams, often with a quite remarkable emphasis on mathematics by lecturers fresh out of North American doctoral programmes, seemed to have made it difficult for students to keep sight of the relevance of economic theory to making sense of practical problems. It must have been difficult for the first-year students to find time to read and think about contemporary economic issues if they were struggling to keep abreast of technical ones in their introductory courses (compare Siegfried *et al.* 1991: 21–2).

The resistance that I encountered was partly associated with difficulties that I had in recommending a single textbook that bore any obvious relationship with the range of materials being covered in the lectures. Given their lack of experience in taking notes in lectures that emphasized ideas and how they might be used and appraised, students craved a convenient printed source that they could compare with their own notes. My attempt at providing a solution to this difficulty was to write and distribute detailed lecture summaries (which were eventually turned into books: see Earl 1990, 1995). However, this strategy seemed counter-productive until I was introduced to Perry's work and in turn began to introduce my classes to the Perry progression at the outset and to remind them from time to time that in addition to teaching economics I was trying to help them advance along the Perry progression.

Without the Perry background, the problem: was that students, — particularly those from countries whose school systems reinforce dualistic thinkers — tended to memorize entire summaries and regurgitate them in the examination. Such students would home in on particular words in the questions as signs of which lecture summary they should regurgitate, rather than make any systematic attempt to answer the question in the way that one would expect of someone thinking at Level 5 in Perry's progression. All my warnings that this would be a disastrous way of tackling the examination went unheeded, for that was the only way they had. None of these students took up my invitation to discuss with me the results of experimenting with additional practice essays from past examination papers, to see whether they were succeeding in getting out of this habit prior to the examination.

By contrast, Barone and his colleagues built their course around a set of half a dozen or so key books from different schools of thought in economics and a 'contending perspectives reader' (which I presume consisted of Xeroxed articles and extracts). In the absence of suitable multi-paradigm textbooks, this strategy has much to commend it, particularly since it may help students to get away from thinking of a textbook as a bible. However, texts may still be indispensable for large classes unless small groups of students can be persuaded to pool their resources, for it is probably unreasonable to expect them each to purchase several books (and unreasonable to expect that libraries would purchase very many sets of the key texts) unless they happen to be, say, cheap Penguin paperbacks, each of which is representative of a particular school of thought. At the minimum, what is likely to be needed is a text which provides an overview and thereby enables diverse prime sources to be tackled with confidence.

At the intermediate to advanced level, I have recently sought to fill the gap in microeconomics (Earl 1995) but a decade and a half has already passed since an exemplary multi-paradigm text on macroeconomics was first published, namely, Dow (1985). Dow's pioneering book is most unusual in beginning with a careful analysis of methodological issues and then presenting, in as unbiased a way as possible, guides to neo-Austrian, mainstream, Post Keynesian and Marxian thinking on macroeconomics. Dow quite deliberately avoided making any attempt to appraise these rival world-views and was criticized for this by Weintraub (1985) on the basis that she was leaving unanswered the question of why at least 98 per cent of economists in the US are members of the mainstream school. Although Dow's text came under fire rather on the basis that it is an unduly relativistic (Level 4) treatment of macroeconomics it may also be seen as a device for helping students to make informed choices between the rival paradigms or between these existing paradigms and ones which they might themselves be trying to put together. Dow teaches students about different ways of thinking and then leaves them to make commitments of their own.

From the standpoint of Perry's work, two rather different comments appear to be in order about Dow's text. First, it is perhaps unfortunate that she chooses to label one paradigm as 'mainstream' rather than 'neoclassical', for she may thereby be encouraging students who do not feel confident about making appraisals of their own to end up conforming with 98 per cent of economists in the US on the basis of nothing more than what the remaining two per cent might prefer to call the 'million lemmings can't be wrong principle'. Such users of the text would not be making a commitment in Perry's and Shackle's senses. Secondly, she might have helped her readers to make commitments (with a capital 'C') if she had presented some personal accounts by macroeconomists of each school who had examined a variety of approaches to macroeconomics before ending up making a commitment to a particular world-view. In the absence of such exemplars, student readers who have previously had mainly dualistic training in this area (via a typical IS–LM/aggregate supply and demand-based text) may tend to retreat towards a Level 3 view of macroeconomics ('really, these debates just come down to discovering the underlying parameters') rather than advancing towards Level 5 and Level 6 viewpoints.

Neither of these comments applies to a more recent, excellent text by Snowdon, Vane and Wynarzcyk (1994). None of the eight schools of macroeconomic thought covered by these authors is labelled as mainstream and the book features interviews with leading members of each school. However, this text has less coverage of methodology than Dow offers. Taken together, the texts by Snowdon *et al.* (1994) and Dow (1985, republished in revised form in 1996) provide a splendid basis for teaching macroeconomics in terms of contending perspectives. The 'no textbook' excuse for continuing deterministic teaching is looking increasingly feeble.

7 CONCLUSION

In this chapter I have explored tensions between three things that George Shackle advocated: the construction and debate of rival scenarios, studies of the stereotypes that people use for coping with uncertainty, and the teaching of economics in a way which encourages students to develop for themselves effective ways of thinking about economic problems. Studies of stereotypes used by students for coping may be taken to suggest that economists who are committed to undertaking the sort of teaching programme that Shackle advocated may be unwise to think that they are 'home and hosed' once they have overcome opposition from colleagues who would prefer to see students being taught the gospel only according to neoclassical precepts. The problem then becomes one of dealing with the range of expectations that one's students have, which may largely have been formed in the light of experiences in courses taught in a deterministic manner. Lecturers cannot force their students to change their ways of thinking even when they have been given the opportunity to provide students with materials that may be construed as showing that the Truth is not obvious and that context-specific commitments may nonetheless be made to particular ways of looking at things. But they may be able to help their students to progress to higher levels of learning in the following four ways:

(i) by challenging those of their colleagues whose styles of teaching involve spoon-feeding and who reward primarily skills in dealing with 'objective tests';

(ii) by spending more of their time giving feedback after requiring students to construct for themselves experimental answers to relatively risk-free assignments;

(iii) by looking for instances of higher-level analysis outside of economics that may be used as metaphors for the kind of thinking styles that might be helpful in economics; and

(iv) by using their own experiences and the experiences of other economists to show that they can understand the struggles which their audiences are undergoing.

NOTE

* I am indebted to Neil Fleming, former Director of the Education Unit at Lincoln University, for introducing me to the work of Perry. The paper has also benefited from comments from and/or references supplied by Ross Cullen, Martin O'Connor, Jody Nyquist and Bert Ward. However, the usual disclaimer applies.

REFERENCES

Andrews, P. W. S. and Brunner, E. (1975) *Studies in Pricing*, London: Macmillan.

Barone, C. A. (1991) 'Contending perspectives: curricular reform in economics', *Journal of Economic Education* 22 (Winter): 15–26.

Baxter Magolda, M. and Porterfield, W. (1988) *Intellectual Development: Linking Theory and Practice*, Washington, D.C.: American College Personnel Association.

Buchanan, J. M. and Thirlby, G. F. (eds) (1973) *L.S.E. Essays on Cost*, London: L.S.E./Weidenfeld and Nicolson.

Caldwell, B. J. (1982) *Beyond Positivism: Economic Methodology in the Twentieth Century*, London: George Allen & Unwin.

—— (1989) 'Post-Keynesian methodology: an assessment', *Review of Political Economy*, 1: 43–64.

Colander, D. (1991) *Why Aren't Economists as Important as Garbagemen? Essays on the State of Economics*, Armonk, NY: M. E. Sharpe, Inc.

Dow, S. C. (1985) *Macroeconomic Thought: A Methodological Approach*, Oxford: Blackwell.

—— (1992) 'Post-Keynesian methodology: a comment', *Review of Political Economy*, 4: 111–13.

—— (1996) *The Methodology of Macroeconomic Thought*, Cheltenham: Edward Elgar.

Earl, P. E. (1983) 'A behavioral theory of economists' behavior', in Eichner, A. S. (ed.) *Why Economics is not yet a Science*, Armonk, NY: M. E. Sharpe, Inc.

—— (1990) *Monetary Scenarios: A Modern Approach to Financial Systems*, Aldershot: Edward Elgar.

—— (1995) *Microeconomics for Business and Marketing: Lectures, Cases and Worked Essays*, Aldershot: Edward Elgar.

Jefferson, M. (1983) 'Economic uncertainty and business decision-making', in Wiseman, J. (ed.) *Beyond Positive Economics?* London: Macmillan.

Lee, F. S. (1984) 'Full cost pricing: a new wine in a new bottle', *Australian Economic Papers*, 23 (June): 151–66.

Loasby, B. J. (1990) 'The use of scenarios in business planning', in Frowen, S. F. (ed.) *Unknowledge and Choice in Economics*, London: Macmillan.

Parvin, M. (1992) 'Is teaching of neoclassical economics as *the* science of economics moral?' *Journal of Economic Education*, 21: 65–78.

Perry, W. G., Jr. (1970) *Forms of Intellectual and Ethical Development in the College Years: A Scheme*, New York: Holt, Rinehart and Winston.

—— (1981) 'Cognitive and ethical growth: the making of meaning', in Chickering, A. (ed.) *The Modern American College*, San Francisco, CA: Jossey-Bass.

—— (1985) 'Different worlds in the same classroom', *On Teaching and Learning: The Journal of the Harvard-Danforth Center*: 1–17.

Shackle, G. L. S. (1953) *What Makes an Economist?* Liverpool: Liverpool University Press (reprinted in Shackle, 1990).

—— (1963) 'General thought schemes and the economist', *Woolwich Economic Papers*, No. 2: 1–20 (reprinted in Shackle, 1990).

——(1967) *The Years of High Theory: Invention and Tradition in Economic Thought, 1926–1939*, Cambridge: Cambridge University Press.

—— (1990) *Time, Expectations and Uncertainty in Economics* (edited by J. L. Ford), Aldershot: Edward Elgar.

Siegfried, J. J., Bartlett, R. L., Hansen, W. L., Kelley, A. C., McCloskey, D. N. and Tietenberg, T. H. (1991) 'The economics major: can and should we do better than a B-?' *American Economic Review*, 81, May (supplement): 20–5.

Snowdon, B., Vane, H. and Wynarzcyk, P. (1994) *A Modern Guide to Macroeconomics: An Introduction to Competing Schools of Thought*, Aldershot: Edward Elgar.

Weintraub, E. R. (1985) 'Review of *Macroeconomic Thought* by S. C. Dow', *Economic Journal*, 95: 1116–8.

Wolnizer, P. W. (1987) *Auditing as Independent Authentication*, Sydney: Sydney University Press

3

SHACKLE AND INSTITUTIONAL ECONOMICS: SOME BRIDGES AND BARRIERS

*Geoffrey M. Hodgson**

1 INTRODUCTION

George Shackle's economic thought has clear links with the economics of Friedrich Hayek and of John Maynard Keynes. Given his celebrated linkage of Post Keynesianism and the economics of the Austrian School, it may seem a little far-fetched to claim some connection with institutional economics as well.[1]

Institutional economics became prominent in the United States in the early decades of the twentieth century but failed until very recently to establish itself in Europe. There are prominent institutionalists of European origin, such as John Hobson, K. William Kapp, Gunnar Myrdal and Karl Polanyi, but their impact on European economics has been slight.

As his career developed, Shackle eventually established himself as a trenchant critic of neoclassical theory but he did not turn to institutional economics for inspiration. Although Gunnar Myrdal emerges as one of the heroes of Shackle's magnificent narrative in *The Years of High Theory*, it is the Myrdal of the 1930s — not the Myrdal who embraced institutionalism in the 1940s after a long stay in the United States. Significantly, Shackle's personal ascendancy as an economic theorist — from the mid-1930s on — coincides precisely with the period in which the 'old' institutionalism suffered a severe decline in its American heartland. In truth there is little or no overt connection between the work of Shackle and that of the institutionalist school.

Neither is it claimed here that Shackle was a covert institutionalist. The goal of this chapter is more modest, to show what Shackle's work and that of the institutionalists can offer to each other, in part by outlining some of the limitations of each research programme. This essay is in five sections. Section 2 briefly examines the core assumptions of neoclassical economics and portrays the similarities between the Shacklean and the institutionalist rejection of these tenets. It is shown that in terms of the major criticisms of the core assumptions of neoclassical economic theory, Shackle shares a great deal with the institutionalists. This section also discusses the concept of uncertainty and relates it to both institutionalist and Shacklean economics.

The third section discusses problem with the Shacklean concept of purposeful behaviour. Although Shackle's vigorous anti-determinism contrasts with some statements by the founders of institutionalism, modern developments in chaos theory suggest a basis upon which determinism and indeterminacy can be reconciled. Unlike much of Marxian and Sraffian theory, both Shackle and the institutionalists see the theoretical conceptualization of human agency as central to the project of economic analysis. However, there are major differences between the Shacklean and the institutionalist conceptions of human agency.

In the fourth section it is shown how the institutionalist emphasis on habit and routine offers a potential way out of the impasse of what has been uncharitably described as Shackle's 'nihilism' (Coddington 1983). This involves a recasting of the conception of the human agent, to bring an appropriate balance between habit and imagination. Although this amendment is substantial, it has clear linkages with the Shacklean treatment of norms and conventions. In fact, the economics of the institutionalists, of Shackle and of Keynes all share a common concern with the role of norms and conventions in economic life. Section 5 concludes the essay.

2 FROM RATIONALITY TO UNCERTAINTY: THE IMPLAUSIBILITY OF ECONOMIC MAN

Neoclassical economics may be defined as an approach that has the following attributes:[2]

1   it assumes rational, maximizing behaviour by agents with given preference functions;

2   it focuses on attained, or movements towards, equilibrium states;

3   it excludes chronic information problems (there is, at best, an inclusion of probabilistic risk or of partial ignorance: notions of radical uncertainty, and divergent perceptions of a given reality, are absent).

Notably, these three attributes are inter-connected. For instance, the attainment of a stable optimum under (1) suggests an equilibrium (2); and rationality under (1) connotes the absence of severe information problems alluded to in (3).[3]

Both Shackle and the institutionalists reject the aforementioned core postulates of neoclassical theory. Shackle was an eloquent and forceful critic of the notion of rational economic man. Consider the following quotation:

> [T]here are some ... queer things about economic man. He is utterly free from all feelings of emulation ... His tastes do not change, he learns nothing and forgets nothing ... He is, perhaps, a sort of Model T economic man, and a few gadgets fitted on here and there during the last hundred years have made him a little more subtle. ... Keynesian economics, the economics of unemployment and depression found the Model T economic man quite useless. ... What makes Keynesian man utterly different from Model T man is in greatest measure the supreme gift of imagination.
>
> (Shackle 1966: 123–4)

These words here are clearly redolent of Veblen. First, Shackle used the word 'emulation', which is a favourite Veblenian term and a core concept of his *Theory of the Leisure Class* (Veblen, 1899). Second, and more generally, the whole quotation is reminiscent of Veblen's famous attack on the notion of the human actor as a 'lightning calculator of pleasures and pains, who oscillates like a homogeneous globule of desire'. Veblen elaborated:

> In all received formulations of economic theory, whether at the hands of English economists or those of the Continent, the human material with which the inquiry is concerned is conceived in hedonistic terms; that is to say, in terms of a passive and substantially inert and immutably given human nature.
>
> (Veblen 1919: 73)

This is the very same idea of the mechanically functioning and immutably given human agent that was likewise rejected by Shackle. Veblen would have probably endorsed the following statement by Shackle:

> Perfect rationality belongs only to the timeless equilibrium in which all actions conform to a general simultaneous solution of the pooled statements of the tastes and resources of all participants.
>
> (Shackle 1967: 295)

We can find very similar arguments in Veblen's essays. It is significant that both Shackle and the institutionalists eschewed mechanical conceptions of human agency. There is a common insistence on the importance of real time and the changing world of economic experience. As Shackle (1972, p. 27) put it: 'Time is a denial of the omnipotence of reason.' The deterministic optimiser known as 'rational economic man' is thereby rejected in both theoretical traditions.

The limitations of equilibrium

Shackle and the institutionalists also share a critique of the predominance of equilibrium notions in economics. For Shackle, the obsession with equilibrium in economics meant the calamitous banishment of the concept of time. As he argued at length in his *Epistemics and Economics*, the demotion of the concept of equilibrium was part and parcel of the rejection of mechanical determinism and the reinstatement of the imaginative, choosing and creative individual. Shackle saw the source of this concept in the slavish emulation by economists of classical mechanics:

> perhaps it is not too fanciful to suppose that the immense prestige and ascendancy in men's minds which mechanics, and in particular celestial mechanics, came to possess during the seventeenth, eighteenth, and nineteenth centuries must have suggested to economists the search for some simple and all-inclusive principle to explain the world.
>
> (Shackle 1953: 6)

Again there is an unwitting echo of Veblen, who repeatedly observed how economics had emulated mechanics, thus limiting itself with a conception of the agent as 'an isolated, definitive human datum, in stable equilibrium except for the buffets of the impinging forces that displace him in one direction or another' (Veblen 1919: 73). For both Shackle and Veblen, the conception of the agent in neoclassical theory was akin to a Newtonian particle subject to deterministic laws. Both authors repeatedly insisted that the use of such a metaphor to conceptualize human agency was highly unsatisfactory.

Veblen argued that the appropriate metaphor for economics is not mechanics but Darwinian evolution. The goal of economics should not be to muse upon equilibrium conditions: 'The question is not how things stabilize themselves in a "static state", but how they endlessly grow and change' (Veblen 1934: 8).

Notably, there is a slight difference of emphasis here. Veblen wished to upgrade economics into an 'evolutionary' or 'post-Darwinian' science (Hodgson 1992, 1993b). Accordingly, he saw the phenomena of economic development and change as central. It is for these reasons that he insists on the limitations of the concept of equilibrium. In contrast, Shackle's rejection of this concept is based on a concept of radical indeterminacy of which there is little or no trace in Veblen. It is the concept of the spontaneous and 'uncaused' action of the human agent that overturns equilibrium in Shackle's theory. This topic shall be raised later below.

The place of uncertainty

Problems of information and uncertainty took some time to reach the forefront of economic theory. The British historical school economist Thomas E. Cliffe Leslie (1888) alluded to some of them in the nineteenth century. But his discussion is exceptional. Problems of knowledge and information did not become prominent until the twentieth century. Such issues were raised in the early institutionalist contributions of Thorstein Veblen (1919) and John Commons (1924, 1934).

However, it is with the work of Frank Knight that the concept of uncertainty first assumed a central role in economic theory. One of the earliest contexts in which such severe information problems were raised is in his classic work on the theory of the firm. In fact, Knight regarded himself as an institutional economist. Although he was never in the institutionalist mainstream there are strong institutionalist elements in his work (Hodgson 1988: 20, 66, 125, 132; Hodgson forthcoming; Tilman 1992: 58). In his *Risk, Uncertainty and Profit* (1921) Knight makes the distinction between risk, to which an estimated probability may be attached, and uncertainty, in regard to which it is impossible to calculate a definite and meaningful probability. However, for some time, the Knightian concept of uncertainty was neglected.

Institutionalists reacted more energetically to Keynes's *General Theory of Employment, Interest and Money* (1936) in which the concept of uncertainty also plays a major role. The most informed and substantive endorsement by an institutionalist of Keynes's economics was to come in the 1940s in two important articles by Allan Gruchy (1948, 1949). Just as Keynes's work was formative for Shackle, in recent decades it has become commonplace for institutionalists to rub shoulders with 'Post Keynesianism'. In fact, the Post Keynesian label is applied to work that could equally and historically be described as institutionalist. There is no apparent reason why a modern version of institutional economics should not also incorporate Keynes's and Shackle's understanding of the pervasiveness of true uncertainty and its affects on human behaviour.

Shackle, Keynes and several institutionalists have argued that mathematics can play only a limited role in economic analysis.[4] Their intuitions in this respect are very similar. Shackle (1983: 116) wrote: 'I do not believe that human affairs can be exhibited as the infallible and invariable working of a closed and permanent system.' A similar notion appears in a famous article by the institutionalist Kapp. Therein Kapp (1976: 71) denied 'that economic processes can be adequately understood and analysed as closed, *i.e.* self-contained and self-sustaining systems'.

Partly for this reason, and like many institutionalists, Shackle (1967: 255) insisted that: 'Economics is inherently and essentially imprecise.' Many institutionalists would also share Shackle's argument that

> Mathematics can explore the meaning of what is already implicitly stated, of what is already *given*. A mathematical model of society in its economic affairs can treat the members of that society as gaining access steadily or step-by-step to items in a bank of knowledge which the model in some sense specifies ...

Such a model has no place for what we are calling *novelty*.
(Shackle 1972: 26)

Accordingly, there is much actual and potential communality between Shacklean and institutional economics in this area. However, at a deeper level some problems are revealed. These are discussed in the next section.

3 CAUSALITY, PURPOSEFUL BEHAVIOUR AND INDETERMINACY THE PROBLEM OF CAUSAL DUALISM

Shackle took a position on the nature of causality that is very different from that of Veblen. At first sight, their differences seem irreconcilable. However, after a summary of the problem, I shall suggest that some modern ideas indicate that the gulf between Shackle and Veblen might possibly be bridged.

Essentially, Shackle aligned himself with a radical version of the causal dualism that is traceable back to Aristotle and more recently to René Descartes. Aristotle distinguished between 'efficient' and 'final' causality. Efficient causality is similar to the materialist or mechanical causality of the modern natural sciences. Final causality, or 'sufficient reason', is teleological in character: directed by an intention, purpose or aim. Much later, despite many other philosophical differences with Aristotle, Descartes retained the same division, with his dualistic separation of physical matter from the volitional and allegedly immaterial human soul.

This distinction persists in modern thought, where the natural sciences embrace materialist cause and effect, and the social sciences find their causal fuel in human intentions or purposes. For the natural scientist, causal relations always involve physical matter. But in the social sciences intentional and purposeful behaviour are seen as the exclusive hallmark of the human and social realm: humans alone are bestowed with intentionality. Cartesian dualism thus persists today in the compartmentalization of the natural from the social sciences.[5]

Few social scientists have asked how their notion of intentional causality is to be reconciled with the materialist causality of the natural sciences. Intentions are taken for granted. But what causes them? Faced with this intractable problem, George Shackle (1959) and Ludwig Lachmann (1969) went so far as to regard human intentionality as an 'uncaused cause'. For the scientist this must mean the abandonment of all scientific investigation into the sources of intention: we arrive at a causal and explanatory dead end. But the assertion of an uncaused cause was not a universal response. Others, such as Hayek (1948: 67), simply took for granted the separate compartmentalization of the social sciences, on the one hand, from psychology and biology, on the other. Nevertheless, the result was the same: further investigation into the causes of human intention was abandoned. Other social scientists — indeed the majority — ignored the problem entirely. Again, the outcome was much the same.

The fact that the sciences are still saddled — well over two millennia after Aristotle — with more than one version of causality, is rarely a subject for discussion. The wall between the natural and the social sciences has averted us from this question. Such an evasion is understandable, as we would enter the realm of such interminable and intractable disputes as between determinism and free will. Neither view can be proved or disproved by evidence. Determinists regard the 'uncaused cause' as a mystical and unsatisfactory escape route, taken because of lack of evidence of a cause: suggesting that in fact there may well be a causal process working beneath the surface. On the other hand, we can provide no decisive evidence of a causal process, because we can only observe effects. Mere evidence can confirm the existence of neither a caused nor an uncaused cause.

There can be no satisfactory review of all the arguments here. But it has to be said that a retention of a complete and ultimate distinction between two or more types of the causality in the real world is untenable. The Cartesian dualism of materiality and volition is unacceptable, for several reasons. In a forceful critique, Mario Bunge (1980) pointed to the evasiveness of the causal dualist position; its fuzziness over causality in the social realm and its use of the indeterminist bolt-hole when convenient. Dualism, he pointed out, refuses to acknowledge the evidence of the molecular and cellular roots of mental abilities or disorders. Dualism, generally downplays or ignores the biological roots of human behaviour, and plays fast and loose with the physical sciences. If human volition can move masses and volition itself has no prior cause, doesn't this violate the law of the conservation of energy?

A related and serious problem concerns interactions and transformations between the two types of causality. As John Searle (1997: xii–xiii) put it: 'dualism ... seems a hopeless theory because, having made a strict distinction between the mental and the physical, it cannot make the relation of the two intelligible.' Essentially, the problem is to explain how the immaterialist form causality of human volition gets converted into a materialist form. This is a core problem with causal dualism. As Barry Hindess (1989: 150) asked pertinently: 'If human action is subject to two distinct modes of determination, what happens when they conflict, when intentionality pushes one way and causality pushes another?' We do not and cannot know the answer, because to reach it would involve the reconciliation of irreconcilables. As Bunge (1980: 20) puts it in a nutshell: *'Dualism is inconsistent with the ontology of science.'* In fact, Veblen many years earlier had said much the same. In 1919 he argued that:

> The two methods of inference — from sufficient reason [or intention] and from efficient [or materialist] cause — are out of touch with one another and there is no transition from one to the other: no method of converting the procedure or the results of the one into those of the other.
>
> (Veblen 1919: 237, material in square brackets added)

In contrast, Veblen favoured the following approach:

> The modern scheme of knowledge, on the whole, rests, for its definitive ground, on the relation of cause and effect; the relation of sufficient reason being admitted only provisionally and as a proximate factor in that analysis, always with the unambiguous reservation that the analysis must ultimately come to rest in terms of cause and effect.
>
> (Veblen 1919: 238)

As a possible solution to the problem of human intentionality, Bunge proposes an 'emergentist materialism' where human consciousness and volition are emergent properties of the material world. This retains a single type of materialist causality but endows it with additional, irreducible, emergent properties at higher ontological levels. Human intentionality is thus an emergentist transformation of materialist causality. It depends upon, and is fuelled by, materialist causality, but as human consciousness it acquires irreducible properties of its own.

The difference between Veblen and Shackle on this question is that Veblen tried to retain a place for purposeful behaviour in his theory but insisted that it must be subject to the same kind of causal principles as operated in the material world. There is no place in Veblen's thought for the Shacklean concept of the 'uncaused cause'. Similarly, the institutionalist John Commons (1934: 739, emphasis added) concluded that 'there can be no science of political economy if the will is free, in the sense of being *wholly capricious and undetermined.*'

Their differences on this point have an important consequence. Shackle saw the individual as rising above causality, as the imaginer of the future and the fount of novelty. In contrast, Veblen and Commons saw agency as more the prisoner of its past. The problem with Shackle's viewpoint is that it is based on a causal dualism, along Cartesian lines, between on the one hand, sufficient reason, or intentionality, and, on the other hand, efficient, mechanical or materialistic causality. The institutionalist viewpoint contains a different problem: it is subject to a determinist temptation. If causal dualism is to be abandoned then the pitfalls of determinism have to be avoided.

Chaos theory and emergence

Neither determinacy nor indeterminacy can be demonstrated by an appeal to evidence. However, what we do know from the mathematical theory of chaos is that if the world were deterministic it would almost certainly behave in an apparently random, even non-probabilistic, and unpredictable way. The possibility of 'deterministic chaos' is thus established.[6]

Nevertheless, this does not give either determinism or indeterminacy victory in their feud against each other. On the contrary, chaos theory suggests that the rules of engagement have changed. If the world is deterministic, the theory suggests that we would have to treat it as if it were indeterministic and unpredictable. If novelty is caused, it may appear as entirely spontaneous and free. Thus the traditional distinction between determinacy and indeterminacy is undermined. We can never know for sure if any event is caused or uncaused, but chaos theory suggests that we have to treat complex systems as if they were indeterministic. The seemingly 'uncaused cause' may have chaotic origins. Chaos theory undermines the whole edifice of predictive and reductionist science. With these developments the Shackleans and the institutionalists can begin to find more common ground.

However, lacking in both Veblen's and Shackle's accounts of intentionality is the language of emergent properties. I have argued elsewhere (Hodgson, 1998b) that Veblen's contact with the concept of emergence — devised originally by the British philosopher of biology Conway Lloyd Morgan — was decisive to the formation of institutional economics in the 1890s. As Morgan himself defined the concept:

> Briefly stated the hypothesis is that when certain items of 'stuff', say o p q, enter into some relational organization R in unity of 'substance,' the whole $R(o\ p\ q)$ has some 'properties' which could not be deduced from prior knowledge of the properties of o, p, and q taken severally.
>
> (Morgan 1932: 253)

The concept of emergence denies the possibility of reductionism, where phenomena at one level are explained entirely in terms of entities at a lower level. My argument is that Veblen's implicit appropriation of the concept of emergence in 1896 was crucial in his rejection of both (the then prevalent) biological reductionism and of methodological individualism. Accordingly, it gave Veblen licence to focus on institutions as units of analysis and objects of evolutionary selection. Regrettably, however, Veblen did not make the concept of emergence explicit in his analysis.

Likewise, in the work of Shackle, there is no recognition of the concept of emergence. If this defect had been rectified then there would have been a less exclusive focus on the role of the individual in Shackle's work. Shackle's admiration of Keynes could have been given even more substance, because Keynes took the methodology of macroeconomic aggregates from Veblen's institutionalist student Mitchell. Mitchell had also implicitly appropriated the concept of emergent properties and thus legitimated the causal powers of macroeconomic structures (Hodgson 1999).

Furthermore, the concept of emergence provides a basis for understanding the role of consciousness and intentionality. In this approach, will and consciousness are regarded as emergent properties of the human nervous system. William McDougall (1929) and others developed these ideas in the interwar period. However, at that time, positivism and behaviourism were on the rise in Anglo-American social science. Consequently, concepts such as consciousness were dismissed as metaphysical, and the issues were sidelined. However, similar ideas are making a comeback today (Bunge 1980; Searle 1997; Sperry 1991).

The limits to indeterminacy

On these grounds, there is a place for genuine novelty and creativity. Emergent properties are genuinely novel, precisely because they are emergent. However, they are not strictly indeterminate, nor an 'uncaused cause'. Accordingly, it is possible to see human action as potentially creative, but also channelled and moulded by circumstances. A complete indeterminism of action is rejected, without succumbing to the limitations of determinism. We escape from the traditional dichotomy of determinism versus free will.

Although novelty and creativity is possible, each human mind has limited powers of imagination and expectation. However, these limits will be a result of experiences and habits of thought, which are bounded and framed by the culture of which the individual is a part.

Accordingly, Veblen and the institutionalists saw action and decision as being moulded by both psychology and culture. It is one thing to suggest with Shackle that human agency presents uncaused causes, another to claim that there are no factors moulding decision and action at all. Although Shackle did not deny that decisions could in part be explained by antecedents, he saw economics as primarily addressing the spontaneity of expectation:

> In so far as economics is about choice as a *first cause*, that is the coming into being of decisive thoughts not in all respects to be explained by antecedents, it is *essential* to talk in terms of what is foreseen, expected and intended.
>
> (Shackle 1989: 51)

Here Shackle takes an extreme position, along with the Austrian School, seeing human action as based exclusively on decision and choice that are themselves wholly uncaused. The emphasis is on expectation and imagination: on action in an uncertain world. In such a view, the external world of institutions and natural resources impinges on the actor principally as a constraint, not as factors affecting choice itself. The sphere of choice in the human mind is sacred, undetermined and free: unsullied by the relations of cause and effect to be found in the external world. As Fernando Carvalho (1983–84: 270) points out, Shackle's work shares a limitation of the Austrian approach: 'it over-emphasizes the freedom of the agent and under-estimates the influence of conditions other than his own imagination'.

Despite its limitations, Shackle's position here is not exceptional. Just as neoclassical theorists put the formation and moulding of individual tastes and preferences beyond the scope of their analysis, for Hayek (1948, p. 67) the task of explaining them is not a matter for economics or any other social science. It is thus argued that it is beyond the scope of economic theory to inquires any further as to how purposes and actions may be determined. Whilst the Austrian and neoclassical analyses may be different they have a common effect: to exclude entirely such matters as the determination of preferences and expectations from the domain of economic inquiry. Despite his theoretical radicalism, Shackle follows both the neoclassicals and Austrians by taking it for granted that choice is the 'first cause', without asking what are the preconditions of and influences on choice itself.

While creating a space for real choice, Shackle and the Austrian theorists seem to deny the legitimacy of inquiry into the framing or moulding of purposes or preference functions. For instance, the role of institutions and culture in shaping human cognitions and actions is downplayed or even ignored. Institutions appear primarily as the (unintended) results of, and constraints upon, human action. Arguably, therefore, Shackle and the Austrian theorists go too far, proposing that it is beyond the scope of economic theory to inquires as to how *any* purposes and actions may be framed or moulded by circumstances. It seems untenable to deny any possible external influence on the thought processes and purposes of the individual, other than as mere constraints.

Such a view neglects the forces that themselves may mould — but not necessarily or completely predetermine — some individual purposes and goals. The individual is taken as a given. He or she descends on the social world, already formed and without a natural or social history. There is no theoretical model of the economy where the formation or moulding of some individual purposes and goals is taken into account, to complement the complex portrayal of social institutions as the unintended consequences of interacting individuals. Half the picture is missing.

In Shackle's subjectivist analysis the role of institutions and culture in shaping human cognitions and actions is downplayed. 'Institutional questions tend to be obscured by the Shacklean approach, losing place to a growing emphasis on the process of imagination' (Carvalho 1983–84: 271). Instead of shapers of the imagination, institutions appear primarily as constraints on pre-formed aspirations.

Furthermore, by seeing individual action and decision as a completely 'uncaused cause', Shacklean analysis takes a one-sided view of the historical process. True, it looks forward and sees the gulf that separates the unknown future from the present. But it does not look backwards and appreciate the full significance of the past. As Stephan Böhm (1989: 76) argues: 'In Shackle's non-determinist account, there is a yawning abyss separating the past from the present; the past is a closed book not making itself felt on the present.'

A more plausible view, and one consonant with institutionalism, is that there are external influences moulding the purposes and actions of individuals, but that action is not entirely predictable from knowledge of them. The environment is influential but it does not completely determine either what the individual aims to do or what he or she may achieve. There are actions that may seem uncaused, but at the same time there are patterns of behaviour that may relate to the cultural or institutional environment within which the person acts. Action, in short, is partially determined by circumstances, and partially a result of emergent human will: partly determined but partly unforeseeable. The economic future is still uncertain, in the most radical sense; at the same time, however, economic reality displays a degree of pattern and order.

I have argued at length elsewhere that intentional explanations may rely on cultural and institutional props (Hodgson, 1988, 1997, 1998a). Imagination and choice, although not culturally determined, may be culture-bound. This creates an analytical symbiosis between rigidity and freedom, between institutions and choice, and between the weight of the past and the potential novelty of the future. This symbiosis does not undermine the Shacklean emphasis on irreversible and historical time. As Shaun Hargreaves Heap (1986-87, p. 276) elegantly puts it: 'Recognition of historical time matters, not only because it forces an acknowledgment of uncertainty, but also because history's legacy to the present is a set of institutions which structure our perceptions and hence influence our behaviour with respect to that uncertain future.'

It may be accepted that there is non-probabilistic indeterminacy and space for choice. Nevertheless, the indeterminacy is partial. Consequently, the set of possibilities is limited and accordingly there is even some scope for prediction. Such a standpoint avoids the extremes of either traditional determinism or complete indeterminacy.

In sum, it is desirable to assert the importance of spontaneity in human action but also to recognize its limits at the same time. In some ranges or dimensions, action may seem indeterminate, but in others it is not. Some apparent indeterminacy can exist alongside actions that are bounded and moulded by the influences of culture, institutions and the past.

4 'INVENTION IS HELPLESS WITHOUT TRADITION': THE PRAGMATIST CHALLENGE

Deep at the root of the difference between the Shacklean and the institutionalist conceptions of human agency are very different philosophical presuppositions. Shackle's conceptualisation of the choosing agent emanates from mainstream European philosophy, invoking leading names such as Immanuel Kant and David Hume. In contrast, institutionalism has different philosophical roots, emanating from the challenge to the whole post-Cartesian tradition that was mounted by the American pragmatists. Indeed, by finding its philosophical basis in the work of pragmatist philosophers such as Charles Sanders Peirce, William James and John Dewey, institutionalism dissents explicitly from the entire Cartesian and Newtonian framework of modern science.

The conception of the agent adopted by Veblen and later institutionalists is strongly influenced by the pragmatist philosophy of Peirce and others. Pragmatists reject the Cartesian notion of the rational, calculating agent, to replace it by a conception of agency propelled by a bundle of habits and routinised behaviours. For Peirce (1934: 255–6) habit does not merely reinforce belief; the 'essence of belief is the establishment of habit'. Accordingly, as the institutionalist John Commons (1934: 150) put it, Peirce dissolved the antinomies of rationalism and empiricism at a stroke, making 'Habit and Custom, instead of intellect and sensations, the foundation of all science'. As a result, institutionalism rejects the continuously calculating, marginally adjusting agent of neoclassical theory or the boundless imaginer in the Shacklean vision, to emphasise inertia and habit instead.

Accordingly, it is reasonable to criticise the one-sided emphasis on the uncertainty of the agent in Shackle's work. Consider, for example, the following observation by Tony Lawson:

> It is noticeable ... that economists who are concerned with realism of analysis, and who focus explicitly on the knowledge that individuals possess, tend to emphasize almost exclusively the fact of *uncertainty* surrounding economic activity. Now it is the case, of course, that uncertainty is a pervasive fact of human agency. Nevertheless, an over-preoccupation with emphasizing and describing it can mask the fact that certainty is also a pervasive feature of human agency.
>
> (Lawson 1987: 952)

Lawson goes on to relate belief and certainty with rule following and convention, in a manner reminiscent of Peirce. The Peircian linkage of habit and belief connotes a process by which habits of action connect with habits of thought and help to establish knowledge or skill. As Veblen (1934: 88) wrote: 'A habitual line of action constitutes a habitual line of thought, and gives the point of view from which facts and events are apprehended and reduced to a body of knowledge'. Institutions create and reinforce habits of action and thought: 'The situation of today shapes the institutions of tomorrow through a selective, coercive process, by acting upon men's habitual view of things, and so altering or fortifying a point of view or a mental attitude handed down from the past' (Veblen 1899: 190–1).

Incidentally, the idea of the pre-eminence of habit does not imply any conformity with the neoclassical notion of fixed preference functions. For instance, with a changing price environment, fixed preference functions imply endless marginal adjustment in demand. In contrast, habitual consumer behaviour suggests that adjustments are minimized in the face of price changes (Arrow, 1986). Fixity of preference functions implies infinite incremental adjustment in behaviour, whereas fixity of habit implies behaviour of a rigid and less flexible kind.

Such rigidities should not be regarded wholly as a negative impairment. A number of recent developments in modern anthropology and psychology also suggest that individual habits and social routines play an essential role in providing a cognitive framework for interpreting sense data and for transforming information into useful knowledge (Bourdieu 1990; Douglas 1973, 1987; Hutchins 1995; Lloyd 1972; Plotkin 1982, 1994). Given that it is impossible to deal with and understand the entire amount of sense data reaching the brain, we rely on concepts and cognitive frames to select aspects of the data and to make sense of these stimuli. These habituated procedures of perception and cognition are learned and acquired from our social surroundings. Many psychologists and cultural anthropologists argue that routines, culture and social institutions give rise to certain ways of selecting and understanding the world around us.

In addition, recognition of the pre-eminence of habit and routine does not exclude a notion of purposeful behaviour, particularly at the higher levels of mental activity. But there should be no false dichotomy between habit and purpose: even purposeful behaviour is guided and framed by habits of thought. Institutionalism emanates from an attempt to transcend such dichotomies. This creates a foundation for a conception of the economy in which there is a place for the influence of past tradition as well as expectation of the future. The philosophical foundations of institutionalism offer a means by which the rather one-sided Shacklean emphasis on expectation and imagination can be rectified.

From uncertainty to conventions and institutions

This does not mean that the Shacklean concerns are downgraded. Indeed they could be enhanced. For instance, Robert Dixon (1986) has noted the failure in Shackle's work to draw out the full implications of the concepts of uncertainty and expectation. The fact that we are uncertain of the future, he argues, results from the fact that it is not under our control. The need for expectation and the existence of uncertainty is not a subjective and asocial datum of the human condition; it results from lack of control over our futures and an inability to shelter from the consequences of the decisions of others. Cast in such a mould, 'Shackle's train of thought leads inexorably to a discussion of control and of power' (p. 589). Such an emphasis on the centrality of power in social life would be at the heart of institutionalist concerns.

There is another clear instance where institutionalism can offer a positive development of Shacklean economics. This concerns the treatment of norms and conventions: ideas that are common to both Shackle and Keynes.

As Keynes wrote in 1937: 'Knowing that our own individual judgement is worthless, we endeavour to fall back on the judgement of the rest of the world which is perhaps better informed. That is, we endeavour to conform with the behaviour of the majority or the average' (Keynes 1973:114). Like Veblen, Keynes sees such conventions as self-reinforcing. Even when they are not, 'other factors exert their compensating effects' (Keynes 1936: 162). In recognizing the importance of durable conventions, this argument clearly dovetails with institutionalism.

There is a similar argument in Shackle's *Epistemics and Economics*. Shackle (1972: 112) wrote: 'Stability by convention ... has to serve instead of stability determined by reason and knowledge.' Also Shackle (1972: 227) argues in his chapter on 'Prices as Conventions', that prices which 'have stood at particular levels for some time acquire thereby some sanction and authority'. In addition, Shackle (1972: 226–7) approvingly notes the work of Hugh Townshend, a pupil of Keynes, in this context. Townshend writes that:

> in regard to actual money-prices, there is nothing save the force of habit, operating through conventional prejudices about the normality, or propriety, of certain price-levels for certain particular variables, ... and through habits and conventions which limit the velocity of circulation of money on the one hand and its volume on the other, to prevent them from varying arbitrarily, even in the shortest period. In long periods they do in fact vary arbitrarily — that is to say, in a way not governed by regular law, and therefore unpredictable. Thus a convention of stability is necessary for any dynamic economic theorising.
>
> (Townshend 1937: 168)

This is clearly redolent of institutionalism. Through a conception of uncertainty more radical than that of the founding institutionalists,

Keynes, Townshend and Shackle are brought to a recognition of the role of norms and conventions in imparting essential meaning and stability in economic life.

Overall, this line of argument has a modern ring. For instance, chaos theorists have shown that the disorder generated out of orderly, non-linear, mathematical functions may often lead to a kind of order at a higher level. Other scientists such as Prigogine and Stengers (1984) and Stuart Kauffman (1993) start from chaotic interactions and show that self-organization and order can arise in complex systems. In both these cases the traits of the self-organizing system emerge from its basic structure, despite the chaos at the micro level. Just as chaos can be spun from the 'order' of simple non-linear functions, order can emerge from chaos. Likewise, the work of Ronald Heiner (1983) suggests that uncertainty may be a major cause of predictable behaviour and institutional rigidity.

Accordingly, both Shackle and modern institutionalists converge on a conception of the economic system in which order and stability is possible despite the radical uncertainty faced by human agents. What needs elaboration from a modern institutionalist viewpoint is the way in which institutions have an informational and cognitive function. Instead of being mere constraints, institutions convey information about the likely actions of other agents which is essential to form expectations (Hayek 1973; Newman 1976; Schotter 1981). As Lawrence Boland put it in the institutionalist *Journal of Economic Issues*:

> One of the roles that institutions play is to create knowledge and information for the individual decision maker. In particular, institutions provide social knowledge which may be needed for *interaction* with other individual decision makers.
>
> (Boland 1979: 963)

Accordingly, institutions are not to be regarded simply as constraints. They are enablers of action as well as curbs upon it (Giddens 1984; Hodgson 1988). Notably, Commons (1934: 73) clearly saw institutions as a liberating as well as a constraining force.

Despite his emphasis on indeterminacy, Shackle saw clearly that individual action depends upon convention and tradition. This perception is most explicit when Shackle discusses the genesis of scientific ideas. For example, Shackle (1967: 258) wrote: 'Without an underlying discernible repetitiveness, science is impossible.' Peirce could have written these words. Consider another example. The full title of Shackle's magnificent volume on the development of the Keynesian revolution is *The Years of High Theory: Invention and Tradition in Economic Thought 1926–1939*. Shackle charted the interplay of 'invention and tradition' in the evolution of economic thought itself. Shackle put it lucidly as follows:

> The innovating theoretician needs ruthless self-belief. He must overturn the intellectual dwelling-places of hundreds of people, whose first instinct will be resistance and revenge. Yet reconstruction must inevitably use much of the old material. Piety is not only honourable, it is indispensable. Invention is helpless without tradition.
>
> (Shackle 1967: 295)

No institutionalist could have put it better.

5 CONCLUSION

This essay has explored a number of differences, commonalities and complementarities between institutional and Shacklean economics. In the first place, both schools of thought reject the underlying, mechanistic presuppositions of neoclassical economic theory and the related theoretical artefact of 'rational economic man'.

The primary potential contribution that Shackle's writing can make to institutional economics is the extension and clarification of the concept of uncertainty. In addition, Shackle underlines the importance of the concept purposeful behaviour. However, the Shacklean emphasis on indeterminacy is a problem for institutionalism. Nevertheless, as the concept of emergence and modern developments in chaos theory both suggest, the dichotomy between determinism and indeterminacy can be transcended.

The primary contribution that institutionalism can make to the Shacklean conception of the human agent is to correct the one-sided emphasis on novelty and imagination. Shackle puts supreme emphasis on the explanation of the decision-making of a single agent, neglecting problems that arise when agents interact with one another. Without dispensing with the concept of purposeful behaviour, and with the quite different philosophical foundations of the American pragmatists, it is possible to reconcile Shacklean imagination and creativity with the binding and creative functions of institutions in economic life. As we have seen, there are passages in Shackle's work which utilise Keynes's notion of the 'convention' in a sense that is very close to institutional theory.

Shackle's own thought exhibits both novelty and tradition. On the one hand it is trapped by Cartesian causal dualism. On the other, Shackle moved our thinking forward in way that will remain at the forefront of social science. Not only institutionalists, but also all other social scientists, can greatly benefit from an engagement with his thought. His works are not only beautifully written, they are also brimming with engaging and relevant ideas.

NOTES

* The author is very grateful to Stephan Böhm, Peter Earl and Knut Mittendorfer for helpful comments on an earlier version of this paper.
1 The terms 'institutionalism', 'institutionalist' and 'institutional economics' employed in this essay refer to the tradition of institutional economics emanating from Thorstein Veblen, John Commons, Wesley Mitchell, Gunnar Myrdal and others, but not the 'new' institutionalism of Douglass North, Mancur Olson, Richard Posner, Andrew Schotter, Oliver Williamson and others. For comparative surveys of the 'old' and 'new' institutionalism see Hodgson (1993a, 1998a).
2 For a useful Lakatosian specification of the 'hard core' and 'protective belt' of neoclassical economics, each with its respective 'heuristics', see Lavoie (1992: 76–8).
3 This particular definition of neoclassical economics clearly excludes members of the Austrian School, particularly because of their explicit critique of attributes (2) and (3), and also because of their rejection of typical conceptualizations of rationality under (1). There is also the question as to whether some recent developments in game theory can also be described as 'neoclassical economics'. This question can only be answered by close inspection and refinement of the boundary conditions in the above definition.
4 Keynes's own views on mathematical modelling are clear in a letter to Roy Harrod of 16 July 1938: 'In economics . . . to convert a model into a quantitative formula is to destroy its usefulness as an instrument of thought' (Keynes 1973: 299).

5　My own position has changed on this issue. In Hodgson (1993b) I declined the opportunity to reject the notion of human intention as an uncaused cause. However, I also noted that chaos theory suggests that even if the world is deterministic, it may appear as entirely spontaneous and free. I noted that chaos theory suggests the possibility of emergence, even in a system that is deemed to adhere to deterministic rules. On reflection, I now believe that the admission of an uncaused cause is not only unnecessary, for the reasons just suggested and already given in my *Economics and Evolution* book, but also untenable, for the reasons given here. The concept of emergence makes the compatibility of determinism and free will possible, but that does not sustain the notion of an uncaused cause. Since 1993 my position has become compatibilist and also, incidentally, more Veblenian on this issue. See Hodgson (1999; unpublished).

6　Institutional economists have been quick to recognize the impact of chaos theory for economics (Coricelli and Dosi, 1988; Dopfer, 1988; Mirowski, 1990; Radzicki, 1990).

REFERENCES

Arrow, K. J. (1986) 'Rationality of self and others in an economic system', *Journal of Business* 59(4.2): S385–S399. Reprinted in volume 2 of Eatwell, J., Milgate, M. and Newman, P. (eds) (1987) *The New Palgrave Dictionary of Economics*, London: Macmillan.

Böhm, S. (1989) 'Subjectivism and post-keynesianism: towards a better understanding', in Pheby (1989: 59–93).

Boland, L. A. (1979) 'Knowledge and the role of institutions in economic theory', *Journal of Economic Issues* 13, 4: 957–72. Reprinted in Hodgson (1993c).

Bourdieu, P. (1990) *The Logic of Practice*, translated by R Nice, Stanford, CA: Stanford University Press/Cambridge: Polity Press).

Bunge, M. A. (1980) *The Mind-Body Problem: A Psychobiological Approach*, Oxford: Pergamon.

Carvalho, F. (1983–84) 'On the Concept of Time in Shacklean and Sraffian Economics', *Journal of Post Keynesian Economics* 6,2): 265-80.

Coddington, A. (1983) *Keynesian Economics: The Search for First Principles*, London: Alan and Unwin.

Commons, J. R. (1924) *Legal Foundations of Capitalism*, New York: Macmillan. Reprinted 1968 (Madison, WI: University of Wisconsin Press), 1974 (New York: Augustus Kelley), and 1995 with a new introduction by J. E. Biddle and W. J. Samuels (New Brunswick, NJ: Transaction Publishers).

—— (1934) *Institutional Economics — Its Place in Political Economy*, New

York: Macmillan. Reprinted 1990 with a new introduction by M. Rutherford, New Brunswick, NJ: Transaction Publishers.

— — (1950) *The Economics of Collective Action*, New York: Macmillan.

Coricelli, F. and Dosi, G. (1988) 'Coordination and order in economic change and the interpretative power of economic theory', pp. 124–47 in Dosi, G., Freeman, C., Nelson, R., Silverberg, G. and Soete, L. L. G. (eds) *Technical Change and Economic Theory*, London: Pinter.

Dixon, R. (1986) 'Uncertainty, unobstructedness and power', *Journal of Post Keynesian Economics* 8, 4: 585–90.

Dopfer, K. 1988) 'Classical mechanics with an ethical dimension: Professor Tinbergen's economics', *Journal of Economic Issues* 22, 3: 675–706.

Douglas, M. (ed.) (1973) *Rules and Meanings*, Harmondsworth: Penguin.

— — (1987) *How Institutions Think*, London: Routledge and Kegan Paul.

Giddens, A. (1984) *The Constitution of Society: Outline of the Theory of Structuration*, Cambridge: Polity Press.

Gruchy, A. G. (1947) *Modern Economic Thought: The American Contribution*, New York: Prentice Hall.

— — (1948) 'The philosophical basis of the new Keynesian economics', *Ethics* 58, 4: 235–44.

— — (1949) 'J. M. Keynes' concept of economic science', *Southern Economic Journal* 15, 3: 249–66.

Hargreaves Heap, S. P. (1986-87) 'Risk and culture: a missing link in the Post Keynesian tradition', *Journal of Post Keynesian Economics* 9, 2: 267–78.

Hayek, Friedrich A. (1948) *Individualism and Economic Order*, Chicago, IL: University of Chicago Press.

— — (1973) *Law, Legislation and Liberty: A New Statement of the Liberal Principles of Justice and Political Economy. Vol. 1: Rules and Order*, London: Routledge and Kegan Paul.

Heiner, R. A. (1983) 'The origin of predictable behavior', *American Economic Review* 73, 4: 560–95.

Hindess, B. (1989) *Political Choice and Social Structure*, Aldershot: Edward Elgar.

Hodgson, G. M. (1988) *Economics and Institutions: A Manifesto for a Modern Institutional Economics*, Cambridge: Polity Press.

— — (1992) 'Thorstein Veblen and post-Darwinian economics', *Cambridge Journal of Economics* 16, 3: 285–301.

— — (1993a) 'Institutional economics: surveying the "old" and the "new"', *Metroeconomica* 44, 1: 1–28. Reprinted in Hodgson (1993c).

— — (1993b) *Economics and Evolution: Bringing Life Back into Economics*, Cambridge: Polity Press.

— — (ed.) (1993c) *The Economics of Institutions*, Aldershot: Edward Elgar.

— — (1997) 'The ubiquity of habits and rules', *Cambridge Journal of Economics* 21. 6: 663–84.

— — (1998a) 'The approach of institutional economics', *Journal of Economic*

Literature 36, 1: 166–92.

— — (1998b) 'On the evolution of Thorstein Veblen's evolutionary economics', *Cambridge Journal of Economics* 22, 4: 415–31.

— — (1999) *Evolution and Institutions: On Evolutionary Economics and the Evolution of Economics*, Cheltenham: Edward Elgar.

— — (forthcoming) 'Frank Knight as an institutional economist', in Medema, S. Davis, J. and Biddle, J. (eds), title to be confirmed.

— — (unpublished) 'Structures and institutions: reflections on institutionalism, structuration theory and critical realism', University of Hertfordshire, mimeo, 1999.

Hutchins, E. (1995) *Cognition in the Wild* (Cambridge, MA: MIT Press).

Kapp, K. W. (1976) 'The nature and significance of institutional economics', *Kyklos* 29, Fasc. 2,: 209–32. Reprinted in Samuels, W. J. (ed.) (1988) *Institutional Economics*, Aldershot: Edward Elgar, vol. 1.

Kauffman, S. A. (1993) *The Origins of Order: Self-Organization and Selection in Evolution*, Oxford and New York: Oxford University Press.

Keynes, J. M. (1936) *The General Theory of Employment, Interest and Money*, London: Macmillan.

— — (1973) *The Collected Writings of John Maynard Keynes, Vol. XIV, 'The General Theory and After: Defence and Development*, London: Macmillan.

Knight, F. H. (1921) *Risk, Uncertainty and Profit*, New York: Houghton Mifflin.

Lavoie, M. (1992) 'Towards a new research programme for post-Keynesianism and neo-Ricardianism', *Review of Political Economy* 4, 1: 37–78.

Lawson, T. (1987) 'The relative/absolute nature of knowledge and economic analysis', *Economic Journal* 97, 4: 951–70.

Leslie, T. E. C. (1888) *Essays in Political Economy*, 2nd edn (1st edn 1879), London: Longmans, Green. Reprinted 1969, New York: Augustus Kelley.

Lloyd, B. B. (1972) *Perception and Cognition: A Cross-Cultural Perspective*, Harmondsworth: Penguin.

McDougall, W. (1929) *Modern Materialism and Emergent Evolution*, London: Methuen.

Mirowski, P. (1990) 'From Mandelbrot to chaos in economic theory', *Southern Economic Journal* 57, 2: 289–307.

Morgan, C. L. (1932) 'C. Lloyd Morgan', in Murchison, C. (ed.) (1932) *A History of Psychology in Autobiography, Volume 2*, New York: Russell and Russell, 253–64.

Newman, G. (1976) 'An institutional perspective on information', *International Social Science Journal* 28: 466–92.

Peirce, C. S. (1934) *Collected Papers of Charles Sanders Peirce, Volume V, Pragmatism and Pragmaticism*, edited by C. Hartshorne and P. Weiss, Cambridge, MA: Harvard University Press.

Pheby, J. (ed.) (1989) *New Directions in Post-Keynesian Economics*, Aldershot: Edward Elgar.

Plotkin, H. C. (ed.) (1982) *Learning, Development and Culture: Essays in Evolutionary Epistemology*, New York: Wiley.

—— (1994) *Darwin Machines and the Nature of Knowledge: Concerning Adaptations, Instinct and the Evolution of Intelligence*, Harmondsworth: Penguin.

Prigogine, I. and Stengers, I. (1984) *Order Out of Chaos: Man's New Dialogue With Nature*, London: Heinemann.

Radzicki, M. J. (1990) 'Institutional dynamics, deterministic chaos, and self-organizing systems', *Journal of Economic Issues* 24, 1: 57–102.

Schotter, A. (1981) *The Economic Theory of Social Institutions*, Cambridge: Cambridge University Press.

Searle, J. R. (1997) *The Mystery of Consciousness* (London: Granta Books).

Shackle, G. L. S, (1953) 'Economics and sincerity', *Oxford Economic Papers* 5,1,: 1–12. Reprinted in J. L. Ford (ed.) (1990) *Time, Expectations and Uncertainty in Economics: Selected Essays of G. L. S. Shackle*, Aldershot: Edward Elgar.

—— (1966) *The Nature of Economic Thought: Selected Papers 1955–1964*, Cambridge: Cambridge University Press.

—— (1967) *The Years of High Theory: Invention and Tradition in Economic Thought 1926–1939*, Cambridge: Cambridge University Press.

—— (1972) *Epistemics and Economics: A Critique of Economic Doctrines*, Cambridge: Cambridge University Press.

—— (1983) 'A Student's Pilgrimage', *Banca Nazionale del Lavoro Quarterly Review* no. 145: 107–16. Reprinted in Shackle (1988).

—— (1988) *Business, Time and Thought: Selected Papers*, edited by S. F. Frowen, London: Macmillan.

—— (1989) 'What Did the *General Theory* Do?', in Pheby (ed.) (1989) 48–58.

Sperry, R. W. (1991) 'In defense of mentalism and emergent interaction', *Journal of Mind and Behavior* 12, 2): 221–46.

Tilman, R. (1992) *Thorstein Veblen and His Critics, 1891–1963*, Princeton: Princeton University Press.

Townshend, H. (1937) 'Liquidity-premium and the theory of value', *Economic Journal*, 47, 1: 157–69.

Veblen, T. B. (1899) *The Theory of the Leisure Class: An Economic Study in the Evolution of Institutions*, New York: Macmillan.

—— (1919) *The Place of Science in Modern Civilization and Other Essays*, New York: Huebsch. Reprinted 1990 with a new introduction by W. J. Samuels, New Brunswick, NJ: Transaction Publishers.

—— (1934) *Essays on Our Changing Order*, ed. L. Ardzrooni, New York: The Viking Press.

4

GEORGE SHACKLE AND
POST KEYNESIANISM

G. C. Harcourt and Claudio Sardoni*

1 INTRODUCTION

George Shackle is to Post Keynesianism what John Hicks (or, rather, JR) was to mainstream neo-classical economics. Both made fundamental contributions and provided deep insights which were accepted and acted upon, often by people who knew not from whence (or whom) they came. In Shackle's case, his general influence is associated with the treatment of time, expectations and uncertainty, with which is associated as well, his unique interpretations of both Keynes and Walrasian general equilibrium analysis. He hoped that his own major analytical contribution, the theory of potential surprise, would be taken up and extended by others. His biographer, Jim Ford, is inclined to argue that with the exception of a small group (including himself), this has not happened and that in so far as such a gentle and unassuming person as George Shackle could have had a disappointment, this was it. But they might have been too pessimistic in their assessment.[1] George's ideas are both respected *and* being looked at anew within the mainstream itself.[2] But this is not our main story for in this essay we shall not follow it up any further here.

To write this chapter we looked at the writings of a number of people who come under the Post Keynesian umbrella and who have explicitly acknowledged the influence of Shackle on their work. They include the late Alan Coddington (an observer rather than a Post Keynesian), Victoria Chick, Paul Davidson, Sheila Dow, John Hicks and Jan Kregel. By looking up their references to Shackle's work, we gained an impression of how his ideas have permeated their work and others. In addition, we read or reread much of Shackle's work. We found especially helpful the 1957 de Vries Lectures, *Time in Economics* (1958), *The Years of High Theory* (1967) (our favourite Shackle book),

Epistemics and Economics (1972), and George's superb essay in the Arestis/Sawyer volume of dissenting economists (1992). In addition, Jim Ford very kindly let us see a pre-publication version of his (1993) obituary essay on George for the *Economic Journal* and some of his papers on Shackle's early work on the trade cycle, together with Ford's interpretation and extension of it (Ford and Peng 1993).

2 EXPECTATIONS AND INVESTMENT

When writing on Shackle's influence on Post Keynesianism we need to remember that Post Keynesianism is a portmanteau term which embraces a diversity of ideas and a collection of heterogeneous people. In Hamouda and Harcourt (1988), they were divided into three broad groups, with some individuals, including Shackle himself, spanning more than one group, and so contributing to more than one strand. The principal groups include the American Post Keynesians, the Neo-Ricardians, and the Robinsonians *cum* Kaleckians. Shackle's influence on most members under the Neo-Ricardian grouping is minimal for they do not regard uncertainty or expectations as central to either their understanding of the economy or the nature of economic theory.

We feel that in this regard they were unfaithful to themselves. For they argue that *general* theory may only relate to an account of the possible interrelationships between sustained, persistent, dominant and permanent features of an economic system, the long-period method is the only possible mode of theorizing. The concept of the long-period position which is central to their approach carries a connotation of realized expectations so that uncertainty and reactions to it seemingly have no role to play in this theoretical schema. Yet what could be more sustained and all-pervading than the inevitable, inescapable presence of uncertainty? It is true that each individual uncertain event is unique and once-and-for-all. Yet an *environment* of a continuous stream of such unique uncertain events is, paradoxically, a certain, obvious and inescapable fact of life. It is surely an inescapable task of a theorist is to tackle the effects of and responses to these kinds of events and George Shackle had more profound things to say about them than most economists in the twentieth (or any other) century.

No more so is this relevant than in the theories of investment and theories of the rate of interest in Keynes and, then, the Post

Keynesians. Shackle had the highest regard for Hugh Townshend (who reviewed his first book) and who wrote a remarkable article in the *Economic Journal* in 1937, 'Liquidity-Premium and the Theory of Value'. The article drew out the implications of the theory of liquidity preference and of the arguments of chapter 17 of *The General Theory*, which Keynes himself initially had missed or, at least, had not taken in their full significance. Victoria Chick has put the essence of all this very well in her *New Palgrave* entry on Townshend:

> [Townshend's] note takes issue with Hicks' [subsequent] attempt...to transform the theory of liquidity preference into a mirror image of the loanable funds theory by Walras's Law. Townshend saw that this was an attempt to retain the link between prices and the flow concepts of cost and demand.... [He argued] that it was in the nature of Keynes's ... theory that expectations of the future could change the value of assets overnight and be reflected in the market prices of those assets even in the absence of actual trading. Thus current prices could be determined by subjective as well as objective factors and future prices were indeterminate.
>
> (Chick 1987: 662)

Shackle himself enlarged on these themes in a number of places, especially in *The Years of High Theory*.[3]

> The interest-rate in a money economy. This was the enigma that led Keynes to the nihilism of his final position, made explicit by him in the *Quarterly Journal of Economics*, and by his interpreter Mr Hugh Townshend in the *Economic Journal*, virtually at the same moment. The interest-rate depends on expectations of its own future. It is expectational, subjective, psychic, indeterminate, And so is the rest of the economic system. The stability of the system, while it lasts, rests upon a convention: the tacit general agreement to *suppose* it stable. This stability, once doubted, is destroyed, and cascading disorder must intervene before the landslide grounds in a new fortuitous position. Such is the last phase of Keynesian economics. But Keynes had shown governments how to prolong the suspension of doubt..
>
> (Shackle 1967: 217)

Shackle and Townshend are here expositing a theme which Nicholas Kaldor was to set out in 1939 in what is generally regarded as his greatest theoretical article, 'Speculation and economic stability'. The theme relates to those markets in which stocks dominate flows, and speculations dominate tangible economic factors, in the determination of prices. The market for financial assets is a prime (but alas, not the only) example. Related to these characteristics is the importance, for the stability of the system, of adoption of certain conventions which in turn, in some concrete situations, can prove to be very fragile.

Again, because of uncertainty and the need to cope with it when making spending and wealth-holding decisions, aggregate demand, especially the component accounted for by investment expenditure, could falter. Because of the peculiar properties of the liquidity variable, themselves attributable in turn to the presence of uncertainty, the faltering demand could be siphoned off into the holding of a non-employment and non-employment-creating asset.[4] If moreover, at the same time as the desire to accumulate is falling off, the desire to hold the liquidity variable was increasing, there would be a directly reinforcing effect on the initial contractionary forces, for not only would the marginal efficiency of capital schedule move to the left (or even collapse) but one effect of the liquidity preference schedule moving to the right could be to tend to raise the rate of interest (complex of) which in turn would have a further contractionary effect on investment spending.

Of course, the whole thrust of Shackle's arguments was that in these realms, the effects of movements of schedules were not only qualitatively and quantitatively much more important than the effects of movements *along* schedules — hence his dislike of IS–LM Keynesianism — but also much harder, if not impossible, to predict. Carried to its logical extreme this insight has the nihilistic implications of the sort which Alan Coddington detected in the work of both Shackle and Joan Robinson and which created the sense of terrible, unresolved tensions in the pages of his last book, *Keynesian Economics: The Search for First Principles* (1983). Coddington fervently hoped that the contributions of Robert Clower and Axel Leijonhufvud would provide a safe route out of the impasse which he saw threatening economics as a discipline, but we do not believe that he persuaded himself that it was a creditable one. He was thus faced with accepting a position that [appeared] to be consistent but analytically nihilistic ... If subjectivist logic is followed to the point of becoming convinced that there is nothing for economists to do but to understand certain (praxiological) [*sic*] concepts, then the only problem remains is that of subjugating one's conscience long enough to draw one's salary in exchange for imparting this piece of wisdom. One could, of course, having got into this state of mind, spend a good deal of time and energy in trying to convince those who engage in macroeconomics, econometric model building, mathematical economics, general equilibrium theory and so on, of the folly of their ways. But, that task accomplished, there would be nothing left but for the whole profession to shut up shop.

(Coddington 1983: 61)

Although such inferences also led Shackle to be ambivalent concerning macroeconomic policy and its chances of success, reinforcing a scepticism borne out of his war-time experiences (see Ford 1993: 686) and to Joan Robinson feeling that, after over 50 years as an economic theorist, economic theory had come to pieces in her hands, that she no longer believed in it, Shackle also offered some interesting insights concerning the way in which macroeconomic policy could be at least partly successful. He did this by referring to Keynes's own position in *The General Theory*. Keynes's conviction that the inducement to invest is 'capricious and incalculable' and that there is a tendency for the economy to remain below full employment required policy interventions. But the 'capricious and incalculable' nature of the inducement to invest also implies an improbable ability to control and foresee such a volatile variable. He tried to solve this dilemma in a 'Marshallian' way. In dealing with investment in a formal way by using the marginal efficiency of capital schedule Keynes adopted the Marshallian method of *ceteris paribus*.

He adopted the method, natural and obvious to a Marshallian, of regarding the marginal efficiency of capital, for the analytic purpose in hand, as dependent only on the size of the aggregate flow of investment, and of treating that size itself as determined by that numerical value of the marginal efficiency at which the latter was equal to the prevailing rate of interest. This analytical scheme had a number of advantages. A superficial one was the suggestion it offered for influencing the size of the investment flow by manipulating the interest-rate.

(Shackle 1972: 432)

But all the *cetera* of the analysis are extremely unstable and precarious. If they change the marginal efficiency schedule shifts 'bodily, abruptly and widely'. If the schedule is subject to such movements how can we hope to control the economy through the rate of interest?

> The legitimate answer seems to be that no matter what the shape and position of the curve, we can always try to push investment one way or the other along the curve. If the curve shifts, the effect of this on the size of investment flow must be counteracted, if desirable, by a movement along the new curve. Keynes was justified, we may think, in urging that monetary policy should do what it can in any circumstances to bring the aggregate investment-flow to an appropriate full employment level.
>
> (Shackle 1972: 433)

Shackle's approach here differs from both that of the general equilibrium and mechanical business cycle models, both with respect to theory and to policy.

> The method implicit in the *General Theory* is to regard the economy as subject to sudden landslides of re-adjustment to a new, precarious and ephemeral, pseudo-equilibrium, in which variables based on expectation, speculative hope and conjecture are delicately stacked in a card-house of momentary immobility, waiting for 'the news' to upset everything again and start a new dis-equilibrium phase.
>
> (Shackle 1972: 433)

3 TIME, HUMAN ACTION AND
GENERAL EQUILIBRIUM ANALYSIS

We have mentioned Shackle's view that many of the relationships in economics are prone to, *in principle*, unpredictable instability. A corollary of this is, of course, his scepticism, to put it at its mildest, concerning general equilibrium analysis principally as a means of capturing the essence of the economic process, just because it excludes the essential characteristics of time as he saw them as a human being and as an economist. We quote Shackle himself at this point:[5]

> In the classical dynamics of the physicist, time is merely a mathematical variable. The essence of his scheme of thought is the fully abstract idea of function, the idea of some working model or coded procedure which, applied to any particular and specified value or set of values of one or more independent variables, generates a value of a dependent variable. For the independent variable in a mental construction of this kind, *time* is a misnomer... The solution to the differential equation, if it can be found, is complete in an instantaneous and timeless sense.
>
> This timelessness...abolishes the distinction between past and future. The physicist has, within the stated limits of his problem, complete, perfect and indisputable *knowledge* of where his particle will be at any instant; the very nature of human consciousness ... depends ... upon *ignorance* of the future ... upon the necessity to live in one moment at a time.
>
> (Shackle 1958: 23–4; italics in the original)

Later on, he amplified this last insight.

> For the individual human consciousness time is not a mathematician's space nor a historian's panorama but a moment. In this solitary moment all the consequences that the decision-maker seeks or accepts must necessarily be contained. These consequences must therefore be experiences by imaginative anticipation. As the basis of these anticipations the individual cannot avail himself of a unique self-consistent picture free of doubts or counter-suggestions, but has in mind a set of rival diverse hypotheses ... [which, in Shackle's view, should be

regarded as] the essential freedom of the individual imagination to create afresh from moment to moment. ... [I]f this freedom were unbounded, if there were no discernible links between action and consequence, decision would be needless and useless. To afford enjoyment by anticipation, imagination must work within a sense of the possible, of the rules of the game, of the essential artistic constraint.

In speaking of freedom, what do we imply? That decisions can be creative acts each injecting something essentially new into the world process: we imply the possibility of *inspiration*. In the universe without inspiration, decisions are empty; in the universe without order, without links between action and consequence, decisions are meaningless. Between these two extremes...is there room for the world of inspiration and order, the world of continuing creation by the instrument of decisions made by men?

(Shackle 1958: 33–4)

The essential weakness of general equilibrium analysis, as Shackle understood it, stemmed from these views. His is a rather idiosyncratic interpretation of general equilibrium, certainly not one which accords either with what Walras himself thought it was or with the view of the best modern practitioners, for example, Frank Hahn.[6] But Shackle's interpretation does go right to the heart of the weakness and abuse of general equilibrium theory in the hands of those less gifted than either its founder or its leading modern expositors. For Shackle it

is the natural and even the logical arrival point of that procedure of theorizing which assumes that men pursue their interests by applying reason to their circumstances ... reason can only be applied to circumstances in so far as those circumstances are taken as known. But the circumstances relevant to the choice of actions include other men's chosen actions. If the solution is to be general or symmetrical; if it is to accord to any and every person, no matter whom, a freedom and knowledge formally identical with those of every other person, if the rules of the games are to be precisely the same for all, the various actions of all these persons must be pre-reconciled. But choices which are pre-reconciled are effectively simultaneous ... Sequential actions, transformations of one situation into a subsequent and different one, occurring successively, are excluded in the nature of things from being studied as the consequences of pure reason, unless these successive transformations all belong to simultaneously pre-reconciled plans.

(Shackle 1972: 90–2)

In Victoria Chick's critique (1978) of Clower's attempt to derive Keynesian results starting from a Walrasian general equilibrium framework which is then modified, she expressed succinctly a view which would have been dear, we believe, to Shackle's heart. After having outlined the main features of Walras's exchange model, she notes:

In contrast, the *General Theory* presents a model of a *production* economy, using *money*, moving through *time*, subject to *uncertainty* and the possibility of *error*. Is it any wonder that Walras' Law does not hold? ... Production, unlike exchange, *necessarily takes time...* it imposes an *ordered sequence of economic decisions*, necessarily over lapping continuously in time at the macroeconomic level but quite distinct at the micro level

(Chick 1978/1992: 59)

Perhaps the most profound comment made on Shackle's understanding of the inappropriateness of ancient and modern general equilibrium analysis for illumination of actual economic processes is to be found in Jan Kregel's paper at the Shackle Conference in 1984 (Kregel 1990). There, Kregel links Shackle's highly original work on imagination, and its central role in economic decision-making and the functioning (or malfunctioning) of the economic system (parts and whole), to Adam Smith's similar discussion. In doing so, Kregel argues, convincingly in our view, see especially pp. 81-89, that modern general equilibrium theorists have misunderstood Smith's views on the roles of self-interest, the invisible hand and the price mechanism, so that modern general equilibrium theory is as illegitimate an heir of our founder's *Theory of Moral Sentiments* and *Wealth of Nations* as the Bastard Keynesians are of Keynes's *General Theory*. The link with Shackle arises from Smith's argument that we can only *know* what we ourselves think and feel; therefore we build into our behaviour the supposition that others have similar sensations and functions and that this gives rise to both norms in, and constraints on the working of the system, especially with regard to price formation, distribution and accumulation. Shackle took this insight further, concentrating his sights principally on business people's decision-making under uncertainty and the process of accumulation, inspired, in Kregel's view, implicitly by Smith and, of course, explicitly by Keynes.

> It is in the explanation of the nature of the motivation of human action that Shackle takes up his investigations, providing the most important extension of the Smithian conception, which he calls 'the human predicament', to the analysis of the predicament facing business enterprise in modern capitalist economies. This represents the shift in the source of the desire for accumulation from Smith's time to the present day, from individual acquisition predominated by exchange, to business enterprise in which the investment decision dominates accumulation.
>
> (Kregel 1990: 93)

Paul Davidson found in Shackle's work staunch support for Davidson's spelling out of the implications of the economic system being made up, in large part, of non-ergodic processes. In recent years Davidson has stressed that this insight is one of Keynes's principal contributions. Non-ergodic processes are characteristic of systems of relationships where the stability of key parameters cannot be guaranteed and where both cross-section and time series averages are spurious measures — spurious in the sense that the values of the variables in the system have no necessary tendency to converge on the values of the averages. As Davidson puts it, 'the outcome of an economic process can never be forecast with statistical accuracy at the start of the process'. He adds: 'it is only in a non-ergodic environment, where people recognize that the future may be non-predictable in any stochastic sense, that the sensibility of human beings prevails. Sensible expectations rely on diverse organizations that have evolved to permit human beings to cope with the unknowable. Only in such a world are the attributes of dignity and human motivation necessarily geared not to rationality but to sensibility' (Davidson 1990: 327; italics in original).[7]

This distinction between 'sensible' and 'rational' is both Marshallian and Shacklean.

4 MATHEMATICS AND THE LANGUAGE OF ECONOMICS

It would be wrong to allow Shackle's deep intuitions and influence to be reduced to the bare bones of 'movements of are more important than movements along schedules'. We know that his genes and his intelligence made him in principle a capable mathematician. He has left us some fine technical articles in which both algebra and geometry are exploited in the best possible way by a master craftsman in complete command of his tools of trade. But he did not think mathematics *was* the appropriate language for large parts of economics. He thought that the written language could best indicate the multi-dimensional aspects of key factors at work in the economic system. Because he was such a kind and generous person, when he distinguished between two sorts of economics (and economists!), he refrained from saying, at least very emphatically, which he preferred. Thus in his 1983 autobiographical essay in the *Banca Nazionale del Lavoro Quarterly Review*, he wrote:

> I think there are two kinds of economics. One of them aims at precision, rigour, tidiness and the formulation of principles which will be permanently valid: an economic science. The other is ... rhetorical. ... often used disparagingly [—] a modern unscholarly abuse. The rhetorician employs reason and appeals to logic, but he is a user of language at its full compass, where words are fingers touching the keyboard of a hearer's mind. I do not believe that human affairs can be exhibited as the infallible and invariable working of a closed and permanent system'.
>
> (Shackle 1983: 116)

But increasingly it became clear from his writings that he preferred the second sort of economics. Sheila Dow especially has taken up this theme in her writings on the economics of the tower of Babel (see, for example, Dow 1990). She argues that

In practice, this mode of thought [the Babylonian approach] involves approaching any issue from a variety of starting-points, using a range of partial analyses in order to build up a picture. Each chain of reasoning may be said to start from axioms, but the axioms of one chain of reasoning may be the conclusions of another. One aspect of Babylonian thought is the rejection of formalism in the sense that not all knowledge can be expressed formally.

... For example, Feynman ... , who applied the term 'Babylonian' to a style of mathematical reasoning, demonstrated that three statements of the law of gravitation which are mathematically equivalent are philosophically and psychologically unequivalent. To express all economic theory in terms of a common language, as advocated by Hahn would thus be to eliminate knowledge.

(Dow 1990: 146–7)

In his earliest work Shackle argued that Keynes's ideas needed to be presented in a framework which included the concepts of *ex ante* and *ex post* (to which he had been introduced by Brinley Thomas's 'thrilling' lectures on the Swedish School at the L.S.E. (see Harcourt 1990: xix). But, then, his emerging views on time made him very critical indeed of deterministic mechanical period analyses of economic processes, including the trade cycle. Especially was this so of any analysis past one period — the next. Jim Ford has succinctly described Shackle's principal objections:

The interpretation of time germane to economics [as] 'inside' or 'subjective' time, rather than 'outside' or 'mechanical' time led Shackle to make two related contentions: the first was that it was impossible to construct a dynamic model of an economic system except for one period at a time; and the second was that the formal, mathematical models of growth and of business cycles which were based upon such mechanisms as difference equations were otiose, having no meaning being necessarily built on mechanical, non-expectational, time.

(Ford 1993: 690–1)

He adds: 'The implication that economics would not be a predictive science was not entirely welcome', a view that is nevertheless being reached from such diverse sources as the critical realists, Frank Hahn, and the evangelical wing of the modern Austrian School![8]

What Shackle seems to have in mind is that, though each moment of time is a separate miracle, if we know what has led up to it, we can discuss what may happen next, in the sense of next period. However, after that, the number of possible interrelated scenarios for each decision-maker taken in isolation and then looked at collectively are so many and so complex that they may not be handled intelligently even by the on-looking economist. This viewpoint is related to an argument which Tom Asimakopulos had with Joan Robinson, an argument that goes back to Keynes's own despair of ever finding a determinate time unit with which to analyze obviously interrelated economic processes, the component parts of which nevertheless take different stretches of actual historical or calendar time to work themselves out. Asimakopulos did not like her later argument, in *Economic Heresies* for example, that 'Marshall's short period is a moment in a stream of time...It is better to use the expressions "short period" and "long period" as adjectives, not as substantives. The "short period" is not a length of time but a state of affairs' (Robinson 1971: 17–18). Asimakopulos by contrast insisted that both Marshall *and* Keynes (one in a partial setting, the other in an economy-wide setting), *did* have a definite length of actual time in mind so that there was 'time available to permit variations in the utilization of productive capacity in response to changing short-term expectations' (Asimakopulos 1988: 196). The simplification then required for Keynes's theory (which he shied away from) is to suppose that most production periods and gestation periods in the economy are of similar lengths and that decisions about production, and about investment, are synchronized.[9]

This was basically Kalecki's solution and it allowed him to string together successions of short periods in order to tell his many stories of cyclical growth in capitalism and, as Richard Goodwin also did, to dismiss the distinction between trend and cycle as bogus.[10] Thus, these Post-Keynesians are not held back, or at least explicitly troubled by Shackle's basic misgivings. It would be fascinating to know whether Shackle and Kalecki ever broached this theme when they worked together in London in the 1930s (see Harcourt 1990: xxi). It would have been even more fascinating to have eavesdropped if they had.

We are aware that temperament has much to do with which stand is taken. Because Shackle thought that liquidity preference was Keynes's most profound contribution, and because Shackle had such respect for Townshend's insights, he may have let his consequent understanding of finance capital dominate his views on the boundaries and limitations of theory.[11] Kalecki was more influenced by the characteristics of industrial capital, partly because of his early personal experience, partly by inclination, and so Shackle's hesitations would not have been such a clamp on his attitudes to and mode of theorizing.

5 SHACKLE AND HICKS

We began this essay by comparing the role George Shackle played for Post-Keynesians with the role Hicks played for mainstream economists. In this section we consider briefly the relationship between Shackle's and Hicks's positions concerning some crucial aspect of Keynesian economics.

J R. Hicks and George Shackle first met in 1930 at LSE. They were two of the group of young economists who worked with Lionel Robbins and Friedrich von Hayek: a group of eminent economists who, in Hicks's words, shared a common 'faith' from which most of them were soon to depart:

> We seemed at the start, to share a common viewpoint, or even, one might say, a common faith. Some of us, especially Hayek, have in later years maintained that faith, others, such as Kaldor, Abba Lerner, George Shackle and myself, have departed from it, to a greater or less extent. (...) The faith in question was a belief in the free market, or 'price-mechanism' — that a competitive system free of all 'interferences', by government or by monopolistic combinations, of capital or of labour, would easily find an 'equilibrium'.
>
> (Hicks 1982: 3)[12]

Keynes's *General Theory* played, of course, a decisive role in making them depart from the old faith. However, despite this initial common faith and the common factor that contributed to its loss, Hicks has been very spare in his reference to Shackle's work, whereas Shackle has always emphasized the importance of Hicks's contributions to economics (see, e.g., Shackle 1967).

In fact we have to wait until *John* Hicks came to reconsider *J.R.* Hicks's IS–LM model in 1980-81 to find an explicit reference to Shackle's work and an acknowledgment of its relevance.[13] The reference to Shackle is only a short footnote but it is significant because of the relevance of the topic being examined: the interpretation of the concept of equilibrium in relation to Keynes's theory.

In his 1980–81 article Hicks was concerned with the conceptual difficulties raised by his 1937 IS–LM model with which he had by then become dissatisfied. In particular, he dealt with the time dimension of the IS–LM model and the compatibility of the *flow-equilibrium* in the commodity market and the *stock-equilibrium* in the money market.

The equilibrium method plays an important role in *The General Theory*; therefore, the IS–LM model which is based on the equilibrium method cannot be regarded as a totally misleading interpretation of Keynes. Such a model, in the same way as *The General Theory*, raises a number of difficulties especially connected with a coherent treatment of time and of stocks and flows. They are difficulties that are inherent to the equilibrium method itself, which is based on contemporaneous causality. The way out from all this is to abandon altogether the method. For Hicks,

> If one is to make sense of the IS–LM model, while paying proper attention to time, one must, I think, insist on two things: (1) that the period in question is a relatively long period, a 'year' rather than a 'week', and (2) that, because the behaviour of the economy over that 'year' is to be *determined* by propensities, and suchlike data, it must be assumed to be in an appropriate sense, *in equilibrium*.
>
> (Hicks 1980-81: 147–8)

To assume equilibrium in the product market (i.e. a flow-equilibrium) makes it possible to establish a Keynesian functional relationship between current output and current input.[14] Equilibrium in the product market (the IS side of the model) is a flow equilibrium which refers to a span of time, a period. In considering equilibrium, in the money market (the LM side) we are concerned with stock relations and equilibrium must be in a point of time rather than in a period. Thus, the IS–LM model must necessarily combine two different sort of equilibrium. A way to reconcile these two different kinds of equilibrium might imply converting the stock relation into a relation which holds over the whole period to which the flow equilibrium applies.

> If we adopt the equilibrium interpretation, on the IS side, the economy must be treated as *if* it were in equilibrium, over the period; that means, on the IS side, that the economy must remain in flow equilibrium, with demands and supplies for the flows of outputs remaining in balance. It would be logical to maintain that on the LM side the economy must be treated similarly. There must be a *maintenance* of stock equilibrium.
>
> (Hicks 1980–81: 151)

A stock equilibrium over the period implies the flow equilibrium over the period.[15] This is the concept of full equilibrium over time. This concept of equilibrium, however, is not acceptable in the Keynesian context; it is at odds with the very notion of liquidity preference — on which the LM schedule is based.[16]

Thus the notion of equilibrium seen above must be amended. Hick's amendment derives from his analysis in *Causality and Economics* (1979). In order to make liquidity compatible with equilibrium,

> We must evidently refrain from supposing that expectations as they were before April of what is to happen after April, were precise expectations, single-valued expectations; for in a model with single-valued expectations, there can be no question of liquidity. And we must also refrain from the conventional representation of uncertain expectations in terms of mean and variance, since that makes them different in kind from the experiences which are to replace them. There is, however, a third alternative. Suppose we make them expectations that the values that are expected ... will fall within a particular range. This leaves room for liquidity, since there are no certain expectations of what is going to happen, but it also makes it possible for there to be an equilibrium in the sense that what happens falls within the expected range. A state of equilibrium is a state in which there are no surprises.
>
> (Hicks 1979: 85; quoted in Hicks 1980–81)

This, for Hicks, is the only notion of equilibrium over time which is compatible with the concept of liquidity. It is in this respect that he acknowledges Shackle's contribution: 'I should here make an acknowledgment to G.L.S. Shackle, who in much of his work has been feeling in this direction' (Hicks 1980–81: 330n).

Before looking at Shackle's reply to Hicks, it is interesting to look at how Hicks proceeded in his analysis after having introduced his 'amended' notion of equilibrium over time. In *Causality in Economics*, after having introduced the notion of equilibrium depicted above, Hicks argues that if the equilibrium method is to be used within the Keynesian model, such a notion of equilibrium must be adopted but,

> Even so, it appears that the weakest part of the Keynesian model; the conventional Keynesian model, is after all the Liquidity Preference relation, which from other points of view, perhaps more important points of view, is its characteristic feature. Liquidity, it turns out, is not at home with Equilibrium; and is therefore not at home with Contemporaneous Causality.
>
> (Hicks 1979: 85–6)

Hicks finds a 'better place' for liquidity in the context of sequential causality in which effect follows cause. Sequential analysis is the analytical method followed by Swedish economists and is regarded by Hicks as the most promising way forward:

> the further development of theory, which I agree is required, should begin with an attempt to identify the questions it will have to be concerned with. These, I have tried to show, are in essence questions of sequential causality. We have so far no more than the beginning of a theory which will help us with such questions; but we do have a beginning.
>
> (Hicks 1979: 101–2)

In a short comment on 'Hicks's explanation', Shackle (1982) returns to his distinction between the two approaches to economics; he ascribes to Hicks great merits in the construction and development of equilibrium economics; and clearly puts himself in the other camp, where the 'theme of the unknowable or not yet originated future' is dominant. More specifically on Hicks's 1980-81 paper, Shackle argues that there Hicks has not yet fully acknowledged the incompatibility between Keynes's theory and equilibrium economics.[17]

As for the reference to his own work, Shackle, not surprisingly, discards Hicks's interpretation:

> I do not think his suggestion in footnote 12 that 'Shackle ... has been feeling in this direction' at all represents my course of thought. I am not sure what 'this direction' is; but the conception I described in Chapter 28 of *Decision, Order and Time* (1961) ... was not meant to underpin any notion of equilibrium. My proposal ... was part of an attempt to elucidate the nature of uncertain expectation. Perhaps my repudiation of the equilibrium frame of analysis can best be summarised by saying *all markets are in some degree speculative.*
>
> (Shackle 1982: 438)

In Shackle's view the truest interpretation of Keynes's thought is to be found in his 1937 article in the *Quarterly Journal of Economics*, Keynes (1937)[18] as *The General Theory* was still largely affected by Keynes's struggle to escape from old ideas. It is in the light of Keynes's position in this article that the equilibrium method of *The General Theory* must be interpreted.

It was Marshall's influence upon Keynes which led him to use the equilibrium method in *The General Theory*.[19]

> The *General Theory* was necessarily at odds with itself. For its author had been brought up to believe that in order to make sense of things we must have 'as many equations as there are variables', we must have a determinate 'equilibrium'. But equilibrium was the antithesis of the *General Theory*'s inward vision of business life. ... How could the two 'necessities' be reconciled? Only by the method of studying the abstract adjustment which the expectations and beliefs ... prevailing at some moment would lead to, given a breathing-space or moratorium to work out their logical inter-active consequences, and then of imagining, so far as possible, the cascade of real events which must flow from the inevitable upset of any such state of rest accidentally attained.
>
> (Shackle 1972: 435)

This is what Shackle called the 'kaleidic' method. Such a method provides us with a notion of equilibrium.

> It presents us with descriptions of equilibrium positions for the economic society as a whole, which differ from those of the value-construct in not being optima, but merely positions which do not contain within their structure an immediate source of movement. It shows how in the nature of things, and in their own nature, these 'equilibria' are vulnerable in the extreme to any expectation-changing news; for they rest upon expectations which naturally and necessarily conflict with each other (speculative prices can only stay at rest on conditions of conflict expectations) and are ready at a touch to break up and dissolve.
>
> (Shackle 1972: 437)

If this is the only acceptable notion of equilibrium ('kaleidic' equilibrium), what role is left for economic theory to play? Is, in particular, theory able to provide us with answers concerning the way in which relevant variables move and change when such fragile positions of rest are upset?[20] Such a view of the economy and the consequent vision of economics can

> offer diachronic insights of a very tentative, modest and short-range kind, not seeking to show what must happen, but what is the range of diversity of the immediate developments that various situations are capable of. ... The notion of kaleidic equilibrium is an explicit recognition of, and draws attention to, the overwhelming evident fact that *economic* affairs of society are not self-contained and independent. They may be compared to a sailing-boat in tempestuous and tide-swept waters. Certainly the boat itself has unity of structure, but what happens to it will be the outcome not only of its design (its capacities for response to impacts of various kinds, its *elasticities*) but of the policies, training and local knowledge of the crew and the behaviour of vast forces of the environment (...) We may be able to gain knowledge of how the economic boat will respond to this or that shift of the surrounding forces, we cannot hope to know what those shifts will be.
>
> (Shackle 1972: 438)

Both Hicks and Shackle see the difficulties that are inherent in the method which Keynes use in *The General Theory*, in particular the difficulty to reconcile the notion of liquidity preference and a tradition notion of equilibrium. However, they point to and develop alternative approaches. Hicks, once he became convinced that the IS-LM model represents an unsatisfactory representation of the essential spirit of Keynes's theory, moved towards the sequential approach which was first started and developed by Swedish economists. Shackle developed a vision of economic theory according to which it is impossible to capture the richness and unpredictability of actual economic systems by recourse to any rigid formal model. It is from this point of view that Shackle criticized also the sequential approach which Hicks regarded as the way out from the difficulties of the equilibrium method. As we have seen, in his critique of the sequential approach, Shackle remained closer to Keynes than Hicks was to Keynes.

6 CONCLUSION

In the appendix to *Time in Economics* (Shackle 1958: 92), Shackle set out the five qualities 'which an economic theory should possess in some degree'. They were:

1. logical rigour
2. realism
3. immediacy
4. inclusiveness
5. human reference.

These five qualities may be recognized in all strands of Post Keynesianism, though clearly different weights are given to them in each. Again, Post Keynesians differ very much in their attitudes to policy and with regard to what policies are morally and politically acceptable. Shackle himself became more and more passive concerning policy as he grew older. An essential clue as to why may be contained in the conclusion to this appendix. He wrote: 'In sum, we have our choice, *predicted man* is less than human, *predicting man* is more than human. I conclude, in an expression of mere personal conviction, that man in his true humanity can neither predict nor be predicted' (Shackle

1958: 105).

Keynes worried about whether it was possible both to do good and to be good. His own life suggests emphatically that it is. That George Shackle was a good man has been attested to over and over again. Provided, therefore, that proper note is taken of his caution and reservations, we believe that Post Keynesians should try to do good, and that in this endeavour, we would surely have the blessing of the person whose example, wisdom and insights have so profoundly affected us all.

NOTES

* Though originally written for this volume, this chapter was first published in G. C. Harcourt (1995) *Capitalism, Socialism: and Post-Keynesianism: Selected Essays of G. C. Harcourt* (Aldershot, Edward Elgar), and although it is a joint paper, the first versions of Sections 1, 2, 3, 4 and 6 were written by G. C. Harcourt and C. Sardoni wrote the first version of Section 5. We are indebted to Stephan Boehm, Jim Ford, Wendy Harcourt, Prue Kerr and Jochen Runde for helpful comments on a draft of this essay.

1 Jochen Runde for one confirms this in his fine chapter in this book.

2 Fernando Carvalho recently published a paper (Carvalho 1992) which spans Shackle's work, the work of two maverick mainstreamers, Bob Clower and Axel Leijonhufvud, and Post Keynesianism. He has linked Shackle's concept of potential surprise to Clower and Leijonhufvud's economy-wide concept of the 'corridor' in order to give precision to the latter. His main results are, first, that the disappointment of individual's expectations is related to the degree of convergence between the expectations of different individuals, and, secondly, that the width of the corridor may be defined in terms of this divergence.

3 See also Shackle (1972: 206–19).

4 As Shackle told G. C. Harcourt in their 1980 talk, 'investment is a highly hazardous business, a gambling question, for the businessman at the time of his decision does not know whether he will make profits or not, especially in future years. In these circumstances, businessmen are swayed by the current state of the news and can lose their nerve, keep their money in the bank and so unemployment starts - it's as simple as that' (Harcourt 1990: xxi).

5 We fervently agree with Jim Ford (1993: 689): 'I let Shackle's words speak for themselves, for I am unable to improve upon them.'

6 But, as general equilibrium analysis is intrinsically linked to and based upon the hypothesis of perfect competition, Shackle's critique of general

equilibrium seems to recall Schumpeter's denotation of perfect competition as a hypothesis which implies the exclusion of any strategy. Prices in the competitive framework are determined by 'the mass effect of the actions of all households and all firms in 'markets', the mechanism of which are relatively easy to describe as long as the households and firms have no choice but to adapt the quantities of commodities and services they wish to buy or to sell to the prices that rule. We may call this the Principle of Excluded Strategy' (Schumpeter 1954: 972). And Schumpeter concluded: 'But exclude "strategy" as much as you please, there still remains the fact that this adaptation will produce results that differ according to the range of knowledge, promptness of decision, and 'rationality' of actors, and also according to expectations they entertain about the future course of prices, not to mention the further fact that their action is subject to additional restrictions that proceed from the situations they have created for themselves by their past decisions' (Schumpeter 1954: 973).

7   Jochen Runde has pointed out to us that Shackle allows for degrees between zero and one in the 'epistemic interval'; in other words, there is a place in his system for *degrees* of belief. Davidson's dichotomy does not — which seems to sever the link between Davidson and Shackle.

8   Stephan Boehm, however, has pointed out to us that 'the evangelical wing of the modern Austrian School' is not the only one to reject the notion of economics as a predictive science. All non-instrumentalists, such as realists, hermeneuticists, proponents of rhetoric, and moderates like himself, reject such a notion.

9   Something that, as Jim Ford reminds us, 'assumes away the problem.'

10 It is ironical that the real business cycles theorists also make this argument, for I am sure they would be horrified to know that they had *anything* in common with the subversives above, if only they had ever heard of them.

11 This is *not* to say that he did not make important contributions to the theory of the firm and of investment, for example.

12 Shackle talked of this period in the following terms: 'Chance brought me to the London School of Economics at the moment when Hayek was reforming and reformulating Böhm-Bawerk's theory of capital; when Hicks was (in that very term) going to propound the production plan and the role played in it by the rate of interest; when Brinley Thomas (in that very term) was going to tell a minute class how the seeds sown by Wicksell were blossoming in the work of Lindhal and Myrdal; and when rumours about the book that Keynes was writing were drifting up from Cambridge. Thus by a blessing of chance I entered L.S.E. to begin my PhD dissertation at an electric moment of charged and tingling intellectual excitement' (Shackle 1983: 112–13).

13 An exception is a reference to Shackle's work in a footnote to *Capital and Growth* (1965), where J. R. Hicks, in dealing with the relationship between

the concept of temporary equilibrium and uncertainty, mentions Shackle's alternative approach to the treatment of uncertainty and expectations (Hicks 1965: 70n).

14 'For once we assume that production plans, during the period, are carried through consistently we have the relation between current input, during the period, and current output, during the period (which has been made equal to effective demand within the period) for which we have been looking' (Hicks 1980–81: 148).

15 By quoting from *Capital and Growth*, Hicks states: 'Equilibrium over time requires the maintenance of stock equilibrium; ... Thus when we regard a 'long' period as a sequence of 'short' periods, the 'long' period can only be in equilibrium over time if every 'short' period within it is in equilibrium over time. Expectations must be kept self-consistent; so that there can be no revision of expectations at the junction between one 'short' period and its successor, ... That can only be possible if expectations - with respect to demands that accrue within the 'long' period — are *right*. Equilibrium over time thus implies consistency between expectations and realisations within the period. It is only expectations of the further future that are arbitrary (exogenous) as they must be' (Hicks 1965, 92–3, as quoted in Hicks (1980–81: 151).

16 [T]here is no sense in liquidity, unless expectations are uncertain. But how is an uncertain expectation to be realised? When the moment arrives to which the expectation refers, what replaces it is fact, fact which is not uncertain' (Hicks 1980–81: 330).

17 'In this "explanation" Sir John still does not seem to me to acknowledge the essential point: the elemental core of Keynes' conception of economic society is uncertain expectation, and uncertain expectation is wholly incompatible and in conflict with the notion of equilibrium' (Shackle 1982: 438).

18 A point of view shared by several Post-Keynesians. See, for example, Minsky (1975, 55–68).

19 'Keynes gave a wide berth to both the achronic method of general equilibrium, and the pan-chronic method of supposing that all dates have an equal and co-valid reality, and are in a peculiar sense contemporaneous with each other, so that there are two kinds of time, one for the all-seeing analyst and one for the participant painfully crawling from one sudden contingency to another with no bird's-eye view' (Shackle 1972: 430).

20 'Can theory or measurement throw light on the character of the disintegrative movements which flow from the break up of a kaleidic equilibrium? Can such an equilibrium be described in such terms as will suggest the directions in which variables will move, and how fast and far their reactions will go?' (Shackle 1972: 437).

REFERENCES

Arestis, P. and Dow, S. C. (eds) (1992) *On Money, Method and Keynes. Selected Essays of Victoria Chick*, Basingstoke: Macmillan.

—— and Sawyer, M. (eds) (1992) *A Biographical Dictionary of Dissenting Economists*, Aldershot: Edward Elgar Publishing Limited.

Asimakopulos, A. (1988) *Investment, Employment and Income Distribution*, Cambridge: Polity Press.

Carvalho, F. J. (1992) 'Equilibrium and co-ordination with Shacklean expectations', *Revista Brasileira de Economia* 46: 319–37.

Chick, V. (1978) 'The nature of the Keynesian revolution: a reassessment', *Australian Economic Papers*, June, 1978, reprinted in Arestis and Dow (1992): 55–79.

—— (1987) 'Townshend, Hugh (1890–1974)', in Eatwell, Milgate and Newman, Vol. 4: 662.

Coddington, A. (1983) *Keynesian Economics: The Search for First Principles*, London: Allen & Unwin.

Davidson, P. (1990) *Money and Employment. The collected writings of Paul Davidson*, Volume 1 (edited by Louise Davidson), Basingstoke: Macmillan.

Dow, S. C. (1990) 'Beyond dualism', *Cambridge Journal of Economics* 14: 143–57.

Eatwell, J., Milgate, M. and Newman, P. (eds) (1987) *The New Palgrave. A Dictionary of Economics*, Basingstoke: Macmillan.

Ford, J. L. (1993) 'G. L. S. Shackle (1903–1992): A life with uncertainty', *Economic Journal* 103: 683–97.

—— and WenSheng Peng (1993) 'Shackle on expectation, investment, the business cycle and economic development', *Review of Political Economy* 5: 138–64.

Frowen, S. F. (ed.) (1990) *Unknowledge and Choice in Economics. Proceedings of a conference in honour of G.L.S. Shackle*, Basingstoke: Macmillan.

Hamouda, O. F. and Harcourt, G. C. (1988) 'Post Keynesianism: from criticism to coherence?', *Bulletin of Economic Research*, 40. Reprinted in Harcourt (1992: 209–32).

Harcourt, G. C., (1990) 'Introduction: notes on an economic querist — G. L. S. Shackle' in Frowen (1990: xviii–xxvi).

—— (1992) *On Political Economists and Modern Political Economy*, London: Routledge.

Hicks, J. R., (1965) *Capital and Growth*, Oxford: Clarendon Press.

—— (1979) *Causality in Economics*, Oxford: Basil Blackwell

—— (1980-81) 'IS-LM — An Explanation', in *Journal of Post Keynesian Economics* 3: 139–54.

Hicks, John (1982) *Collected Essays on Economic Theory, Volume II: Money, Interest and Wages*, Oxford: Basil Blackwell.

Kaldor, N. (1939) 'Speculation and economic stability', in *Review of Economic Studies* 7: 1–27

Keynes, J. M., (1937) 'The general theory of unemployment', in *Quarterly Journal of Economics* 51: 209–23, reprinted (1973) in his *Collected Writings*, Vol. XIV, London: Macmillan/Royal Economic Society: 109-23.

Kregel, J. A., (1990) 'Imagination, exchange and business enterprise in Smith and Shackle', in Frowen (1990: 81-95).

Minsky, H. P. (1975) *John Maynard Keynes*, New York: Columbia University Press.

Robinson, J. V. (1971) *Economic Heresies: Some Old-fashioned Questions in Economic Theory*, Basingstoke: Macmillan.

Schumpeter, J. A. (1954) *History of Economic Analysis*, New York: Oxford University Press.

Shackle, G. L. S. (1958) *Time in Economics*, Amsterdam: North-Holland.

— — (1967) *The Years of High Theory. Invention and Tradition in Economic Thought 1926-1939*, Cambridge: Cambridge University Press.

— — (1972) *Epistemics and Economics: A Critique of Economic Doctrines*, Cambridge: Cambridge University Press.

— — (1982) 'Sir John Hicks' "IS-LM: an explanation": a comment', in *Journal of Post Keynesian Economics* 4: 435-8.

— — (1983) 'A student's pilgrimage', in *Banca Nazionale del Lavoro Quarterly Review*, no. 145: 107-16.

— — (1992) 'George L. S. Shackle (born 1903)', in Arestis and Sawyer (1992: 505-10).

5

ON SOME CONCEPTS OF RATIONALITY IN ECONOMICS

Ian Steedman

1 INTRODUCTION

It is perhaps in the nature of fundamental concepts that they are somewhat illusive, multi-faceted and hard to pin down; almost by definition they are not readily amenable to simple definition. It is always likely, then, that they will at one and the same time be dismissed, with some irritation, as 'mere words' and yet will refuse to 'go away'. The concept of rationality exhibits just these characteristics, in social theory generally and, specifically, in economics. The purpose of the following incomplete notes (and they are no more than that) is to promote discussion of the place of 'rationality' within economic theory by bringing together, first, some of the uses of that concept in conventional choice theory; second, some familiar criticisms of that theory; third, some notes on 'rationality' within Austrian economics. It is to be noted that no attempt will be made to consider any concept of 'group rationality', nor to assess the idea of rationality of goals and purposes, for the following notes will still be (at least) long enough. — on 'rational goals' see, for example, Hollis (1977, 1979) together with Williams (1979) for a contrary position.; on 'expressive rationality' see Hargreaves Heap (1989: ch. 8). Nor will attention be paid to the specific claims of revealed preference theory: here I can only assert my view that Wong's critique thereof (1978) is essentially sound (albeit rather pretentious in parts). Within our restricted scope, however, we shall feel free at certain points to draw attention, albeit briefly, to the contributions of G. L. S. Shackle.

It will be suggested throughout that whatever criticisms may justly be made of particular, narrow interpretations of rationality in economic theory, the fundamental idea of *acting for reasons* — and

101

reasons which others can, in principle, understand — cannot be given up in any serious attempt to understand social phenomena. (Meeks 1991, has usefully emphasized the distinction between rationality as narrowly defined by many economists and rationality as being reasonable, as being sensible, in her discussion of Keynes's 'Chapter 12' argument).

2 CONSUMER CHOICE THEORY

Standard treatments of the now conventional consumer choice theory are shot through with references to rationality, rational behaviour, the rational consumer, and so on. Interestingly, however, the now conventional nature of the theory has not led to completely consistent usage of such terms and, indeed, has not overcome a certain embarrassment about their use. For example when, in introducing a discussion of consumption theory without transitive indifference, Chipman wrote 'There has been increasing recognition in recent years that the hypothesis of so-called "rational" behaviour (behaviour which can be represented in terms of a total binary preference ordering) is by no means coterminous with the hypothesis that consumers act so as to maximize a real-valued function. In fact, neither supposition implies the other' (1971: 224), he added the following note: 'The word "rational" is enclosed in quotation marks in order to avoid the appearance of approbation'. Walsh too, in commenting on his own 'Axioms of Rationality' (1970: 84), leaves one wondering 'Why then does he use the word Rationality?' (See also the editorial introduction to Hahn and Hollis 1979: 12). There frequently seem to coexist an eagerness to make 'rational' and its cognates a purely technical term and a reluctance to abandon those particular words!

It is not always easy to pin down even a single author on the precise meaning attached to rationality and related concepts. In part, this is no doubt simply because the concept is such a fundamental one. Perhaps because of this, one often finds that rational behaviour is said to involve this or to imply that, without any definition of rationality having been provided. The issue is then often further complicated by the move from references to rationality in the context of preference orderings to such references in the context of the maximization of utility functions. Thus one can find (at least) the following uses of the term Rational Choice..

(It should be noted that the different uses are clearly all members of a fairly close-knit family and it is not surprising that they are all to be found; for a taxonomy and discussion of a far wider family of perspectives on rationality, see Singer 1996.)

1   '[T]he idea of consistency (or rationality): the *same* ordering is used to make choices in all manner of different situations' (Layard and Walters 1978: 124). The authors then go on immediately to define an ordering in terms of completeness, comparability, reflexivity and transitivity, so probably they are saying the same as 2) below, albeit less clearly than they might. Be that as it may, we may note here that there does sometimes seem to be a temptation to relate rationality very strongly to consistency, where this latter is reduced to transitivity alone. Richter (1971: 30) rejects the reduction of 'rationality' to 'transitivity' as being 'egocentric' — a point I do not understand. Readily understandable, however, are the following statements by Sonnenschein (1971): 'We have been able to demonstrate that the properties of consumer behaviour that are necessary to prove the existence, optimality, and unbiasedness of competitive equilibrium depend only on the fact that consumers are maximizing. It follows that the transitivity axiom is both an unnecessary and limiting assumption in the theory of consumers' behaviour for competitive equilibrium' (pp. 220-1); 'The economics profession appears to be so well-indoctrinated with the concept of transitive preference that statements about behaviour arising from intransitive preferences are sometimes interpreted as making no sense. Indeed, such behaviour is referred to as "irrational". Suffice it to say that the rationality of consumer behaviour is not based on empirical observation' (p. 223).

2   Henderson and Quandt (1971: 8) describe as 'The postulate of rationality' the assumption that there is a complete, transitive preference ordering. In similar vein — but more cautiously! — Sen (1970: 2-3) refers to the transitivity, reflexivity and completeness of the relation 'at least as good as' as *conditions of* rationality.

3   By contrast, the terms rationality and rational behaviour are used by some authors to refer not to completeness, etc. of a preference ordering but rather to the consumer's actually selecting an element of the attainable set to which no other attainable element is preferred. (The 'negative' formulation is used in order to allow for

indifference between 'best' elements.) This usage can be found, for example, in Green (1971: 24); Shone (1975: 25); Walsh (1970: 84–6). It may be noted that Walsh describes the Axiom of Rationality (in the present sense) as 'perhaps the least controversial' of the axioms of choice theory and that this can be related to von Mises's *a priorism* mentioned below.

4 '[E]veryone more or less agrees that rational behaviour simply implies consistent maximization of a well-ordered function, such as a utility or profit function' (Becker 1962: 1). Many similar statements could be quoted but it will be clear from the above quotations from Chipman and from Sonnenschein that, by 1971 at the latest, by no means everyone agreed with Becker. Defining rationality in terms of the properties of an ordering is *not* equivalent to defining it in terms of maximising and many authors do the former.

Authors who use 'rationality' etc. in rather different ways from one another nevertheless often have one, very important, thing in common: they fail to make it explicit whether 'rational behaviour' is a conceptual construct used by the theorist to describe individual behaviour, or whether it is 'more' than that, providing a substantive account of how individuals act. (Economists usually refer to behaviour rather than to action but they are not, I think, thereby adopting a specific position with regard to the philosophers' behaviour/action distinction. Indeed, the whole drift of their discussion, with references to consistent pursuit of goals, rationality, etc., clearly implies that, in terms of that distinction, they refer to action and <u>not</u> to behaviour). When the matter is treated explicitly, the usual view is that rational behaviour is descriptive, rather than explanatory, and is a construct used by the theorist. (Compare the discussion of. von Mises below). Thus J. de V. Graaff writes 'It should be emphasized that [a utility function] *describes* choices, and it in no way seeks to *explain* them' (1967: 34), while Knight (1933: 236n.) insists that the means/ends framework is the form of thought about behaviour, not the form of behaviour itself. And Friedman and Savage, in their famous paper on choice and risk (1948), consistently refer to the aim of 'rationalizing' the (supposedly) observed behaviour of choice-makers faced by risk. The (perhaps) implied concept of rational choice as choice which is rationalizable — that is to say, choice of which a coherent account can be given by the theorist —

is made quite explicit and given great emphasis by Richter (1971) (in what seems to me — and to Sen (1992: 1, n.3) — to be one of the best discussions of conventional choice theory). He writes, '... if we start with observations of choices, it would be etymologically proper to call them rational if there were *some* preference ranking ("point of view") which rationalized them. This is the intuitive notion of rationality to be formalized and studied in this chapter' (p. 30). As Richter points out (p. 31, n.3) the precise resultant definition of rationality will depend on how one characterizes the preference rankings considered as candidates for rationalizing observed choices and, indeed, Richter goes on to generate weaker and stronger forms of rationalization by 'nice' preferences. (It is worth noting that rationalization by transitive preferences is Richter's <u>strongest</u> form of rationalization, which provides yet another reason for not linking rationality too closely to transitivity). For our purposes, however, the important point to be taken is the idea of rational as rationalizable.

3 CRITICISM OF RATIONAL CHOICE THEORY

Before turning, in my next section, to concepts of rationality in Austrian theory, I bring together in the present section some of the familiar criticisms of conventional rational choice theory, for these criticisms are not only of interest in their own right but also serve to show that there is really no unbridgeable gulf between Austrian economists and others. As will soon emerge, the 'consumer' will no longer be so exclusive a focus of attention as in the previous section but this is important for our purposes only in so far as the relevance of standard rational choice theory may be greater in some spheres of economic activity than in others. (I shall not discuss whether this is in fact so). Of greater significance is the point that, because the conventional economic model of rational behaviour is so well entrenched, criticism of that specific interpretation of rationality can easily appear (perhaps, on occasion, even in the mind of the critic) to be criticism of the relevance of rationality itself. Any such appearance must certainly be resisted; one can quite consistently raise all sorts of questions about that specific, conventional interpretation of rational action without in the least denying the importance of rational action theory as such.

Not surprisingly, the various 'different' kinds of criticism often made of conventional rational choice theory tend to link up with one another in various ways, with the result that any categorization of such criticisms will be somewhat arbitrary. No great significance should therefore be attributed to the way in which some of those criticisms are grouped below; indeed it is important to keep in mind their inter-relationships. It is also to be considered how far the thrust of the following criticism turns on their authors' having rejected the view that the purpose of rational choice theory is only to describe observed choices in a coherent way, in favour of the (perhaps implicit) view that it is designed to assist our understanding and/or explaining of such choices.

3.1 The nature of the choice set

In the theory of individual choice the choice set is usually held to consist of physical objects. (This is not the case, of course, for Lancaster's 'characteristics' approach, nor for his predecessors such as Menger and Wicksteed; nor, again, in social choice theory.) Yet it is clear that, since choice, decision and action are intrinsically future-directed, the choice set would more properly be presented as a set of expected experiences and other consequences, as Shackle was tireless in reminding us. This immediately leads to a number of questions about the conventional rational choice theory (several of which will spill over into sections 3.2 and 3.3 below).

First, the choice set — and the attainable choice set within it — immediately comes to be seen as subjective and peculiar to the choosing/deciding agent and there is no automatic presumption that the perceived choice set either is, or can be described as, the same for all agents. It does *not* follow, of course, that actors' perceived choice sets will have nothing in common with each other or with 'the way things really are'; indeed a major issue within social theory is precisely to show how (and how far) actors' perceptions do or do not 'come into line'. But it remains of great importance that action takes place within the *perceived* environment (compare Simon 1959/1966: 4).

Secondly, once the relevant choice set is seen in this way, it is open to question whether there exist any ends or purposes which are truly data for the agent (Knight 1963: 128–9, 172), which clearly leads to a further question about the interpretation of rational action in terms of 'reasoned and efficient movement towards *given* ends'. In similar vein, it may be queried whether the choice set, seen as a set of perceived possible consequences, is either bounded or closed (Knight 1933: 207; and Shackle in all his works!).

Thirdly, once the place of expectations in the perceived choice set is emphasized, the question inevitably arises whether those expectations can be 'rationally' grounded. Some would argue not — compare Shackle (1967: 124–33), who there attributes the same view to the Keynes of the *Quarterly Journal of Economics*, 1937 (plausibly enough) — while others would be less sceptical.. (However, Matthews (1991) has noted that in so far as agents are motivated by activity as such, for its own sake, expectations may be less important than economists often suppose)

Fourthly, the suggested characterization of the choice set leads easily to the type of criticism of conventional choice theory made by, for example, Schick (1976) and Sen (1977). They argue that 'rational' behaviour is all too often identified with 'selfish' behaviour (in other words, behaviour concerned solely with one's own consumption/leisure bundle) and point out that it is perfectly normal (and hardly 'irrational') to be influenced in one's choices by *commitments* to principles and to the welfare of others (Sen) and by *sociality* (Schick). This line of argument then leads naturally to the consideration of rationality as including consideration of, say, Kantian moral principles; of rationality as involving hierarchically ordered 'levels' of reasons of different reach. (See also Harsanyi (1955); Kolm (n.d.); Steedman (1989); Zamagni (1992). Collard (1991) considers the importance of knowledge for successful altruistic action.)

It should be clear, I hope, that neither Schick nor Sen is rejecting the concept of acting *for reasons* (that is to say, rationally) but is only rejecting the restriction of the relevant set of reasons to 'selfish' ones. We can most certainly understand choices, made by others, when they are motivated neither by purely selfish reasons nor by exactly the set of reasons which might motivate our own choices. Thus the scope for rationalizing and understanding choices is by no means restricted to 'rational choices' as characterized by conventional choice theory.

3.2 Knowledge, belief and learning

It is commonly observed, with good reason, that the agent in rational choice theory, for example, a consumer, is generally attributed the most amazing range and depth of knowledge, for example, about *all* commodities and their attributes, *all* possible occupations, and so on. This observation, linked to the distinction made in section 3.1 between actual and perceived environments, leads at once to the point that rational behaviour is (without exception?) based on very *partial* beliefs/knowledge. Indeed Knight, who seems to regard the absence of error as one defining condition of 'rational' behaviour (1963: 175), argues that, since economic action (like all other problem-solving activity) is necessarily concerned with the less than fully-known, 'perfect economic rationality ... is as a real concept self-contradictory' (Knight 1963: 128). Acting and deciding as we know it would not exist in the presence of perfect knowledge. In our world, the choosing agent will never know of all the truly available alternatives (together with all their relevant attributes and consequences) and will often not know how to compare all the known alternatives. (Indeed, absence of knowledge is sometimes *valued*, as in the desire for novelty and/or surprise (Knight 1933: 53).) This has led Simon, of course, to propose the concept of 'bounded rationality', rational action within severely circumscribed sets of alternatives, the limitations (informational, institutional, and so on) being taken as data by the agent (1957a; 1957b; 1959/1966; 1982).

Simon has also stressed that once attention is turned to rational humans — as opposed to models which represent them as perfectly informed, computationally unlimited machines — emphasis must be placed on *learning*. (Compare the reference in section 3.1 to the grounding of expectations). This leads at once to further interesting questions about rationality. Thus one can consider rational behaviour in the acquisition of information, not forgetting that a rational agent may have a 'want' not to bother with too fine a calculation (Knight 1933: 62n); that the value of information is often known only *after* it has been acquired; and that, consequently, talk of equating the marginal cost of information to its marginal value is probably empty formalism. More generally, one can consider the rationality of the agent's perceptions as well as that of his actions given his perceptions (Simon 1957b: 278). (Philip Pettit has suggested the term 'attitudinal rationality' to refer to the attempt to keep one's beliefs in line with the evidence.)

Of course, some writers take the view that adequate attention to the absence of relevant knowledge makes nonsense of economic rationality (at least as conventionally portrayed). Thus Shackle, for example, urges that perfect rationality (note the adjective) is possible only when the consequences of an action are fully known — which is *never*, since consequences lie in the future. The concept of perfect rationality thus has meaning, he argues, only in the strictly timeless world of simultaneous equilibrium (1967: 294–5). (For the relation of this to concepts of equilibrium, see Shackle (1967: 90–3) and below, on both Shackle and Hayek).

3.3 Preference orderings

It has already been noted, in sections 3.1 and 3.2, that it is not self-evident that the choice set defined over the agent's perceptions of possibilities will be either bounded or closed, or that the choice set defined over all the actual possibilities will be known to the agent. Here we need only refer briefly to the familiar and important doubts about the agent's ability to make comparisons between all alternatives and about the assumption of transitivity of preferences — because of thresholds, time lapses, multi-criteria decisions (May 1954), etc. (It must not be forgotten, of course, that Sonnenschein, for example, would be quite unconcerned about non-transitivity of preferences).

Less familiar (perhaps) will be Walsh's (1970: 120) criticism of standard choice theory that it fails to capture the *dispositional* nature of the verb 'to prefer', at least as that verb is used in English. Again, of course, this is not a criticism of the very concept of rational action but only of a specific (and limiting) interpretation of it; one can give a reasoned account both of an agent's doing something and of his not doing something which he has a disposition to do. (I take it that Walsh is here concerned with explanation and not simply with description.)

3.4 Uncertainty and interdependence

In a neoclassical decision problem the outcomes in which the agent is interested (a) depend only on his own choices, and (b) depend on his own choices in a known way ... [But] the two 'impurities' [of interdependence and uncertainty] are no mere trace elements, they are the stuff of economic decisions.

(Bacharach 1976: 3, 5)

The criticisms of standard rational choice theory implicit in this quotation are so important and far-reaching that they cannot possibly be adequately surveyed here — how could the burgeoning game theoretic literature, say, be covered in a few pages? — but neither can they be ignored. It must suffice simply to point towards them, on the assumption that the reader needs only to be reminded of the areas thus sign-posted. The central issue for our purposes is that the meaning to be attributed to rationality in the presence of uncertainty and (perhaps even more) of interdependence requires careful consideration. (Unless, of course, one simply so defines rational behaviour that it is impossible in such circumstances. But that is hardly helpful, since one still needs to consider what action is reasonable — capable of being grounded in reasons — and it would be odd to deny oneself the use of the term rational to describe reasoned action!)

Deliberately averting our gaze from the distinction between risk and uncertainty, we may note that Bacharach (1976: 23–4), for example, gets close to proposing adherence to the five axioms of von-Neumann/Morgenstern choice theory as a definition of rationality in risky choice — though he immediately points out that the axioms are not all uncontentious, particularly the postulate of substitutability of indifferent consequences in a lottery. Interestingly, this latter postulate, and the transitivity of preferences, together provide for Raiffa the 'two principles of consistent behaviour' (1970: 127). (It is to be noted that Raiffa's whole discussion of decision analysis is explicitly *normative* (1970: 127–8) as, of course, is much decision theory, game theory, statistical sampling theory, etc. Unfortunately there is not space here to pursue the significance of normative discussion of rationality).

When the consequences of an agent's decision and action will depend on the actions of another agent (or other agents) it is clear that it becomes incoherent to rationality on the part of *each* agent as involving the supposition that *others* react in a purely mechanical way, as in all 'conjectural variation' analyses of, for example, oligopoly (see, for example, Hurwicz 1945; Simon 1959/1966: 13; Bacharach 1976: 71). Thus Hurwicz notes that such considerations lead to 'the rejection of a narrowly interpreted maximization principle as synonymous with rational behaviour' and he proposes maximin behaviour as a definition of rational action. (Note that he does not suggest that it is *the* definition and as Bacharach (1976: 57), for example, points out, maximin behaviour can lead to 'regret'). It is, of course, open to debate how far game theory can be used to represent decision taking subject to interdependence — for example, it supposes, if anything, even more knowledge and ratiocinative capacity than does standard rational choice theory — but that debate cannot be entered here. Rather it is important to point to the way in which game theoretic considerations can explicate the rationality of cooperation/collusion between individual agents and bring out the role of inter-agent *communication* in rational action. This line of thought could, no doubt, bring one back again to the arguments of Schick and of Sen considered in the section. 3.1

Such thoughts might well remind one also of Shackle's insistence that choice, time and interdependence are intimately related. If choice and decision relate to the future, if the consequences of one's decisions depend, in part, upon the past, present and (to some extent) future decisions of other agents and if the current and future decisions of those other agents cannot at present be known to one then, clearly enough, one *never* has full relevant information when making a choice. Under what definition(s) of rationality, then, can economic (and 'other') choices be rational? It is not necessary to answer that question in order to see that 'rationality' is impossible according to any definition requiring that one's decision be fully informed. As Coddington (1975: 153) observed, in reviewing Shackle's *Epistemics and Economics*, 'To be "fully informed" about the consequences of one's own decision, one would have to know what everyone else is deciding *at the same time*'; he could have added 'and at all relevant future times', of course. He went on to note that 'equilibrium market prices' can only provide an interesting solution to this problem if equilibrium can both be reached and be recognized for what it is (p. 154).

It would need a substantial essay in itself to present Shackle's various statements on the matter; here just three may be quoted from *Epistemics and Economics*. 'Rationality cannot span a temporal succession of situations', Shackle writes (1972: 84) and 'Thus if economics is to be the pure logic of choice, the dismissal of time was necessary' because 'Time is what brings new knowledge ... Time is alien to reason' (1972: 151). In sum, 'in a non-timeless world, a world of earlier and later, there can be no pre-reconciliation of choice, therefore no fully rational choice, therefore no rigorous analysis of conduct as reasoned response to fully-known circumstances' (1972: 265).

In the same work Shackle also draws attention to the importance in any *contest* of unexpected actions: 'The most dramatic and spectacular secret of success is novelty, and novelty is that which an infallible algorithm must, by definition, exclude' (1972: 426). This observation is, presumably, of some significance for many 'rational' theories of competition, of bargaining and of games generally. It also prompts us to ask the following question: if it is rational in some sense for individual actors to seek to change conditions in a way unexpected by other actors — for example, to change the law, the property distribution, technical knowledge, more general beliefs — then what, if anything, can appropriately be regarded as given when one defines rational action along the lines suggested by the conventional choice theory of economics?

In brief, then, it has been argued by many (no doubt correctly) that the analysis of rational behaviour should take account of the actor's limited capacities for knowledge acquisition, imagination, attention and calculation; should face up to the subjective nature of the 'data' which are relevant to decision taking; should recognize that subjectivity is an expression of, and not in contradiction with, the social nature of individual choosing; and should give a central place to learning, expectations, uncertainty and inter-agent dependence and communication. It remains crucial, however, not to misinterpret any of these points as grounds for abandoning the concept of rationality. Human beings (at least) do act for *reasons*, reasons which, with effort, we can understand (independently of whether we approve of them). This is the root of the concept of rationality and it must not be confused with specific interpretations thereof, just because these latter have been influential amongst some economists for a few decades.

4 RATIONALITY IN AUSTRIAN ECONOMICS

It must be said at once that 'Austrian' economists differ from one another, both in matters of emphasis and (sometimes) in matters of substance, just as do the members of any other tendency of thought. This must be borne in mind throughout the following since, while it would be important for other purposes to make clear distinctions between the views of various Austrian writers, it will be appropriate to our purpose to glide over such distinctions and to emphasize the common features of Austrian economics in relation to rationality. It should also be noted that explicit reference will be made to the work of only four, albeit important, Austrian economists, namely von Mises, Hayek, Lachmann and Kirzner. It is hoped that neither of our simplifications will lead to any undue distortions.

By contrast with orthodox choice theory, writers in the Austrian tradition emphasize a broader and more active conception of human action; for them, allocating given means to given ends by no means exhausts the scope of human action. Indeed they often adopt the view that there is little or no genuine human choice either necessary or possible in the type of situation portrayed by orthodox choice theory; the necessarily unknown nature of the future is, for them, crucial to genuine human decision-making. Not surprisingly then, great stress is laid on expectations and, more generally, on the radically subjective nature of the 'data' relevant to choices. A great stress on the inherently rational nature of human action coexists, within the Austrian tradition, with an equal emphasis on the fact that the 'knowledge' on which actions are based is constantly changing, largely as a result of those very actions themselves. This, in turn, underpins a distinctive Austrian emphasis on the market *process* as a real process in time and on an active conception of competition and entrepreneurship. Equilibrium is regarded as a useful analytical device with respect to an individual's actions but Austrians tend to be dubious about the concept of a social equilibrium. (This is, however, an important issue over which different Austrian writers adopt significantly different stances).

In examining the above issues in somewhat more detail below, I shall not keep referring back to the related points presented above as 'conventional criticisms' of conventional choice theory but it is to be hoped that the reader will do so; there is not a chasm between Austrian and non-Austrian theory.

4.1 Human action, rationality and a priorism

Austrian writers, especially those closest to von Mises, lay great stress on the intrinsically purposive nature of human action and on the idea that action consciously aimed at a purpose must, necessarily, be rational from the standpoint of the purposes and beliefs of the actor at the time of the action. Indeed von Mises says bluntly that 'Human action is necessarily always rational. The term "rational action" is therefore pleonastic and must be rejected as such' (1949: 18). A few further quotations will help to show the thrust of this line of thought.

An action unsuited to the end falls short of expectation. It is contrary to purpose, but it is rational, i.e., the outcome of a reasonable — although faulty — deliberation and an attempt — although an ineffectual attempt — to attain a definite goal.

(Mises 1949: 20)

The doctors who a hundred years ago employed certain methods for the treatment of cancer which our contemporary doctors reject were — from the point of view of present-day pathology — badly instructed and therefore inefficient. But they did not act irrationally; they did their best.

(Mises 1949: 20)

Man, before setting out on his course of action, has to make a plan ... otherwise his action is not (rational) conduct but (non-rational) mere behaviour.

(Lachmann 1977: 68)

In the praxeological view, action is rational by definition; and this has been attacked from two directions. On the one hand, it has been branded as palpably false .... On the other hand, it has been interpreted as a vicious misuse of language, in which the word "rational" has been emptied of all meaning ....

(Kirzner 1976: 167)

As might be expected, Kirzner (1976: 167–72) goes on to argue that the rationality of action is indeed empirically non-falsifiable but that the concept of (pleonastically rational) action is of crucial importance in the understanding of social phenomena. Since the term 'a priorism' often has incendiary effect, it is worth noting here that Kirzner explicates it as referring simply to the possibility of our reasoning about the reasoned action of others, there being no implication whatever that one can dispense with empirical knowledge about the world in which that action takes place (1976,: 179–80).

(We noted above Shackle's view that time and interdependence make perfectly rational action impossible. It may thus be of interest to recall here that in a *relatively* early work, *Time in Economics* (1958), he appeared to approach the view that choice is always rational! Thus he argued that it makes no sense to compare the agent's feelings at the time of a decision with his feelings at any later time (1958: 18–19) and drew the conclusions that this 'destroys the distinction between rational and irrational conduct' and that there can never be adequate grounds for declaring that the wrong decision was made (p. 20).)

Austrian writers, it need hardly be said, do not describe goals and purposes as either rational or irrational and they simply take them to be what they are and not something to be explained within their analysis. It is important to note, however, that this does not commit them to the view that purposes are constant over time or that individuals are 'given atoms', outside history and society. Indeed Kirzner goes so far as to say that 'Unquestionably the most "interesting" [level of discussion] ... is the consideration of the ways in which men have acquired their particular interests ... the forces that determine people's value judgements and the emergence of their sense of absolute moral appraisement' (Kirzner 1976: 177). This does not alter the fact that Austrian writers always insist that their concern is with actions and their consequences (intended and unintended) and not with historical, social, psychological, etc. sources of those actions.

4.2 Subjectivity, expectations and knowledge

It was seen earlier that fully rational behaviour is sometimes taken to be impossible in the absence of complete knowledge but within the Austrian tradition the insistence that all action is (necessarily) rational is counterpointed by great emphasis on the acquisition of knowledge, on its necessary variability over time and on its differential dispersion amongst individuals. (The 'knowledge' which informs an action is, of course, always taken to be constituted by the subjectively held beliefs of the actor, whether those beliefs are well or ill-founded.) This leads Hayek, in particular, to draw a sharp distinction between the 'tautologies' on the one hand, which define the equilibrium plan of an individual, on the one hand and, on the other, empirical propositions about how the individual acquires knowledge. Thus:

> It is important to remember that the so-called 'data', from which we set out in this sort of [equilibrium] analysis, are (apart from his tastes) all facts given to the person in question, the things as they are known to (or believed by) him to exist, and not in any sense objective facts. It is only because of this that the

propositions we deduce are necessarily *a priori* valid ... the equilibrium relationship comprises only his actions during the period during which his anticipations prove correct..

(Hayek 1937: 36)

[T]he assumptions from which the Pure Logic of Choice starts are facts which we know to be common to all human thought. They may be regarded as axioms which define or delimit the field within which we are able to understand or mentally to reconstruct the processes of thought of other people. They are therefore universally applicable to the field in which we are interested — although of course where *in concreto* the limits of this field are is an empirical question. They refer to a type of human action (what we commonly call rational, or even merely conscious, as distinguished from instinctive action) rather than to the particular conditions under which this action is undertaken. But the assumptions or hypotheses, which we have to introduce when we want to explain the social processes, concern the relation of the thought of an individual to the outside world, the question to what extent and how his knowledge corresponds to the external facts. And the hypotheses must necessarily run in terms of assertions about causal connections, about how experience creates knowledge.

(Hayek 1937: 46; compare pp. 33, 53–4)

In this respect, then, the Austrians do not regard the conventional choice theory as wrong but as receiving an amount of attention out of all proportion to its relative importance. 'Unfortunately, the Pure Logic of Choice has filled the minds of economists to such an extent that the study of the actual means and ways by which men try to realize their aims has come to be sadly neglected' (Lachmann 1977: 70). 'Neoclassical' theory is sharply criticized for simply assuming that so much knowledge is immediately and equally available to all: 'By contrast, Austrian economics takes no form of knowledge for granted. The market appears to it as a continuous process, in the course of which the knowledge possessed by some participants becomes diffused to many, while new knowledge is acquired by some, and some earlier knowledge becomes obsolete' (*ibid*: 35). Furthermore, knowledge is not wholly exogenous with respect to the market but is 'at least partly, a product of the market process' (*ibid*). While such statements have, perhaps, the air of being rather radical with respect to, say, general equilibrium theory, they look decidedly less so with respect to Shackle's insistence on the importance of the speculative element in markets, an element which ensures, by its very meaning, that agents cannot all have 'knowledge' or, indeed, even have the same beliefs as one another. (See, for example, Shackle 1972: 93, 159, 235, 266, 412; 1979: 64.)

4.3 Time, process, entrepreneurship and equilibrium

While it is not possible here even to mention, let alone discuss, all aspects of the Austrian emphasis on the market process, attention must quickly be drawn to a few points which bear fairly directly on the picture of rational behaviour presented in conventional choice theory. For the Austrians, competition is a process (not a state) which necessarily unfolds in real time. Since the market process is, in part, an unending learning process, the presumption must always be that the subjective (and different) expectations of all the economic agents are *constantly changing*. Unchanging (and thus relevantly complete) knowledge is thus, for Hayek (1937), not a precondition for the existence of equilibrium in an economic system but rather its defining characteristic. Insofar as there exists a real tendency towards a system equilibrium — and the concept has no significance unless there is such a tendency — a major role in its creation is played by entrepreneurial action (Hayek 1937; see Kirzner 1973 for an extended discussion of these themes). (Some Austrians, such as von Mises and Lachmann, share Shackle's even more doubting attitude towards the meaningfulness of system 'equilibrium'. I understand that amongst American Austrians reference is sometimes made to 'Lachmannian nihilism'). It will be clear that this vision of an ever-moving, ever-changing process, whose movement results from the very actions of the rational agents whose conduct is being theorized, is not completely identical to the vision of the world which underlies standard rational choice theory.

4.4 Austrian criticism of orthodox choice theory

It may be useful to note explicitly a few Austrian criticisms of conventional choice theory (a number have, of course, already been implied above). First, it is considered that no 'real choice' is faced by an omniscient agent with a complete, etc. preference ordering — there is no genuine *decision* to be made and an identically informed machine could pick out the preferred set(s) just as well as the rational actor. Genuine choices and decisions arise precisely because there are no omniscient agents with 'nice' preference orderings. (Compare Shackle's insistence that genuine decision involves a 'cut' relative to the past.) Second — and this is an extension of the previous point — the means/ends picture of choice, as portrayed by, for example, Robbins, is too narrow in its focus properly to capture all the major aspects of (economic) action. Allocating is but one (albeit important) aspect of acting and *homo agens* rather than *homo oeconomicus* should be placed at centre-stage (Kirzner 1976: 148, 161–2, 184).

Third, von Mises in particular has argued vigorously against making transitivity (consistency) of preference part of the meaning of rationality. Since an individual's actions occur in temporal succession, he argues, no conceivable observed sequence of actions can ever be used as a basis for imputing irrationality to that individual: if we successively observe that a person prefers x to y, y to z and z to x, then those three observations refer to three distinct instants in time, however close they may be, and the only valid inference is that preferences have changed over time (Mises 1949: 103). 'Constancy and rationality are two entirely different notions' (*ibid*).

Fourth, and more generally, von Mises is strongly opposed to any idea of a preference ordering as something existing independently of, and explaining, real actions — 'the scale of value is nothing but a constructed tool of thought' (1949: 102). This, of course, is not an objection to those theorists who see a preference ordering simply as 'our' description of an actor's choices.

4.5 The object and scope of Austrian theory

As was mentioned above, Austrian theorists are not concerned to explain (rational) action but rather to understand social phenomena as the (intended and, even more, unintended) consequences of such action (Hayek 1942: 288). The emphasis is generally placed quite strongly on understanding phenomena rather than on predicting them. Thus Hayek writes: 'We "understand" the way in which the result we observe can be produced, although we may never be in a position to watch the whole process or to predict its precise course and result' (*ibid*: 289) and: 'The distinction between an explanation merely of the principle on which a phenomenon is produced and an explanation which enables us to predict the precise result is of great importance for the understanding of the theoretical methods of the social sciences' (*ibid*: 290–1). While Lachmann states flatly that 'Economists should, in our view, openly admit that they are unable to make positive predictions about the world ... But [they can] give an intelligible account of the world with which they are dealing' (1977, p.89). This stress on 'understanding' and 'intelligibility' is, of course, intimately related to that on the necessarily rational nature of human action; it is because action is rational that 'we' can understand another's action, quite independently of whether or not we share his beliefs and purposes (compare Kirzner 1976: 150, 173, 181). Shackle (1972: 346) too, it may be recalled, argued that explanation is easier than prediction, in part because it can draw on recognized stereotypes.

> All this does not prevent the praxeologist from maintaining a becoming modesty with regard to his own contribution. He does not in any way believe that his theorems can exhaust all that can be known about social phenomena.
>
> (Kirzner 1976: 181)

> The most popular objection raised against economics is that it neglects the irrationality of life and reality ... No censure could be more absurd. Like every branch of knowledge economics goes as far as it can be carried by rational methods. Then it stops
> ....
>
> (Mises, 1949: 21)

5 RECAPITULATION

In drawing this chapter to a close it is useful to begin with some passages from the Austrian/American phenomenologist Alfred Schütz, whose view of choice has recently been compared and contrasted by Koppl (1992, 1994) and Augier (1998) with that of Shackle:

We shall never understand why the mercury in the thermometer rises if the sun shines on it. We can only interpret this phenomenon as compatible with the laws we have deduced from some basic assumption about the physical world. Social phenomena, on the contrary, we want to understand and we cannot understand them otherwise than within the scheme of human motives, human means and ends, human planning — in short — within the categories of human action.

(Schütz 1943:146)

[O]nly action within the framework of rational categories can be scientifically discussed. Science does not have at its disposal other methods than rational ones and it cannot, therefore, verify or falsify purely occasional propositions.

(Schütz 1943: 148)

As has been implied at various points above, economists should try (it will be hard work) to bring into their basic rational choice theory many of the considerations which can at present properly be presented as criticisms of what is now the conventional analysis. The subjective nature of the choice set; the processes of learning and of the formation of perceptions and of expectations; the social nature of many beliefs and desires and of many constraints on individual decision-making; the active, problem-solving (and not just passively allocating) nature of decisions and actions in an uncertain, changing and interdependent world (in other words, the actual world): all these and other central aspects of genuine human choosing and deciding demand to be taken seriously and to be brought within the (future) conventional theory, not to be left on the fringes as persistent, gnawing criticisms. At the same time, economists should be clear that carrying out this (difficult) programme of work would not in any way be tantamount to abandoning the concept of rationality. Rather it would involve taking *more* seriously the proposition that people act for reasons, since the task would be precisely to consider more closely the range and type of reasons for which people are able to and do decide to act. (See, for example, Hargreaves Heap (1989: *passim*) and Sen (1992: 6–7).)

As Pettit (1978) has argued at some length, 'rational man theory' is inherently 'soft-edged'; because beliefs and desires can change, such theory is not primarily predictive, even though it does often possess some limited predictive power. Its use is rather that of providing a coherent framework within which we can understand the (economic and other) actions of other agents. The suggested development of the economists' rational choice theory will thus seem frightening only to those who both exaggerate the predictive, as opposed to interpretative, capacities of present micro-economics and simply assume that those capacities would be weakened by that development.

REFERENCES

Augier, M. (1998) Typicality and novelty: Schütz and Shackle on the paradox of choice', paper presented at a session on 'Alfred Schütz and the Economists' at the 1998 Eastern Economic Association meeting in New York.

Bacharach, M. (1976) *Economics and Theory of Games*, London: Macmillan.

Becker, G. S. (1962) 'Irrational behavior and economic theory', *Journal of Political Economy* 70: 1–13.

Chipman, J. S. (1971) 'Consumption theory without transitive indifference', in Chipman, J. S., Hurwicz, L., Richter, M. K. and Sonnenschein, H.F. (eds) *Preferences, Utility, and Demand*, New York: Harcourt Brace.

Coddington, A. (1975) 'Creaking semaphore and beyond: a consideration of Shackle's *Epistemics and Economics*', *British Journal for the Philosophy of Science* 26: 151–63.

Collard, D. (1991) 'Love is not enough,' in Meeks, J.G.T. (ed.) *Thoughtful Economic Man*, Cambridge: Cambridge University Press.

Friedman, M. and Savage, L. J. (1948) 'The utility analysis of choices involving risk', *Journal of Political Economy* 56: 279–304.

Graaff. J. de V. (1967) *Theoretical Welfare Economics*, Cambridge: Cambridge University Press.

Green, H. A .J. (1971) *Consumer Theory*, Harmondsworth: Penguin.

Hahn, F. H. and Hollis, M. (eds) (1979) *Philosophy and Economic Theory*, Oxford: Oxford University Press.

Hargreaves Heap, S. (1989) *Rationality in Economics*, Oxford, Blackwell.

Harsanyi, J. (1955) 'Cardinal welfare, individualistic ethics, and interpersonal comparisons of utility', *Journal of Political Economy* 63: 309–21.

Hayek, F.A. (1937) 'Economics and knowledge', *Economica* 4: 33–54.

—— (1942) 'Scientism and the study of society, part I', *Economica* 9: 267–91.

Henderson, J. M. and Quandt, R. E. (1971) *Micro-Economic Theory* (2nd edn), New York: McGraw-Hill.

Hollis, M. (1977) *Models of Man,*. Cambridge: Cambridge University Press.

—— (1979) 'Rational man and social science', in R. Harrison (ed.) *Rational*

Action, Cambridge: Cambridge University Press.

Hurwicz, L. (1945) The theory of economic behavior, *American Economic Review* 35: 909-25.

Kirzner, I. M. (1973) *Competition and Entrepreneurship*, Chicago, IL: University of Chicago Press.

— — (1976) *The Economic Point of View.*, Kansas City: Sheed and Ward.

Knight, F. H. (1933) *Risk, Uncertainty and Profit*, L.S.E. reprint, London: London School of Economics.

— — (1963) On the History and Method of Economics. Chicago, University of Chicago Press.

Koppl, R. (1992) 'Alfred Schütz and George Shackle: two views of choice', unpublished manuscript.

— — (1994) 'Lachman on Schütz and Shackle', *Advances in Austrian Economics* 1: 289–302.

Kolm, S.-C. (n.d.) 'Psychanalyse et Theorie des Choix', Paris: CEPREMAP.

Lachmann, L. M. (1977) *Capital, Expectations, and the Market Process*, Kansas City,: Sheed Andrews and McMeel.

Layard, P. R. G. and Walters, A. A. (1978) *Micro-Economic Theory*, New York: McGraw-Hill.

Matthews, R. C. O. (1991) 'Animal spirits', in Meeks, J. G. T. (ed.) *Thoughtful Economic Man*, Cambridge: Cambridge University Press.

May, K. (1954) 'Transitivity, utility and aggregation in preference theory,', *Econometrica* 22: 1–13.

Meeks, J. G. T. (1991) 'Keynes on the rationality of decision procedures under uncertainty: the investment decision', in Meeks, J. G. T.. (ed.) *Thoughtful Economic Man*, Cambridge: Cambridge University Press.

Mises, L. (1949) *Human Action*, New Haven: Yale University Press.

Pettit, F. (1978) 'Rational man theory', in Hookway, C. and Pettit , F. (eds.) *Action and Interpretation*, Cambridge: Cambridge University Press.

Raiffa, H. (1970) *Decision Analysis*, Reading, MA: Addison-Wesley.

Richter, M. K. (1971) 'Rational Choice', in Chipman, J., Hurwicz, L. Richter, M.K. and Sonnenschein, H.F. (eds) *Preferences, Utility, and Demand*, New York: Harcourt Brace.

Schick, F. (1976) 'Rationality and sociality,' mimeo, Rutgers University, P.S.A.

Schütz, A. (1943) 'The problem of rationality in the social world', *Economica* 10: 130–49.

Sen, A. K. (1970) *Collective Choice and Social Welfare*, Edinburgh: Oliver and Boyd.

— — (1977) 'Rational fools: a critique of the behavioural foundations of economic theory', *Philosophy and Public Affairs* 6: 317–44.

— — (1992) 'Internal consistency and social choice', mimeo.

Singer, A. E. (1996) *Strategy as Rationality*, Aldershot: Avebury.

Shackle, G. L. S. (1958) *Time in Economics*, Amsterdam: North-Holland.

— — (1967) *The Years of High Theory*, Cambridge: Cambridge University Press.

—— (1972). *Epistemics and Economics: A Critique of Economic Doctrines*, Cambridge: Cambridge University Press.

—— (1979) *Imagination and the Nature of Choice*, Edinburgh: Edinburgh University Press.

Shone, R. (1975) *Microeconomics: A Modern Treatment*, London: Macmillan.

Simon, H. A. (1957a) *Administrative Behaviour*, New York: Free Press.

—— (1957b) Models of Man. Social and Rational. New York, Wiley.

—— (1959) 'Theories of decision-making in economics and behavioral science', *American Economic Review* 49. 253–83, reprinted (1966) in the American Economic Association and Royal Economic Society *Surveys of Economic Theory*, Vol. III, London: Macmillan (page references to reprint).

—— (1982) *Models of Bounded Rationality*, Cambridge, MA: MIT Press.

Sonnenschein, H. F. (1971) 'On the lower semi-continuity of utility functions derived from demand data', in Chipman, J. S., Hurwicz, L., Richter, M. K. and Sonnenschein, H. F. (eds) *Preferences, Utility, and Demand*, New York: Harcourt Brace.

Steedman, I. (1989) 'Rationality, economic man and altruism in P. H. Wicksteed's *Common Sense of Political Economy*', in Steedman, I. *From Exploitation to Altruism*, Cambridge: Polity Press.

Walsh, V. C. (1970) *Introduction to Contemporary Microeconomics*, New York: McGraw-Hill.

Williams, B. (1979) 'Internal and external reasons', in Harrison, R. (ed.) *Rational Action*, Cambridge: Cambridge University Press.

Wong, S. (1978) *The Foundations of Paul Samuelson's Revealed Preference Theory*, London: Routledge and Kegan Paul.

Zamagni, S. (1992) 'Extended rationality, altruism and the justification of moral rules'. Johns Hopkins Bologna Centre, Occasional Paper, No. 72.

6

SHACKLE AND THE PROJECT OF THE ENLIGHTENMENT: REASON, TIME AND IMAGINATION

*Stephen D. Parsons**

1 INTRODUCTION

Despite exhibiting a powerful and evocative prose, the writings of G. L. S. Shackle have generally not been well received within the economics profession. This may well reflect a perception that Shackle's writings are animated by different concerns than those deemed relevant by most economists. Unfortunately it is probably also indicative of the increasingly insular nature of contemporary economic pedagogy, where economists scribble away in blissful ignorance of the metaphysical underpinnings of their own theories.

These two problems of perceived different agendas and institutionalized myopia are not unrelated, as there is a dual aspect to the relationship between Shackle and mainstream economics. On the one hand Shackle does invoke a different set of philosophical discourses from those underpinning mainstream economics, occasionally pushing divergences to an extreme. On the other hand, Shackle also shares, to a large extent, a common philosophical heritage with mainstream economics. Unfortunately, defenders of the mainstream position are, in the main, unaware of this shared heritage.

For example, take Coddington's remark that, if ideas such as those advanced by Shackle are taken seriously, then:

> We would then be faced with a situation akin to one in which there was an outbreak of Christian Science among the medical profession, or a passion for telekinesis among airline pilots.
>
> (Coddington 1983: 61–2)

Coddington is here indicating a suspicion that, if Shackle's emphasis on uncertainty is embraced, it must be concluded that economic problems are not amenable to rational solution.[1] Given this suspected 'irrationality' of Shacklean economics, it is instructive to situate Shackle's writings within the various strands of discourse comprising the project of the Enlightenment, understood in terms of the belief that 'it is not tradition, but reason that constitutes the ultimate source of authority' (Gadamer 1979: 241). Through exploring Shackle's relationship to the Enlightenment project, it is possible to recognize that the charge of 'irrationality' is not founded. This also permits an appreciation of where Shackle does follow the philosophical agenda pursued by the majority of economists, and where he departs from it. A suitable place to start the inquiry is with Cartesian philosophy.

2 DESCARTES, SHACKLE AND ECONOMICS

Three main elements can be taken as comprising the Cartesian vision (Flew 1986):

1   Knowledge is only possible where it is inconceivable that there might be error, and reason for belief in any knowledge claim is entitled only where this entails the truth of the proposition asserted as known;

2   We are immediately and non-inferentially aware only of successive moments of our logically private consciousness;

3   As we are confined to immediate knowledge of our own private consciousness, and statements concerning such do not have the logical strength to entail conclusions about a mind-independent public world, then the status of this world, including our possession of a body, is problematic.

The first element means that, for Descartes, all arguments are either deductive or defective, and mathematics is identified as the system of knowledge par excellence. Most economists define themselves in terms of (1), working within the confines of an axiomatic deductive system where reason is taken as more reliable than experience (Clarke 1982). However, the acceptance of (1) does not merely indicate that logical coherence, rather than experiential evidence, serves as the criterion of

125

truth: rather, the axiomatic system defines in advance the nature of the object of knowledge:

> Descartes's admiration for and appropriation of mathematics must be understood first and foremost in the abstract sense — as a new set of rational relations whose axiomatic character creates the logical context which 'defines' the object to which it is applied. From this perspective, the object has no room to intervene experientially and challenge its axiomatic definition.
>
> (Judovitz 1988)

Consequently, it is only objects that can be defined within the axiomatic structure that are deemed suitable for study. With this, the status of the axiomatic structure is itself inevitably problematic: as it is regarded as a means to elucidate the nature of economic reality, it is always other than this reality, and hence the inter-relationship between the axiomatic structure and the reality being investigated is intrinsically indeterminate.

Element (1) raises certain problems for Shackle. Although clearly recognizing the restrictive nature of axiomatic reasoning, he is also aware that, unless his insights can be formulated thus, most economists will not take them seriously. Economics is regarded as either an art form, and therefore dismissed by the majority of economists, or as an axiomatic system, where the nature of the object of investigation is defined in advance.

On the whole, Shackle tends to reject element (1), and does this through employing element (2). Hence Shackle defers to the Cartesian emphasis on 'cogito', or I think, and speaks of the (mental) 'impressions' created by external objects (see especially Shackle 1979). Initially, this may appear puzzling, as it seems to indicate merely a move *within* the Cartesian system. However, employing (2) over (1) gives Shackle the required space from mainstream economic reasoning, for two reasons. Firstly, element (2) is not restricted to the Cartesian system, but remains prominent throughout the majority of Enlightenment philosophy. This allows Shackle to incorporate insights from different strands of Enlightenment thought, as explored below. Secondly, the dominance of (1) in mainstream thought is such that any reference to consciousness is deemed to be no longer required. Thus Lucas and Sargent (1981) adopt a behavioural perspective on economic agents, whereby any reference to consciousness is regarded as unnecessary, and individuals can thus be defined within the axiomatic structure.[2] Consequently, one of the disagreements between Shackle and the majority of economic theorists concerns the relative importance of emphasizing either (1) or (2).[3]

However, both Shackle and the majority of economists accept (3) — or, rather, their respective starting positions entail the acceptance of (3). Consequently, neither Shackle nor mainstream economists develop a substantive theory of the self. In mainstream economics, as the axiomatic structure defines the object of knowledge in advance, the 'economic subject' can only appear in a mathematically tractable form — as essentially a 'bundle' of tastes or preferences. With Shackle, although the intention is to offer an account of lived experience, the 'economic subject' also remains undeveloped. This is because the emphasis on the 'cogito' leads, as Husserl recognized, to the absurd position where an ordinary being ('the subject') is the ground of the possibility of all other ordinary beings (Husserl 1960). As the subject constitutes the ground of knowledge, it can only appear as a purely formal notion, not as an anthropological entity with material, social and historical substance. I shall argue later that the adoption of (3) as a consequence of adopting (2) raises problems for Shackle's economics.

However, the Cartesian emphasis on the 'cogito' by no means exhausts Shackle's philosophical heritage. In order to situate this more adequately, it is necessary to appreciate two counter-veiling strands to Cartesian philosophy arising within the Enlightenment. These are:

4   A radical conception of freedom, cogently articulated by Kant;

5   A romantic strain, where, according to Taylor (1979: 1–2), 'human life was seen as having a unity rather analogous to that of a work of art, where every part or aspect only found its meaning in relation to all the others'.

Both of these tendencies can be seen as a reaction to the Cartesian vision, exemplified in Hobbes, according to which individuals are analogous to objects, and can thus be scientifically studied. The Kantian insistence on freedom emphasized that the individual is essentially a moral being, possessing a will, whose actions are intrinsically free, hence not the result of causal effects, whether emanating from nature or from within (e.g. desires or inclinations). Similarly, the romantic strain rejected a mechanical view of the individual, emphasizing the aesthetic over the mechanical, art over science. Hence, for Schiller 'the 'political problem' of a better organization of society 'must take the path through the aesthetic realm, because it is only through beauty that one arrives at freedom' (Marcuse 1968: 117). The intention here was to revitalize the cultural conditions of Ancient Greece, which Enlightenment thought had neglected, in order to overcome the fragmentation of the individual identified as arising through the division of labour (Kain 1981).[4]

Unlike the majority of economists, Shackle accepts the force of (4) — the emphasis on radical freedom. However, despite some suggestive remarks, Shackle does not take on (5) — the expressive element. This is automatically ruled out by the vision of the subject entailed by the Cartesian starting point.

3 REASON, FREEDOM AND IMAGINATION

In one of his more iconoclastic statements, Shackle admits that:

> If there is a fundamental conflict between the appeal to rationality and the consideration of the consequences of time as it imprisons us in actuality, the theoretician is confronted with a stark choice. He can reject rationality or time.
>
> (Shackle 1972: xviii)

Given Shackle's emphasis on the importance of time, it is not difficult to discern the choice he thinks ought to be made: rationality must be rejected. It is no doubt this apparent rejection of rationality that leads Coddington, as noted earlier, to equate any adoption of Shackle's economics with 'an outbreak of Christian Science amongst the medical profession'. However, Shackle's statement that the theoretician is forced to choose between reason and time, with the implicit inference that reason must be abandoned, can be set against the following: 'A theory which denied men reason would be an abdication from our claims of humanity' (Shackle 1972: 446)

Shackle is either flatly contradicting himself or attempting to develop a particular perspective on reason. Essentially, Shackle is objecting to two related characteristics of reason that predominate in current economic theorizing: (ii) the defining of reason in relationship to the technical, rather than the practical; (ii) the dogmatic employment of reason. The objection to the first characteristic is evident in the following:

> The thought-practice of those who conduct our affairs, unknowledge is treated as alien, intolerable, unbelievable. There must... be a method and means of foreknowledge. Military aggressions on a vast scale, unthinkably evil in aim and method, have been based on the supposition that calculation can tell men what action will produce what effect... The procedure of calculation... is some form of calculus of probability.
>
> (Shackle 1979: 57–8)

Shackle is specifically objecting to the understanding of reason in terms of calculation, or technical expertise *(techne)*, as illustrated in Hobbes's (1968: 111) claim that 'Reason... is nothing but Reckoning'. Hobbes exemplifies the transformation of the classical Greek understanding of politics as an arena of the practical *(praxis)* governed by judgment *(phronesis)* into politics understood as the realm of the technical *(techne)*.

This introduces the second characteristic of reason in contemporary economics — its dogmatic employment. As economic theorizing embodies reason understood as *techne*, then the scope of reason so understood must be reduced in order to incorporate practical concerns. Shackle does so much redefine reason as restrict its scope in order develop his insights into practical action. This is achieved through drawing attention to the significance of imagination:

> Imagination and Reason are the two faculties that make us human. But whereas Reason has its laws that are the same for all men, Imagination is brought under constraint only when men turn to practical affairs, in which it is only useful to imagine what is deemed to be possible. Reason is sure, safe, even in a sense simple. The economic analyst has opted for Reason. His guide is a single principle. He assumes that men pursue their interest by applying reason to their circumstances. And he does not ask how they know what these circumstances are. It is the effort and consequences of asking this last question, and of going on to inquire what we substitute for knowledge in that vast and limitless area where we are eternally denied it, 'tomorrow', that

is my object of study in this book.

(Shackle 1972: xiv)

Shackle's interest in imagination in contrast to reason as calculation is explicitly linked to the concern with practical, not technical, affairs. The attempt to limit reason can thus be seen as an attempt to resurrect the enlightenment ideal of 'specialized culture for the enrichment of everyday life' (Habermas 1983) through explicitly focusing on questions of human practice in economic affairs. This is in direct contrast to mainstream economics which, through concentrating on formalization, shears 'economic knowledge' away from the self-understanding of ordinary citizens.[5]

Coddington's jibe illustrates the very different conceptions of economics that he and Shackle are appealing to. For Coddington, economics is essentially technocratic, with economists formulating predictions according to economic models divorced from the self-understanding of individuals. In contrast, for Shackle, economics is practical, necessarily tied to individual perspectives and self-understanding. Consequently, Shackle's economics is concerned with the judgments facing the individual decision-maker in unique situations: 'What is the best action? is wholly dependent on the unique historical situation' (Shackle 1972: 86). With this inherently practical orientation, economics can no longer be conceived as a science, akin to the natural sciences. Such a position is anathema to most economists, who assume that economics is 'scientific', without inquiring as to either the possibility or the desirability of this state of affairs. In contrast, attending to the 'unique historical occasion' indicates that economics is a branch of 'historiography':

> The business of choice, I am maintaining, is the business of imagination. The business of historiography, therefore, is the effort to penetrate one man's imagination by another's. Evidently, such art of historiography will be precarious and unsure, it will be 'poetry'. The Greeks believed it was the poet who could get nearest the truth.
>
> (Shackle 1979: 60)

However, despite a variety of pregnant suggestions throughout his writings, it is ultimately through appealing to freedom, not art, that

Shackle grounds his critique of mainstream economic theorizing. The incorporation of reason as *techne* in economic reasoning indicates the inherent objectification of mainstream thought. Individuals are identified as analogous to objects and consequently the appeal to reason precludes any consideration of real choice: 'We have to assume that reason dictates at each moment to each individual interest (each person or firm) only one course of action' (Shackle 1988: 141).

Through appealing to 'reason', the economist can predict how any one individual will, in acting 'rationally', behave in a given situation:

> The theoretician has only to apply his own reasoning powers to a general, universally applicable description of men's basic predicament in order to know not only the essential character of a correct policy for the individual in each of his various business capacities but also what, in fact, the individual will do.
>
> (Shackle 1988: 136)

Reason as *techne* provides economists, as technicians, with the means to formulate predictions concerning behaviour within specific 'policy options'. As Habermas remarks:

> The engineers of the correct order can disregard the categories of ethical social intercourse and confine themselves to the construction of conditions under which human beings, just like objects within nature, will necessarily behave in a calculable manner. This separation of politics from morality replaces instruction in leading a good and just life with making possible a life of well-being within a correctly instituted order.
>
> (Habermas 1974: 43)

It is also through appealing to the 'disregard for the categories of ethical life' that Shackle mounts his challenge. Reason as *techne* omits the one concept that must, as Kant argued, be presupposed in order that ethical concerns can be raised in the first place — the concept of freedom. For Shackle:

> Rationalism, the belief that conduct can be understood as part of the determinate order and process of Nature... is a paradox. For it claims to confer upon men freedom to choose, yet to be able

to predict what they will choose.

(Shackle 1972: 239)

The identification of reason with technique prohibits any exploration of the question of freedom: as reason dictates only one outcome from any given set of circumstances, freedom is illusory. In emphasizing the relevance of freedom through restricting the claims of reason, Shackle is directly following the precedent set by Kant, for whom:

> The dogmatism of metaphysics, that is, the preconception that it is possible to make headway in metaphysics without a criticism of pure reason, is the source of all that unbelief, always very dogmatic, which wars against morality.
>
> (Kant 1787: B xxx)

If the project of the Enlightenment is conceived, following Kant, in terms of 'man's emergence from self-incurred immaturity' (Kant 1971), the freedom must be recognized as crucial. The faith in reason embodied in the cry 'have courage to use your own understanding!' itself presupposes freedom. For enlightenment of this kind, all that is needed is freedom (Kant 1971: 54). The dogmatic employment of reason endemic in economic theorizing does not allow space for the consideration of freedom, and thus practical concerns are cut off at source.[6] For Shackle, as for Kant, emphasizing the limitations of reason allows for the possibility of freedom.

Unfortunately, the relationship between freedom and the limitations of reason in Shackle is frequently misconstrued. For example, Boland subsumes Shackle's concerns within a generalized 'problem of induction', stating that, for Shackle:

> Neoclassical economics is wrong in assuming that individuals are maximizers, since the supposedly needed inductive knowledge of the successful decision-maker is a practical impossibility.
>
> (Boland 1982: 38)

The emphasis on the limits of reason thus becomes merely an acknowledgment of the problem of induction. Shackle does draw attention to the problem of rational action given the limits to our

132

knowledge. For instance, concerning the 'theory of value', Shackle (1972: 446) writes: 'It shows men as acting rationally, whereas to be human is to be denied the necessary condition of rationality, complete relevant knowledge.' However, his emphasis on the lack of 'completely relevant knowledge' does not necessarily entail a reference to the problem of induction. Indeed, there are good reasons for not relating Shackle's concerns to the 'problem of induction'. For one thing, the 'Humean problem of induction' is only a problem in the manner construed if one accepts Cartesian element (1) — that all knowledge must be of a rigorous form. But Hume's reasoning concerning induction can be construed as follows: 'Where and so long as all known X's are or have been Y, to presume that all X's have been or will be Y, until and unless some positive reason is found for revising this particular assumption' (Flew 1984: 59).[7]

Now this does not constitute 'knowledge' in the Cartesian sense, but there is no compelling reason to assume knowledge in this form of exhausts all knowledge criteria.[8] Secondly, for Shackle the major problem with mainstream economics is not that it does not acknowledge the problem of induction, but that it does not acknowledge the possibility of freedom:

> Beginning I use here as the term for a taking-place in which some element, aspect or character is ex nihilo. No knowledge of antecedents, however complete and exact, would make possible a foreknowledge of that aspect or character.
>
> (Shackle 1979: 48)

The problem is not that of justifying our beliefs that the future will resemble the past, but that any such belief is mistaken. We cannot predict how individuals will act, and thus the form of the future, because actions are the product of freedom, not causality.[9] Again, Shackle's argument is perfectly understandable in the context of Kant's conception of freedom:

> We must, then, assume a causality through which something takes place, the cause of which is not itself determined... by another cause antecedent to it, that is to say, an absolute spontaneity of the cause... This is transcendental freedom.
>
> (Kant 1781/1787: A 446/B 474)[10]

The claim in mainstream economics that reason allows action to be predicted neglects the essential spontaneity, the uncaused causality, of freedom. Mainstream economics is not mistaken because it assumes that individuals have 'solved' the problem of induction, but because it neglects the essential creativity of freedom:

> Reason can find novelty. But if we wish to claim that reason by itself is a sufficient guide to conduct, we need to claim, not that reason can find novelty, but that it can find *all* novelties and *exhaust* novelty.
>
> (Shackle 1972: 96, emphasis in original)

Again, Shackle is drawing attention to the limitations of reason understood as *techne*. Such reason cannot predict the actions that any individual will undertake because actions are the result of freedom, not technical reason — hence Shackle's definition of 'beginning':

> A taking place not wholly knowable from antecedents no matter how completely themselves known, a taking-place not implicit in antecedents, a taking-place such that the sequel would be different if this taking-place were different, a taking-place thus originating *ex nihilo* some characters of a train of events in history, an uncaused cause.
>
> (Shackle 1979: 8)

However, if action is not the result of an exercise of technical reason, but of freedom, how is it guided? It is because acts of freedom are not determined by reason that Shackle appeals to imagination:

> Having opted for the supremacy of reason, it rejects what conflicts with reason... thus it has cut itself off from the most ascendant and superb of human faculties. Imagination, the source of novelty, the basis of mens' claims, if they have one, to be makers and not mere executants of history, is exempted.
>
> (Shackle 1979: 44)

Shackle's emphasis on the significance of freedom is intimately related to his objection to the dogmatic employment of reason and the subsequent neglect of imagination. Having argued that Shackle's objection to reason as *techne*, and the emphasis on freedom, is prefigured within Enlightenment thought, it is instructive to appreciate the significance of imagination in the Enlightenment project.

4 SHACKLE, HUME AND KANT

The philosophers of the Enlightenment followed the Cartesian lead in linking the question of awareness with the question of consciousness. As Warnock (1976: 13) notes, 'In order to answer questions about knowledge, belief, perception, or indeed about causation and substance, one had to turn one's attention inwards, and examine the objects of one's consciousness.' However, the rejection by Locke, Berkeley and Hume of the Cartesian justification of only deductive knowledge witnessed an interest in the relationship between thought and perception, in keeping with the emphasis on experience.

In the case of Locke, with 'having ideas and perception being the same thing' (Locke 1977: 36), imagination was invoked in explaining the building up of complex ideas from perceptions:

> By explaining the names of actions we never saw, or motions we cannot see; and by enumerating, and thereby, as it were, setting before our imaginations all those ideas which go to making them.
>
> (Locke 1977: 129)

Hence, although simple ideas were equivalent to perception, imagination could build up complex ideas from these simple ideas: imagination could represent objects that were themselves not present. However, imagination could not arbitrarily invent complex ideas, as ideas were ultimately always tied to perception. This acknowledgment of the significance of imagination, coupled with a suspicion regarding its potential, reverberates throughout Enlightenment thought.

Hume followed Locke in characterizing imagination in terms of its capacity to represent an object not itself present. However, this raised the question as to how imagination could be differentiated from memory. Hume focused on two characteristics. Firstly, ideas presented by imagination are livelier and stronger than those presented by memory; secondly, whilst both memory and imagination are dependent on prior perceptions, only memory presented corresponding ideas in the same order and form as originally found. In this sense, 'memory is in a manner ty'd down' (Hume 1978: 9) whereas with imagination, Hume spoke of the 'liberty of the imagination to transpose and change its ideas' (Hume 1978: 10).

Again, this raised the question of the limitations, if any, to imagination. Hume argued that, although 'nothing is more free than this faculty', there is a 'gentle force' which suggests certain associations of ideas, so that one idea 'naturally induces' the other. He lists three 'qualities' through which the mind is 'convey'd from one idea to another' — resemblance, contiguity in time and place, and cause and effect.

Hence, imagination may 'run easily' from one idea to another because these ideas resemble one another, or because imagination becomes accustomed to the senses presenting objects in similar temporal and spatial positions, or because there is some form of causal relationship operating. Regarding the latter, Hume notes that there is nothing in objects themselves that indicates that one object implies the existence of another: hence, the existence of one object can only be inferred from another through experience. Observing that the relationship of cause and effect is founded on the constant conjunction of objects, based on experience, Hume inquires whether reason or imagination is responsible for establishing this connection. Hume rejects that reason can 'shew us the connection of one object with another':

> When the mind, therefore, passes from the idea or impression of one object to the idea or belief of another, it is not determin'd by reason, but by certain principles, which associate together the ideas of these objects, and unite then in imagination.
>
> (Hume 1978: 92)

Imagination, not reason, induces us to identify causal relations. Hume's emphasis on the significance of imagination continues in the section on scepticism. Hume seeks an answer to two, for him related, questions: how can we attribute a continued existence to objects, even when we are not perceiving them, and how can we suppose that these objects have an existence independent of us? He concludes that:

> Since all impressions are internal and perishing existences, and appear as such, the notion of their distinct continu'd existence must arise from a concurrence of some of their qualities with the qualities of the imagination.
>
> (Hume 1978: 194)

Hume thus rejects either experience or reason as the source of the notion of the continued existence of independent objects, leaving imagination to fulfil the role.[11] In the end, even understanding itself is predicated on the activity of imagination: 'The memory, senses, and understanding are, therefore, all of them founded on the imagination, or the vivacity of our ideas' (p. 265).

Relating Hume and Shackle on the imagination reveals on number of points. Shackle's emphasis on the role of imagination has a strong precedent in Enlightenment thought. For both Hume and Shackle imagination becomes significant because of the rejection of the Cartesian vision of knowledge and subsequent emphasis on experience. This leads to the question of the <u>origins</u> of experience — for Shackle 'the economic analyst... does not ask how they know what these circumstances are' (1972: xiv). Shackle thus rejects the 'blinkered vision' of the economics profession, where so many aspects of their models are taken merely as 'given'. Indeed, the neglect of imagination in economic theorising reveals a lack of that faculty in the profession itself:

> Economic theory treats quantity alone as important, and neglects or abjures all interest in the real internal structure or visible conformation of things, in how they work physically or how they appeal to instinct, taste and judgement or fire the human imagination by suggestion of beauty.
>
> (Shackle 1972: 114)

However, although Shackle's concern with imagination is prefigured in Hume's thought, Shackle does not follow Hume's sceptical route. Whereas Hume argued that understanding is ultimately dependent upon imagination, Shackle seeks only to restrict, not undermine, the claims of reason. In this, as noted earlier, Shackle is closer to Kant. It is thus not surprisingly to find that Hume's acknowledgment of the importance of imagination continues in the theories of Kant.

In the *Critique of Pure Reason* Kant sought to rescue reason from

Hume's sceptical onslaught. He accomplished this through redefining the role of imagination. The contrast between the position of Hume and Kant on the imagination can be summarized as follows. Whereas Hume tends to invoke imagination where reason fails, Kant does so where experience fails.[12] In respectively situating Hume and Kant with respect to imagination, it is also possible to appreciate how Shackle's work is itself vulnerable to criticism

Hume argued, in line with his emphasis on experience, that our notion of time was derived from the succession of ideas and impressions, as 'from the succession of ideas and impressions we form the idea of time' (Hume 1978: 35). Kant raised two objections to Hume's argument. Firstly, the experience of successive ideas and impressions cannot give rise to the idea of time because a succession of ideas *presupposes* time. If ideas are successive, they are already situated in temporal relations to each other. Hume's argument, although claiming to explain the origin of our sense of time, already presupposes a sense of time.[13]

To appreciate Kant's second problem with Hume's account of time, it is necessary to distinguish between a succession of perceptions and a perception of succession. To argue that a succession of perceptions exists does not account for our awareness of this succession as a succession. In order for this awareness to occur, there must be some means through which this succession is brought to consciousness. This in turn requires that successive perceptions are retained and united within one consciousness. Yet Hume (1978: 636) could not discover any means through which this was possible: 'All my hopes vanish, when I come to explain the principles, that unite our successive perceptions in our thought or consciousness.'

Kant avoided Hume's two problems through denying that perceptions had a real temporal existence, independent of the mind. Time and space, which Kant termed pure intuition, provided the form within which — in the case of time — all perceptions must be connected. Hence time was not arrived at through experience, but was produced through the imagination: time was 'imaginary': 'The mere form of intuition, without substance, is in itself no object, but the merely formal condition of an object (as appearance), as pure space and pure time (ens imaginarium)' (Kant 1781/1787: A 291/B 347). Imagination was not only responsible for generating perceptual succession, but also for retaining successive perceptions, thus allowing their unification in consciousness. With Kant, Hume's first problem — that of presupposing time, in order to derive it — is avoided through making imagination the source of time. Hume's second problem — uniting successive perceptions in consciousness — is avoided though advocating their unification through imagination.

Given this brief summary of Kant's position, it is possible to explore how relevant Kant's arguments are to Shackle's position. Take Shackle's account of our construction of the notion of 'extended time':

> Real experience 'takes time'. It finds us at one instant and leaves us at another, the experience having filled an interval of time, however short. Experience of the elapsing, extended moment impels us to hypothesize a succession of moments, to construct extended time. Extended time, in one direction, is available to be filled with content, but content is not available to fill it, except it be invented, even if on suggestions offered by experience.
>
> (Shackle 1972: 245)

This implies that we have a succession of temporal experiences, from which we construct the notion of extended time. However, Shackle fails to explain how we generate the experience of succession from a succession of experiences. The problem that Shackle's explanation of time encounters becomes clear in the following:

> The abstract notion of a thought which will succeed my present one, and of one which will succeed that successor, and so on endlessly, is the notion of time-to-come. What frame can formal imagination supply to accommodate the notion of an endless succession of transients?
>
> (Shackle 1979: 1)

Shackle suggests a succession of thoughts. However, he offers no indication as to how this succession of thoughts can generate the thought of succession. Shackle wants to explain how we generate an awareness of time as successive. However, he fails to explain how this awareness, or thought of, succession can be generated from a succession of states of awareness, or thoughts. In the end, thought is itself both the experience of thought and the experience of a succession of thoughts. Shackle fails to differentiate between a succession of awareness and an awareness of succession, and allocates both to the activity of thought. The problem is not so much that Shackle emphasizes imagination, but that he restricts it. Consequently, in contrast to Kant, Shackle attempts to intellectualizes our awareness of succession: it is the product of thought, although somehow generated from a succession of thoughts.

This intellectualization indicates a major problem for Shackle's account of the individual: the individual becomes overburdened. The demand that time must be thought into the future places a significant onus on the cognitive capacity of the individual. Kant's exploration of the relationship between imagination and time indicated that imagination, not thought, was responsible for both the generation of time itself and the generation of time as successive. Consequently, for Kant, the production of an extended temporal horizon works at a pre-conceptual level. This is not so with Shackle, where the production of any time-span is the responsibility of thought itself. Despite acknowledging the limitations of reason, Shackle's argument places a considerable burden on individual cognitive abilities. The extent and ramifications of this are explored in the next section.

5 THE WORLD OF THE INDIVIDUAL CONSCIOUSNESS

For Shackle, choice takes place within the bounds of the possible. As 'possibleness' is not objective (1988: 4), then choice and possibility are referred to the subject. Given that judgments concerning possibility occur within the thoughts of the subject, Shackle is specifically concerned with 'epistemic possibility'. This can be broken down into three components — natural, general, and specific possibility. Natural possibility is defined thus:

> The widest of these, natural possibility, I shall use to refer to all states of the field, and transformations of such states, which do not seem to the chooser to be excluded by the principles of Nature or of human nature, the inherent fibre or constitution of the world.
>
> (Shackle 1979: 36)

General possibility is defined as the above, with the added limitation that the starting point of choice must be the chooser's actual present location, whilst specific possibilities are those that the chooser thinks will be realized, given a certain course of action. The limitations on possibility are necessary in order to differentiate imagination from fantasy, as only constrained imagination is allowed to influence expectation formation. A further restriction is located through 'time available': decisions must be congruent with the time available for transforming the present into the desired future, although this idea is problematic (Parsons 1990).

Shackle thus shares the Enlightenment concern of both acknowledging imagination, yet recognizing it must be restricted. For Shackle, imagination is restricted solely through appealing to what the individual knows concerning certain 'facts' of natural and human nature and time available. This entails an unfortunate emphasis on the cognitive capacities of individuals, and subsequent over-burdening of the subject, as foreshadowed in the discussion of time. To appreciate this, take one of Shackle's favourite examples — the decision by a businessman as to whether or not to invest. Such a decision entails that an individual is capable of investing, and thus a specific form of society within which investing is possible. In order for 'investment decisions' to enter the imaginative framework, certain historical/social/institutional conditions are already presupposed.[14] Consequently, individuals are socially and historically grounded, and this basis must inform their expectation formation. In other words, the realm of the possible is restricted through these conditions, although such limitations may not operate on a cognitive level.

The problem is not that Shackle is unaware of the relevance of these factors — referring, as in the above, to the 'inherent fibre or constitution of the world'. Similarly, he states that:

> The elements in their role as building-blocks of imagined sequels of choice will include such formal evidences as contracts of employment, appointment to office, business accounts, granting of patents, results of elections ...
>
> (Shackle 1979: 122)

The problem is how these factors be incorporated within an analysis that emphasizes the 'cogito'. They cannot be located within the 'inherent fibre and constitution of the world' as this would threaten the creativity of action. As institutions are socially and historically specific, they are essentially the result of human action, and hence creativity. However, as ultimately the outcomes of imaginative acts, then they cannot also limit or constrain the imagination. In other words, Shackle's appeal to principles of nature and human nature is intended to capture only those aspects of the world which are historically immutable, and hence lie outside the range of possibilities for originative acts.

Further, Shackle's emphasis on the Cartesian 'cogito', or 'I think' also obviates any possibility of locating them at a pre-conceptual level.[15] Here, the problem with the Cartesian starting point consists in the assumed transparency of the 'cogito'. As noted earlier, this Cartesian starting point rules out any possibility of Shackle incorporate the 'romantic strand' into his thought. Yet this 'romantic strand' could have been developed in order to reduce the burden on the subject's cognitive powers, through developing a substantive notion of the self. In order to appreciate this argument, it is necessary to explore Shackle's understanding of the self.

At times, Shackle explicitly recognizes the individual as a 'bearer of roles' — hence: For example, He comments that 'Exchange, in the economist's theory of value, is absolutely necessitated by specialization, where one man develops and employs the skills of the builder and another those of the tailor (Shackle 1979: 101). Again, this offers a possible avenue through which the cognitive capacity required of the individual could be reduced. That is, expectation formation could be tied, not only to facts of nature, but to the specific role selected or allotted to the individual. In this case, expectations would be relative to, and mediated through, individual life-histories, and the scope of relevant imaginations reduced. Unfortunately, despite this acknowledgment of the relevance of roles, Shackle's individual is ultimately highly abstract and formalized — it is, again, the Cartesian 'cogito'.

Now Shackle (1979: 37) does acknowledge that any decision maker is limited by the particular resources available to them. However, this is merely fleshed out in terms of the normal neoclassical emphasis on scarcity. For example, when Shackle presents his formal diagrammatic representation of choice, he states (1979: 101) that: 'On such a diagram, an indifference-curve is the locus of all points which, for the chooser with his particular temperament, tastes and material endowments, are equally attractive and equally repellent'. Ironically, given Shackle's criticism of reason as *techne,* he then proceeds to develop an axiomatic structure for understanding his theory of choice. However, my main concern lies with Shackle's understanding of the individual decision maker. Although this individual has a 'temperament', this is only relevant at the level of valuing possibilities, not at the level of *generating* them(1979: 63). Given this limitation, the individual can be reduced to essentially 'a map which Pareto ... called a 'photograph' of the individual's tastes' (1979: 102)

Shackle's individual is thus reduced to a bundle of tastes, which are presumably 'operationalized', subject to a resource constraint. However, this is a remarkably impoverished view of the individual, which again, places a high liability on cognitive abilities. To appreciate this, take the example of my imagining what course of action to take tomorrow evening, given the likelihood of my having leisure time. Now there are certain possibilities I will entertain for spending tomorrow night doing, and some I will not entertain, simply because of the person I am. I would not, for example, imagine watching a football match. Likewise, I would not imagine stealing a car to get to my chosen place, because 'someone who steals cars' does not constitute part of my self-understanding. It is not the that I have entertained the idea of 'stealing cars' , only to disregarded it after weighing up relevant costs and benefits ('gains' and 'losses', in Shackle's terminology). It simply does not arise as a possibility, given my self-understanding.

This is not simply a case of 'preferences', but involves my own (and others) understanding of myself. If I announced to friends that I am going out to buy some books, and return with a needle, syringe, and quantity of heroin, I doubt they would merely remark that I had undergone a change in my preferences.[16] Similarly, if I returned home with my head shaved, dressed in a leather outfit covered in chains, I doubt that my children would simply remark on my 'preference change'. In both these cases questions would be raised concerning my identity and others' understanding of this identity. If I continued purchasing heroin, my friends would be likely to remark that I (not just my 'preferences') had changed, or that they thought they knew me, but really did not, and so on. The point is that my preferences are, at least in part, constitutive of my identity, and my identity influences what I recognize as possibilities-for-me.[17]

Similarly, an individual may not contemplate (in other words, form imaginations concerning) attending, say, a university course because this notion does not constitute part of their self-understanding, even if this is, in an abstract sense, a 'possibility'. These are clearly 'fundamental, irreversible' decisions in Shackle's sense. However, the 'imagined deemed possible' is not simply restricted by 'facts of nature and human nature', but by individuals own understandings of their self-identity. Of course, this self-understanding may change: however, it does limit what the individual considers as 'a possibility'

In the end, the neglect of historical/social/institutional features and the impoverished understanding of the individual results in a highly abstract account of decision-making. In short, the individual is simply not grounded — an implication of the reliance on the 'cogito'. With this, the individual is intellectualized, and the cognitive burden placed on the individual is immense. Consequently, despite emphasizing both the individual decision-maker and the limitations of reason, the upshot of Shackle's Cartesian starting point is that the individual is purely abstract, and must possess considerable cognitive powers. Ultimately, the Cartesian starting point undermines the intentions of the theory.

6 CONCLUSIONS

Shackle's criticisms of the understanding of knowledge and reason prevalent in mainstream economics remains within the tradition of Enlightenment thought. Indeed, Shackle's arguments can be regarded as an attempt to maintain the spirit of the Enlightenment in the face of an economics divorced from the concerns of everyday life. To accuse Shackle of 'irrationality' when he is merely challenging a specific, and limited, understanding of reason is highly indicative of the generalized cultural ignorance criticized by Saul (1997), amongst others.

However, Shackle's over-reliance on the Cartesian 'cogito' in order to criticize mainstream economics results in the over-burdening of the cognitive powers of individuals. The Cartesian starting point severely restricts the possibility of developing a more substantive sense of the self, which would in turn allow the weight placed on individual cognitive abilities to be reduced.

NOTES

* I would like to thank Peter Earl for helpful comments on an earlier version of this paper.

1 It is worth pointing out that Coddington had earlier expressed a more sympathetic view of Shackle.

2 As Shackle recognises, Descartes dualistic approach distinguished between *res cogitans* and *res extensa*, where the latter is subject to mathematical (primarily geometrical) manipulation. For most mainstream economists, economic agents are viewed, not in terms of consciousness, but as elements in *res extensa*.

3 The importance of the attending to the subjective realm, as opposed to developing deductive arguments, has been emphasized in the context of consumer research. See, for example, Holbrook (1995).

4 This romantic strain is obviously significant to Marx's explorations of alienated labour.

5 For a devastating critique of this state of affairs, see Saul (1997). Saul is also acutely aware of the increasingly narrow focus of 'technical economics', again contrasting it with the Enlightenment, where 'change meant a return to the humanist vision with greater openness to reality. The result was a leap in creativity, an enrichment of language and a spreading of knowledge' (Saul 1997: 72).

6 Initially, this may appear to contrast with Etzioni's (1988) claim that the mainstream analysis of rationality stresses individual freedom. However, Etzioni is concerned with individual autonomy, not the relationship between freedom and causality.

7 This way of characterizing Hume's argument can be usefully linked to Keynes's notion of a convention in chapter 12 of *The General Theory*. For an initial exploration, see Parsons (1999).

8 Given this, then the 'problem of induction' does not require any 'solution'. For an attempted 'solution', see Harrod (1956). For a critical examination of Harrod's argument, see Ayer (1970).

9 'If experience could tell us what will come to pass, we should be in a world of determinate history, choice-denying and choice abolishing' (Shackle 1979: 59).

10 Kant responds to Hume by defending the principle of causality – that every event has a cause – not by defending particular causal laws. Consequently, we can know, a priori, that whatever happens can be located within a causal nexus. However, we cannot know that past occurrences justify future inferences.

11 Initially, Hume inquires 'whether it be the senses, reason, or the imagination, that produces the opinion of a continu'd or of a distinct existence' (1978: 188). The senses are rejected, as perceptions of objects are

discrete and discontinuous, whereas it is not through rational arguments that 'children, peasants, and the greatest part of mankind are induc'd to attribute objects to some impressions, and deny them to others' (p. 193).

12 The role played by imagination in Kant's work has been the subject of considerable debate. Heidegger's path breaking interpretation of Kant (see Heidegger 1997) argued that, whereas the first edition of the *Critique of Pure Reason* emphasized the significance of imagination, the second edition withdrew from this, re-emphasizing the importance of reason. However, even in the first edition, the imagination is ultimately subordinate to understanding (Parsons 1998). See also Waxman (1991).

13 It is useful here to recall Bergson's argument that time prevents everything happening at once. If we are of ideas as successive, we are aware that they are not all happening at once, hence time is presupposed.

14 Dawson (1994) utilises Shackle's arguments on decision in order to shed light on questions of decision making within an institutional framework..

15 As Peter Earl notes, 'choice is concerned with alternative images of the future, but, since the future cannot be known before its time, these images are inherently conjectural. As such, they are prone to shaping by unconscious cognitive processes' (Earl 1983: 136). See also Earl (1986: ch. 6); Etzioni (1988).

16 Neither, I suggest, would they assume that the relative prices of books and heroin must have altered.

17 For an exploration of the significance of identity in investigating consumption, see Lunt and Livingstone (1992).

REFERENCES

Ayer, A. J. (1970) 'Has Harrod answered Hume?' in Eltis, W., Scott, M. FG. And Wolfe, J. N.(eds) *Induction, Growth and Trade: essays in honour of Sir Roy Harrod*, Oxford: Clarendon Press.

Boland, L. A. (1982) *The Foundations of Economic Method*, London: George Allen & Unwin,.

Clarke, D. M. (1982) *Descartes Philosophy of Science*, Manchester: Manchester University Press.

Coddington, A (1983) *Keynesian Economics: The Search for First Principles*, London: George Allen & Unwin.

Dawson, R. M. (1994) 'The Shacklean nature of Commons's reasonable value', *Journal of Post Keynesian Economics* 17, 1: 33–44

Earl, P. E. (1983) *The Economic Imagination: Towards a Behavioural Theory of Choice*, Brighton: Wheatsheaf.

—— (1986) *Lifestyle Economics: Consumer Behaviour in a Turbulent World*, Brighton: Wheatsheaf.

Etzioni, A. (1988) *The Moral Dimension: Toward a New Economics*, New York: Free Press.

Flew, A. (1986) *David Hume: Philosopher of Moral Science*, Oxford: Blackwell.

Gadamer, H-G (1979) *Truth and Method*, 2nd. edn, London: Sheed & Ward.

Habermas, J. (1974) *Theory and Practice*, London: Heinemann,.

—— (1983) 'Modernity — an incomplete project', in Foster, H. (ed.) *Postmodern Culture*, London: Pluto Press,.

Harrod, R.F. (1956) *Foundations of Inductive Logic*, London: Macmillan.

Heidegger, M. (1997) *Kant and the Problem of Metaphysics*, 5th edn, Bloomington, Indiana, IA: University Press. (Originally published in 1929).

Hobbes, T. (1968) *Leviathan*, edited by C. B. Macpherson, Harmondsworth: Penguin

Holbrook, M. B. (1995) *Consumer Research: Introspective Essays on the Study of Consumption*, Thousand Oaks, CA: Sage.

Hume, D. (1978) *A Treatise of Human Nature*, edited by L. A. Selby-Bigge, 2nd. edn, Oxford: Clarendon, Press, (Originally published in 1739/40).

Husserl, E. (1960) *Cartesian Meditations*, The Hague: Nijhoff.

Judovitz, D. (1988) *Subiectivity and Representation in Descartes: The Origins of Modernity*, Cambridge: Cambridge University Press

Kain, P. J. (1981) 'Labour, the state and aesthetic theory in the writings of Schiller', *Interpretation* 9: 263–78.

Kant, I (1781/1787) *Critique of Pure Reason*, translated by N. K. Smith (1929), London: Macmillan.

—— (1971) 'An answer to the question: what is enlightenment?', in *Kant's Political Writings*, edited by H. Reiss, Cambridge: Cambridge University Press.

Locke, J. (1977) *An Essay Concerning Human Understanding*, edited by J. W. Yolton, London: Dent (Originally published in 1690).

Lucas, R. and Sargent, T. (eds) (1981) *Rational Expectations and Econometric Practice*, London: George Allen & Unwin.

Lunt, P. K. and Livingstone, S. M. (1992) *Mass Consumption and Personal Identity*, Buckingham: Open University Press.

Marcuse, H. (1968) *Negations: Essays in Critical Theory*, Harmondsworth" Penguin.

Parsons, S. (1990) 'The philosophical roots of modern Austrian economics: past problems and future prospects', *History of Political Economy* 22:. 295–319.

—— (1998) 'Kant and pure intuition', mimeo, Milton Keynes: De Montfort University.

—— (1999) 'Challenging the Keynesian consensus: organicism, conventions and probability', mimeo, Milton Keynes: De Montfort University

Saul, J. R. (1997) *The Unconscious Civilization*, Harmondsworth: Penguin.

Shackle, G. L. S. (1972) *Epistemics and Economics: A Critique of Economic Doctrines*, Cambridge: Cambridge University Press.

—— (1979) *Imagination and the Nature of Choice*, Edinburgh: Edinburgh University Press,.

—— (1988) *Business, Time and Thought: Selected Papers of G. L. S. Shackle*, edited by S. F. Frowen, London: Macmillan.

Taylor, C. (1979) *Hegel and Modern Society*, Cambridge: Cambridge University Press.

Warnock, M. (1976) *Imagination*, London: Faber & Faber.

Waxman, M. (1991) *Kant's Model of the Mind*, New York: Oxford University Press.

7

HOW FAR CAN YOU GET WITH HERMENEUTICS?

Shaun P. Hargreaves Heap[*]

1 INTRODUCTION

Quite plausibly, George Shackle was the most important exponent of hermeneutics in economics the twentieth century. This chapter is concerned with whether such an attribution constitutes a criticism or a compliment. In other words, should admirers of George celebrate the connection with hermeneutics or quietly forget about it?

There is a prior question which needs some sorting out: what is hermeneutics? The answer is not straightforward and it will be helpful to say a little on this at the outset so as to avoid any misunderstandings which might otherwise develop (for a fuller discussion, see Gadamer 1975, Ricouer 1981, and Bernstein 1983). In its most general sense hermeneutics is associated with taking the 'internal point of view seriously': that is, with understanding what people think they are doing. Unfortunately, the injunction has been variously interpreted. The so-called romantic, nineteenth century version of hermeneutics identified it with reading texts in the context of their times in order to recover their true meaning. In contrast, modern hermeneutics, which is how the term will be used in this paper, takes the internal point of view seriously by complicating the relation between the internal and external views (or the subjective and the objective accounts of action and events).

To appreciate what this complication amounts to, it is helpful to recall a view of science that may be 'old hat', but which is no less popular for that in economic circles. It posits that the difference between the objective and subjective accounts is like the difference, which arises when there is fog between how the landscape really is and our imperfect vision of it. The point of science on this account is, so as to speak, to remove the fog and thereby render the subjective identical

149

to the objective. Modern hermeneutics rejects this because the objective and subjective views of what is going on in the social world are mutually constituted. In so doing, it denies that the aim is to purge the subjective until it is indistinguishable from the objective.

The key claim, then, is that we cannot do without a more substantial sense of the internal point of view. To see why the claim might be warranted in a general way, consider what is entailed by seeking the objective view. It comes by putting distance between ourselves and our subjective views so that we can reflect on the relation between those views and the world they purport to describe. However, the very process of 'being objective' here presupposes a subjective starting point or ingredient. The same relation holds in social science since the attempt to explain the social world 'objectively' must recognize that the social world is partially constituted by people with 'internal points of view'.

Indeed, if this contribution is purged, then we are eventually likely to do some injustice to what we understand of ourselves. And of course, Shackle gave us a prime example of this danger in his discussion of choice. The objective approach to choice seeks causes for the actions which we take and, as Shackle presciently argued, if this was all that there was to choice then it would belie the name.

> To suppose that choices to come are thus predetermined destroys the meaning of choice, robbing human choices of all power of their own. The notion of choice would be empty and the act of choice sterile.
>
> (Shackle 1988: 1)

Instead, some measured recognition of 'free will' (that comes from distinguishing action from reaction or to use Shackle's words that 'choice can be in some respects an uncaused cause') entails conceding something to the subjective which can never be fully explained objectively.[1]

Thus hermeneutics broadly encourages us to take the subjective or internal point of view seriously in the sense that we should not attempt to reduce or explain it objectively in terms of some external point of view. This is enough on the preliminaries to get an argument going on the real question of the chapter: how far can one get with hermeneutics in this sense?

The next section turns to this and argues that one gain from the hermeneutic turn is methodological — although some care is required on this point because I shall dispute at least two popular views on the methodological implications of hermeneutics, those of Weber and modern Rhetoric. The third section addresses the practical contribution from hermeneutics: firstly with respect to the appreciation of the role of institutions in economic life; and secondly in the arena of normative decision making.

2 EPISTEMOLOGY AND METHOD

2.1 Goodbye to empiricism

This section focuses on one constituent of the 'internal point of view': the beliefs or theories about the world which agents hold. The fact that such beliefs can inform actions (thus helping to constitute the world which social science wishes to study) is potentially damaging to a traditional view of science. This has already been noted in the introductory section and it is worth glossing in more detail now. The recognition has two principal effects. The first is to undermine any simple form of empiricism as a method because the 'facts' do not generally supply an 'independent' ground where we can test our theories.

Some care is required, however, over this interdependence between observation and theory because the recognition of interdependence need not be as damaging as it might seem at first glance. Theory may chase the facts which are themselves chasing the theory, but so long as this process converges on a *unique* fixed point where theory helps inform actions which confirm the theory and the process of empirical testing helps move us to this fixed point, then the simple view of science will still be in business. There remains an 'objective' set of beliefs and the purpose of science is to close the gap between those objective beliefs and the subjective ones which we now entertain. I have deliberately worded this in a way which echoes Muth's (1961) version of rational expectations because the developments of his ideas have revealed very clearly why the interdependence between fact and theory cannot, in general, be rendered benign. It is now well known that there are quite often multiple rational expectations equilibria: so there is not a unique fixed point to the chase between theory and observation. Furthermore, it is also well known that even when there is a unique fixed point, convergence to it is not guaranteed by many standard forms of empirical updating of beliefs.[2]

The importance of both these developments in the rational expectations literature should be clear. First, once there are multiple equilibria, the selection of one rather than another is scarcely a triumph of 'objectivity' since 'objectivity' (in the modified form now of the property of fixed point in the relation between theory and observation) is shared by all the potential rational expectations equilibria. In fact, equilibrium selection will depend very largely on the character of the original subjective beliefs and the subsequent learning procedures which are adopted. Thus, 'the internal point of view' matters in exactly the manner of hermeneutics: it cannot be reduced to the demands of what is objective; rather it contributes to the very definition of what is 'objective'. Of course, George Shackle saw the whole point very well when he argued that our theories help to create order in the world, they rarely simply describe some pre-existing order (see for instance Shackle 1967).

Secondly, the general failure of empirical updating to yield convergence on equilibrium suggests that even in the case of a unique fixed point, it would not be wise methodologically to rely exclusively on the usual forms of empirical updating of belief.

Thus the first implication of the mutual constitution of theory and observation is the undermining of simple forms of empiricism as exclusive methodological guides for social science. The second implication follows from this. In particular, it would not be surprising to find that what begins as a point about the collapse of the fact/theory distinction spreads to corrode the fact/value distinction, with the result that the traditional separation of normative and positive questions in social science becomes less than watertight. The further corrosion can occur because it is not unreasonable to allow normative considerations, in the form of views with respect to the desirability of the world portrayed by a theory, to become criteria governing theory selection when theories not only represent the world but also help to create the world. In effect the selection of a theory in these circumstances can entail a choice of the type of world to live within and we are quite naturally likely to prefer the world which we regard as the most desirable and select our theory accordingly.

Again some care is required here so as not to overstate the case. To introduce the internal point of view in this way does not mean that it always plays such a role, nor does it mean that the selection of a theory is only a matter of consulting our sense of what is desirable since something being desirable does not guarantee that it is attainable. But, it does mean that the selection of theories is not as simple as exclusively empiricist methods would have us believe; and it hints that a part of the complication comes through the potential licence of normative considerations.

The hint is returned to later. For now, it is time to address briefly two specific approaches to method that have been premised on the need to go beyond empiricism and which have at one time or another allied themselves with hermeneutics. Both will be rejected because each fails to maintain a healthy respect for *both* internal and external points of view. Instead, they seem to reproduce the mistake, found in that traditional model of science, of reducing one to the other; and the next sub-section sketches this failure.

2.2 Weber and rhetoric: two false starts

Weber famously argued for the internal point of view when suggesting that an account of an event would have to be satisfactory, both at the level of explanation and understanding. Satisfaction at the level of explanation came through empirical evidence and satisfaction at the level of understanding came by providing an account of what the agents themselves actually thought that they were doing. Such an account he argued would rest on a view of rational agency, and he gave four ideal types of agency through which we might understand an agent's behaviour. According to Weber, like all action, social action may be orientated in four ways:

1 Instrumentally rational.....
2 value rational, that is, determined by a conscious belief in the value for its own sake of some ethical, aesthetic, religious, or other form of behaviour, independently of its prospects of success;
3 affectual (especially emotional), that is, determined by the actor's specific affects and feeling states;

4   traditional, that is, determined by ingrained habituation.

(Weber 1922: 24–5)

What seems right about this famous proposal is the requirement of a theory of agency for the project of understanding. By putting matters in this way, Weber turns 'understanding' into a bridge which connects epistemology and ontology (and I shall develop it in a different way later). Where Weber seems on decidedly weaker ground is with respect to his particular four-fold classification of ideal types of action. Why should we believe that these are the correct four or that four is the right number? Or to take the problem one stage further, even if there was agreement on this, how would we decide which ideal type was to be used in any situation?

Weber is silent on these questions and one is left with a suspicion that the only warrant for one interpretative understanding rather than another will come from the empirical evidence which is adduced from adequacy at the level of explanation. If this is so, then we are firmly back with the problems of empiricism. In this sense, Weber's attempt to take the 'internal point of view seriously' fails to escape the difficulties of empiricism because it merely encounters them one stage later (see Hollis 1987).

Those who fly the (post) modern flag of rhetoric (see McCloskey 1983) are also often associated with the interpretative turn of hermeneutics (see Lavoie 1990). Yet they seem to fall foul of the opposite tendency. While Weber's incorporation of the subjective seems to takes us eventually back to what is supposed to be objective, those who subscribe to rhetoric seem unable to escape a pure form of subjectivism. For rhetoricians, theories are simply stories about the world which we find more or less persuasive because of the more or less judicious deployment of rhetorical devices. In particular, there is nothing objective to distinguish one narrative from another. What is called 'objective' now is simply the conventions used by the scientific community (or more often what we think they use). Style is what counts in argument and about all that can be said about this is that persuasive style often varies with time and place. This may be unfair to some rhetoriticians, but it is difficult not to smell a retreat into relativism (see Hollis 1985 and Gerrard 1990).

Of course, a retreat into relativism may be all that is available. I shall argue below, however, that it is not the only route. Furthermore, there are some well known difficulties with the relativist route which should provide reason for delay. In particular, relativism seems to involve a conceptual contradiction of the sort captured by the famous declaration 'I, a Cretan, declare that all Cretans are liars'. After all, why should we believe a view which says that views are relative? Indeed, if this view were correct, then we would never have any reason for believing in the truth of relativism.

2.3 The positive methodological programme of hermeneutics

This depiction of Weber and the contemporary rhetoriticians takes certain liberties with both, but it serves to highlight the difficulty of resisting the reduction of the internal to the external point of view, or vice versa. Yet without such resistance, hermeneutics loses its distinctiveness and its potential for making a constructive contribution (see Bernstein 1983). In this section, I shall briefly sketch a way of avoiding the reduction which has epistemological and ontological implications for theory construction.

The resistance to the epistemological either/or of relativism and objectivity (which the rhetoriticians and Weber seem to reproduce) comes from advancing a particular ontological claim. The claim is that we are interpreters and that it is through self interpretation that our sense of identity arises. In Taylor's(1989) words, 'the human agent exists in a space of questions' or in Shackle's words from the *Nature of Economic Thought* we need 'flesh and blood', in the form of 'hopes, doubts and fears' to distinguish us from the 'Model T' version of human agency which gives us only tastes. Of course, the frameworks which agents have used to answer these questions vary over time and space with the result that our sense of identity is historically and culturally specific. But this does not undermine the general claim that all human agents seek an identity through interpreting their existence.

There is a further feature of our existence that follows from our interpretative character: our sense of identity can never be fully articulated. There is always some uncertainty over who we are because every framework that we use for interpretation consists of givens which can only be justified with reference to further frameworks, with further givens and so on. This is a familiar philosophical insight that is often mistakenly taken to lead to relativism. Of course, it might with further argument lead in that direction, but, since there are internal difficulties with respect to the doctrine of relativism (as noted earlier), it seems sensible not to take it in that direction. The great virtue of drawing the inference that there is ineliminable uncertainty associated with the value of any interpretative scheme (because every interpretative scheme relies on unsubstantiated premises) is that this inference does not involve us in an internal inconsistency. To say that 'everything is uncertain' is not self undermining in the way that saying 'everything is relative' is.

This argument can be expressed in specifically 'modern' terms by drawing on the idea we have a 'free will', in Shackle's sense, that we like to exercise and which enables us in some degree to create ourselves. This is, so as to speak, a version of what can be recognized as the modern, individualist approach to identity. In this light, the task of theory in social science could never simply be one of discovering something which is already there, as it would be on an objective reading, because our behaviours are not fixed. Equally, theory cannot aim solely at being internally coherent, as it would on a relativist account, because we care about the kind of people and world which our theory helps to make (as this is why we care about identity) — and anyway there are bound to be natural constraints on our abilities to create who we are. Instead, the task of theory is to help make the world a better place for people like us to live in and we will judge theories accordingly. But how are we to judge what is better in this context? Here is the rub. We have certain preferences and moral views now which inform a judgement of what constitutes better, but we know that our preferences and moral views are likely to change in the future. It is the exercise of free will which makes us care about the influence which theory has on our world, but, to return to famous Shackle observation, it is that same free will which casts uncertainty over what kind of people we will be in future worlds. So, how is one to judge whether the theory makes the world a better place when we do not know what kind of people will inhabit that world?

This is a genuine dilemma which we return to later. For now, suffice with the thought that as with all genuine dilemmas, it never goes away. When we select those theories which seem most likely to serve us best, the practice of those theories yields unexpected outcomes including changes in ourselves which lead to renewed theory construction and so on. Thus, the dilemma occasions the sort of restlessness between our theories, values and practices which is sometimes referred to as dialectical and which requires an historical appreciation because one can only understand where one is now with reference to where one has recently been.[3]

In short, the argument here is that the ontological claim regarding interpretative character of human life (or specifically the individualistic concern with exercising 'free will' in modern times) supplies an external point of reference which prevents the retreat into relativism: we know we want to be able to value/choose who we are and so not every internally coherent theory is as good as another. However, the claim also forestalls a full move into objectivity because it also denies that we can know with certainty whether a transformation of the world is an improvement or is even possible. This leaves us, then, through the recognition of uncertainty neatly suspended between objectivity and relativism with our theories, values and practices evolving together in what amounts to a continuing dialogue amongst themselves.[4]

It is perhaps useful to pause to note the similarity between what is being suggested here and the contemporary revival of methodological realism (see Maki 1988 for a survey of forms of realism, and Hardy and Clegg 1997 for a more general taxonomy of methodological approaches). At first glance, any similarity seems unlikely since realism has traditionally been premised on the idea that the world exists independently of our thoughts about it and, in important respects, this is precisely what the hermeneutic turn denies. However, what distinguishes so called 'critical realism' is that it concedes that in at least some respects reality is inter-subjectively constructed. Quite whether this concession meets the hermeneutic argument is a moot point. Nevertheless it bridges some of the difference and there is an additional similarity when realists make use of a form of transcendental argument (for example, Lawson 1997). In effect, this is exactly the form of argument that I have used here. I have taken as self-evident the fact that we are interpreters and I am concerned to see what must be presupposed about the character of our interpretations by this fact (that is to say, their uncertain nature). Actually there is more to be said in this vein and it tells us something further about the material of theory construction in the social sciences.

Consider how individuals are able to form an internal point of view. There is a puzzling relation between the whole and its parts that is crucial to hermeneutic argument in this respect (see Gadamer 1975).

For instance, take a simple form of the question of how an understanding is achieved: ask how we come to understand the meaning of a sentence in a text. Of course, we understand it partially with reference to what we take to be the meaning of the whole paragraph in which it is embedded. Yet at the same time the meaning of the whole paragraph consists only of the meaning of the sentences which comprise it because there is nothing in the paragraph apart from the sentences which make it up which could give it meaning. It seems that the part and the whole are mutually constituted in an hermeneutic circle.

The same sort of puzzle surfaces in the relation between individual meanings and shared social meanings and suggests that the individual and society, like the whole and its parts, are mutually constituted. Consider the meaning of an action to an individual undertaking it. It depends in part on how it is received by other agents. But the reception by other agents will only correspond to the meaning which the individual gives to the action if all agents share the same understanding of the action. In other words, it seems that each individual, if they are to achieve understanding must relinquish some part of their idiosyncratic interpretation of their actions. This is something social as distinct from individual, but where does it come from? There are only individuals attempting to understand their actions and consequently it seems again that we can understand neither the whole nor the parts in isolation: the individual and society are mutually constituted. [5]

The importance for contemporary theory construction of this puzzling relation between the whole and its parts is that it undermines a reduction of the whole to the sum of its parts. This has a direct bearing on theory construction in economics because this reductionism is precisely what is entailed by the commonly understood, and commonly pursued, goal of methodological individualism (see Levine, Sober and Olin Wright 1987). Recall the standard model of individual agency. The individual has a well behaved set of preferences and action is taken to satisfy best those preferences. Of course, we know there are institutions in the world which constrain and mould individual action but this notion of the individual is not compromised by the observation so long as the institutions can be understood as a result of the interactions between individuals; and the goal of methodological individualism (at least, the currently fashionable rational choice versions) has been precisely to explain these apparent social constraints in these terms.

In fact, the caution sounded by the hermeneutic understanding of the organic relation between the whole and its parts is increasingly echoed within economics. For instance, the discovery of multiple equilibria in repeated games and the related frequent discovery of multiple rational expectations equilibria suggests that the shared practices or shared beliefs which constitute an institution cannot be solely understood through interaction between instrumentally rational individuals. Common knowledge of instrumental rationality might point to the achievement of an equilibrium (although even this is increasingly disputed), but it cannot explain the selection of one equilibrium rather than another. Thus it seems that there is something irreducibly social about institutions which should feature in theory construction — and of course, this explains why institutionalists have often been the first to ally themselves with hermeneutics. Or to put it another way, there is something inescapably social about individuals which the standard model of rational agency overlooks.

Thus to summarize the methodological contribution of hermeneutics, it has two parts. The first is to bring uncertain normative values back into the evaluation of theories because theories cannot aspire to mere descriptive accuracy or internal coherence (see for instance Gadamer 1975, and his requirement for 'effective history'). The second is to focus theory construction on the puzzling relation between whole and its parts (again see Gadamer 1975); and in economics, this is reflected in the contemporary concern with new models of rational agency and their relation to institutions.

3 THE PRACTICAL CONTRIBUTION
OF HERMENEUTICS

Hermeneutics may make a distinctive and important methodological contribution, but for many this has only a passing interest (and apparently for some it is of no benefit and is not to be recommended, see Hahn 1992). The real test of any approach is often more practical. What does the approach actually tell us about the world and how to change it for the better? In this section, I offer a partial answer to this question. It is qualified in a variety of respects.

Firstly, there is not the space to attempt even to begin to consider what hermeneutics adds to economics *in toto*. Of necessity, the discussion must be selective. In fact, in this instance, I focus on what the 'hermeneutic turn' tells us about the selection of institutions for coordinating and regulating economic life. This seems a natural area to look at since hermeneutics has been identified methodologically with an appreciation of the independent (ie non-reductive) role of institutions.

Secondly, there is a problem with identifying the contribution of the 'hermeneutic turn' in even a selected area. Or to put this concretely, there is some difficulty in sorting out what we would have known about institutional selection without hermeneutics. It would *not* be right to refer only to contributions from people who self consciously fly the flag of hermeneutics. Important ideas surface along a number of seemingly unrelated and different paths and this does nothing to dent their importance. In short, many roads lead to hermeneutics and not just the one that is clearly labelled 'hermeneutics'. On the other hand, one cannot give hermeneutics a blank cheque: it would only be right to include those contributions which turn on taking the internal point of view seriously. To cut through this problem, at least as clearly as possible as far as bias is concerned, I shall propose a non-hermeneutic conventional wisdom on the question of institution selection from which we can judge the hermeneutic contribution. It has the following (obviously controversial) form.

The wisdom distinguishes sharply between positive and normative aspects of the question. On the positive side of the question it focuses on the efficiency attributes of markets versus planning and how the definition of property rights affects both systems. The principal conclusions of this analysis is that, with perfect information, markets and plans are as efficient as each other: perfect planning is no less perfect than perfect competition. The big difference between them emerges when information is imperfect. In these circumstances, private property rights provide the essential complement to markets and once the combination is made it outperforms the planning plus social ownership arrangement. The importance of private property rights is simply that they provide the incentive for agents to seek out mutually beneficial exchanges because they guarantee that the individual gains from discovering such exchange. The contrast is clearest when property rights are so socially defined that an individual's reward is severed from individual action: for example, as in the literature on planning which has focussed on the problems of 'soft' budget constraints. A corollary of this conclusion seems to be the presence of a trade-off between efficiency and equity since any form of intervention which alters the relation between individual action and individual reward reduces the incentive to seek out mutually beneficial exchanges.[6]

On the normative side, the conventional wisdom has been concerned with how to weight different normative principles, in particular principles like equity and liberty. Here I associate it with the conclusion that there is no magic formula for doing this. If people in a community agree on the combination of moral principles then there is no difficulty. But if there is disagreement, then there is no simple way of deciding how to weight the various viewpoints. For example, voting (at least as a general mechanism) falls foul of the Arrow Impossibility Theorem. Indeed, one might fairly describe the attempt in mainstream welfare economics to generate social welfare functions as fully reflecting the problems of modernity which have been responsible for the drift to post-modernity. It seems there are no over-arching principles which all rational agents will subscribe to in virtue of being rational, there are merely a diverse set of local agreements on what is the good.[7]

Of course, precisely because hermeneutics denies the neat separation between positive and normative, its contribution does not map exactly on to the same ground as the conventional wisdom. Nevertheless, there is sufficient overlap here to make the comparison meaningful. For instance, hermeneutics has contributed to the understanding of how institutions affect the economy. It simply denies that this understanding is a neutral or value-free exercise. Likewise hermeneutics has contributed to the post-modern problem of how to accommodate competing conceptions of the good in institutional design and this fits substantively with the conventional normative discussion, it is just that hermeneutics again denies the strict separation of such normative discussion from so-called positive analysis. I consider each of these possible contributions in the next two sub sections.

3.1 Understanding the role of institutions

On the 'positive' side of things, that is understanding what are the options, two hermeneutic contributions seem worth mentioning.

Firstly, there is an argument that bolsters the conventional wisdom in its support for markets. The ability of a planning system to replicate what goes on in market is based on an assumption that the preferences for goods exist prior to the planning exercise or market interaction, whereas as Buchanan(1991), acknowledging his debt to Shackle, has argued, many preferences are created through choice and so could never be planned for in advance. In other words markets do not just help satisfy existing preferences, they help agents to experiment and acquire their preferences and planning by definition can not serve the latter function.

Secondly, there are a group of arguments which undermine (or at least qualify in important respects) a wholesale enthusiasm for the market. They turn on a possibility of market failure which is rarely recognized by the conventional wisdom.

Two principal sources of failure are externalities or spillovers which either create prisoner dilemma or coordination game like interactions. In the latter, it is perfectly possible for agents to coordinate their actions on a Pareto-inferior outcome and in the former the pursuit of individual goals is collectively self defeating. To avoid such outcomes, we need supplementary non-market institutions; and this is a major insight.

Some care is required, however, in tracing this insight to the hermeneutic turn. Consider first the case of coordination games. These arise whenever there are multiple equilibria. To appreciate this and the part played by the hermeneutic turn, return to the phenomenon of multiple rational expectations equilibria mentioned earlier. In general in such circumstances, any of the potential equilibria will be a rational expectation for an agent to entertain provided all other agents entertain the same expectation. Thus, the trick to selecting one equilibrium is to coordinate your belief with that of other agents. Now the point to notice is that this act of coordinating belief changes the character of agent beliefs. It makes them matter in way which the conventional wisdom overlooks. With the conventional wisdom the beliefs which agents hold are about the world and rational agents are supposed to close the gap between those 'subjective' beliefs and what is 'objectively' the case. The problem is that the recipe of closing the gap does not fix the beliefs for the agents when there are multiple rational expectations. Agents beliefs have to do more, they have to select the equilibrium from among the set which satisfies the recipe. In this way, agents expectations are *creative* and add to the situation in a way that the conventional wisdom neglects. (This is, in effect, why it is broadly plausible to associate the insight with the hermeneutic turn because it is bound up with taking the internal point of view seriously.)

It is worth pausing to reflect on the character of the creative element in these expectations so as to make some connections with the earlier argument. The creative (or the 'extraneous' to strictly instrumental calculation) part must be shared, otherwise it will not do the job of coordinating. In this sense, the expectations embody a convention and to do the selecting it must treat something within the interaction as relevant which lies outside the traditional economic description. As a matter of observation — although see Gilbert (1989) for an argument that makes it more than a contingent feature — conventions of this sort often seem to have a quasi-moral character in the sense that those who do not obey them are often regarded as deficient in a moral way. As a result, it is tempting to locate the something extra in some shared sense of what is loosely regarded as morally appropriate. In other words, it seems as a matter of fact quite likely that the extra dimension to belief is moral.

The link between hermeneutics and the appreciation of prisoner dilemma interactions is weaker. Indeed, it is really a derivative of the argument above regarding equilibrium selection. It is not so much that taking the internal point of view seriously in some sense makes prisoner's dilemmas more likely. Rather it is that overcoming the dilemma involves institutions in way that again recognizes the importance of the internal point of view. An example will help to bring out the point.

Trust enters in many market interactions and without it, agents often find themselves in a prisoner's dilemma, unable to undertake a potentially mutual beneficial exchange. The transactions cost part of the new institutionalist literature has made much play of this and argued that the market must be supplemented by other institutions, like the firm, which are capable of introducing the requisite trust. What is less often recognized in those transaction cost arguments is that 'firm' works because it institutionalises repetition of exchange and it is repetition which is responsible for each agent adopting quite rationally the cooperative strategy in the prisoner's dilemma. Now once such games are repeated, there are typically multiple equilibria (vide various Folk Theorems) and consequently the institution (the firm) does rather more than just overcome the dilemma: it selects the equilibrium. And one aspect of the selection is, of course, bound up with the distribution of the gain which comes from trust. In effect, there is a form of bargaining game embedded in a repeated prisoner's dilemma and fewer and fewer economists believe that such bargaining games have a unique solution.

The hermeneutic turn, then, really only enters here in the same way as before. Nevertheless, the example is useful because it reinforces the earlier observation on the character of the creative element of people's expectations. Where the shared beliefs are settling the distribution of income in this fashion, again it would not be at all surprising to find that they encoded some shared sense of justice.

It is difficult to judge how significant these non-market institutions really are. There is a large literature which attests to the importance of the institution of money (see for instance, Davidson 1978). Furthermore, there are many hints of importance in the recent literature which is concerned for instance with the difference between Japanese firms and North American ones and in bankruptcy laws and the constitution of financial markets (see for instance Aoki 1990, Aghion, Hart and Moore 1992). Equally there is a large literature on the importance of shared rules for interpreting acts of consumption and these shared rules, in effect, constitute a non-market institution (see Douglas and Isherwood 1978, for the seminal original argument, and for a survey of the more recent advertising/marketing literature that applies these insights by focussing on the symbolic aspect of consumption, see Ozanne 1998, and Venkatesh 1998).

This is not the place to attempt a serious evaluation of the role played by such non-market institutions. These references are at best pointers. Nevertheless there is an enduring message from the hermeneutic turn in these respects which should *not* be overlooked as it signals a further contribution. It is that changing institutions is never likely to be easy because people are not just instrumentally attached to them, they are also likely to be normatively attached to them and the interaction between instrumental concern and normative allegiance requires careful study (see Frey 1997)

3.2 Making the world a better place for people like us

At first glance, the hermeneutic turn seems both to give and take away a standard which might be helpful to the normative concern with how to reconcile competing views of the good. The standard comes from positing that we are particular kinds of people, But then it turns out that 'people like us' are an uncertain commodity and so we seem bereft of a standard for judging institutions. It is the dilemma which was left in Section 2 and which resurfaces now to leave us in an apparently post-modern predicament of being unable to adjudicate between value systems when they conflict.

But are matters really as bad as this? Can we really say nothing, for instance, about Nazism if it satisfies a minimal test of internal coherence? And if we cannot adjudicate between disputes over the good, are we resigned to let force become the arbiter? In this section I argue that hermeneutics actually does rather more than return us to the post-modern predicament. We are agents who are concerned to exercise 'free will' (or more generally to have identities through interpretation) and I shall claim two things as a result. Firstly, that this tells us something about the attributes of institutions which are to be valued — the desiderata so as to speak. Secondly, that while this list is far from exhaustive or decisive, it also tells us something about what we should do when people's ideas over the list and their respective weights differ.

On the first issue, the capacity to exercise free will has notoriously generated controversy because there seems to be an unbridgeable gulf between the positive sense (emphasizing the autonomous choice of ends) and the negative sense (emphasizing the absence of restraint on the pursuit of ends) of liberty. Since both seem to have a clear claim on the attention of agents who wish to exercise free will, it seems as a result that there will be plenty of scope for the value conflicts (which are to be discussed later). On a more substantive note, though, the 'hermeneutic turn' does help in the sense that it draws attention to the incoherence or at best incompleteness of a singular commitment to negative liberty. In this way, hermeneutics provides a negative result on institutional attributes which may indeed be a useful corrective in the current circumstances.

There are two ways to bring out this negative result. One is to appeal to the notion of self creation as something more than preference satisfaction. The other is to notice that the exercise of liberty in the negative sense, say through market exchanges under institutions of well defined property rights as some have argued (for instance Nozick 1974), does not yield a determinate outcome. (This is the problem of multiple equilibria again — the keen appreciation of which, I have associated with hermeneutics.) Thus a commitment to negative liberty does not tell us how to choose between one libertarian outcome and another and since libertarian claims are to be licensed it will not settle the ensuing disputes between those who favour one outcome rather than another. To do this requires the application of some other morally relevant principle (see Varian 1975, and Hargreaves Heap 1989). Naturally, the further moral principle does not have to be drawn from considerations of positive liberty, but given the overall commitment to the exercise of free will, this would seem to be the obvious place to look for such principles.

To arrive at this conclusion from a different route, and indeed a rather more specific and familiar one, it is tempting to endorse the common thought that the capacity to create one self in both the positive and negative sense will depend on material resources. Consequently, Pareto optimality should be considered a desirable attribute of institutions. However, it is well known that most societies face a number of potential optimal outcomes. So this criteria is not decisive and, given the nature of the choice, it seems that selection principle must entail some notion of just distribution. This is certainly familiar enough and would not be worth re-stating were it not for the fact that rather extravagant claims have been recently made on behalf of the negative sense of liberty (for instance, Fukoyama 1989; note that his later work — such as Fukoyama 1995 — is much more sensitive to the normative allegiances which go beyond a simple commitment to negative freedom).[8]

To turn to the issue of what to do when values conflict producing different evaluations of institutions within a community, I shall argue that the hermeneutic recognition of uncertainty which attaches to each individual's values is likely to promote institutions which favour a form of equality between individuals' points of views. There are two strands to this argument (see Hargreaves Heap 1997, for a more general discussion).

Firstly there is always some uncertainty both over the outcomes of a particular set of institutions and over what values an agent will come to hold. As a result, no individual agent can be sure in what degree a particular institution will favour his or her conception of what is valuable. The individual thus finds him or herself behind a modified form of Rawls's (1972) 'veil of ignorance'. And although there are cases where Rawls's veil does not always favour egalitarian outcomes, the thrust of his arguments seem to be in that direction.

Of course, uncertainty need not generate a consensus over the selection of institutions in this fashion. For instance, agents may not adopt the same decision rule behind the veil of ignorance or they may not suffer from uncertainty in quite the same way. Nevertheless, the fact that we recognize that our own values are uncertain ought to entail a respect for values which are different from ours — and this is the nub of the second strand of the argument. How could one deny values to other people when one might come to hold those same values at a later date? Such an action would entail either dynamic inconsistency or regret at a later date or amount to simple foolishness since other people's values are valuable experimental evidence; and so such intolerance should be avoided.

Indeed, several recent political and moral philosophers have argued similarly that the post-modern appreciation that value systems do not have some absolute foundation should not signal a retreat into relativism. Instead, the recognition of diversity should entail a respect for other points of view. For instance, Macintyre (1981, 1988) argues that although value systems are no more than traditions, traditions in good working order must be open to emendation and this involves dialogue with other traditions. In other words, a tradition in good working order presupposes the existence of other traditions. Likewise Hampshire (1989), echoing what I have called the ontological claim of hermeneutics, argues that if there is anything peculiar about the human species, it lies in the individuality of the person. He goes on to suggest that this sense of singularity comes from our individual capacities to form idiosyncratic conceptions of the good. Everyone has an evolving conception of the good and his or her life is organized in some degree around that conception. Thus, what distinguishes us in part as a species is our commitment to singularity and this necessarily entails recognizing that there will be a great diversity of conceptions of the good. Hence, to settle problems of diversity with the use of force, that is essentially by snuffing out the diversity, is to deny something which marks us out as a species. By contrast, the accommodation of diversity through fair procedural mechanisms is re-affirmation of our humanity.

To bolster this claim, Hampshire observes that the clearest example in modern times of those who have tried to settle the conflicts with force are the Nazis; and they precisely demonstrate his thesis. They had no concern with any notion of fairness or justice. It was action rather than argument or talk that was their order of the day and the exercise of power was to require no justification and admit no constraint. There were no arguments with respect to the good, these were only ever the arguments of the weak. Thus, by denying the language of the 'good' to people (rather than disagreeing over the content of a particular language), the Nazis were turning their backs on what it is to be human.

O'Neill (1989a, 1989b) makes a similar point when she argues that Nazis denied the Jews any moral status. She builds her argument by suggesting that the discussion in moral philosophy is often wrongly polarized between idealized and relativized standards of rationality and agency. Neither extreme offers a satisfactory account of moral values. Instead, she argues that we can build a theory of justice on the basis of an acceptance that there is a plurality of potentially interacting and diverse agents.

> What does justice require of such a plurality? At least we can claim that their most basic principles must be ones that *could* be adopted by all. If they were not, at least some agents would have to be excluded from the plurality for whom the principle can hold, whose boundaries would have to be drawn more narrowly.
>
> (O'Neill 1989b: 18)

Thus to accept the existence of a plurality of agents necessarily commits one to be guided by principles which are capable of being universalized, otherwise the application of the principle would undermine the plurality. This seems reasonable enough and offers a practical way of exploring what might be entailed by respect for other opinions. This is not the place to follow the suggestion in any serious way, save to note that O'Neill (1989a) presents some counters to the common criticism of universalizability (namely that it fails to give much bite in the sense of ruling out many value systems, other than extreme cases such as Nazism).

5 CONCLUSION

How far can you get with hermeneutics? The glib answer is further than you would get without it. The importance of hermeneutics lies, of course, in how much further it takes us. I have argued that, in the area of institutional selection, it specifically draws our attention to the role of non-market institutions which are, in part, normatively constituted and I have suggested that it may provide some insight over how to accommodate differences in value systems.

Of course, these are no more than suggestions in this paper, but there is perhaps no better guide to how important the 'hermeneutic turn' might be, if these suggestions are right, than what has occurred (and is happening now) in Eastern Europe and what was the Soviet Union. Nobody needs lessons in what can happen when different value systems cannot be accommodated and one can only gasp at the conventional wisdom which has been responsible for 'selling' the simple institutional recipe of markets plus private property rights to these economies. After all, you really do not need a hermeneutic appreciation of non-market institutions to see the point: a cursory glance at the very diverse economic records of economies during the post-war period which embody markets and private property ought to have cautioned against the simple mindedness of this institutional recipe.

NOTES

* My Thanks go to Stephan Boehm, Peter Earl, Martin Hollis and Serap Kayatekin for comments on an earlier draft and to other participants of the conference at Aldeburgh. The research for this paper was partially supported by the ESRC grant R 000 23 2269 for the project on the Foundations of Rational Choice.

1 Nagel (1986) eloquently argues that it is the tension which comes from recognising the claims of both subjectivity and objectivity which underpins many of the hard philosophical problems which emerge, for instance, in the discussion of 'free will', the relation between mind and body, ethics, scepticism and so on.

2 Multiple rational expectations equilibria abound in models of financial markets and in overlapping generations models because of their recursive structure. They also abound in game theoretic representations of the interactions which comprise the economy largely because coordination

games seem unavoidably embedded in these interactions (see Hargreaves Heap 1992a). The problem of convergence with empirical updating has been widely discussed (see for instance, Bray 1985).

3 This restlessness has obvious Hegelian resonances and Stephan Boehm reminds me in a manner reminiscent of Hegel's discussion of consciousness and self consciousness that the very quest for identity breaks down the dichotomy between subject and object because the subject needs something outside itself to authenticate that its sense of self is something more than a private whim or deception.

4 It is fair to point out that there is some dispute over quite what form of objective constraint there is on self creation in this sense. It is plain that a desire for self creation is unlikely to provide a constraint which singles out one theory rather than another. In this spirit, some might argue that there are objective features of human existence other than the fact that we are interpreters which place further constraints on who we might become. Alternatively, those such as Rorty (1986) seem more inclined to argue that the only constraint is a practical one which arises because any individual act of self creation requires a basically settled sense of who you are. Thus wholesale self creation is an impossibility and only marginal adjustments are possible.

5 Taylor (1989) expresses a similar tension when he discusses the relation between frameworks and individual identity. He argues that the latter requires the former and yet a framework can only operate in this way when it is external to the individual.

6 The same point applies even to those proposals which deal in equalizing initial endowments because they reduce certain incentives since you can no longer pass on your gains to a later generation.

7 Although, this seems as far as it is fair to go. There is perhaps more than a slight suspicion in the conventional account (certainly when it draws on Hayek) that, on evolutionary grounds, we should favour a simple commitment to liberty in Berlin's(1958) negative sense of the absence of restraint.

8 There is a further and less familiar character of institutions which hermeneutics seems to bring out related to the nature of the interaction within the institution. I am somewhat more tentative in advancing this suggestion and so I have confined it to a footnote. The general point here is that a willingness to experiment in new ways of living is not only a function of material resources, although this is important, it is also a positive function of the stability in the background shared commitments in society. This creates a problem in the sense that individual experiments destroy the shared commitments and thus undermine the willingness to experiment. Some institutions may be more or less prone to this kind of collapse (and thus enable more or less experimentation to take place within them) because they encourage in different degrees experiments which

cancel each other out. In other words, institutions which encourage experiments which are self cancelling are to be preferred to those where the experiments cumulate.

REFERENCES

Aghion, P., Hart, O. and Moore, J. (1992) 'The economics of bankruptcy reform', NBER.

Aoki, M. (1990) 'Toward an economic model of the Japanese firm', *Journal of Economic Literature* 28: 1–27.

Berlin, I. (1958) 'Two concepts of liberty', reprinted in his (1969) *Four Essays on Liberty*,. Oxford: Clarendon Press.

Bernstein, R. 1983) *Beyond Objectivity and Relativism*, Oxford: Basil Blackwell.

Bray, M. (1985) 'Rational expectations, information and asset prices', *Oxford Economic Papers* 37: 161–95.

Buchanan, J. (1991) 'Economics in the post-socialist century', *Economic Journal* 101: 15–21.

Davidson, P. (1978) *Money and the Real World*, London: Macmillan.

Frey, B. (1997) *Not Just for the Money*, Cheltenham: Edward Elgar.

Fukuyama, F. (1989) 'The end of history?', *The National Interest*, Summer, 3–18.

—— (1995) *Trust*, Harmondsworth: Penguin.

Gadamer, H-G. (1975) 'The historicity of understanding', in Connerton, F (ed.) (1976) *Essays in Critical Sociology*, Harmondsworth: Penguin.

Douglas, M. and Isherwood, B. (1978) *The World of Goods*, Harmondsworth: Penguin.

Gerrard, W. (1990) 'On matters methodological', *Journal of Economic Surveys* 4: 197–219.

Gilbert, M. (1989) *On Social Facts*, London: Routledge.

Hahn, F. H. (1992), 'Reflections', *Royal Economic Society Newsletter*, April.

Hampshire, S. (1989) *Innocence and Experience*, London: Penguin.

Hardy, C. and Clegg, S. (1997) 'Relativity without relativism: reflexivity in post-paradigm organization studies' , *British Journal of Management* 8, special issue: S5–S17.

Hargreaves Heap S. P. (1989) *Rationality in Economics*, Oxford: Basil Blackwell.

—— (1992) *The New Keynesian Macroeconomics: Time, Belief and Social Interdependence.*, Aldershot: Edward Elgar.

—— (1997) 'The economic consequences of pluralism', in Salanti, A. and Screpanti, E. (eds) *Pluralism in Economics*, Cheltenham: Edward Elgar.

Hollis, M. (1985) 'The Emperor's newest clothes', *Economics and Philosophy* 1: 128–33.

── (1987) *The Cunning of Reason*, Cambridge: Cambridge University Press.

Lavoie, D. (ed.) (1990) *Hermeneutics and Economics*, London: Routledge.

Lawson, T. (1997) 'On criticizing the practices of economists: a case for interventionist methodology', in Salanti, A and Screpanti, E. (eds) *Pluralism in Economics*, Cheltenham: Edward Elgar.

Levine, A., Sober, E. and Olin Wright, E. (1987) 'Marxism and methodological individualism', *New Left Review* 162: 67–84.

Macintyre, A. (1981) *After Virtue*, London: Duckworth.

── (1988) *Whose Justice, Which Rationality?*, London: Duckworth.

Maki, U. (1988) 'How to combine rhetoric and realism in the methodology of economics', *Economics and Philosophy* 4: 89–109.

McCloskey, D. (1983) 'The rhetoric of economics', *Journal of Economic Literature* 21: 481–517.

Muth, J. (1961), 'Rational expectations and the theory of price movements', *Econometrica* 29: 315–35.

Nagel, T. (1986) *The View from Nowhere*, Oxford: Oxford University Press.

Nozick, R. (1974) *Anarchy, State and Utopia*, Oxford: Basil Blackwell.

O'Neill, O. (1989a) *Constructions of Reason*, Cambridge: Cambridge University Press.

── (1989b) 'Justice, gender and international boundaries', WIDER Working Paper 68.

Ozanne, J. (1998) 'Hermeneutics', in Earl, P. E. and Kemp, S. (eds) *The Elgar Companion to Consumer Research and Economic Psychology*, Cheltenham: Edward Elgar.

Rawls, J. (1972) *A Theory of Justice*, Oxford: Oxford University Press.

Ricoeur, P. (1981) *Hermeneutics and Human Science*, translated and edited by T. Thompson, Cambridge: Cambridge University Press.

Rorty, R. (1986) 'Contingency of language', 'Contingency of selfhood', 'Contingency of community', *London Review of Books*, April–July.

Shackle, G. L. S. (1966) *The Nautre of Economic Thought: Selected Papers 1955–1964*, Cambridge: Cambridge University Press.

── (1967) *The Years of High Theory*, Cambridge: Cambridge University Press

── (1988) *Business, Time and Thought*, edited by S.F. Frowen, London: Macmillan.

Taylor, C. (1989) *Sources of the Self.*, Cambridge: Cambridge University Press.

Varian, H. (1975), 'Distributive justice, welfare economics and the theory of fairness', *Philosophy and Public Affairs*: 223–47.

Venkatesh, A. (1998) 'Postmodernism', in Earl, P. E. and Kemp, S. (eds) *The Elgar Companion to Consumer Research and Economic Psychology*, Cheltenham: Edward Elgar.

Weber, M. (1922) *Economy and Society*, edited by G. Roth and C. Wittich, 1968, New York: Bedminster Press.

8

UNCERTAINTY, PRIVATE PROPERTY AND BUSINESS ENTERPRISE IN THE TRANSITION TO A MARKET ECONOMY

J. A. Kregel

1 DIFFERENT CONCEPTIONS OF CHOICE

Traditional microeconomic theory is often described as the theory of choice. However, George Shackle, a life-long critic of traditional theory, also insisted that economic theory be grounded in the problem of choice. His conception of choice was rather different. For traditional theory, choice was related to the problem of allocating scarce means amongst multiple ends. Choice was denial — there is no such thing as a free lunch, so we have to decide what we have to give up in order to have lunch. The market was the instrument of allocating denial amongst the population. Those least willing to be denied, were willing to pay more to satisfy their ends with the scarce means.

For Shackle choice was freedom — the origination of an idea in the imagination that would overcome existing constraints and which would bring something new and unexpected to the table.[1] Choice was liberating, not constraining. The market existed because there was uncertainty over the viability of the various schemes for overcoming the constraints of the existing situation. It indicated new directions.

There has been a great deal of discussion of the macroeconomic stabilization policies most appropriate to the transformation of the Eastern and Central European economies from centralized command systems to decentralized market systems. However, even though they are macroeconomic in nature, they are based on the traditional conception of choice as denial due to scarcity of existing resources relative to the multiplicity of ends to be achieved. Indeed, it is not always clear what those multiple ends are, aside from a generic reference to the 'transformation' of the economy from a command system to a 'free' market-based system of decision making. Usually they are simply to eliminate inflation and produce economic recovery.

The content of these policies, now generally known as 'shock treatment' or the 'big bang' approach, has been quite uniform across countries; they usually involve action to balance the government budget, control of the money supply to produce positive real interest rates, eliminate all State price and output subsidies, tariffs and controls, the introduction of free trade in goods and capital, and convertibility of the currency.

The results of these policies have not been encouraging. As a rough rule of thumb, industrial output has fallen by around 50 per cent in those economies that have initiated the process of transformation via the big bang. As a result of their negative influence on demand and income, means that were scarce, have got much scarcer. Granted, there was a great deal of production that was incapable of meeting any of the multiple ends and there was no level of price at which it could be sold;[2] it existed just to ease the fulfillment of centrally planned production targets. The famous jokes about the nail factory that met its output quotas by producing one-hundred-pound nails gave a new meaning to the idea of the benefits associated with economies of scale. Informed estimates now place such unmarketable production as high as 25 per cent of total industrial output.

But, that still leaves unexplained half of the decline in the output of industry. Where is the missing output? Part of it can be explained directly by the macro impacts of the transformation policies which, as already mentioned, were designed to decrease purchasing power and real wages. This is the problem of eliminating the 'currency' overhang. In rough terms, the overhang was created by the unsold, unwanted output of hundred pound nails and so forth which produced incomes, but not expenditures. Reducing it by means of inflation, as occurred in Poland, meant reducing demand for saleable goods as well. Thus some of the additional decrease in output can be explained by the attempt to reduce the means of purchasing to the available ends.

2 THE THEORY OF CHOICE AND MACROECONOMIC STABILIZATION POLICY

These macro policies were justified on the basis of the belief that the production inefficiencies of the Eastern economies stem from the prolonged period of protection from the necessity of making choices caused by the absence of price competition under central planning. The basic problem to be resolved was how to best introduce the economics of 'choice', in other words, to introduce the market allocation process based on freely determined prices. The first step was thought to be the introduction of private ownership of State property to break the control of the State on private economic decision making.[3]

After the privatization of the economy, the next problem to be resolved in converting the planned economy to market conditions was the introduction of a rational, market-based domestic price structure. It was also generally thought that this should take place as rapidly as possible, since it is a precondition for the reallocation of resources necessary for the reconstruction of domestic industry. It is evident that the new price structure could not be introduced by means of central direction, but in the early stages of transformation there is no domestic market capable of producing the correct, market determined, competitive prices. The resolution of this dilemma was to open the economy to foreign competition: the competition from international producers was to impose international market prices on the domestic economy and thus instantly produce competitive market prices in internal markets.

It is for this reason that convertibility of the currency is also an integral part of the macroeconomic policy required to produce transition to a market-based allocation process, rather than as a final step to be undertaken after the completion of reconstruction, as was the case of post-war reconstruction in western European in the 1950s. International prices can only prevail in the internal market if there is free trade; free trade can only take place if domestic residents are free to buy foreign goods and they have this freedom of choice only if the domestic currency is convertible into foreign currency to permit the unconstrained purchase of foreign goods. Convertibility is thus required, as a minimum, for current account transactions. And, convertibility must be at stable exchange rates to ensure that exchange rate fluctuations do not create instability and uncertainty in domestic relative prices. The introduction of market choice thus implies instant introduction of convertibility of the currency at stable exchange rates and the elimination of any impediments to international trade such as government price subsidies or production support schemes.[4]

There are a number of superficial criticisms that might be made of this reasoning. For example, it is based on the presumption that internationally traded goods are exchanged at competitively determined market prices, when a substantial proportion of internationally traded goods trade at administered or subsidized prices. Agricultural goods, textiles, steel and automobiles are just a few examples of goods which trade at prices which are influenced by government subsidies or formal or informal quality controls. Indeed, the idea that there is an international market which serves as an exemplar for the kind of competitive market system the transforming countries are trying to introduce seems unfounded since a large proportion of trade in the global economy now takes place between the international branches of multinational firms, but the evidence on transfer pricing suggests that the conditions which determine them are far from freely competitive.[5]

The same sort of criticism may be made of privatization. The rationale for rapid privatization was to introduce private decision making into the production process. But the absence of domestic buyers with sufficient capital to combine ownership with effective management control has meant that there is no more effective market control over firm managers than under central planning. Foreign buyers have been motivated to defend market share and many have not even bothered to operate the production facilities that they have acquired, or have simple used them as assembly points for actual production done by skilled labour in plants located in the western economies. Thus, there has been little 'transfer' or market skills and practices and few of the spin-offs and linkage effects normally associated with the introduction of a full production operation.

3 PRIVATIZATION, BUSINESS ENTERPRISE AND THE 'MISSING' OUTPUT

The effects of the big bang macro policy effects cannot explain the entire fall in industrial output that the transforming economies have experienced, nor does it apply in countries that did not resort to devaluation of the domestic currency. East Germany is an example of a transforming country in which the domestic currency was even revalued. But, there is something more fundamental in the way the dispersion of State-owned assets was undertaken which helps to explain the extreme fall in output.

If the naive belief that private property and the elimination of controls would automatically produce transformation as the 'market' replaced economic commands is discarded, again, the basic idea behind the policy of privatization was the application of the traditional theory of choice. Most industries in the Eastern European socialist planned economies were part of large, vertically integrated production structures meant to exploit the economies of scale and centralization of information and control. From the point of view of traditional theory, this production structure was thus viewed as an agglomeration of productive assets, the given means, that were combined in ways which were inappropriate to meeting the multiple ends of consumers exercising their freedom of choice via the market. Since socialist managers were not free to combine factors of production in the most optimal way to maximize output or return — this was done by the central planners rather than by consumers expressing their sovereignty in the market — the introduction of free choice should have eliminated inefficiency and thus increased the productivity of the existing factors of production. This was one of the theoretical arguments in favour of the privatization of State-owned enterprises via the rapid sale of State-owned assets. The problem was particularly acute in Eastern Germany where State industry, following the logic of economies of scale, was organized in the form of extremely large production monopolies. Thus the large 'kombinats' had to be broken up in order to promote the necessary conditions for market competition, as well as to allow the reorganize of the given means to better meet the multiple ends chosen via the market mechanism.[6]

But, privatization carried out in this way meant that the evaluation of the assets and their place in a productive structure was determined by the existing productive and market conditions of the buyers, which in almost all cases were western (usually German) firms, rather than as part of an efficient independent evaluation of optimal production. The most frequently given examples relate to peculiar conditions of vertical and horizontal integration within State owned enterprises.

In general, since it was difficult to insure supplies and replacement parts, many production units developed very efficient 'procurement' agents, and highly skilled technical repair shops. The latter became the equivalent of highly skilled machine tool producers. If any equipment broke, since it was unlikely that replacements could be procured rapidly, if at all, they were required to produce the spare parts, and in some cases to completely build and rebuild production equipment via a process known as 'reverse engineering'.[7]

However, the western buyer of State-owned assets was usually interested in acquiring or defending market share by buying out a potential competitor, or in acquiring the site value of plant, or even less often, the productive capacity for the basic product. Thus the engineering shops that had been built up had no market value and the skilled labour employed in them immediately laid off.[8]

The same arguments apply to the unofficial procurement departments, which were the equivalent of supply and sales-marketing departments in market oriented firms. They had no value to the firm acquiring State assets, which obviously had already existing facilities for this purpose; thus another set of skilled workers were lost. Both of these types of labour might have been employed productively if the privatization of State assets had been organized differently. Thus, the value of the privatized productive assets was primarily influenced not by their optimal combination in forming a national production structure, but in how they fit into existing western production organizations — usually very badly.

This is where Shackle's alternative conception of the problem of choice as an imaginative act might have been employed to great benefit to the transformation process. For example, only a little imagination would be required to see the engineering–repair shops as embryo machine tool producing firms, or the procurement sections as wholesale trading firms. But, this would have required the provision of capital, and above all management organization to form a production unit and to identify a potential market. In this context, the 'scarce' factor is not the financial capital or the physical capital equipment, but the 'organizational' capital (see Tomer 1987, Tremblay 1995) and the time required to form the factors into a new combination in which the existing factors would have a higher productive potential than if they were sold piecemeal into an already existing western firm.

The same arguments apply to physical productive structures which were not of the latest vintage or highest productivity and thus of no value to a western firm, but which might have been able to be reorganized into a production unit to sell into international markets, given differences in labour costs.[9]

4 THE 'OPTIMAL' POLICY OF THE PRIVATIZATION AGENCY

From the point of view of the 'liberating' theory of choice the privatization agency should try to think as a potential entrepreneur, starting afresh 'to conceive a scheme which will best take advantage of the evolving environment' and to act 'like a palaeontologist seeking to re-construct a vast skeleton from a few bones' of existing information (Shackle 1988: 106). It should thus form new units, or offer the blueprints of business plans, to potential entrepreneurs. Western expertise has been used extensively in privatization agencies, but usually only to determine the 'free market' value of assets or combinations or assets, not to formulate business plans and organization for the best utilization of State assets. The privatization agency has, in a sense to replace the central planning agency, but it has to do so by learning the same business organization and planning that is practised by any large corporation operating in a free market economy. It should also adopt the same sort of actions that are practised by every industrial development agency in the US which actively seeks industrial investment by indicating the potential value of local assets if combined according to an imaginative business scheme.

The business plans would then be really free choices, and the valuations would come close to market value. Again, to take a simple example, the valuation of a manufacturing plant, with clearly outdated equipment, would be close to zero and possibly negative if introduced into the production structure of a western firm, while it may be in a location in which a minimum investment in an alternative use would produce an increase in potential value. It is the maximum potential value in any use, not the existing value in existing use, which should be the aim of the privatization agency. It should be the responsibility of the planning agency not only to value the assets according to the alternative potential uses, but to draw attention to these uses.

The results would be different from the values placed on the assets by potential acquirers who are working from existing business plans and with already acquired assets and strategies. Although it need not always be the case, but it seems likely, that these latter valuations will be different from those produced under conditions of free choice as indicated in Shackle's approach.

The pressure to introduce competitive international prices and to raise foreign exchange by means of the sale of State-owned assets thus has meant that these assets are being sold at below their potential value and combined in less than optimal ways. The result is a loss in the productivity of the existing assets compared to their use before the elimination of central planning. This helps to explain the great paradox of the transformation process: in most countries the standard of living is now lower than it was under command economy socialism. It helps explain the additional losses in output which occurred in excess of those linked to the decline in demand due to the policies to eliminate inflation and the monetary overhang. Many potentially productive assets were sold at knockdown prices and then simply junked, when they might have continued to contribute to saleable output had the privatization been carried out under the Shacklean conception of choice.

5 THE ROLE OF THE STATE IN TRANSFORMING STATE PROPERTY

In the absence of indigenous entrepreneurial activity, the privatization agency will have to combine the tasks of 'privatizing' state property with the formulation of the business organizations and strategies required to produce their maximum value. However, this application of Shackle's approach to the transformation problem raises what is a seemingly unsurmountable impediment to the success of transformation from planning to the market. The progressive, democratic forces in the transforming countries generally identify the role of the State in economic affairs with the influence of the Communist party and centralized planning. Thus, transformation to the market means the complete elimination of the government from the operation of the economy.

However, the elimination of the State planning apparatus has not automatically introduced markets, nor the market forces required to replace the organizing activities of the central planner. Nor is it obvious that market forces are any more capable of spontaneously producing transformation and recovery than they were in the western economies in the 1930s. Indeed, the eagerness to introduce market prices has impeded measures to introduce the institutions and initial conditions necessary for the creation of markets. As a result, it is the most progressive forces in the transforming economies which have embraced the policies based on the traditional theory of choice and which have produced both depression and the preclusion of the State to intervene even when the free operation of market forces is incapable of producing recovery and transformation. Thus, the very government policies that allowed the industrialized world to recover from depression in the 1930s are excluded on political grounds.

But, if we follow Shackle's approach to the theory of choice, it is clear that the importance of the government in the economy is not in its direct interference with market forces, but first in indicating the way imagination should be used in formulating business plans and evaluating business outcomes. This might include the provision of training in techniques of scenario planning (see Jefferson 1983; Loasby 1990) or creative and open-minded thinking (a useful starting point would be Nolan 1981). Beyond that, the role of the State is limited to setting the confines within which the rival business hypotheses envisaged by the privatization agency or the private entrepreneurs are formulated by defining the range between what Shackle called 'focus' gains and losses. To influence these factors does not require either government ownership of means of production, nor control or economic activity. Rather the appropriate use of the privatization agency and government expenditure policy is necessary. The role of government is not to set or influence prices, but to indicate business plans, and in placing limits on focus losses, by engaging in active policy to assure a minimum level of activity and thus a maximum focus loss on business projects.

6 STATE DEVELOPMENT AGENCIES

One possibility would be for the government to form investment banks which would take joint-ventures, meeting all up-front capital costs, and being repaid only after the company becomes self-sustaining, by sale to the operators or to other private investors. Indeed, even the formation of new investment banks could be joint-ventures of this type. This is not a new proposal. The Reconstruction Finance Corporation Act of the Hoover administration, used to great effect by the Roosevelt administration in the United States in fighting the depression, is a precedent. In Italy the Institute for Industrial Reconstruction, formed in 1932 to remove from private banks' balance sheets the shares of firms in difficulties resulting from the depression, provides another variant on the same theme. The German government used the Golddiskontobank to take equity positions in failing banks and extend emergency credits in the bank crisis of 1931. In all three cases, government was used on the micro level to indicate and lead the process of industrial transformation and reconstruction in the private sector, and to provide the assurance of a sufficiently buoyant economy to support these initiatives through aggregate expenditure policy.

While these historical examples were more concerned with reorganizing existing productive units, they were usually motivated by the belief that efficient firms were experiencing difficulties which were not of their own causing, but due to macroeconomic effects over which they had no direct control. In the transforming economies energy must be concentrated on the creation of new firms, on the recombination of assets in new ways, rather than on the preservation of the old.[10]

There will inevitably be losses in these ventures. Indeed, the whole point is to allow losses to be made without creating excessively negative impacts on individual investment decisions, and on the overall level of output, for it is only in this way that true innovation and reconstruction can take place.

Such an approach means, however, that the policies of instant privatization and complete absence of the government in economic affairs must be abandoned without this being interpreted as a return to the old system of State control. Until this internal contradiction concerning the role of the government in economic activity is resolved, not only will there be no recovery, there will be no transformation. The expectations of the economic and social benefits that the market mechanism were to produce will be disappointed. History has taught that government intervention in conditions of instability is necessary, but that it can take widely divergent forms. By denying this role to government the transforming economies have made the task allocated to the market doubly difficult. Not only must the market produce recovery from depression, it must also transform their productive structure to compete with western producers. The spontaneous action of the market has already been shown to be inadequate to the first task. The second takes the form of a series of crucial experiments whose outcomes can only be concentrated on focus gains if the role of government is reconsidered in the Eastern European economies.

NOTES

* Some of the points contained in this chapter represent an elaboration of arguments I presented in Kregel, Matzner and Grabher (1992). I am also grateful for detailed comments from Peter Earl., out of which have grown some of the notes below .

1 Shackle's alternative view of the nature of choice can be linked to a variety of themes in the heterodox literature that relate to the problem of achieving economic growth.. At the macro level, Shackle's conception links to the contrast between the neoclassical growth-accounting literature, whose supply-constrained view contrasts with the Post Keynesian demand-constrained analysis that rejects the full employment assumption At the level of the firm, the link is to the Stirling school (for example, Loasby 1976) who see the supply side as dependent on the use of the imagination for solving problems. Somewhere between the micro- and macro-levels of analysis comes the question of the extent to which policy makers can shape consumer confidence and business sentiment and how far manufacturers can move their demand curves to the right by changing the scale and/or content of their promotional campaigns in a way that fired up the imagination of potential buyers (compare Galbraith 1958, Katona 1960, and the Shackle-inspired contribution by Littlechild 1982).

2 Instances of output which could not be sold at any price do not mesh well with the neoclassical economists' faith in the principle of gross substitution. However, they are perfectly compatible with the emphasis accorded to lexicographic and checklist-based decision rules in behavioural economics (see Earl 1995: ch. 4).

3 The economics of the transition are not confined to former socialist economies. The deflationary policies and post-protection shock therapy have a major parallel in the case of New Zealand, a country which prior to the 1970s oil shocks was characterized by both a high degree of regulation and negligible unemployment. Since 1984, extreme free-market policies and tight money have been associated with very poor productivity growth, high unemployment and a chronic current account problem, with many of the privatized enterprises becoming foreign owned (see Hazledine 1998, Jesson 1999). Notable technological success stories seem far less related to the reforms rather than to 'Kiwi ingenuity' (in other words, imagination):

examples include world-class computer graphics products and the Britten motorcycle, built almost entirely in-house in a small workshop and which won the Daytona 500 with technology way ahead of the major international teams.

4   This raises the subsidiary problem of the particular exchange rate which is to be set. Why will the National Bank be any better at fixing the 'correct' price of foreign currency than the planners would have been at setting the 'correct' goods prices? It also raises the problem of the appropriate accumulation of exchange reserves to offset variations from the fixed parity.

5   It is interesting to note that those countries which have been granted associate status by the EEC have in many cases had to reintroduce controls and tariffs which they had only recently eliminated in the belief that international market prices were determined without government intervention.

6   In other countries, such as Hungary, the creation of individual enterprise units on the pattern of free market firms had started more than a decade earlier, and there privatization could proceed on the basis of individual production units. (see also note 9 below and Stark 1998).

7   This is a technique that was used to great benefit by Japanese corporations. The difference was that in Japan the process took place on leading edge technology whereas in the Eastern European countries it was on 1950s technology.

8   Once again, there are striking parallels with New Zealand. Prior to the reforms of the past decade or so, import controls ensured that New Zealanders had expensive cars, mostly assembled locally from imported kits. Geographical isolation and a small market made imported spare parts supplies unreliable. However, motoring was actually quite cheap (enabling the country to have the third highest number of vehicle per capita) because cars had glacial depreciation rates: they were kept going for many years longer than in the rest of the developed world   via expertise in reconditioning and repair. With the removal of tariffs and the closures of assembly plants, consumers switched to cheap but rapidly-depreciating used Japanese imports and the reconditioning market largely collapsed (though exports of classic car restoration services are a telling vestige of the former regime).

9   For a more encouraging perspective one can turn to Stark (1998), who has recently examined the reform process in Hungary with a focus on the ways in which 'actors in the post-socialist context are rebuilding organizations and institutions not *on the ruins* but *with the ruins* of communism as they redeploy available resources in response to their immediate practical dilemmas' (Stark 1998: 117, italics in original). He suggests that this 'recombinant' approach is producing a new kind of mixed economy. This approach links readily to Shackle's view of the way

that the imagination works in a kind of alphabet soup manner using a limited repertoire of elements to come up with new ideas (Shackle 1979: 24) (see also the chapter by Potts in this volume). It also runs parallel with recent work by Pavitt (1999) on the way that modern giant firms in the West strategically employ multiple technologies in novel combinations to produce new products for newly perceived market niches.

10 Here, lessons might be learned by examining the role played in Japanese reconstruction and development after 1945 (see Gao 1998) and in structural adjustments during the 1970s (see Dore 1986) by bodies such as the Headquarters of Productivity and MITI. The Japanese system has not been based on free-market neoclassical thinking. According to Gao (1998: 97–8), the Japanese system for promoting innovation and corporate change was directly linked to work on industrial dynamism by Schumpeter via a number of senior public servants (most notably Nakayama Ichiro, vice president of the Headquarters of Productivity in the late 1950s) having studied with Schumpeter.

REFERENCES

Dore, R. (1986) *Flexible Rigidities: Industrial Policy and Structural Adjustment in the Japanese Economy, 1970–1980*, London: Athlone Press.

Earl, P. E. (1995) *Microeconomics for Business and Marketing*, Aldershot: Edward Elgar.

Galbraith, J. K. (1958) *The Affluent Society*, London, Hamish Hamilton.

Gao, B. (1998) 'Efficiency, culture, and politics: the transformation of Japanese management in 1946–66', Callon, M. (ed.) *The Laws of the Markets*, Oxford, Blackwell./Sociological Review.

Hazledine, T. (1998) *Taking New Zealand Seriously: The Economics of Decency*, Auckland: HarperCollins.

Jefferson, M. (1983) 'Economic uncertainty and business decision making', in Wiseman, J. (ed.) *Beyond Positive Economics?*, London: Macmillan.

Jesson, B. (1999) *Only Their Purpose is Mad: The Money Men Take Over NZ*, Palmerston North: Dunmore Press.

Katona, G. (1960) *The Powerful Consumer*, New York: McGraw-Hill.

Kregel, J. A., Matzner, E. and Grabber, G. ((1992) *Market Shock: An Agenda for the SocioEconomic Reconstruction of Central and Eastern Europe*. Ann Arbor, MI, Michigan University Press (in German as *Der Markt Schock*, Sigma: Berlin),).

Littlechild, S. C. (1982) 'Controls on Advertising: An Examination of Some Economic Arguments', *Journal of Advertising* 1: 25–37.

Loasby, B. J. (1976) *Choice, Complexity and Ignorance*, Cambridge: Cambridge University Press.

—— (1990) 'The use of scenarios in business planning', in Frown, S.F. (ed.) *Unknowledge and Choice in Economics*, London: Macmillan.

Nolan, V. (1981) 'Open to change', *Management Decision* 19, 2 (monograph).

Pavitt, K. (1999) 'Divisions of labour in the innovating firm', in Dow, S. C. and Earl, P. E (eds) *Contingency, Complexity and the theory of the Firm*, Cheltenham: Edward Elgar.

Shackle, G. L. S. (1979) *Imagination and the Nature of Choice*, Edinburgh: Edinburgh University Press.

—— (1988) 'On the nature of profit,' reprinted in Frowen, S.F. (ed.) *Business, Time and Thought*, London: Macmillan.

Stark, D. (1988) 'Recombinant property in East European capitalism', in Callon, M. (ed.) *The Laws of the Markets*, Oxford, Blackwell./Sociological Review.

Tomer, J. (1987) *Organizational Capital: The Path to Higher Productivity and Wellbeing*, New York: Praeger.

Tremblay, P., (1995) 'The organizational assets of the learning firm', *Human Systems Management* 14: 7–20.

9

UNCERTAINTY, COMPLEXITY AND IMAGINATION

Jason Potts

Time comes into it.
Say it.
Say it.
The Universe is made of Stories,
Not of Atoms
(Muriel Rukeyser 1960: 111)

1 INTRODUCTION

Epistemics or axiomatics: that is the question. Axiomatics defines information, knowledge, and expectations as identical constructs. Furthermore, it denies that there exists choice beyond the pale of perfect rationality and consequently finds no place for the faculty of imagination. Shackle rejected axiomatics because he believed that these epistemic constructs were distinct and that uncertainty and imagination were legitimate objects of inquiry. He was clear about where things had gone wrong, too (Time comes into it...). Specifically, he suggested that theorists had misconstrued the temporal structure of the economic universe and the locus of the agent in the space–time continuum. Death and taxes aside, events generally have to happen before we know about them with certainty. He also observed that agents are not isotropic entities smeared uniformly over the space-time continuum. The agent does not exist at all points in space-time but rational choice theory is mathematically set up as if this is so, a fiction that is arguably the most fundamental in economic theory.[1]

This problem has been 'solved' in various ways. Debreu's (1959) contingent commodity markets allow agents to exist over the entire space–ime continuum. Rational Expectations defines the future as

187

complete sets of probability functions, thus also collapsing it back into the present. Shackle instead made an absolute distinction between two sorts of information entering the calculus of choice. One sort is constructed from known events and exists as objective information. The other sort is constructed from unknown imagined events and consists of subjective possibilities. Shackle insisted that this latter class, known generally as *expectations*, could not be treated in the same way as real data because they are simply not made of the same thing. Expectation is a vast parallel network of interdependent belief constructed from what is objectively speaking nothing but imagination and inertia — immanence and imminence. Axiomatics can deal with what is already given (Shackle 1972: 26), but only epistemics can analyze the space in between.

Most analysts found this distinction untenable and declared Shackle's epistemics hopelessly nihilistic. It cannot be denied that Shackle's writing was provocative and almost solicitous of nihilism, but to read this as the content of his message is both unfair and misleading. For Shackle, all information (entering into the moment of choice) is both cognitively and socially constructed. Specifically, some information is constructed from real events, some from imaginary events. The implication was that although construction from real events may afford a reasonable stability to the framework of choice, and even underpin a scheme of axiomatics and equilibrium analysis, a system constructed from imaginary events will be of an entirely different nature. In a word, it will be *kaleidic*. So there are two streams feeding into the moment of choice — a calm stream of known events and a turbulent stream of expectations. But the superposition of the two will still retain the character of turbulence.[2] Shackle argues that this turbulence is epistemic in origin.

In this chapter I set out to elucidate the nature of this instability from the perspective of complex systems theory. In Section 2, show the relationship between epistemics and complex systems theory. In Section 3, the topographical format is used to show the reflexive relationship between micro and macro uncertainty. Section 4 then shows how the mathematics of Genetic Algorithms may provide a formal basis for the concept of the economic imagination.

2 KALEIDICS AND COMPLEX SYSTEMS THEORY

Shackle's 'kaleidic' image refers to the dynamic properties of a system. Its message is that small rearrangements in the micro-configuration of the system can (although do not necessarily) produce quite spectacular changes in the pattern of the system as a whole. Shackle never really attempted to go beneath this metaphor, to ask *why* small local changes can sometimes escalate so dramatically. He simply noted that it is a pervasive phenomenon in economics, operated principally through expectations (and hence was epistemic in nature), and that due to its direct affect on variables such as investment and consumption was of fundamental importance. Elsewhere in science, and particularly in the past twenty years or so, a powerful integrative force has drawn the synthesis of combinatorial and non-linear mathematics into dynamical systems theory.[3] One of the key discoveries in this field has been the existence of the regime of Complexity (also known as 'the edge of chaos') which has dynamical properties that can well be thought of as 'kaleidic'. In this section I will show that Shackle's Kaleidic Epistemics can be translated directly into Complex Systems Theory once the concept of uncertainty is interpreted as a statement about the topography of connections within the system.

Dynamical systems theory is a mathematical framework for the study of emergent properties in (potentially vast) networks of interconnected elements.[4] Boolean networks are a particular class of dynamical system in which the state of each element in the lattice is represented as a binary variable (for example, on or off) as a function of the prior state of some set of specific other elements elsewhere in the lattice.[5] The theoretical biologist Stuart Kauffman describes the characteristic dynamics of Boolean networks as follows:

Random Boolean networks are a vast family of disordered systems. Yet we find that they exhibit three broad regimes of behaviour: ordered, complex, and chaotic. In the ordered regime, many elements in the system freeze into fixed states of activity. These frozen elements form a large connected cluster, or frozen component, which spans, or percolates, across the system and leaves behind isolated islands of unfrozen elements. In the chaotic regime, there is no frozen component. Instead, a connected cluster of unfrozen elements, percolates across the system, leaving behind isolated frozen islands. In this chaotic regime, small changes in initial conditions unleash avalanches of changes which propagate to many other unfrozen elements. ... The transition region, on the edge between order and chaos, is the complex regime. Here the frozen component is just percolating and the unfrozen component just ceasing to percolate. In this transition region, altering the activity of single unfrozen elements unleashes avalanches of change with a characteristic size distribution having many small and few large avalanches.

(Kauffman 1993: 174)

Now compare this with Shackle's description of kaleidics.

The 'facts' at best are like a few pieces of coloured stone or glass intended for a mosaic, and the task of expectation is to design the mosaic as a whole from the suggestions offered by those few disconnected fragments. A slight, accidental rearrangement of the scattered fragments can reveal new possibilities and configurations, can call for new *tesserae* of hitherto unthought of kinds and colours to fill out what is to hand, and can produce novelty in a moment of inspiration. The kaleidoscope ... seems to epitomize in some sense the limitless richness of mutations and the incalculable instability of the task of expectation-forming. The economic society whose affairs depend upon on its valuations of desirable equipment can perhaps be suggestively labelled *kaleidic*.

(Shackle's 1972: 428)

The crucial point is that both images differ from the 'conventional' space of dynamics — the real field R^n — by allowing the connective structure of the space to be the essential variable governing the macro-dynamics of the system. What the topographical framework of complex systems theory allows us is a way of revealing the sorts of microstructure that would generate different characteristic patterns of macro-dynamics. Shackle's kaleidics is an image of the macro: Kauffman shows the sort of microstructure that would generate it. Of course this mapping of kaleidics into topographic complexity is only suggestive,[6] but it does serve to highlight what is really going on with

Shackle's Epistemics. The sort of dynamical behaviour that is observed in Boolean networks is a direct function of how many other elements the behaviour of each element depends on: as the density of connections in a system increases, so does its chaotic potential. Shackle comes at this from the other direction, first witnessing turbulence in expectations, then asking what might be causing it. Keynes also approached the matter in this way, and arrived at a relation between choice, expectations and uncertainty that found radical uncertainty as the origin of instability.[7] Keynes wrote:

> In abnormal times in particular, when the hypothesis of an indefinite continuance of the existing state of affairs is less plausible than usual even though there are no express grounds to anticipate a definite change, the market will be subject to waves of optimistic and pessimistic sentiment, which are unreasoning and yet in a sense legitimate where no solid basis exists for a reasonable calculation.
>
> (Keynes 1936/1973: 154)

For Keynes, then, the investment decision always has a component of uncertainty that is irreducible to known probabilities. Keynes (1936/1973: 162) accepted that the system was fundamentally incomplete, and so introduced a psychological force to keep the system alive; such that 'if the animal spirits are dimmed and spontaneous optimism falters, leaving us to depend on nothing but mathematical expectation, enterprise will fade and die.'[8] So for Keynes it was not the existence of uncertainty *per se* that accounted for instability, but that the space opened by uncertainty was then filled with an unstable compound, just as a fissure opened in bedrock is invariably filled by the most fluid substance nearby. So the principle that nature abhors a vacuum can be considered true in psychics as well as in physics. Two questions are now important: (1) Why is there uncertainty?; and (2) Why, given this, are expectations necessarily an unstable mass? I will treat these in turn.

In an ergodic, knowable, fully time-reversible world, expectations necessarily refer to a sequence of unfolding events that can be *ex ante* fitted back to the present.[9] The two obvious limitations to the convergence of expectations and event outcomes are the requirement that initial conditions be perfectly specified and that the dynamic equations used for the projection are the 'correct' ones.[10] Curiously, the tacit acceptance of these respectively impossible and unknowable conditions is termed Rational Expectations (see Richardson 1959). However a more devastating critique of the perfectibility of expectation formation rests on neither of these Laplacean aspects, but on the logical impossibility of accounting for the effects of decisions not yet made. For example, political decisions about taxation and welfare support, managerial decisions about investment, entrepreneurial decisions about new services or products, all such things have the potential for massive impact on the lives of individuals, but before the event they are nothing but the potential for instability. Yet there is no rational means for placing such things on an actuarial basis. You may not be presently able to appreciate the full impact of the as-yet-unknown sport of Feezal-ball, but then few people fully grasped the significance of the computer revolution before it happened either. So while it is perhaps reasonable to suppose that developments in science and technology may go some way toward reducing 'Laplacean' uncertainty, it can never be eliminated so long as future decisions remain undetermined. In fact the historical record shows plainly that in our efforts to know more about the world, and presumably to be better at predicting it, we also learn new and unexpected ways of changing it. Another name for uncertainty is free-will.

The second question — Why are expectations unstable? — was answered by Keynes, Townshend and Shackle alike (see Loasby 1976: ch. 12). In short, when there is no real basis for the prediction of future events, but one nevertheless requires some information on which to base decisions, the next best alternative is to base one's own behaviour on that of others. Coddington (1976: 1260) interpreted this position as such:

> Keynes emphasizes that the basis of choice lies in vague, uncertain and shifting expectations of future events and circumstances: expectations that have no firm foundation in circumstances, but that take their cues from the beliefs of others, and that will be sustained by hopes, undermined by fears and continually buffeted by 'the news'. ... The coordination of such crowd behaviour and its characteristic dynamics arise from the fact that participants are taking their cues directly from one another. Reductionist choice theory as it has been developed

does not shed any light on decisions involving such immediate and strong interdependence as this.

(Coddington 1976: 1260)

Expectations are thus an interconnected and highly reflexive web of conditionals. The dynamics of this sort of highly parallel network structure can be modeled with discrete dynamical networks such as Random Boolean Networks or Cellular Automata, but such work although enormously promising is still very young. Still, the basic principle that has emerged is that such webs can exhibit a vast range of behaviour, as Kauffman described above, and that the class of dynamic observed is a function of how many other elements each element is connected to. Keynes, Shackle and Townshend thought that agents cope with uncertainty by connecting their expectations to others. Complex systems theory tells us that in doing so they set up a network structure with a dynamic life all of its own. Micro uncertainty becomes macro uncertainty.

Suppose we separate the causes of uncertainty into an exogenous and an endogenous component. The exogenous component consists of 'shocks' arising from weather, culture, supply conditions or whatever. Many of these factors can be placed on an actuarial basis and reduced to calculable risk, hence effectively eliminating uncertainty from the model. But uncertainty nevertheless remains in the necessity of dealing with novelty. This is the endogenous component of uncertainty, that which arises from within the system by the normal behaviour of the system, and is synonymous with the entrepreneur. It is the entrepreneur who is identified with the various tasks of shouldering uncertainty (Mises, Knight), seeing through it (Kirzner), and also engendering it (Schumpeter). In this view of things, the entrepreneur is nominally charged with fine-tuning of the system, but in occupying that position may also be the impetus for radical change in the material content and organization of the system. However in all such thinking it is implicit that the entrepreneur is a definitive agent that when variously added or removed from the formal system changes the dynamical properties of that system. In the neo-Walrasian framework there is no place for this agent because there are never disequilibrium states that may present the opportunity for 'alertness'. Conversely, in the Austrian and Post-Schumpeterian framework in which the market is continuously in motion, it is the entrepreneur who is the prime mover. Shackle is unique among theorists in denying both conceptions.

For Shackle, uncertainty is the inverse image of the possibility of origination, so that in a world without uncertainty there is no demand for the faculty of imagination as entrepreneurial 'vision'. Shackle does not then regard the entrepreneur as an agent, a subspecies within the population — as Mises, Schumpeter, Lachmann, and Kirzner do — but rather regards *entrepreneurship as a component of all agency*. Shackle's epistemics proceed on the basis that all agents must deal with uncertainty, and while some may specialize in this function, none are exempt from facing it. Uncertainty, then, is simply a consequence of the impossibility of knowing what other agents will decide to do in the future and filling this with imagination — 'the provision of knowledge surrogates in the face of knowledge deficiencies' (Coddington 1976: 1260). We move into the future by successively fixing these decisions and therefore realizing latent connections between things that were previously unforeseen.[11] Shackle (1972: 341) calls this entire process the 'epistemic cycle', which describes the flux of knowledge across a network in which each action acts as a trigger to further action but the consequences of such then feed back to the original element. In this way the system is in a continual state of activity, perpetually generating novelty and sustaining a complex state of uncertainty.

Equilibrium-based mathematical models cannot cope with the concept of uncertainty in its raw form and minimally require its translation into something tractable, such as risk. Uncertainty becomes risk when the space of event outcomes is bounded, sorted and each state assigned a fixed probability; it is presumed that this operation can always be done (compare Keynes 1936/1973: 210–11). Complex Systems Theory also requires a translation of uncertainty, but instead of reducing the billowing epistemic cloud into an exhaustive statement about each of its individual elements, it begins with the perceptible 'shape' of the cloud, as it were, and recognizes that different topographical forms have different dynamical potential. Uncertainty is translated as a statement about this 'dynamical potential' (in other words, laleidics). Complex Systems Theory is a framework for the analysis of such dynamical potential, defining a state-space of possibilities from extreme order (no feedback connections anywhere in the system) to extreme chaos (a completely inter-connected system). The more the behaviour of every element depends on the behaviour of other elements, which is a response to uncertainty, the more chaotic the dynamics are likely to be, which is a further cause of uncertainty. To make sense of the dynamics of such a system, we shall require a more formal approach.

3 THE UNCERTAINTY PRINCIPLE OF UNCERTAINTY

We represent this problem of interdependent expectations using the framework of Graph Theory (Kirman 1987: 558–9), which is the branch of combinatorial mathematics that underpins all modelling of discrete dynamical systems (Green 1996). A graph-theoretical model consists of two primitives, a set of elements (**V**) and a set of connections (**E**). Suppose we have a set of n elements such that:

$$\mathbf{V} = (V_1, \dots, V_i, \dots, V_n) \tag{1}$$

We suppose that each element V_i represents an individual agent and can be connected to $(n-1)$ other elements (agents). In this way we can describe a specific network of interconnected agents. If an element V_i is connected to another element V_j then we define this with the existence of a connection E_{ij}. To describe the set of all potential connections between all elements in **V** we define the set **E**.

$$\mathbf{E} = (E_{1,\ 2}, \dots, E_{i,j}, \dots, E_{n,(n-1)}) \tag{2}$$

The set of elements **V** plus the set of connections **E** defines a system **S** (for example, Figure 9.1 below).[12]

$$\mathbf{S} = (\mathbf{V}, \mathbf{E}) \tag{3}$$

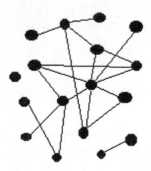

Figure 9.1: A System

It is supposed that there will be a given number of elements and hence the prime variable is the number of connections in the system, represented by the cardinality of the set **E** and illustrated diagrammatically by the individual lines in Figure 9.1 above. Let this equal h: $(0 \leq h \leq j)$. For $h = 0$ no elements are connected and therefore the set **E** is the empty set (no agent is connected to any other agent). For $h = j$ every element is connected to every other element (every agent is connected to every other agent). Given n, the value of j is given by equation 4 below.

$$j = \frac{n!}{(n - 2)2!} \tag{4}$$

There are two ways of viewing the above conception, either from the perspective of the system as a whole, or from the perspective of an individual element within the system. The connective geometry of the whole is described by the variable h, which describes the number of connections in the system.[13] For each element, let k describe the number of other elements it is connected to: $(0 \leq k \leq n - 1)$. A simple relationship holds between h and k if all elements are connected to the same number of other elements. In that case — otherwise known as the NK model (Kauffman 1993: ch. 2):[14]

$$h = \frac{nk}{2} \text{ [for } n \text{ even, } (nk + 1) \text{ for } n \text{ odd]} \tag{5}$$

Before proceeding further, however, we should make explicit what is meant by a connection. This requires that we first distinguish between an *ontological* connection and an *epistemic* connection. If we assume that each agent V_i knows of the existence of all other elements (agents) then we have assumed that all elements are ontologically connected: this is a necessary but not sufficient condition for agents to be epistemically connected. For instance, although few people in Australia would claim to know the current price of yak milk in Tibet, equally few would be astonished to learn of the existence of milk-producing yaks in Tibet. It is thus perfectly possible to know of a thing's existence (an ontological connection) without having any notion of or being directly affected by the *current state* of its existence. It is this latter concept that is inferred by an *epistemic connection*.

Two points should be noted. First, this distinction is only evident in a lattice space. In a field or integral space each point that is in the space (ontologically connected) is also epistemically connected because the very definition of an integral space is, in its topographical expression, a complete set of connections between all elements (see Kirman 1987, 1997). It is only in a lattice space, where we can define some elements as not directly connected to others, that the distinction between an ontological connection and an epistemic connection arises (Potts 1999). Second, ignorance, uncertainty and risk can be distinguished within this framework. Ignorance is defined as the absence of an ontological connection, when we do not actually know the complete set of all elements that we might be connected to. Ignorance relates to a state of simply not knowing the existence of some set of either current elements or future elements or both. Uncertainty refers to those elements which are known to exist, but about which we have no basis for calculating an independent probability distribution for all future states because the set of epistemic connections in the system is incomplete and variable. Risk refers to a situation where such calculations can be made because such epistemic connections are complete and unchanging. If theorizing is done over an integral space, it follows that there cannot possibly be uncertainty in the above sense, only risk.[15].

Formally speaking, a connection exists between, say, *A* and *B* when the state of *A* is conditional upon (is an input into) the state of *B*, and vice versa. This does not say that *B* uniquely determines *A*. For the state of *A* may also be conditional upon *C*, *D* and *E*. In this case, the effect B has on A depends upon the simultaneous state of these other variables. When an agent 'makes a connection' with another agent what they effectively do is to plug a 'conditional for action' (an algorithm) into that agent. When they remove a connection they unplug that algorithm. This web of connections defines the total geometry of a system. So when A is connected to B, at each time step A receives a signal indicating the state of B.[16] The state of A at the next time step will be a function of B (and all other elements to which A is connected) according to some predefined programme.[17] Threshold effects regarding the signal are obviously important here, as is the question of how the set of elements to be connected to are chosen. I return to these themes in the next section. Presently though, we are concerned with the dynamic nature of such a web of conditional expectations.

Key to the large-scale dynamics of expectations is, I suggest, the *uncertainty principle of uncertainty*. This is the argument that, under certain conditions, as the individual attempts to know more of the whole, the whole effectively becomes less knowable.[18] This general principle rests on two premises. The first we have already encountered. If there are n elements in the system, each element will be connected to between zero and $(n - 1)$ other elements. If agents wish to reduce their states of uncertainty, they increase the number of epistemic connections, thus receiving more direct signals about the state of other elements. For example, speculators may decide to follow an increased number of stock prices, with rules relating the composition of their current portfolios to changes in a now increased number of inputs. In the upper limit, then, and neglecting all bounded rationality considerations, these agents may attain a state where they are directly affected by any change in any element in the system. Here the agents have written computer-trading programmes with as many input channels as stock prices such that the portfolio is, like a hungry nocturnal predator, sensitive to any movement anywhere.

Second, the more highly connected a system — the greater the ratio of connections to elements — the more dynamically unstable the system. This is a robust result from the study of discrete dynamical systems and which originated from the study of random graphs.[19] As the density of connections in the system increases, so too does the dynamic instability (the 'chaotic potential' of the system) due to the larger and wider extent of feedback effects. The greater the extent of feedback effects in the system, the greater difficulty in predicting its forward behaviour due to increased sensitivity to initial conditions and increased tendency for small local fluctuations to propagate and escalate across the entire system. As it turns out, the dynamical behaviour of the system is not a linear function of the number of connections in the system. What is generally observed, as connections are incrementally added to or removed from a system, is that the system passes through three 'regimes' or 'macro-states' of behaviour — order, complexity and chaos — separated by abrupt phase transitions. The general point, however, is that as the number of connections increases in a system, the dynamics of the system become more chaotic and increasingly difficult to predict.[20] (And I would emphasize that this is a general result pertaining to *all* dynamical systems, it is not peculiar to the economic circumstance.)

Each agent, in an attempt to gauge the epistemic basis of their uncertainty, requires the estimate of two parameters. First, the extent to which they are connected to all other elements (the degree to which they are connected to the web). Second, the extent to which all other elements are connected to each other (the topographic geometry of the overall web). However, there is something of a dilemma embedded in the situation if the agents then attempt to take steps to redress uncertainty in either dimension. On the one hand, if they attempt to improve their own epistemic position in regard to connectedness to the set of all other elements, they do so by adding further connections to the system. This increases the set of inputs feeding into each agent and connects the agent with events and circumstances in other parts of the system. A change elsewhere in the system that did not previously directly affect the agents now does so. But note the necessary implication: as uncertainty is decreased for the individual agent as k increases, it is simultaneously increased for all agents as h also increases, and vice-versa. The more we try to know, the less we can know, a micro-macro feedback that may be called the uncertainty principle of uncertainty.

What this principle asserts is that the rational individual agent can always improve their position vis-à-vis other agents by increasing epistemic connections. Thus without constraint, as individual agents each pursue their own best interests the overall system would tend towards a state of total internal connectedness ($h \rightarrow j$) and with a network of feedback loops that would manifest purely chaotic dynamics. In theory, the market system would catalyze an escalation of feedback towards total meltdown. But in practice, however, there are several crucial mitigating factors.

(i) *Agents are boundedly rational.* This limits the number of connections to some finite variable — say, x — that each agent can extend to other elements. It is generally recognized that x will be somewhere around seven.[21] I would draw attention to the magnitude of this number (less than one hundred) rather than its exact specification. In contrast, the order of magnitude of elements (potential connections) in the economic system would be placed somewhere between millions and billions (apologies to Carl Sagan) depending upon our definitional criterion. It is clear then that the bounded rationality constraint ensures the system will always be very sparsely connected and thus considerably short of the chaotic state of internal connectedness.

(ii) *It matters where the system already is in state-space.* The state-space of a Boolean network consists of three macro-states — order, complexity and chaos — with dynamics broadly similar within each regime. However, these macro-states are separated by abrupt phase transitions. At or near these phase-transitions increments to the connective geometry (an increase in h) are sensitive in the way described above. But an increase in h does not always leads monotonically to an increase in the chaotic potential of the system. Deep within either the ordered or chaotic regime small changes to the connective structure of the system generally have no noticeable impact at all on the dynamic behaviour of the system. Critical mass arguments apply generally.

(iii) *Extant organizational structure decomposes the system.* It is entirely reasonable to presuppose that there will exist an institutional hierarchy of organization and distribution both within and between firms that effectively constrains local interactions along established pathways. Furthermore, such structure can be supposed to exist widely across the spectrum of behavioural institutions (habits and routines, as discussed in Nelson and Winter 1982) as a kind of social and cultural embeddedness (see Granovetter 1985, Lawson 1997).

So the origins of order in the economic system, where the system is understood to be a vast network of interactions, derives essentially from the large-scale incompleteness in the set of all possible connections. This is not a paradox. The economic system functions *because of* its limitations (Richardson 1960).[22]

The graph-theoretic framework of elements variously connected shows how uncertainty resides in two places at once: in the extent to which each element is connected to the system, and in the extent to which the system is connected to itself. The micro component is synchronic and essentially a statement about the knowledge of the individual. The macro component is diachronic and expresses the 'know-ability' of the system itself.[22] The uncertainty principle of uncertainty is the hypothesis that these two manifestations of uncertainty are linked by an inverse relationship, such that generally considered, any attempt to reduce uncertainty in one dimension simply shifts it to the other. In a system where each agent is connected to only a few others then there will be much individual uncertainty as each agent has very little information upon which to act. But because of this very fact, the macro system will be highly stable due to localization of any disturbance (as in Kauffman's description above). Thus the macro system itself will rarely exhibit 'kaleidic' shifts. Uncertainty in the economic system can be variably apportioned between the individual and the whole but it seems that one cannot be decreased without increasing the other.[24]

However there is still something missing from this framework:, namely the issue of how the agent might come to know the overall state of the macro system. Thus far we have insisted that knowledge is a consequence of being 'connected', as knowledge of the specific state of a set of other elements. But how does the agent decide which elements to be connected to? Furthermore, the agent will also require some estimate of the extent to which connections exist between other elements, and the possible consequence of the existence of specific connections. How is this map constructed? This, I think, is the role of the formal imagination. But what, then, is meant by imagination? From the analytical perspective, graph theoretic expression forced us to confront how connections are chosen. The uncertainty principle, which is also a graph theoretic construction, shows that uncertainty can never be eliminated from the arguments of a discrete dynamical system. Both analytically legitimize the concept of imagination as a search process over a space of constructed combinatorial possibilities. We now consider how imagination can be formally conceptualized.

4 ON THE MECHANISMS OF IMAGINATION

Despite the clear centrality of the concept of imagination in Shackle's framework, a notable gap is the absence of a clearly formulated expression of the mechanisms of imagination as a micro-theory of expectation formation. Shackle seemed to struggle with this aspect, sometimes resting content with the sufficiency of impenetrable terms such as 'origination' (for example, 1958: 21–2; 1972: ch. 1; 1974: 76), and at other times pointedly hostile to any pretension to go beneath such a basis (for example, 1972: sections 30.7, 31.5, 33). In *Expectation, Enterprise and Profit* (1970: 155) we find reference to business R&D as 'systematized imagination' and finally a more abstract micro-theoretical principle in the 'alphabetic' metaphor (1979: 21). As such, the development of Shackle's thinking can be clearly seen to converge upon a concept of imagination as search and search as recombination.[25] This concept is the basis of the evolutionary computational process of recombinant search known as a genetic algorithm (GA). In this section I provide a sketch of how GAs provide a formal underpinning to Shacklean notions of uncertainty and imagination.

GAs have two broad applications, either as optimization functions for problem solving or as models of an evolutionary process. We shall be concerned only with the latter, which defines a GA as an internal component of a Discrete Dynamical Network (DDN).[26] A DDN consists of a set of elements on a lattice each taking inputs from each other (being specifically connected) and changing their state according to some logical function on their inputs. An agent within such a system is defined as a set of internal rules[27] and a set of connections to other elements. The internal rules describe the present state of each element in terms of the state of the other elements. A DDN, then, is a highly reflexive structure that is capable of a vast array of dynamical behaviours depending upon the action conditionals embedded in each element and the extent to which elements are connected. A GA is a systematic (algorithmic) procedure for changing either the internal rules or the space of connections. It does this by defining two operators — cross-over and mutation — that have obvious biological verisimilitude. Although the underlying mathematical logic is quite involved, the basic idea is simple. Each agent is represented as a set of encoded bit strings which represent a candidate solution. These strings are typically written as binary strings (such as 100110, 111000, and so on) but they can also include null variables (#) at any locus (for example, 1#####, and so on).[28] These strings encode properties of the agent such as decision heuristics and connective structure. At each time step each string is subjected to some predefined fitness or selection function which selects some fraction of this population to be carried forward to the next round.[29] The surviving population is then cross-bred and mutated to create a new population.[30] This process is then repeated for however many time steps are defined. In theory, each iteration will be an improvement on the last.

Consider why this process works. GAs are a massively parallel search method that operate on a population of potential solutions by applying the principle of survival of the fittest and breeding new solutions using operators borrowed from natural genetics. It is evident that a solution, as a string (for example,. s_1 = 100110011), can be decomposed into 'building blocks', which are the sub-components of the string (for example, 1001 and 10011, or 100, 110 and 011, etc). Both the string and the sub-components of the string are known as *schemas* or *schemata* (Holland 1975). As Melanie Mitchell (1998: 27) explains, 'GAs work by discovering, emphasizing and recombining 'building blocks' of solutions in a highly parallel fashion.' The intuition, as such, is that *a good solution will be more than likely to contain good components, and it is these components that are sought to create even better solutions.* So GAs work by fixing upon good 'building blocks' (schemata) and combining such building blocks to produce new variations. Each 'solution' is made of component parts just as any system is made of sub-systems. And when we create a new solution, a new system, we do so by recombining the elements of previous solutions or systems. This is a basic mechanism of all evolutionary processes in natural and artificial systems (Holland 1975, 1995).

The process by which expectations cumulatively form and reform as a vast parallel epistemic network can be modeled as an evolving artificial system. Unlike the neoclassical approach to the modelling of expectations, which requires an exhaustive and consistent account of all elements and therefore negates uncertainty and imagination, a GA model of expectations defines the otherwise untouchable concepts of genuine uncertainty and imagination as essential dynamic mechanisms.

For a most interesting and powerful aspect of GAs is that they do not necessarily require complete specification of the initial schema. The logic works equally well and often better on partial solutions. To make sense of this we note that although in the above strings each locus was defined by a definite binary variable (0 or 1) we can also specify a 'don't care' or 'undecided' symbol (#) at any locus (for example, 10##). It is evident that this binary string contains 1011, 1000, 1010, and 1001 as possible instances. In the case that 10## is used as a conditional for action (*if* 10##, *then* ...) all four strings will trigger the action, but in the more restricted case of 101# being the conditional then only two of the strings will work (1011 and 1010). As such, the use of these 'don't care' sites effectively makes the schema more general. It will serve as an input to a larger set of conditionals with a greater likelihood of narrowing in on the active sites contributing to the higher 'fitness' of the total string.

To illustrate this, suppose that we have two strings 100110 and 1##### which score the same on some fitness test. While it is impossible to tell what aspects of the first string contributed to its total fitness, it is perfectly clear in the second case. This concept should seem familiar, because GAs employ the same basic principle underlying experimental science: abstract and test (isolate and evaluate). GAs make use of abstraction in order to isolate the components that actually matter, and it is this property that translates so directly into an epistemic model of the economic agent. Uncertainty (an ontological but not an epistemic connection) plays a positive, constructive role in the choice process by providing the necessary conditions for learning and imagination as algorithmic recombinant processes in Lattice space. I have argued elsewhere (Potts 1999) that this is a fundamental concept in the evolutionary microeconomics.

New issues arise. An important one, I think, concerns the phenomenon of *disorientation* and the process by which agents realign themselves after some general disturbance of the system. This is a general inquiry into the process of adaptation and the mechanisms of adjustment. In the graph theoretic framework, a sense of 'orientation' means making the right connections to other elements so as to be tuned in to signals that matter. GAs provide a way of modelling a systematic search for such 'critical' elements as an iterative process, and one that can be effectively modified to investigate different search strategies. In this same way, GAs also lend themselves well to modelling the dynamics of embedded rules within rules, such that when a general rule is found the search procedure can switch to variations on that rule or conditionals within it (for example, see Earl 1986).

However this micro aspect relating to the individual agent is only part of the story: the process by which expectations are formed is very much a collective self-organizational phenomenon (see Felh 1986). This is what is important about the concept of orientation. For while the rational agent thinking only of the long-term equilibrium will search for the 'fundamentally' correct signals, the speculative agent will be far more concerned to know which signals the herd is orientating themselves with respect to and regardless of how unfounded these may be. And if the long run is just a series of short runs, and optimal behaviour driven to ever shorter horizons of speculative second guessing, then it remains unclear when one actually ever need be concerned with fundamentals (compare Keynes 1936/1973: 156). The fundamental question here is: To which signals do we pay attention?[31]

Currency traders, for example, obviously look to such things as credit ratings or current account debt ratios as published by private and governmental sources, but they also look to each other. For various reasons, George Soros may be considered such a critical element; when he moves, so do others. Indeed, it may be possible that some traders base their behaviour on nothing but what Soros is doing. The tabloid press would have it that Ronald Reagan sought out the timing (if not the substance) of major policy initiatives with astrological guidance. Irrespective of how much one may have known about macroeconomic theory, the smart trader may have required as inputs nothing more than a similarly-schooled astrologer (see also Gimpel and Dakin 1984).

These points are perhaps verging on the facetious, but I mean something serious. However the economy might work in theory, at some point we inevitably have to ask how it works in practice. The first issue we then meet is epistemics — how and what people know. And when the issue is confronted in this way our arguments for rationality and information seem backwards. Agents do not endeavor to eliminate all ignorance and uncertainty. Rather, they strive to see how much ignorance and superstition they can get away with (Hayek 1945). This is a perfectly reasonable behavioural axiom: Where short cuts can be taken they will be taken.[32] By a 'short-cut' I mean the use of abstraction, the connection to a minimal set of other elements hypothesized to be useful for estimating the current state of the system and for projecting its future movements (see Loasby 1991). This is an experimental behaviour (Kelly 1963) over a platform of decision heuristics (Simon 1959). But a clear consequence of this behaviour is that the macro-system exhibits a degree of stability that it would not otherwise have (Heiner 1983). A further consequence is that this stability is only meta-stable: the large-scale dynamics of a loosely connected system will exhibit a 'kaleidic' character analytically represented by the complex regime of state-space. Genetic Algorithms provide a direct and powerful tool for the modeling and analysis of epistemic behaviour within this space.

Finally, we must not lose sight of the fact that a general framework for the analysis of economic evolution (an evolutionary economics) requires, among other things, a deep rethink of the theory of expectations. The challenge is to synthesize the following elements into a coherent framework.:

1 The Uncertainty Principle of Uncertainty, as recognition of the irreduciblity of expectations to the expectations held a 'representative agent'.

2 Recognition that expectations are things that are actively constructed by agents, and in so doing they construct the forward space of 'potential' for an economic system. The future is constructed in parallel in the distributed minds of its agents before it is then actualized by the actions of the agents. The theorist must clearly understand that the concept of a 'representative imagination' makes no sense at all, and that the origins of diversity and variety and evolutionary potential must ultimately stem from a heterogeneous set of expectations. Furthermore, coordination can now be seen to occur (or fail to occur) in two distinct places: (i) in the coordination of expectations as acts of imagination, and (ii) in the coordination of actions then based upon these expectations.

3 Lastly, we must recognize that the concept of probability (used to weight possible outcomes) is only well defined for closed, ergodic systems. The theory of expectations must be sensitive to the fact that currently we simply do not have a general theory of the probability structures that applies in a well defined sense to open complex adaptive evolutionary systems.

I am reasonably confident that these problems are in some sense solvable, and that an evolutionary theory of expectations is on the horizon. However I also surmise that in doing so we will find that an evolutionary theory of expectations is in fact a general theory of heuristic search and meta-level learning (for example, pattern recognition), and thus deeply related to the cognitive and computer sciences (Herbert Simon's 'sciences of the artificial').

5 CONCLUSION

Shackle serves many roles in heterodox economics. He is a Patron Saint of Post-Keynesian,[33] Austrian[34] and behavioural economics, a bridge between Keynes and Hayek, a fundamental critic of reductionism and exponent of uncertainty in expectations, an exemplar of nihilism and literary theorizing, and more. My purpose in this chapter has been to put a new spin on Shackle, to bridge his epistemics into a vast and exciting new territory of modelling and analysis, namely complex systems theory, computational economics and the evolutionary microeconomics. I have not been overly concerned with formalism but instead have seen my primary task as the conceptual translation of epistemics into algorithmics. The question, I suggest, is not axiomatics or *epistemics*, but rather axiomatics or *algorithmics*.

Shackle rejected axiomatics outright as a basis for economic theory. Some incorrectly read this posture as nihilistic, with the false presumption that all mathematical analysis must be axiomatic. But the lattice or topographical based framework of complex systems theory does in large measure accommodate the substance of Shackle's epistemics. Kaleidics translates as the complex regime of state-space. Uncertainty translates as both a micro and macro statement about the topographical geometry of connections. It also shows the way in which these are reflexive and interdependent. Imagination is abstractly schematic recombination with random variation, which is a dynamic that can be modelled with Genetic Algorithms. The graph theory framework legitimizes Shackle's conceptualizations of imagination and uncertainty. Complex Systems theory analytically legitimizes kaleidics. Post-Shacklean economics — Shackle's epistemic questions framed in terms of complex systems theory type modelling — is a way of looking at the economic process from the bottom up, and seeing a complex skein of knowledge and belief that somehow manages to weave imagination into reality.

NOTES

1 See Potts (1999).

2 An excellent examination of the metaphor of turbulence in economics can be found in Louçã (1997).

3 This story has been often told; arguably, Waldrop's (1992) account is the best.

4 *Dynamical Systems Theory* is sometimes referred to as *Complex Systems Theory* when the focus of attention is upon the emergence and behaviour of self-organizing systems. Self-organization only occurs at or near the complex regime, hence the surrogate title. It is also sometimes known as *Evolutionary Systems Theory*.

5 Note that *Cellular Automata* are a restricted class of network in which the 'other elements' are constrained to be immediate neighbours.

6 Shackle's (1972: 433) description of the kaleidic economy 'as subject to sudden landslides of re-adjustment to a new, precarious and ephemeral, pseudo-equilibrium' is strikingly similar to what the physicist Per Bak (1996) calls *self-organized criticality*. See also Kauffman (1993: 255).

7 This was also Townshend's (1937) interpretation of the *General Theory*, which greatly influenced Shackle (see Rotheim 1993).

8 I have always considered 'animal spirits' an ironic term. Was Voltaire not correct in making the preference for action over inaction and for imagination over resignation the most characteristic mark of the human being?

9 Needless to say, the projection is done with internal models of the economy or whatever. An explicit account of this otherwise covert assumption is one of the good things to have come from the New Classical school, with their blatant presumption that all agents are New Classical economists.

10 The now standard criticism (since Poincaré's discoveries early in the twentieth century) is that the validity of this formulation is conditional upon there being no non-linearities embedded anywhere in the system.

11 Uncertainty refers to the absence of an epistemic connection, but this does not imply that the connection does not therefore exist. A connection may well exist, but we are simply unaware of it. Callon (1998) refers to the importance of this concept in terms of market externalities, which he argues are essentially connections unaccounted for.

12 The standard graph theoretical expression is $G = (V, E)$, where G stands for Graph, V for Vertex, and E for Edge. I shall preserve the symbols V and E, which represent respectively the set of elements and the set of connections, but shall replace the symbol G with S, such that what would otherwise be termed a graph I shall term a System.

13 Equation 2 describes where these connections are, but our concern now is

only with the cardinality of that set.

14 For this to be an equality for all values of n and k, we require that an element can be connected to itself.

15 See Lawson (1988) for discussion of the various interpretations of uncertainty by Knight, Keynes and others.

16 Such algorithmic-based systems are invariably modeled with discrete time.

17 For example, an algorithm might be (for binary state variables) $If <B = 1,$ $C = 1, D = 0>$ $then$ $<A = 1>$.

18 A specific form of this argument can be found in Darley and Kauffman (1997: 48). They hypothesize that 'in a persistent attempt to optimize prediction about the behaviour of other agents, adaptive agents will alter their finite optimally complex models of one another so that the entire system approaches the edge of chaos.'

19 It is well established that the connective properties of Random Graphs exhibit abrupt phase transitions as the ratio of edges to vertices passes through certain thresholds (Erdos and Renyi 1960). See Kauffman (1993: 307).

20 Another way of thinking about this is that the system becomes increasingly *non-ergodic* (*á la* Davidson 1996).

21 This is known in the behavioural literature as 'Miller's rule' (Miller 1956). This concept has been instrumental to all finite heuristic based approaches to consumer decision making which emphasize that structural decomposition, selective attention to information sources and rules of thumb in processing information act to give order to what would in its informational and structural potential interactions be massively chaotic. (for example, Simon 1962, Hey 1982, Heiner 1983, Earl 1986).

22 Another way of looking at this is to recognize that the very possibility of distributive calculation as the basis for rational coordination requires of absolute necessity some preexisting unambiguous framing of events. Callon (1998: 260) points out that this is only possible in 'cold' situations where the interconnections between events are few and unquestioned. In other words, mass ignorance of the actual connective structure of the system is a precondition for 'rational' calculation within that system.

23 Again we distinguish two forms of uncertainty: (1) the inability to foresee the arrival of new elements (novelty) or the redundancy of existing elements (selection); and (2) the inability to foresee changes in the matrix of connections (structural evolution).

24 It is unclear as of yet whether this is a zero- or positive-sum game or upon what this might depend. For instance, an important counter-effect would occur when epistemic connections can be locked in to induce large-scale, coordination-assisting planning, thus reducing uncertainty at the micro as well as macro level (see Richardson 1981).

25 Curiously, Shackle nowhere admits any debt of inspiration or pertinence

of example to Evolutionary Genetics.

26 Discrete dynamical networks are also known as Automata Networks. Sub-species include Random Directed Graphs, Random Boolean Networks and Cellular Automata.

27 In the mathematics of an automata network this is the 'look-up table', but in the behavioural, evolutionary and institutional economic literature this corresponds to the set of behavioural heuristics or the choice algorithm. Either way, it refers to the same thing: the rules that determine the state of a given element in terms of the state of a set of other elements.

28 These abstract strings are highly plastic in their meaning. For instance the just- mentioned situation might refer to a set of product characteristics, where we would interpret 100110 as having characteristic 1, 4 and 5 but not 2, 3 or 6. Similarly, 1##### has characteristic 1 but information about characteristics 2-6 is deemed irrelevant. The circumstance of the application or some given convention is assumed to determine the particular ordering. Another interpretation might be to regard sites 1-6 as other elements in the system, such that the first string describes a connection to elements 1, 4 and 5 but not to 2, 3 or 6. In the second case the agent is definitely connected to element 1 and doesn't care whether or not she is connected to elements 2-6. In this instance the agent predefines the ordering.

29 The specification of the fitness function depends on the problem to be solved, but in any case it takes the individual string as an input and returns a real number as an output. The complete set of these forms a topographical concept known as a 'fitness-landscape'. The GA then manipulates this structure to produce a new population of strings that is better adapted to the environment.

30 When two 'parent' solutions are combined into a hybrid 'daughter' solution the parameter setting will specify where along the string the 'cut' is made. When an existing string is mutated the parameter settings will describe where along the string the mutation occurs (usually random) and the distribution (Gaussian or Cauchy) that the mutation is drawn from. It is reasonably well established that while the cross-over operator does most of the work initially, in the long period the performance of a GA is conditional upon mutation, as this operator ensures that the probability of searching a particular sub-space is never zero. For example, suppose we have a population of binary strings, all of which end in 0 (that is, 110100, 101110, 001010, and so on). It is evident that no amount of reshuffling (cross-over) will ever generate a new candidate solution with a 1 in the final place.

31 It was of course Leijonhufvud (1968) who first clearly asked this question and recognized its fundamental importance.

32 According to Hahn (1981: 128) 'The fundamental element of neoclassical

theory [is] that agents will, if open to them, take actions they consider advantageous.' I consider the axiom above to fall within this meaning.
33 See Coddington (1976). Also Loasby (1976), Davidson (1996).
34 In classic instance see Lachmann (1976).

REFERENCES

Baas, N. (1997) 'Self-organization and higher order structures', in F. Schweitzer (ed.) (1997) *Self-Organization of Complex Structures: From Individual to Collective Dynamics.*, Amsterdam: Gordon and Breach.

Bak, P. (1996) *How Nature Works — The Science of Self-Organized Criticality*, New York: Springer Verlag.

Callon, M. (1998) 'An essay on framing and overflowing: economic externalities revisited by sociology', in Callon, M. (ed.) *The Laws of the Markets.* Oxford: Blackwell, 244–69.

Coddington, A. (1976) 'Keynesian economics: the search for first principles', *Journal of Economic Literature* 14: 1258–73.

Cyert, R. M. and March, J. G. (1963) *A Behavioral Theory of the Firm*, Englewood Cliffs, NJ: Prentice-Hall.

Darley, V. and Kauffman, S. (1997) 'Natural rationality', in Arthur, W. B., Durlauf, S. and Lane, D. (eds) (1997) *The Economy as a Complex Evolving System II*, New York: Addison-Wesley.

Davidson, P. (1996) 'Reality and economic theory', *Journal of Post-Keynesian Economics* 18: 479–508.

Debreu, G. (1959) *Theory of Value.*, New York: Wiley.

Earl, P. E. (1986) *Lifestyle Economics.*, Brighton: Wheatsheaf.

Epstein, J. and Axtell. R. (1996) *Growing Artificial Societies: Social Science from the 'Bottom-Up'*, Cambridge, MA: MIT Press.

Erdos, P. and Renyi, A. (1960) *On the Evolution of Random Graphs*, Institute of Mathematics: Hungarian Academy of Sciences, 5.

Felh, U. (1986) 'Spontaneous order and the subjectivity of expectations: a contribution to the Lachmann–O'Driscoll debate', in Kirzner, I. (ed) (1986) *Subjectivism, Intelligibility, and Understanding*, London: Macmillan, 72–86.

Gimpl, M. and Dakin, S. (1984) 'Management and magic', *California Management Review* 27: 125–36.

Granovetter, M. (1985) 'Economic action and social structure: the problem of embeddedness', *American Journal of Sociology* 91: 481–510.

Green, D (1996) 'Towards a mathematics of complexity', in Stocker, R., et al. (eds) (1996) *Complex Systems: From Local Interactions to Global Behaviour*, Amsterdam: IOS Press, 97–105.

Hahn, F. H. (1981) 'General equilibrium theory', in Bell, D. and Kristol, I. (eds) (1981) *The Crisis in Economic Theory*, New York: Basic Books, 123–38.

Hayek, F. A. (1945) 'The use of knowledge in society', *American Economic Review* 35: 519–30.

Heiner, R. (1983) 'The origin of predictable behavior', *American Economic Review* 73: 560–95.

Hey, J. D. (1982) 'Search for rules of search. *Journal of Economic Behavior and Organization* 3: 65–81.

Holland, J. (1975) *Adaptation in Natural and Artificial Systems*, Ann Arbor, MI University of Michigan Press

Holland, J. (1995) *Hidden Order: How Adaptation Builds Complexity*, New York: Helix Books.

Kay, N. M. (1982) *The Evolving Firm: Strategy and Structure in Industrial Organization.*, London: Macmillan.

Kelly, G. A. (1963) *A Theory of Personality*, New York: Norton.

Kauffman, S. (1988) 'The evolution of economic webs', in P. Anderson, K. J. Arrow and D. Pines (eds) *The Economy as a Complex Evolving System*, New York: Addison Wesley, 125–46.

Kauffman, S. (1993) *The Origins of Order: Self-Organization and Selection in Evolution.* New York: Oxford University Press.

Keynes, J. M. (1973) *The General Theory of Employment, Interest and Money* (1st edn 1936), London: Macmillan/Royal Economic Society

Kirman, A. (1987) 'Graph theory', in Eatwell, J., Milgate, M. and Newman, P. (eds) (1987) *The New Palgrave: A Dictionary of Economics.* London: Macmillan, 558–9.

— — (1997) 'The economy as an interactive system', in Arthur, W.B., Durlauf , S. and Lane, D. (eds) (1997) *The Economy as a Complex Evolving System II*, New York: Addison-Wesley, 491–530.

Lachmann, L. (1976) 'From Mises to Shackle: an essay on Austrian economics and the kaleidic society',. *Journal of Economic Literature* 14: 54–62.

Lawson, T. (1988) 'Probability and uncertainty in economic analysis', *Journal of Post Keynesian Economics* 11: 38–65.

Lawson, T. (1997) *Economics and Reality*, London: Routledge.

Leijonhufvud, A. (1968) *On Keynesian Economics and the Economics of Keynes*, New York: Oxford University Press.

Loasby, B. J. (1976) *Choice, Complexity and Ignorance.*, Cambridge: Cambridge University Press.

— — (1991) *Equilibrium and Evolution: An Exploration of the Connecting Principles in Economics.*, Manchester: Manchester University Press.

Louçâ, F. (1997) *Turbulence in Economics: An Evolutionary Appraisal of Cycles and Complexity in Historical Processes*, Cheltenham: Edward Elgar.

Miller G. A. (1956) 'The magic number seven plus or minus two: some limits on our capacity for processing information. *Psychological Review* 63: 81–97.

Mitchell, M. (1998) *An Introduction to Genetic Algorithms.*, Cambridge, MA: MIT Press.

Nelson, R. and Winter, S. (1982) *An Evolutionary Theory of Economic Change.*, Cambridge, MA: Harvard University Press.

Potts, J. (1999) 'First principles of evolutionary microeconomics', unpublished Ph.D. thesis, Lincoln University, New Zealand.

Richardson, G. B. (1959) 'Equilibrium, expectations and information', *Economic Journal* 69: 225–37.

— — (1960) *Information and Investment.* Oxford: Oxford University Press.

— — (1981) 'Planning versus competition.', in Wagner, L. (ed) (1981) *Readings in Applied Microeconomics*, London: Oxford University Press.

Rotheim, R. (1993) 'On the indeterminacy of Keynes's monetary theory of value', *Review of Political Economy* 5: 197–216.

Rukeyser, M. (1960) 'The speed of darkness, IX', in *The Speed of Darkness*, New York: Random House

Simon, H. A. (1959) 'Theories of decision-making in economics and behavioral science.' *American Economic Review* 49: 253–83.

— — (1962) 'The architecture of complexity.' *Proceedings of the American Philosophical Society* 106: 476–82.

Shackle, G. L. S. (1958) *Time in Economics*, Amsterdam: North-Holland.

— — (1968) *Expectations, Investment and Income.*, 2nd edn (first published 1938), Oxford: Clarendon Press.

— — (1970) *Expectations, Enterprise and Profit: The Theory of the Firm*, London: George Allen & Unwin

— — (1972) *Epistemics and Economics.*, Cambridge: Cambridge University Press.

— — (1974) *Keynesian Kaleidics*, Edinburgh: Edinburgh University Press.

— — (1979) *Imagination and the Nature of Choice.*, Edinburgh: Edinburgh University Press.

Townshend, H. (1937) 'Liquidity premium and the theory of value', *Economic Journal* 47: 157–66

Waldrop, M. (1992) *Complexity: The Emerging Science at the Edge of Order and Chaos*, New York: Simon & Schuster.

10

SHACKLE ON PROBABILITY

Jochen Runde[*]

1 INTRODUCTION

Perhaps the most distinctive feature of George Shackle's work is his preoccupation with how best to conceive and represent what he calls the standing of uncertain hypotheses. By standing he means an actor's assessment of the capacity of an hypothesis to 'come true'. Shackle is well known for his opposition to probability, the conventional measure of such assessments in economic analysis, and for his alternative measure of potential surprise.[1]

Unfortunately Shackle was proposing his highly original ideas just when the orthodox notion of mathematical expectation was experiencing a powerful new lease of life through von Neumann and Morgenstern's (1947) axiomatization of the expected utility hypothesis.[2] Although his constructive proposals did attract some initial interest, therefore, they attracted less attention than they might otherwise have done. But the orthodox theory is currently itself under fire (Machina 1987, 1989) and Shackle's ideas have found some distinguished proponents, most notably Ford (1983, 1985, 1987, 1990) in economics and Levi (1966, 1967, 1972, 1979, 1980, 1991) in philosophy. It is possible that Shackle-type measures may yet have their day (see appendix). But however this may be, Shackle's critical writings on probability merit attention in their own right. It is these on which I shall concentrate here.

I begin by comparing Shackle's 'general framework of decision' with that of the orthodox model. Shackle's two main lines of argument against probability are then introduced and assessed. The first, which receives more emphasis in his earlier writings, concerns the use of frequency-ratios in one-shot decision situations. The second concerns the use of additive 'distributional' measures of uncertainty where the set of hypotheses, events or states over which they are defined cannot be assumed to be exhaustive. I argue that the standard model largely avoids the first set of Shackle's criticisms, but not the second. Shackle's views on the degree of belief interpretations of probability, the subjective or 'personalist' approach on the one hand and the Keynesian logical approach on the other, are then considered. I show that whereas the subjectivist approach escapes only the first line of Shackle's critique, the Keynesian approach escapes both.

2 EXPECTATION, DESIREDNESS AND STANDING

The basic components that Shackle regards as fundamental to the theory of choice under uncertainty are uncontroversial. The 'formal' scheme he has in mind is the familiar one in which an actor must choose one from a number of actions, each of which lead to one of a number of mutually exclusive sequels. The problem is that the actor does not know with certainty which sequel will follow every course of action. Shackle emphasizes that such sequels necessarily exist only in thought and therefore prefers to refer to them as 'hypotheses' or 'answers' (to the question: 'What will be the sequel if I take such-and-such a course of conduct.')[3] These hypotheses may of course be about quite objectively verifiable outcomes, such as that the next toss of a coin will land heads up.

Shackle argues, again uncontroversially, that each of the hypotheses will be evaluated in at least two respects. First, they will be judged in terms of their relative 'desiredness'. Shackle does not dwell on the measurement of desiredness, save to say that it may be possible to order hypotheses in respect of desiredness and, in some cases, to measure desiredness on a scale (Shackle 1972: 367–8). Second, the hypotheses will be judged in terms of their standing. The fundamental problem for the theory of choice under uncertainty is how these judgments should be combined (for each possible action) so as to be able to choose between alternative actions. As Shackle puts it:

> The main task of the analyst of expectation is to evolve some scheme in which these three elements, the formal, the psychic and the inferential, are satisfactorily fused. This scheme must in effect be able to rank or order the skein of expectations, each

taken as a whole, one skein for each course of action, so as to show why the businessman or other decision-maker chooses one course out of many possible ones.

(Shackle 1970: 106–7)

Most economists would agree with this characterization of the problem facing the decision theorist. I now turn to its orthodox solution.

The expected utility hypothesis

The expected utility hypothesis is that economically rational actors possess a von Neumann-Morgenstern (VNM) utility function defined over some set of consequences and, when faced with alternative risky acts ('gambles' involving those consequences), choose that act which maximzes the expected value of that utility function.

The idea that money gambles should be evaluated in terms of their expected value can be traced to the seventeenth century writings of such authors as Pascal and Fermat. This injunction could in turn be justified by appeal to the law of large numbers, that the average payoff of an indefinitely and independently repeated gamble eventually converges to its expected value. But this leaves open the question of what happens when the gamble is not indefinitely repeated. The St Petersburg game provides a graphic illustration of the problem. Here the bettor is offered \$2 if a fair coin lands heads up on the first toss, \$4 it lands heads up on the second toss, and so on. The famous paradox is that although the gamble has an infinite expected value $\Sigma 2^n(1/2)^n$, no-one would pay more than a finite amount to take it. The solution proposed by Gabriel Cramer and Daniel Bernoulli consists of calculating a 'moral' expectation in terms of utilities rather than amounts of money. With declining marginal utility, $u(\$x) = \log(x)$ for example, the St. Petersburg game has finite expected utility. The first axiomatic treatment of this approach, that of Ramsey (1926/1978), attracted little attention from economists. But the subsequent one of Von Neumann and Morgenstern (1947) did, so much so that it has come to be called the cornerstone of the economics of uncertainty.

The basic components of the expected utility model are much the same as those identified by Shackle. The main difference is that probabilities are not attached to final consequences, but to a jointly exhaustive list of exogenously determined and mutually exclusive 'states of the world' s_j (j = 1, 2, ..., n) on which the consequences associated with each act depend. The decision problem may then be represented in terms of the familiar acts/states/consequences matrix shown in Figure 10.1.

The set of acts a_i (i = 1, 2, ..., m) correspond to Shackle's rival courses of action and the set of consequences c_{ij} to his hypotheses. The specification of a state entails a complete description of all decision-relevant attributes, save for those that depend on the actor's actions.[4] In order to minimize confusion in what follows, I shall refer to probabilities being attached to hypotheses when referring to Shackle and probabilities being attached to states when referring to the orthodox model.

States of the World

	s_1	s_2		s_n
a_1	c_{11}	c_{12}		c_{1n}
a_2	c_{21}	c_{22}		c_{2n}
a_m	c_{m1}	c_{m2}		c_{mn}

Acts

Figure 10.1 Acts/states/consequences matrix

The expected utility theorem is that, subject to certain postulates of 'rational choice', a cardinal utility $U(a)$ may be attached to each act. There are two stages to the argument. First, numerical indicators of utility $u_i = u(c_{ij})$ are assigned to each consequence. The procedure is based on comparisons between a sure consequence on the one hand and a random pair of consequences on the other. Suppose that the consequences are $c_1, c_2, ..., c_n$ arranged in increasing order of preference. Arbitrary numbers are assigned to the worst (w) and the best (b) consequence, say $u(c_w) = 0$ and $u(c_b) = 1$ (giving the origin and units of the utility index). The utility of any intermediate consequence c_i is found by asking the actor at what value of p he or she would be indifferent between c_i for certain and a gamble with probability p of obtaining $u(c_b)$ and probability $(1 - p)$ of obtaining $u(c_w)$. (Since the c_i lie between c_w and c_b, then, by continuity, there exists some such a value of p for every c_i.) Suppose that the actor expresses such indifference at $p = r$. The utility of c_i is then:

$$u(c_i) = pu(c_b) + (1 - p)u(c_w) = r$$

The same procedure is used to assign utilities to the remaining consequences. The index thus derived is the VNM utility function, which is unique up to a positive linear transformation.

At the second stage of the argument, the utility of each act is expressed as the mathematical expectation of the utility of the final consequences

$$U(a_i) = \sum_{j=1}^{n} p_j u(c_{ij})$$

The decision rule is to select that act which offers the highest expected utility.

The curvature of the VNM utility function is often interpreted as reflecting the actor's 'attitude towards risk' (where the consequences are members of the real line, e.g. monetary values).

For example, many people prefer an amount of money x for certain to the gamble G of a 50 per cent chance of an amount $x + a$ and a 50 per cent chance of an amount $x - a$ $(a > 0)$, or

$$x \succ [0.5, x + a), (0.5, x - a)]$$

As the expected value of the gamble $EG = x$, this gamble is actuarially fair. But for the risk averter, $U(EG) \succ EU(G)$. On the standard definition, then, an actor is 'risk averse' if he or she prefers the expected money value of a gamble to the gamble itself and 'risk prone' if he or she displays the opposite preferences. It can be shown that an actor is risk averse (risk prone) with respect to a given gamble if and only if his or her VNM utility function is concave (convex) in the region around the mean value of the gamble. This definition of risk implies that risk aversion is fully captured by the curvature of the utility function, which may be unacceptable to those who feel that the utility curve and risk attitudes should be kept apart (see below).

So far nothing has been said about the conception of probability used in the model. Von Neumann and Morgenstern (1947: 19) assume the 'perfectly well founded interpretation of probability as frequency in long runs', but recognize that 'probability and preference' could be axiomatized together. There have since been several axiomatizations of this kind (see Fishburn 1981), the classic one still being that of Savage (1954). These contributions adopt the subjectivist or personal interpretation of probability as the actor's subjective degree of belief in an hypothesis or state. Subjective probabilities may be elicited in much the same way as described above. Let $p(s_1)$ denote the actor's personal probability of state s_1. To find $p(s_1)$ the set of all possible states is divided into s_1 and its complement $\neg s_1$. A gamble is then devised such that the actor receives a one unit increment of utility if s_1 obtains and a zero increment of utility otherwise. The problem then reduces to finding the utility number q (fraction of 1) at which the actor would be just indifferent between q for sure and that gamble. We would then have:

$$q = p(s_1)(1) + (1 - p(s_1))(0) = p(s_1)$$

So long as they satisfy a condition of 'coherence' (see below), degrees of belief assigned in this way have all the usual properties of probabilities.

We are now in a position to turn to Shackle. I begin with his first line of argument, which is based on his distinction between divisible, unique and crucial experiments.

3 DIVISIBLE, UNIQUE AND CRUCIAL EXPERIMENTS

In his early writings, Shackle takes the frequency view of probability as more or less coextensive with numerical probability.[5] According to this interpretation, if the relative frequency of some outcome A in a 'large' number of trials made in 'similar' circumstances tends to p, then the probability of A is said to be p. Statements of probability based on frequency-ratios are admissible, according to Shackle, subject to two sets of conditions. The first set consists of the conditions that must be satisfied in order for frequency-ratios to be derived, such as the number and uniformity of trials.[6] I shall say no more about these requirements here, save that Shackle does not deny that they may sometimes be met. His more urgent concern is with the second set of conditions, which has to do with the kind of experiments that statements of probability pertain to. In particular, he maintains that statements of probability based on frequency-ratios are admissible only when made in respect of divisible experiments or, in special cases, of seriable experiments.

Divisible experiments

Shackle (1955: 5) defines a divisible experiment as one 'which consists in the totality of the contemplated series of performances considered all together in one whole.' Unfortunately, this statement is somewhat ambiguous. Shackle's use of the word 'contemplated' suggests that his 'series of performances' consist of future trials, an interpretation consistent with the example he subsequently presents. But he does not specify what he means by the 'totality' of the contemplated series. It is not clear whether he is referring to an infinite series (in which case divisible experiments could never be more than a hypothetical possibility) or whether he is referring to all trials of a particular kind remaining to be made (which may in some situations not be very many).

Yet it is perhaps not too difficult to see what he has in mind. In terms of the frequency interpretation, the statement 'the probability that the next bottle to come off the production line will be defective is 1/100' is not really a statement about that bottle at all, but about the sequence of bottles of which the next is just one member. This statement says no more than that the proportion of defective bottles in the sequence tends to be one out of every hundred. Strictly speaking, statements of probability based on frequency-ratios are admissible only to the extent that they adopt a frequency interpretation, namely when made in respect of the whole (or at any rate a good part of the whole) of a long series of trials. A divisible experiment consists of a series of this kind. A non-divisible experiment consists of just one trial in the sequence, whether or not the next bottle on the line will be defective.

Few would deny that many economic decisions cannot be treated as divisible experiments. But this still leaves the possibility that non-divisible experiments may be combined so as to transform them into divisible experiments in the aggregate. Shackle calls such experiments seriable experiments, of which he identifies two kinds. The first occurs where people are able to pool the results of their individual non-divisible experiments, so that, taken together, they will face a divisible experiment. This, of course, is the familiar principle on which insurance is based. The second occurs where the actor feels sure that he or she will repeat the non-divisible experiment 'many times'. By many times, presumably, Shackle means sufficiently often for the law of large numbers to come into operation.

Unique experiments

A 'unique experiment' is non-divisible and non-seriable (a one-shot experiment that is not insurable). Notice that uniqueness in this sense has nothing to do with an absence of (knowledge of) frequency-ratios; when Shackle discusses unique experiments he usually invokes examples which involve well-defined frequency-ratios.

In his earlier writings on the subject, Shackle contends that knowledge of frequency-ratios is strictly irrelevant in the case of unique experiments (for example, Shackle 1952: 110). His position appears to be based on the premise that statements of probability are admissible only if they provide certain knowledge of the relevant outcomes.[7] The only situation in which this requirement is met, save for degenerate cases, is where the statement of probability pertains to the outcome of a divisible experiment. As knowledge of the relevant frequency-ratio cannot tell us what the outcome of the next trial will be, according to Shackle, such knowledge must be entirely irrelevant with respect to the outcome of that trial. He provides the following quotation from Peirce in support of this view:

> If a man had to choose between drawing a card from a pack containing 25 red cards and a black one, or from a pack containing 25 black cards and a red one; and if the drawing of a red card were destined to transport him to eternal felicity and that of a black one to consign him to everlasting woe, it would be folly to deny that he ought to prefer the pack containing the larger proportion of red cards, although from the nature of the risk, it could not be repeated. It is not easy to reconcile this with our conception of chance. But suppose he should choose the red pack and should draw the black card, what consolation would he have? He might say that he had acted in accordance with

reason, but that would only show that his reason was absolutely worthless. And if he should choose the red card, how could he regard it as anything but a happy accident? He could not say that if he had drawn from the other pack, he might have drawn the wrong one, because an hypothetical proposition such as 'if A, then B', means nothing with reference to a single case.

(Peirce 1923: 69-70)

But Shackle could have perhaps have chosen a better passage to help fortify his argument. For the opening sentence suggests that a knowledge of the relevant frequency may after all be relevant even in a one-shot case: it is hard to see how it could possibly be 'folly' to deny that the actor ought to prefer the pack containing the larger proportion of red cards when a statement of probability 'means nothing' with respect to the outcome of a single trial. In a similar if slightly less dramatic example, Weckstein (1959: 110) suggests that if we had the choice between a revolver loaded with one bullet and one loaded with two in a game of Russian Roulette, there could hardly be any question about which we would choose. The point, to paraphrase Keynes, is that although the use of probability as a guide to conduct cannot confer the certainty of success, it may nevertheless be rational to be guided by it in action. In the above examples it is difficult to escape the conclusion that least some account should be taken of probability.[8]

The expected utility model is widely used to represent what Shackle calls 'unique' choices. The question that arises, then, is what he would make of this approach. In terms of this theory, choices are not between the expected value but the expected utility of random consequences. It was shown in Section 2 how the utilities in question may be elicited from choices over gambles. As this procedure presupposes that the doctrine of mathematical expectation is applicable in one-shot decision situations, one might have expected Shackle to reject von Neumann and Morgenstern's approach on this basis alone.[9] But in his 1956 commentary on their proposals (and Ellsberg 1954), he takes a somewhat different line:

My contention is, then, that if von Neumann and Morgenstern's operation, by which they seek to define utility, refers to a unique lottery drawing, the resulting observed behaviour will spring from the combined effect of two subjective judgments, one concerned with degrees of belief in outcomes and the other concerned with degrees of satisfaction arising from given face-values of outcomes, and that it will be impossible, by observation alone ... to disentangle the effects of these two elements. If, on the other hand, von Neumann and Morgenstern have in mind an infinitely long series of drawings of the same lottery, then risk and uncertainty are eliminated and the proposed method breaks down ...

(Shackle 1956: 87)

Shackle raises two points here. First, he correctly observes that when VNM utilities are assigned on the basis of choices between one-shot gambles (as they are), they will comprise of a compound mixture of two judgements which it will not in general be possible to separate by observation alone. He does not develop this criticism but, in raising it, aligns himself with those who have raised problems concerning the interpretation of conjoint measures. For example, someone who considers himself risk neutral may nevertheless have a concave 'risk averse' VNM utility function due solely to diminishing marginal utility (Hansson, 1988).

Shackle's second point is that considerations of risk are eliminated completely where the same gamble is repeated indefinitely. This observation is correct, but does not lead the theory to break down in the way Shackle seems to have in mind. For this situation corresponds to that in which the actor is sure to receive the equivalent of the expected value of each individual gamble ex post (Shackle's divisible experiment case), so that $U(EG) = EU(G)$ for each individual gamble. The reasoning here is analogous to that which underlies the assumption often made in the asymmetric information literature, that, because they can spread their risks, insurers have linear (risk neutral) VNM utility functions.

We come now to the third of Shackle's trichotomy of definitions. Thus far I have assumed that the actor knows the relevant frequency-ratios. I now turn to the situation in which such knowledge is not to be had.

Crucial experiments

A 'crucial' experiment is one in which the relevant act irreversibly destroys the conditions under which it is performed. For example, a firm's decision to make a large investment in fixed capital equipment may result in large profits or in bankruptcy. But either way, once the choice has been made the firm will never find itself in similar circumstances again. The non-replicable or 'self-destroying' nature of crucial experiments precludes the frequency interpretation of probability, which is based on repetitions of similar events. But it does not preclude the degree of belief interpretations (see below).

Summary

Although I shall return to some of the themes raised in this section, it may be useful to summarize the argument so far. In his earlier writings, Shackle adopts a strict frequency interpretation of probability, which informs his distinction between divisible and non-divisible non-seriable experiments and his view that frequency-ratios are irrelevant in one-shot decision situations. Although Shackle does consider the expected utility model, which is widely used to represent such decision situations, the criticisms he raises against it cannot be said to be decisive. Finally, the fact that 'crucial' experiments preclude the frequency interpretation of probability does not disturb the subjectivist interpretation of probability.

4 PROBABILITY AS A DISTRIBUTIONAL MEASURE

In terms of the standard model the list of hypotheses or states to which probabilities are assigned must be a complete list. Shackle's most telling objection to the use of probability in economic analysis is that this assumption is seldom met. He expresses the matter as follows:

> [T]he whole probability calculus is founded on this assumption. This calculus assumes that one or other contingency out of some fully specified set must occur whenever a certain type of trial or experiment is made. When one such trial is contemplated, the assertion that its outcome will belong to this set has the status of certainty, and this is represented by unity. The status of an assertion that the outcome will be some particular member of

the complete set must then be represented by some proper fraction, and since all members of that set, taken together, compose the set, so the corresponding proper fractions must sum to unity. The probability unity attaching to the complete set of contingent outcomes is thus distributed over the component outcomes, and we may therefore call probability a distributive uncertainty variable.

(Shackle 1966: 89)

Probability, in other words, is an additive measure distributed over an exhaustive list of hypotheses or states. In some situations there may be no particular difficulty in compiling such a list. Savage's (1954) famous omelette, for example, admits of only two possibilities: either the eggs are good or they are bad. Similarly, the outcomes of a head or a tail exhaust the possible outcomes of a toss of a coin, as do the six numbers on the six faces of a die. But if the relevant hypotheses or states consist of alternative future possibilities in the context of an investment decision, for example, then there is reason to doubt that an actor would be able to list all the relevant possibilities.[10] We certainly do not find it strange that otherwise reasonable people sometimes say that 'I did not foresee such-and-such a possibility'.

Where there is a 'residual' of unimagined hypotheses or states the standard model runs into difficulties.[11] Shackle fastens on the fact that when the probability of an existing hypothesis is revised upwards or when a new item is added to a list of hypotheses, the probability of at least one of the remaining members of that list must fall. He attacks the descriptive validity of this implication of the probability calculus, on the grounds that nothing need have occurred to affect the 'intrinsic' standing of the original hypotheses. This point informs four further arguments Shackle raises against probability in economic analysis (Shackle 1955: 26–7).[12]

Shackle begins by pointing out that there is an important epistemic state that is not easily represented by a probability measure, that of 'perfect possibility' or 'perfect credibility' (what Levi (1977/1984, 1979/1984) calls 'serious possibility'). An hypothesis H is perfectly possible if and only if the truth of H is consistent with the actor's stock of knowledge. Note that this is not to say that H is true, merely that relative to what the actor knows, he or she has no reason to disbelieve H. Shackle argues that maximum probability ($p = 1$) cannot be used to represent perfect possibility as this would exclude all but one hypothesis as perfectly possible when there may be more. Alternatively, if from the actor's point of view more than one hypothesis qualifies as perfectly possible, then these could be assigned values of less than unity. But this move has the consequence, unpalatable from Shackle's point of view, that the degree of belief assigned to perfectly possible hypotheses may not be independent of the number of rival hypotheses countenanced.[13]

It is of course true that there is no particular reason that perfect possibility should be assigned the number one. The actor might just as well specify some minimum probability k above which the hypothesis qualifies as perfectly possible. But again, and this is Shackle's second point, this move suffers from the drawback that the value of k may be sensitive to the number of rival hypotheses countenanced. If an additional hypothesis is added to the list, perfect possibility may now have to be represented by a lower numerical probability.

Shackle's third point is similar to the second. He begins by arguing that the actor must assign at least one hypothesis in every experiment or act a perfect or highest degree of possibility:

> If, for any given experiment, he can think of no hypothetical outcome which does not seem to him to conflict with the nature of the universe as he conceives it, or with the character of the particular existing situation as he conceives that, we can only say that he has not yet brought his thoughts into an internally self-consistent and harmonious picture; there is a logical contradiction within his own ideas.
>
> (Shackle 1955: 27–8)

Now it seems reasonable, as Shackle contends, that if the actor is deciding between acts, the degree of belief assigned to outcomes considered perfectly possible should be the same for each act. But if probability is taken as a measure of possibility this will generally not be possible. Compare the toss of a fair coin with the toss of a fair die. The outcomes of a head and an ace are both perfectly possible on Shackle's definition, although the respective probabilities are different. It is not possible to scale these probabilities to bring them into equality without relaxing the additivity requirement (or, when the probability distributions are not uniform, and as Shackle demonstrates diagramatically, without changing their shape).

Finally, Shackle argues that probability is not well suited to representing the situation in which, from the actor's point of view, both H and its contradictory $\neg H$ are equally possible, when both the hypothesis and its contradictory are consistent with his or her stock of knowledge. The orthodox view in this case, is that H and $\neg H$ should be assigned equal probabilities of 1/2. But this move presupposes that $\neg H$ is not a disjunction of hypotheses of the same form as H (see Keynes 1921/1973: ch. 4).[14] And this condition, of course, is unlikely to be met in the situations in which Shackle is interested, namely, when there is a residual hypothesis.

The orthodox response

I have not been able to find many orthodox responses to Shackle's objections to the assumption about the absence of a residual hypothesis.[15] In most economic applications of the expected utility model this assumption is simply taken for granted and not justified in any way. Yet it is not difficult to think of situations in which the possibility of learning something as yet unimagined may have consequences for economic choice. A firm may postpone a decision to replace computer equipment on the basis that a major supplier is about to announce a new product, for example, even though the nature of that product may as yet be unknown. There is a branch of the orthodox literature, building on A. G. Hart (1942), which attempts to formalise the idea that there may be benefits to postponing decisions until more information has been acquired (Hahn, 1988; Jones and Ostroy, 1984; Makowski, 1989). But this approach assumes that the actor can list all possible states ex ante; the benefits from waiting stem from the intertemporal resolution of uncertainty via Bayesian 'learning' rather than from learning something that had not been thought of before. Shackle's concerns therefore remain unaddressed (see Hahn 1988: 24; Runde 1994).

5 SHACKLE ON SUBJECTIVE AND LOGICAL PROBABILITY

Subjective probability

Although the subjective conception of probability has been standard in microeconomics and game theory for some time, Shackle has relatively little to say about it. As has already been noted, subjectivists interpret probability as the actor's 'personal' degree of belief in an hypothesis or state. It was shown how such degrees of belief can be mapped onto real numbers via the odds the actor would be prepared to accept on an hypothesis 'coming true' or state coming about. The only constraint placed on beliefs is that they conform to the probability calculus. This requirement is often defended by the so-called Dutch Book argument. A Dutch book is a sequence of bets that yields a non-positive outcome for every state and a negative outcome for at least one. It can be shown that someone who fails to accept the laws of probability could be induced to accept a Dutch book (de Finetti 1990), which, as this would lead to a certain loss, would be irrational.

The idea that probabilities may be identified with betting odds is a seductive one, not least because it is sometimes seen as making it possible to transform 'uncertainty' in Knight's (1921) sense into (calculable) 'risk'. But the theory is based on two strong assumptions: that actors' beliefs are adequately represented by unique real numbers and that they will be prepared to take coherent bets at odds that correspond to these degrees of belief. Both conditions must be met in order for subjective probabilities to be elicited in the way described in Section 2. Shackle is not in a position to object to the first of these two conditions, since his own theory presupposes that actors have unique real-valued degrees of potential surprise. But he would presumably object to the second condition. For it can hardly be a requirement of rationality that people should be prepared to make bets. Of course, if they do do so, they should satisfy the no Dutch Book requirement (on pain of a certain loss). But this still leaves the possibility that they may refuse to bet, which may be a rational course of action when their beliefs do not satisfy the axioms of the probability calculus.

This leaves the two sets of arguments considered in Sections 3 and 4. The first, those based on the distinction between divisible and non-divisible and non-seriable experiments, tell most heavily against the use of frequency-ratios in one-shot expected value calculations. They are less damaging to expected utility theory, where probability is usually interpreted on subjectivist lines and which extends to unique choices and crucial events. Shackle's second set of criticisms are more on the mark, however. The standard model cannot accommodate a residual hypothesis in Shackle's sense, and subjective probability does not appear to be able to capture his notion of possibility.

Logical probability

Shackle devotes somewhat more attention to Keynes's (1921/1973) logical conception of probability than he does to the subjective conception.[16] On Keynes's approach the probability of an hypothesis H is interpreted as arising out of the apprehension of a (partial) logical relation between that hypothesis and a body of evidence E. This probability relation is written H/E and reads 'H relative to E'. Unlike proponents of the orthodox model, however, Keynes does not believe that all probabilities correspond to real numbers. He regards comparative statements of probability of the form $H_1/E_1 \; \varepsilon^* \; H_2/E_2$ as fundamental, where '$\succeq^*$' is the probability relation 'at least as probable as' ($\succ^*$ and $\sim^*$ are defined in the usual way). A distinctive feature of Keynes's approach is that it yields only a partial ordering of probabilities.

Keynes's theory escapes both lines of Shackle's attack on probability.[17] In the first place, logical probability arises out of a balance of the evidence (or arguments) for and against an hypothesis, and is not based on some implicit notion of long-run frequencies.[18] Keynes would agree that probability cannot tell us what the outcome of a unique experiment will be, moreover, although, and as I have already mentioned above, he would not go so far as to say that it is therefore irrelevant as a guide to conduct. But he regards probability as only one of a number of factors to be taken into account when deciding on a course of action and emphasises that the way in which these factors are combined involves more in the way of an intuitive judgment directed at the situation as a whole than it does mathematical calculation (Keynes, 1921/1973: 343–56).

In the second place, the idea that probability should be regarded as corresponding to the strength of the argument from the evidence to some hypothesis, seems to satisfy at least some of Shackle's intuitions about the 'intrinsic standing' of an hypothesis. On Keynes's account, probability is always relative to a specific body of evidence; new evidence E_2 cannot show the probability relation H/E_1 to be wrong, only give rise to a new one $H/(E_1 \ \& \ E_2)$. Thus there is one sense in which a Keynesian probability relation justifies is independent of changes in information about the number and/or probability of competing hypotheses.

But Shackle would want more than this. Suppose we have a list of all the mutually exclusive hypotheses H_i ($i = 1, 2, ..., n$) we can think of concerning the outcome of some action. Then let E_2 be a report that there is an additional competing hypothesis H_{n+1} that had not been thought of prior to arriving at the assessments of the H/E_1, where $P(H_{n+1}/(E_1 \ \& \ E_2)) > 0$. Shackle believes that a theory of standing should permit E_2 to be irrelevant to the probability of the hypotheses H/E_1, or $H_i/E_1 \sim^* H/E_1 \ \& \ E_2$ ($i = 1, 2, ..., n$). This possibility is precluded on the standard approach to probability, according to which

$$\sum_{i=1}^{n} P_i(H_i/E_1) = 1 \text{ prior to the acquisition of } E_2.$$

But it is not precluded on Keynes's (non-distributional) theory, since his basic statements of comparative probability do not presuppose a complete list of states or hypotheses.[19]

Probability, possibility and evidential weight

Although his criticisms leave the *Treatise on Probability* largely unmarked, Shackle remains keen to emphasise his differences from Keynes. The purpose of this section is to suggest that their respective accounts nevertheless do display one striking commonality.

On Keynes's theory, uncertainty arises out of the incompleteness of the body of evidence bearing on an hypothesis (if the evidence were complete, it would have the capacity to provide certain knowledge of the truth or falsity of that hypothesis). As we often cannot wait on certainty before acting, Keynes takes it for granted that it is rational to be guided by the evidence that we do have at our disposal at the time of decision. Keynesian probability thus arises out of knowledge and constitutes of an assessment of the balance of the favourable and unfavourable evidence in respect of an hypothesis. Shackle, in contrast, prefers to emphasize that which is not known regarding an hypothesis, the difference, so to speak, between the body of evidence that would be sufficient to demonstrate the truth or falsity of an hypothesis and the evidence currently at hand. In Shackle's view, therefore, 'probability' should reflect an assessment of the extra evidence that would be required to achieve certain knowledge of an hypothesis:

> I feel it necessary to say that the different degrees of probability, which different bodies of knowledge or evidence entitle us to adjudge to a given proposition, take their effect through the different amounts or forms of extra evidence which we should need to supply, in order to render the proposition, not 'probable' but conclusively proved; and that the effect of starting with one rather than another set of initial propositions, or corpus of evidence or data, is to oppose different kinds of obstacle, or different degrees of severity, in the way of making that set of initial propositions, evidence or data into a sufficient basis for certain inference and conclusive demonstration.
>
> (Shackle 1972: 391)

While Keynes would almost certainly object to the term 'probability' being used in this way, he would not object to the underlying idea. For in the *Treatise* he also introduces a measure that is in many respects similar to what Shackle is proposing, of what he calls 'weight of evidence' (Keynes 1921/1973: 77–85).[20] Evidential weight is often interpreted as reflecting the amount, in some sense, of the evidence on which a judgement of probability is based. Keynes suggests that probabilities may sometimes be compared in terms of weight as well as probability, and, other things being equal, that it is rational to be guided by arguments of greater weight. But he also describes weight as the balance of the relevant knowledge and relevant ignorance or, equivalently, the degree of completeness of the information on which a probability is based. Elsewhere, I have argued in favour of this second interpretation (Runde 1990).

A full account of the links between possibility and weight would warrant a paper on its own. Shackle (1979a: 128–33) does provide a brief discussion of the matter and concludes that Keynes's views on weight 'might ... have been a little more accessible to my theme' than

Keynes's views on probability. This is a rather lukewarm endorsement and most of Shackle's approval seems to stem from the possibility that assessments of weight have more to do with (subjective) 'judgment' than with 'logic'. But Shackle adopts the standard interpretation of weight as a measure of the 'amount' of the evidence relevant to some hypothesis. The alternative conception of weight as the degree of completeness of such evidence, and which thereby introduces questions regarding the extent of our ignorance concerning the factors which will determine the truth or falsity of an hypothesis, is much closer to Shackle's own position on what it is that a measure of standing should represent.[21]

6 CONCLUSIONS

Shackle raises two broad lines of argument against the use of probability in economic analysis. The first questions the relevance of frequency-ratios in one-shot decision situations. However, and although the distinction between divisible and non-divisible non-seriable experiments remains an illuminating one, this part of Shackle's critique has lost some of its force. For the expected utility approach can to some extent accommodate the problem he raises regarding 'unique' choices and the frequency interpretation of probability has been supplanted by the subjectivist interpretation in economic theory.

Shackle's second set of arguments, however, stand. The standard approach does not extend to situations in which there is a residual hypothesis in Shackle's sense and invites replacement or substantial revision on this point. It is somewhat more difficult to assess the overall importance of Shackle's notion of possibility, not least because probability concepts are so deeply ingrained in us. But there is no doubt that probability measures cannot represent the kinds of beliefs Shackle has in mind. Whether these ideas will at some stage become more important in economics remains to be seen.

In his later writings, Shackle devotes increasing attention to the subjectivist and Keynesian conceptions of probability. Both of these approaches interpret probability as a degree of belief and accordingly avoid the criticism based on Shackle's distinction between divisible and non-divisible non-seriable experiments. Keynes's approach also avoids the second of Shackle's criticisms, as it does not presuppose the absence of a residual hypothesis. In terms of Keynes's theory, the standing of hypotheses may be graded both in terms of the balance of the favourable and the unfavourable evidence that bears on them (probability) and in terms of the 'completeness' of this evidence (weight). Shackle would not have much to do with the first measure, but the second, I have suggested, has affinities with his notion of potential surprise.

APPENDIX: THE AXIOMS OF POTENTIAL SURPRISE

Let $S(H/K)$ be the potential surprise (or disbelief) assigned to H relative to the actor's background knowledge K. This measure satisfies the following rules (see Levi 1979, 1980; also Katzner 1986).

(1) If $S(H/K) > 0$, $S(\neg H/K) = 0$ = minimum surprise value
(2) If $K \Rightarrow \neg H$, $S(H/K) = 1$ = maximum surprise value
(3) $S(H \vee G/K) = \min(S(H/K), S(G/K))$
(4) If H_i ($i = 1,2, ..., n$) is an exhaustive list of mutually exclusive hypotheses relative to K, then $S(H/K) = 0$ for at least one i.

For a concise summary of Shackle's decision theory, see Ford (1990: 21–30).

It is easy to see that a measure that satisfies the above requirements avoids the four points raised against probability in Section 4. First, 'perfect possibility' corresponds to a zero value of potential surprise. Thus we have a measure that 'can express perfect plausibility or perfect credibility or perfect possibility without any implication or suggestion of perfect certainty' (Shackle 1955: 33). Shackle's second and third objections are met as the degree of potential surprise assigned to one hypothesis is independent of those assigned all other hypotheses (individually or severally). And finally, it is permitted that both an hypothesis and its contradictory carry zero potential surprise.

Shackle holds that to believe H to some degree is to disbelieve $\neg H$ to the same degree. Given this condition, belief (B) functions satisfy the following requirements (Levi 1979):

(1') If $B(H/K) > 0$, $B(\neg H/K) = 0$

(2') If $K \Rightarrow H$, $B(H/K) = 1$

(3') $B(H \& G/K) = \min(B(H/K), B(G/K))$

These three conditions are satisfied by Cohen's (1977) measure of inductive probability. It should be said, however, that Cohen and Levi interpret this formalism quite differently (see the exchange in Cohen and Hesse 1980: 26–27, 64–66, 171). For a discussion of the links between the theory of inductive probability and Keynes's theory of evidential weight, see Cohen (1977:   36–39; 1985:   276–278; 1989). Others who have developed formalisms similar to Shackle's include Shafer (1976) and Spohn (1988).

NOTES

* I am grateful to Paul Anand, Vicky Chick, John Davis, Peter Earl, Martin Dietrich, Donald Gillies, Geoff Harcourt, Brian Holley, Tony Lawson, Charles McCann and Arnis Vilks for helpful comments on earlier versions of this paper.

1 Save for the section on Keynes, the term 'probability' denotes a measure that satisfies the axioms of the probability calculus. I shall use the notation p(.) for the standard measure and P(.) for the Keynesian one.

2 In a prominent early survey of the theory of choice under uncertainty, Arrow (1951) presents Shackle's theory of potential surprise as rival to those of von Neumann and Morgenstern (1947) on the one hand, and Neyman and Pearson (1933) and Wald (1939, 1950) on the other. But Shackle's theory is not or only barely mentioned in more recent surveys (Hey 1983, 1984, Hirshleifer and Riley 1979, Kelsey and Quiggin 1992, Lawson 1988, Schoemaker 1982, Machina 1987, 1989).

3 'Choice is amongst rivals; and rivals, of their nature, must be both mutually exclusive and co-existent. This is only possible to thoughts' (Shackle 1972: 364–5).

4 It is unlikely that Shackle would accept the idea that completely exogenous states of the world could be conceived ex ante: 'when [the actor] sets himself to choose a course of action out of many which seem open to him, he may implicitly assume himself to be making history, on however a small scale, in some sense other than mere passive obedience to the play of all-pervasive causes' (Shackle 1983: 28).

5 See Shackle (1952: 109). Shackle also mentions the epistemic 'a priori' counterpart to the frequency view (see Hacking 1975). A priori probabilities are based on judgements of symmetry rather than a counting of trials: if on the basis of such rules as Bernoulli's Principle of Insufficient

Reason or Keynes's Principle of Indifference each of an exhaustive and exclusive list of consequences ci (i = 1, 2, ..., n) are judged equally probable, then $p(ci)$ = $1/n$ for each i. In his *Epistemics and Economics*, Shackle (1972) classifies the frequentist and the a priori views as 'objective' and refers to them as the experimental and the structural view respectively. Shackle mentions Keynes in his earlier writings, but as a proponent of the principle of indifference more than anything else. Only later does he take a more comprehensive view of Keynes's contribution (see Shackle, 1972, 1974, 1976, 1979a, 1979b and Section 5 below).

6　Shackle (1955: 4) is reluctant to expand on the terms 'similar' and 'large', but recognizes that these conditions will be fulfilled to varying degrees in practice and will accordingly give answers to varying degrees of precision. Shackle (1972: 385–6) gives a more rigorous set of requirements, including a closure condition: that the system is 'guaranteed from invisible change of its constitution'.

7　Coddington's (1982) characterization of Shackle as a 'nonfallibilist' is thus warranted. Shackle (1955: 28–9) regards it as a flaw of probability that, except in degenerate cases, any assignment of probability to the outcome of a unique experiment will be false: 'Suppose, for example, that a probability of 1/6 is assigned ex ante to some hypothesis concerning the outcome of a non-divisible non-seriable experiment. Then if this hypothesis proves false, the decision-maker was plainly wrong not to assign it a probability zero instead of 1/6, while if it proves true, he was plainly wrong not to assign it a probability of unity.'

8　See also Arrow (1951: 415) and Ellsberg (1961/1988: 246). It should be said that Shackle's position on this issue seems to moderate over time. In a paper first published in 1949 he writes: 'it is plain ... that for a non-divisible non-seriable experiment no frequency-ratio can have any meaning or relevance' (Shackle, 1955: 7). Three years later he writes that for such experiments: 'there can be no straightforward use of frequency-ratios as knowledge which will enable [the actor] to predict with confidence the relevant outcome for himself of the experiment' (Shackle, 1955: 24).

9　See Shackle (1972: 405–7).

10　Shackle (1966: 71–84) provides a forceful account of the undesirable ontological implications of the assumption of a complete list of hypotheses, namely that it is incompatible with surprise. For commentaries on this part of Shackle's writings, see Levi (1986: 53–67) and Schick (1979).

11　Shackle's theory of potential surprise is designed to deal with situations of this kind and has the merit of being able to represent beliefs compatible with the existence of a residual hypothesis (see appendix).

12　Shackle raises five points here. I shall consider all but the fourth, which is included in footnote 7 of the previous section.

13 As Shackle conceives of probability in terms of ratios of equi-probable events, he takes it for granted that the addition of an hypothesis to an existing list of hypotheses must lead to revised probabilities for all of the original members of that list. But this need of course not be the case where the probabilities of individual hypotheses can assume different values.

14 In the absence of evidence either way a (naive) application of the principle of indifference would lead to the hypothesis that a particular book is red being assigned a probability of 1/2. But the same rule could equally well be applied to the hypothesis that the book is black, or to the hypothesis that it is blue. We would then have three mutually exclusive alternatives, the combined probability of which is 1.5.

15 Hey (1990) is aware of Shackle's argument but offers no theoretical counter-argument. Madan and Owings (1988) propose to extend the Savage model to situations in which it is not possible to list all hypotheses, but proceed on the basis that there is a probability of the residual hypothesis (but which cannot be effectively decomposed). Kreps (1992) attempts to introduce 'unforeseen contingencies' by looking at the extent to which the actor attempts to preserve flexibility (to adapt to such contingencies should they arise). There have also been a number of papers on expected utility with nonadditive probability (Gilboa 1987; Schmeidler 1989). But these are addressed at the Ellsberg (1961) paradox, where the problem is one of ambiguous probabilities rather than that of providing an exhaustive list of states.

16 Although interest in logical probability fell off after Carnap (1950), there has since been something of a resurgence (Benenson 1984, Stove 1986, Weatherford 1982, Watt 1989). See also the economic literature surrounding Keynes's *Treatise on Probability* (Carabelli 1988, Davis 1994, Lawson and Pesaran 1985, O'Donnell 1989).

17 Shackle's criticisms do apply to probabilities derived from applications of the Principle of Indifference. But although Keynes has quite a bit to say about this principle, his contribution is better described as one of limiting rather than widening its range of application. Shackle does not appear to recognize that Keynes's theory is primarily one of comparative probability.

18 Keynes in fact developed his theory in response to perceived deficiencies in the frequentist conception of probability implicit in G. E. Moore's (1903) *Principia Ethica*.

19 Madan and Owings (1988: 26–7) even suggest that Keynes's theory implies that one may be forced to live with a residual hypothesis, since one 'can never have taken account of all possible H's, for any assertion to this effect is an H and alternatives can be conceived.'

20 The major difference is that Keynes regards this measure as complementary rather than competing with probability.

21 Levi (1966, 1972, 1979) has long argued that potential surprise should be regarded as an index of the need to increase the weight of evidence. Cohen's (1977) measure of inductive probability, which satisfies the same formal properties as Shackle's measure of potential surprise, also bears close links with Keynesian weight (see appendix).

REFERENCES

Arrow, K. J. (1951) 'Alternative approaches to the theory of risk bearing', *Econometrica* 19: 404–37.

Benenson, F. C. (1984) *Probability, Objectivity and Evidence*, London: Routledge & Kegan Paul.

Carabelli, A. (1988) *On Keynes's Method*, New York: St. Martin's Press.

Carnap, R. (1950) *Logical Foundations of Probability*, Chicago, IL: University of Chicago Press.

Coddington, A. (1982) 'Deficient foresight: a troublesome theme in Keynesian economics', *American Economic Review* 72: 480–7.

Cohen, L. J. (1977) *The Probable and the Provable*, Oxford: Clarendon Press.

—— (1985) 'Twelve questions about Keynes's concept of weight', *British Journal for the Philosophy of Science* 37: 263–78.

—— (1989) *An Introduction to the Philosophy of Induction and Probability*, Oxford: Oxford University Press.

—— and Hesse, M. (eds) (1980) *Applications of Inductive Logic*, Oxford: Clarendon.

Davis, J. B. (1994) *Keynes's Philosophical Development*, Cambridge: Cambridge University Press.

de Finetti, B. (1990) *Theory of Probability, Volume 1*, New York: Wiley.

Ellsberg, D. (1954) 'Classic and current notions of "measurable utility"', *Economic Journal* 64: 529–56.

—— (1961/1988) 'Risk, ambiguity and the Savage axioms', *Quarterly Journal of Economics* 75: 528–56. Reprinted in Gärdenfors, P. and Sahlin, N.-E. (eds) *Decision, Probability and Utility: Selected Readings*. Cambridge: Cambridge University Press, 245–69.

Fishburn, P. C. (1981) 'Subjective expected utility: a review of normative theories', *Theory and Decision* 13: 139–99.

Ford, J. L. (1983) *Choice, Expectation and Uncertainty*, Oxford: Basil Blackwell.

—— (1985) 'Shackle's theory of decision-making under uncertainty: summary, exposition and brief appraisal', *Journal of Economic Studies*, January.

—— (1987) *Economic Choice Under Uncertainty: A Perspective Theory Approach*. Aldershot: Edward Elgar.

—— (1990) 'Shackle's theory of decision-making under uncertainty: a brief exposition and critical appraisal', in Frowen, S. F. (ed.) *Unknowledge and*

Choice in Economics. London: Macmillan.

Gärdenfors, P. and Sahlin, N.-E. (eds.) *Decision, Probability and Utility: Selected Readings*. Cambridge: Cambridge University Press.

Gilboa, I. (1987) 'Expected utility with purely subjective non-additive probabilities', *Journal of Mathematical Economics* 16: 65–88.

Hacking, I. (1975) *The Emergence of Probability*, Cambridge: Cambridge University Press.

Hahn, F. H. (1988) 'Liquidity', Economic Theory Discussion Paper, no. 129, Department of Applied Economics, University of Cambridge.

Hannson, B. (1988) 'Risk aversion as a problem of conjoint measurement', in Gärdenfors, P. and Sahlin, N.-E. (eds.) *Decision, Probability and Utility: Selected Readings*. Cambridge: Cambridge University Press, 136–58.

Hart, A. G. (1942) 'Risk, uncertainty and the unprofitability of compounding probabilities', in Lange, O., McIntyre, F. and Yntema, T. O. (eds) *Studies in Mathematical Economics and Econometrics*, Chicago, IL: Chicago University Press, 110–18.

Hey, J.D. (1983) 'Whither uncertainty.' Supplement to the *Economic Journal*: 129–39.

— — (1984) 'Decision under uncertainty', in van der Ploeg, F. (ed.) *Mathematical Methods in Economics*. London: John Wiley and Sons, Ltd, 433–55.

— — (1990) 'The Possibility of Possibility.' In Frowen, S. F. (ed.) *Unknowledge and Choice in Economics: Proceedings of a Conference in Honour of G. L. S. Shackle*, London: Macmillan, 168–91.

Hirshleifer, J. and Riley, J. G. (1979) 'The analytics of uncertainty and information — an expository survey', *Journal of Economic Literature* 17: 1375–421.

Jones, R. A. and Ostroy, J. M. (1984) 'Flexibility and uncertainty', *Review of Economic Studies* 51: 13–32.

Katzner, D. W. (1986) 'Potential surprise, potential confirmation, and probability', *Journal of Post Keynesian Economics* 9: 58–78

Kelsey, D. and Quiggin, J. (1992) 'Theories of choice under ignorance and uncertainty', *Journal of Economic Surveys* 6: 132–53.

Keynes, J. M. (1921/1973) 'A treatise on probability.' *The Collected Writings of John Maynard Keynes*, vol. VIII, New York: St. Martin's Press.

Knight, F. H. (1921) *Risk, Uncertainty and Profit*. Chicago, IL: Chicago University Press.

Kreps, D. M. (1992) 'Static choice in the presence of unforeseen contingencies', in Dasgupta, P., Gale, D., Hart, O. and Maskin, E. (eds) *Economic Analysis of Markets and Games: Essays in Honor of Frank Hahn*. Cambridge, Massachusetts: The MIT Press, 258–81.

Lawson, T. (1988) 'Probability and uncertainty in economic analysis', *Journal of Post Keynesian Economics* 11: 38–65.

—— and Pesaran, H. (eds.) (1985) *Keynes' Economics: Methodological Issues*, London: Croom Helm.

Levi, I. (1966) 'On potential surprise.' *Ratio* 8: 107–29.

—— (1967) *Gambling with Truth*, New York: Knopf.

—— (1972) 'Potential surprise in the context of inquiry', in Carter, C. F. and Ford, J. L. (eds) *Uncertainty and Expectations in Economics: Essays in Honour of G.L.S. Shackle*, Oxford: Basil Blackwell, 213–36.

—— (1977) 'Four types of ignorance', *Social Research* 44: 745–56. Reprinted in Levi, I. (1984) *Decisions and Revisions: Philosophical Essays on Knowledge and Value*, Cambridge: Cambridge University Press, 128–35.

—— (1979) 'Support and surprise: L. J. Cohen's view of inductive probability', *British Journal for the Philosophy of Science* 30: 279–92.

—— (1979/1984) 'Serious possibility', in E. Saarinen et al. (eds) *Essays in Honour of Jaakko Hintikka*, Dordrecht: Reidel, 219–36. Reprinted in Levi, I. (1984) *Decisions and Revisions: Philosophical Essays on Knowledge and Value*, Cambridge: Cambridge University Press, 147–61

—— (1980) 'Potential surprise: its role in inference and decision making', in Levi, I. (1984) *Decisions and Revisions: Philosophical Essays on Knowledge and Value*, Cambridge: Cambridge University Press, 214–42.

—— (1986) *Hard Choices: Decision Making Under Unresolved Conflict*, Cambridge: Cambridge University Press.

—— (1991) *The Fixation of Belief and Its Undoing.* Cambridge: Cambridge University Press.

Machina, M. J. (1987) 'Choice under uncertainty: problems solved and unsolved', *Journal of Economic Perspectives* 1: 121–54.

—— (1989)'Dynamic consistency and non-expected utility models of choice under uncertainty', *Journal of Economic Literature* 27: 1622–68.

Madan, D .P. and Owings, J.C. (1988) 'Decision theory with complex uncertainties', *Synthese* 75: 25–44.

Makowski, L. (1989) 'Keynes's liquidity preference: a suggested interpretationi', in Hahn, F. H. (ed.) *The Economics of Missing Markets, Information and Games*, Oxford: Basil Blackwell, 468–75.

Moore, G. E. (1903) *Principia Ethica*, Cambridge: Cambridge University Press.

Neyman, J. and Pearson, E. S. (1933) 'The testing of statistical hypotheses in relation to probabilities a priori', *Proceedings of the Cambridge Philosophical Society* 29: 492–510.

O'Donnell, R. M. (1989) *Keynes: Philosophy, Economics and Politics*, London: Macmillan.

Peirce, C. S. (1923) *Chance, Love and Logic*, London: Kegan Paul, Trench, Trubner & Co. Ltd.

Ramsey, F. P. (1926) 'Truth and probability', in Mellor, D. H. (ed.) (1978) *Foundations: Essays in Philosophy, Logic, Mathematics and Economics*, London: Routledge & Kegan Paul, 58–100.

Runde, J. H. (1990) 'Keynesian uncertainty and the weight of arguments', *Economics and Philosophy* 6: 275-92.

—— (1994) 'Keynesian uncertainty and liquidity preference', *Cambridge Journal of Economics* 18: 129-44.

Savage, L. J. (1954) *The Foundations of Statistics*, New York: John Wiley & Sons, Inc.

Schick, F. (1979) 'Self-knowledge, uncertainty and choice', *British Journal for the Philosophy of Science* 30: 235-52.

Schoemaker, P. J. H. (1982) 'The expected utility model: its variants, purposes, evidence and limitations', *Journal of Economic Literature* 20: 529-63.

Schmeidler, D. (1989) 'Subjective probability and expected utility without additivity', *Econometrica* 57: 571-87.

Shackle, G. L. S. (1952) *Expectation in Economics*, 2nd edn, Cambridge: Cambridge University Press.

—— (1955) *Uncertainty in Economics and Other Reflections*, Cambridge: Cambridge University Press.

—— (1956) 'Expectations and cardinality.' *Economic Journal* 66: 211-19.

—— (1958) *Time in Economics*, Amsterdam: North-Holland.

—— (1966) *The Nature of Economic Thought: Selected Papers 1955-1964*, Cambridge: Cambridge University Press.

—— (1970) *Expectations, Enterprise and Profit*, London: George Allen & Unwin.

—— (1972) *Epistemics and Economics*, Cambridge: Cambridge University Press.

—— (1974) 'Decision: the human predicament', *The Annals of the American Academy of Political and Social Science*, Philadelphia 412: 1-10.

—— (1976) 'Time and choice', *Proceedings of the British Academy* 62: 1-23.

—— (1979a) *Imagination and the Nature of Choice*, Edinburgh: Edinburgh University Press.

—— (1979b) 'On Hick's causality in economics: a review article', *Greek Economic Review* 1: 43-55.

—— (1983) 'The Bounds of unknowledge', in Wiseman, J. (ed.) *Beyond Positive Economics?* London: Macmillan, 28-37.

Shafer, G. (1976) *A Mathematical Theory of Evidence*, Princeton: Princeton University Press.

Spohn, W. (1988) 'Ordinal conditional functions: a dynamic theory of epistemic states', in Harper, W. and Skyrms, B. (eds) *Causation in Decision, Belief Change and Statistics*, Dordrecht: Reidel, 105-34.

Stove, D. C. (1986) *The Rationality of Induction*, Oxford: Clarendon Press.

von Neumann, J and Morgenstern, O. (1947) *Theory of Games and Economic Behaviour*, Princeton: Princeton University Press.

Wald, A. (1939) 'Contributions to the theory of statistical estimation and testing Hypotheses', *Annals of Mathematical Statistics* 10: 299-326.

— — (1950) *Statistical Decision Functions*. New York: John Wiley & Sons.

Watt, D. E. (1989) 'Not very likely: a reply to Ramsey.' *British Journal for the Philosophy of Science* 40 223–227.

Weatherford, R. (1982) *Philosophical Foundations of Probability Theory*, London: Routledge & Kegan Paul.

Weckstein, R. S. (1959) 'Probable knowledge and singular acts', *Metroeconomica* 11: 104–118.

11

LIQUIDITY AND POTENTIAL SURPRISE

Moacir dos Anjos Jr and Victoria Chick

1 INTRODUCTION

The need for liquidity may be fulfilled by a wide range of assets, from money and short-term financial assets to old masters and land. However, the chosen assets must be expected to be quickly convertible into the means of payment at terms which enable the holders to discharge their contracts, to face unforeseen needs for money, or to take advantage of unexpected opportunities. To rank the assets according to their liquidity and to choose amongst them, one must form expectations now concerning the terms of immediate convertibility of each of these assets into the accepted means of payment in the future.

Despite many attempts to pin down the meaning of liquidity and to arrive at some description of how an agent might assess the liquidity of assets in an environment of uncertainty, liquidity remains as slippery a concept as its name suggests. More can still be said. In particular, although it is now conventional to bring the classical theory of probability to bear on this question, we see difficulties with this. We shall explore Shackle's twin concepts of potential surprise and focus gain and loss as a framework for evaluating liquidity. We start by looking in some detail at the problem of liquidity and the probabilistic approach to it; then we explore the relevance of Shackle's concepts and the relationship of these concepts to classical probability. Finally we apply Shackle's concepts to an episode in recent Brazilian monetary history.

2 THE NEED FOR LIQUIDITY

The background of liquidity has two elements: uncertainty and the money economy; there is, amongst the stream of anticipated payments, a set of payments which are at the time of the asset-holding decision unforeseen, either in their timing or their extent or both, and a standardized means of payment is required if these payments are to be made. The ease with which, and the price at which, one's assets can be converted into the means of payment is the measure of their liquidity. For this reason, money is taken as the benchmark of liquidity; it is normally the perfectly liquid asset.

The liquidity of a non-money asset, or of a portfolio, lies between two extremes. First, imagine that vehicles for saving in the form of financial assets consist of securities which mature at various dates but for which there are no secondhand markets. Thus these securities are perfectly illiquid up to the day of maturity and perfectly liquid at that date. Suppose also that the means of payment, 'money', is subject to a swinging holding tax ('stamped money'), so that keeping it for any length of time is not really an option.

The problem of managing liquidity under these conditions is to make the best estimates of one's expenditure plans and have the appropriate amount in securities maturing at the relevant dates. A failure to have liquid assets ready when an expenditure falls due will mean that the expenditure is not made or a contract is not fulfilled. To hedge against this eventuality there would of course be an incentive to hold short-term securities and re-invest them if expenditure plans did not materialize. Short-term securities would also permit a delay in buying long-term securities in order to get the best price. Short-term securities thus would, other things equal, command a premium: a liquidity premium. There is an unambiguous ranking of securities in terms of their liquidity narrowly conceived: liquidity falls monotonically with length of time to maturity. In choosing a portfolio, then, the factors which balance the desire for liquidity are the higher rates of return on long-term assets and any transactions costs involved in buying securities and/or claiming money on their maturity.

At the other extreme, we introduce the possibility of borrowing against assets. Then we can include non-financial assets as well, for we do not need maturity dates. Let us, further, have a perfect capital market. Then any expenditure, however unexpected, can be accommodated by borrowing against assets. In this case, all assets are perfectly liquid except for transactions costs (including borrowing costs). The portfolio decision can be based on expected pecuniary and direct returns and associated costs alone; liquidity need not be considered. (It is not surprising that neoclassical economists gravitate to transactions-costs explanations of liquidity.)

The actuality of the liquidity problem is much messier than these simple extremes. First, expenditures vary in their unpredictability. A primary need for liquidity is to meet regular consumption expenditures, yet this is usually ruled out of the discussion, for it is assumed that these expenditures are covered by cash flow from current activities. This is the nature of transactions demand for money, and we follow convention and leave it aside.

Yet the border between regular, well-foreseen and relatively small expenditures and the expenditures for which liquidity is needed is not always clear. At the other end of the spectrum the impossibility of financing a large expenditure, even if foreseen, out of current cash flow is obvious enough. It is also clear that more distant expenditures, even those which are, in their broad outline, foreseen (a deposit on a house, a child's school fees, one's consumption in retirement), cannot be financed with current cash flow; one has to find an abode for one's purchasing power or be confident of one's future borrowing capacity. One may attempt to do some maturity matching, but in an uncertain world it cannot be perfect. And the capital market is neither perfect nor cheap. Hence liquidity will play a role in asset-holding decisions.

The very nature of an unexpected expenditure entails finding the money for it quickly. For other expenditures, even if one cannot plan a portfolio perfectly matched in its maturities to expected expenditures, liquidity allows one to dispose of one's assets in an orderly manner, at favourable prices. One can frame the question of the liquidity of a portfolio in terms of a *hierarchy of budget constraints*, where the more liquid assets are realized first, then the others, trading off speed of realization and favourable prices on one side and risking delaying, or not making, the expenditure, on the other (Chick 1973: ch. 5).

Expenditure need not be construed as the purchase of goods and services; the literature on the term structure of interest rates ascribes a liquidity motive to the wish to be able to take advantage of higher-yielding assets should the opportunity arise.

Insofar as illiquid assets foreclose options, the inclusion of those assets in a portfolio is a *crucial decision* in Shackle's sense: the future may be irrevocably influenced by that choice at a point of time. One could turn this statement around and make the following proposition: *the search for liquidity is an attempt to turn crucial decisions into non-crucial ones.* In real life this can only be done imperfectly: even money may have less liquidity than one expects, as we shall see in the Brazilian example.

3 THE NATURE OF LIQUIDITY

Sir John Hicks (1962) first traced the origin of the concept of liquidity to Keynes. In the *Treatise on Money* and the Macmillan Report a liquid asset was described as 'more certainly realizable at short notice without loss' (Keynes 1930, vol. II: 67). Later (1976), Hicks attributes the earliest and best discussion of liquidity to Menger (1871), who emphasized that liquidity keeps one's options open, not just in a protective way but actively. This idea is reflected in a major survey of liquidity (Hahn 1990). Keynes's definition can be seen as the practical expression of Menger's idea. Keynes's definition has four components: realizability or marketability, which is the *sine qua non*, the degree of certainty (conventionally, the probability) of this marketability, the time horizon, and the amount of loss one might expect.

Realizability is put at the top of this list, for we have taken it for granted that liquid assets are substitutes for money, 'as good to hold and only inferior when the actual moment of payment arrives' (Radcliffe Report). The ease with which assets can be turned into money when the actual moment of payment does arrive is the essence of liquidity. To look at the matter from the other direction, it is being assumed that money is unambiguously the most liquid asset (while recognizing that in an inflation (see Chick 1983: ch. 17) or during war or other dislocation, this assumption would not hold). We shall also take for granted that the par value between different forms of money is maintained. Assets which are not legally marketable at all (such as children or ivory carvings) are ruled out of discussion.

The *degree* of marketability is related to price: one could argue that the person who says he cannot sell his house is simply not lowering its price sufficiently. Or to turn the point around, the fact that selling the house may involve substantial loss marks it as comparatively illiquid.

There is no paradox here. As Carvalho (1992: 85) puts it, 'Liquidity is a bi-dimensional concept. It refers simultaneously to the duration of time required (or expected to be required) to dispose of an asset and to the capacity this asset may have for conserving its value over time.'

This question of finding the 'right' buyer brings in the question of uncertainty, not about the future expenditure but about the sale price of the asset; in usual discussions of liquidity this is treated as a matter of probability. The case of the sale of a house has a kind of spatial dimension which becomes temporal: one can imagine a class of potential buyers, one or more of whom will pay the asking price, but they are spatially disbursed and imperfectly informed. It therefore takes time to sample, let us say by a random process, the 'population' of buyers and for all potential buyers to discover the property. Therefore the shorter the time between the identified need for money and the initiation of the sale of the house, the lower one expects the realized price of the house to be. Of course it may not be necessary to lower the price (remember we are talking about a stable economy): one might be 'lucky' and find the right buyer straight away.

There are other assets for which a secondhand market is not even organized, where the spread between the buying and probable selling price is even more marked than in the case of houses. (See Earl (1995) for an extended discussion of liquidity in relation to secondhand markets and the role played by dealers.)

Houses are not homogeneous: all offer shelter but each is unique, and they have direct use-value. By contrast, financial assets, while they differ by risk-class, by their expected return, and by their length to maturity, are otherwise homogenous. Therefore interest in them is limited to the financial return they produce — and their liquidity. By virtue of their non-uniqueness, their close substitutability with financial assets in other risk classes and maturities, and the breadth of their (organized) markets, they are deemed more liquid than houses. The traditional literature would attribute the difference in liquidity of the two types of asset to differences in *transactions costs*: selling a house involves search, selling a financial asset usually involves paying a commission. (The commission can be viewed as the price each participant pays the jobber/broker for maintaining an organized market.)

While a search for a buyer is of probabilistic duration and cost, a commission may be treated as known. The uncertainty amongst financial assets reduces to the readily-observed variation in the price of those assets. Financial assets have no use-value; hence they pose the question of potential gain or loss in its purest pecuniary form. Other things equal, a general change in interest rates will affect long-term assets more than short-term ones by virtue only of their relative length to maturity. Thus in general one would expect the price of long-term assets to vary more than short-term ones. Add to this the fact that at maturity all assets are equally liquid and short-term assets may be said to be almost always more liquid than long-term ones.

The question of *how much* price variation may be expected has traditionally been the province of classical probability theory; one looks at the past performance of prices of securities of different lengths and from that derives a probability distribution of prices. By establishing some confidence interval, one can then formalize the extent of loss one expects on a quick sale.

4 CONVENTIONAL PROBABILITY IN LIQUIDITY THEORY

The chief area of application of conventional probability theory to the question of liquidity relates to the expected sale price of one's assets: prices are assumed to vary within a pattern which can be discovered by observing the past. One then can attach confidence intervals to different ranges of expected gains and losses. Conceiving the choice between more and less liquid assets in the single dimension of the trade-off between expected interest payments and capital gains on the one hand and capital losses on the other brings liquidity within the ambit of portfolio theory but also exposes it to the criticisms of portfolio theory. Some of the criticisms directed at the use of portfolio theory in the context of speculation (Chick 1983: ch. 10 and appendix) are valid also in the context of liquidity.

The criticisms of portfolio theory have all, one way or another, been made indirectly by Shackle in his critique of classical probability theory (hereafter referred to simply as 'probability'). This critique is the subject of Runde's chapter in this book and is based on the fact that probability theory was devised for repeatable experiments — the tosses of coins or dice, the drawing of balls from an urn — which are divisible or seriable. 'Divisible experiments' are those in which the Experiment was to be seen not as an individual toss or draw but conceived as the entire sequence, taken as a whole. The Experiment is divisible into the individual tosses or draws. These elements of the Experiment may be undertaken by different agents at the same time or may take place sequentially, as long as the passage of time does not affect the outcome, i.e. when the attributes of time are not materially different from those of space. Seriable experiments include events which happen once to the individual but which can be converted into the equivalent of a divisible experiment by insuring. The unity of the Experiment is illustrated by its result: a statement of probability which applies only to the whole or a long series of similar trials.

Stability over time becomes vital when observations are taken from past history. In portfolio theory, it is tacitly assumed that the probability distribution of capital gains/losses must be derived from past experience. It can be seen from the above that only special circumstances render such an extrapolation legitimate. The process which generates the probability distribution must be stationary. (This is a stronger requirement than ergodicity: Davidson 1982–3, 1990, 1991a; Mills 1999.)

Although the stationarity condition is important, it still treats the generation of asset prices as somehow objective and even mechanical. Actually, prices are unknowable because they depend on the future behaviour, necessarily unpredictable, of *other people*, including those acting on behalf of government. ('The economy as a whole is only as liquid as government permits' (Chick 1973: 83).)

Only if the generating process is stable is the distribution a useful guide to present action. Even then it is useful only within limits: the distribution itself is taken from past data but the actual dates of each observation are 'lost in the distribution', so to speak. Thus nothing can be said about prices on actual dates in the future, except that one's best guess is always the mean. All that the probability distribution can indicate is the degree of confidence one ought to place in that single expectation.

Shackle has remarked that in classical probability theory, not only the Experiment but even the time-frame of the Experiment can be conceived as a single whole:

> The mathematician treats time as a space, or as one dimension of
> a space, in which all points have an equal status or importance

or validity *together*. ... [T]hey have ... a simultaneous validity; each of them means the same to him when he thinks about them all in one thought.... In the mathematician's act of writing down his equation, all the instants...are folded up into one indivisible statement.

(Shackle 1959: 14–15)

Classic probability experiments rely on unchanging properties of the objects involved: the experiment does not go on so long as to wear out the die and render it 'untrue'. In that sense time is 'all of a piece' and the probabilities which can be attached to outcomes refer to the population of outcomes, not to specific events. This conception conforms well to portfolio theory, with its unit time period of completely undefined length, no requirement that the portfolio ever be realized, and probabilities which do not indicate what the portfolio would fetch if it *were* sold, any more than (to use Runde's example) the probability of bottles on an assembly line being defective says anything about the soundness of an individual bottle.

Realization, however, is at the centre of the problem of liquidity. The need to consider realization arises from the uncertainty over the size and timing of future expenditures and the price of the assets sold to meet these expenditures. Thus there are actually *two* time frames of importance in liquidity theory: the time horizon for which the portfolio strategy is being formed and the length of time available between knowing there is a need to realize assets and actually doing so. For the first of these, one could (and we shall) argue in favour of the usefulness of probability theory, up to a point. But for the second, one needs to have an idea of the price an asset will fetch *on a particular date*. The 'experiment' is not seriable, it is *unique*.

Moreover, if there is insufficient liquidity, expenditure plans are likely to be frustrated. Some of these plans may be held by the agent as very important, and this is intensified if the opportunity is unlikely to be repeated. To this extent, a portfolio decision may also be *crucial*, in Shackle's technical sense.

Finally, using probability theory for portfolio problems rules out the possibility of genuine surprise. The events comprised by the probability distribution are assumed to be *complete*, since the total probability is equal to unity and the probability of particular outcomes is expressed as a fraction of that unit total. (Shackle calls probability a 'distributional variable', for this reason.) One could argue that the Wall Street crash of 1929 or Black Monday of 1987 are just observations in the lower tail. But what of the response to the devaluation of 1967: 'Nobody told us we could do that'. Is that not an admission of *surprise* — of a possibility the speaker had not thought of? And we shall later give an example which, one of us can attest, involved complete surprise. There is no room for that in probability.

5 APPLICATION OF SHACKLE'S THEORY OF POTENTIAL SURPRISE

So complete is the triumph of the probability approach that one would never have guessed from the literature on liquidity, precautionary demand and speculation that Shackle in 1945 applied his theory of potential surprise to 'speculative choice' and recommended in the article's concluding pages that the approach might be applied to the problem of liquidity. (We did not know this either until the present paper was well underway!) Recall that Markowitz's seminal article was not published until 1952, and the famous Tobin piece came out in 1958. Shackle's approach has clear priority. The time for reasserting it may be ripe, as a new consciousness amongst economists of the importance of the philosophy of probability has been brought about by the important work on Keynes's *Treatise on Probability* initiated by Carabelli (1988) and O'Donnell (1989).

Shackle's theory of choice under uncertainty is based on *possibility*, which he distinguished rigorously from the classical conception of *probability*. (His most extensive exposition is in *Decision, Order and Time*.) An outcome may be envisaged as perfectly possible but yet be improbable. The advantage of possibility is that it is open-ended: as it is not an additive measure it allows for outcomes not originally envisaged, while probability, as a distributional variable, must encompass all outcomes; there can be no surprises. In probability theory all outcomes are treated on equal footing, not as equally *likely* — unless one has a rectangular probability distribution — but as, equally, perfectly possible, however improbable. All outcomes but one, however (the expected value or mean), are in probability theory deemed unexpected. *Possibility*, by contrast, can distinguish, as Shackle does (1943: 69, n. 2), between events which he calls 'contra-expected' — that is, considered, but deemed unlikely — and the totally un-envisaged, for which he reserves the term 'unexpected'.

We begin the exposition of Shackle's framework at the simplest starting point. The agent is faced with trying to assess the liquidity of various assets in a state of uncertainty about the future behaviour of actors in markets and even about his own needs. In such a situation, the agent is assumed to try to list the outcomes which can be related to the decision of maintaining this asset as a store of value. These outcomes refer to the expected terms of immediate convertibility of a specific asset into the accepted means of payment at any moment in the future. This list is not exhaustive (in the sense which is required when one is utilizing distributional probability), nor are its components (in other words, each particular term of convertibility) derived from any statistical method. Instead, this list is comprises those outcomes which the decision maker imagines. For the moment we allow only two mutually-exclusive categories: imagined possible outcomes and those ruled out as not possible.

This list of imagined possible outcomes can be indefinitely extended, the only deadline for additions being given by the moment in which the decision must be taken (Shackle 1979: 86). What is deemed possible is conditioned by the agent's remembered experiences and by the elements which stimulate his imagination: 'Experience suggests what can come to pass. If experience could tell us what will come to pass, we should be in a world of determinate history, choice-denying and choice-abolishing' (ibid.: 59). Knowledge about the institutional features of the markets for each particular asset and the past and present behaviour of the actors in these markets would, we assume, be important elements, as well as the past behaviour of prices in those markets.

Among these imagined, deemed possible outcomes there is one which can be considered as the *neutral outcome*. This is the crucial concept in applying Shackle's framework to liquidity. An outcome is neutral if its value in terms of immediately realizable purchasing power at any moment in the future is the same, including any contractually established interest, as that which would be achieved by maintaining the asset over the originally projected holding period that is, without the need for liquidity.

The concept of neutral outcome may seem to have some affinity with Tobin's critical rate of interest, but there is an important difference. Where Tobin's critical rate refers to an unspecified unit time period, here we see the time-contrast made by Carvalho (see above, Section 3) brought together. This contrast between the return which would have been earned if there had been no unexpected expenditures (the asset is held for the originally projected period) and the immediate realization value not only confronts the Carvalho problem; by posing the problem of liquidation for *any and all* dates short of the expected holding period it also resolves another difficulty with the probability approach to liquidity: that probability can say nothing about values on specific dates.

All imagined outcomes which are larger than the neutral outcome would represent gains for the agent, whereas all imagined terms of convertibility smaller than the neutral outcome would signify losses. Thus, according to the current situation of a specific agent, the distinct prospective outcomes can be ranked in terms of their desiredness or counter-desiredness: the bigger the gains, the more desirable the outcomes; the bigger the losses, the more undesirable the outcomes.

In this simple framework, in which all the terms of convertibility deemed possible are arranged in order of desiredness and counter-desiredness, Shackle proposed that the agent's attention will be arrested by only the best and the worst of these outcomes 'according to his own psychics and circumstances and to the character of the imagined outcomes in any degree of their complexity' (Shackle 1988: 2). He concentrates on these extreme outcomes because

> all others will be eclipsed by one or other of these two extremes.
> It is these two extremes amongst the sequels all equally deemed
> possible which will constitute for the chooser the power of his
> action to benefit or harm him. He cannot know what his action
> will do for him. The two extremes are what, at best and worst,
> he supposes that it can do.
>
> (Shackle 1988: 3)

These two outcomes Shackle refers to as focus hypotheses or focus elements:

> By focus-hypothesis or focus-element we mean an element ...
> which has some special and extraordinary power to command
> and concentrate upon itself the decision-maker's attention. In
> what we shall present as a centrally important group of cases,

there will be two focus-elements, one selecting itself from amongst the hypotheses of success and the other from amongst the hypotheses of misfortune.

(Shackle 1961: 122)

In the present context, the two focal hypotheses associated with the decision of holding a particular asset indicate two extreme expected terms of convertibility of the asset into money (representing both gains and losses) which are deemed possible by the agent at the moment of portfolio decision. They eclipse all the other possible imagined outcomes.

6 POTENTIAL SURPRISE

The above exposition does not distinguish between degrees of possibility. It is to this matter that we now turn. Until now possibleness has been considered as a category; that is to say, outcomes are or are not deemed possible. However, although an agent may see 'no fatal obstruction' to the occurrence of an extensive (and even non-complete) list of outcomes, he would not react in the same way to all outcomes. According to his current knowledge, some outcomes would surprise him more than others. Some would not surprise him at all, being sequels 'entirely unobstructed, wholly free, within the chooser's thought, of any threatened interference' (Shackle 1979: 86); these latter are considered *perfectly possible* outcomes. Such outcomes can be associated therefore with a zero degree of potential surprise, for no doubt or disbelief arises when the agent considers their future occurrence.

The surprise is potential because it represents the degree of disbelief now associated with the possible occurrence of a particular outcome in the future. Therefore, it is a completely different feeling from that which depicts what an agent experiences at the moment when an outcome actually happens. As Shackle (1961: 68) puts it, potential surprise 'is the surprise we should feel, if the given thing did happen'.

Outside the area of perfectly possible terms of convertibility of a specific asset into money there are other outcomes that, if they should happen, would cause some degree of surprise to the agent who decides to keep that asset as store of value, despite the existence of 'no fatal obstruction' to their occurrence. Accordingly, these outcomes are associated with a greater than zero degree of potential surprise. To yet further outcomes is attached a high degree of potential surprise, reaching a maximum for those outcomes the agent believes to be impossible.

In sum, possibleness is no longer treated merely as a category, but as a variable. This situation is represented in Figure 11.1 (Shackle 1961: 141), where the horizontal axis represents the imagined possible terms of immediate convertibility of a specific asset into the accepted means of payment. The neutral outcome is the dotted line; gains are to the right of it and losses to the left. The vertical axis represents the degrees of associated surprise with each of the possible outcomes of the decision to hold a certain asset as store of value. The range of definition of the potential surprise function for a particular agent 'will lie between entire possibility and non-possibility... [The agent's] judgements of possibleness, as of desiredness, will be the product of grounds and intuitions peculiar to himself and his experience' (Shackle 1988: 4).

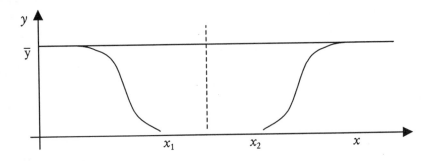

Figure 11.1: A potential surprise curve

The area of perfect possibility (zero potential surprise), in Figure 11.1, is the range of outcomes between x_1 and x_2. In our preliminary discussion, these outcomes limited the range of discourse. Now we consider gains or losses outside this range. These outcomes are deemed less than perfectly possible; they are associated with positive degrees of potential surprise. The larger the gain or the loss outside that interval, the more the surprise the agent feels he would experience if this outcome actually happened.

When considering only the range of zero potential surprise, the largest (net) loss and the largest (net) gain arrested the attention of the agent. With the introduction of degrees of potential surprise, the matter of focus becomes more complex. For while a large deviation from the neutral outcome is more surprising, outcomes with high potential surprise also have less power to command the agent's attention, just because they are deemed so unlikely to occur. Thus the determination of the outcomes which will most arrest the attention of the decision-maker (that is to say, the focus elements) will depend not only on the desiredness or counter-desiredness of each outcome but also on the degree of possibleness which a particular agent attaches to each outcome. The attention-arresting power of the outcomes, which Shackle calls *ascendancy*, 'will assuredly be an increasing function of desiredness, and a decreasing function of potential surprise. There will be, within some range of greater or less desiredness, a constrained maximum of ascendancy; and again within some range of greater or less counter-desiredness, another such constrained maximum' (*ibid.*: 5–6).

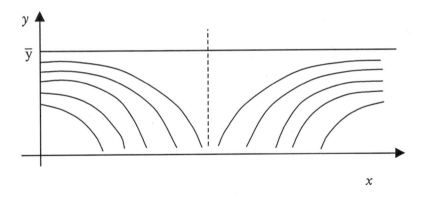

Figure 11.2: The ascendancy function

The ascendancy function (*A*) can be represented as a set of equal-ascendancy curves (Figure 11.2; Shackle 1961: 149). Each of these curves connects points (*x*, *y*) such that the corresponding values of *A* are equal; furthermore, as the increasing attractiveness of larger gains or losses is compensated by the increasing degree of disbelief assigned to the possibility of these outcomes occurring in the future, the equal-ascendancy curves must slope north-eastward or north-westwards (Shackle, 1970: 118). Thus, if one superposes the potential surprise function (*y*) upon the equal-ascendancy map (Figure 11.3), there will be two points of tangency between this function and the equal-ascendancy curves, one in the positive and one in the negative range of valuations. These two points represent the two constrained maxima of ascendancy associated with a specific set of outcomes, which, except by extreme coincidence, are not symmetrical around the neutral outcome. They refer to different levels of disbelief. By replacing these points by those which lie in the same equal-ascendancy curve but which also lie upon the x axis, it is possible to determine the *standardized focal hypotheses*, which will describe a specific asset for a particular agent (Shackle 1979: 107).

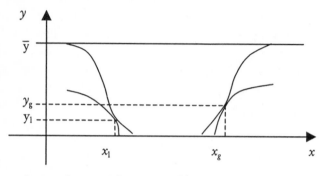

y_l = degree of potential surprise of focus loss
y_g = degree of potential surprise of focus gain
x_l = standardized focus loss
x_g = standardized focus gain

Figure 11.3: The equal-ascendancy map

The standardization allows the focal expected gains and losses of different assets to be compared and the assets to be ranked for their combination of liquidity and return. If one considers the segment of gains depicted in the diagram of the potential-surprise function, it follows from what was said that the larger the gains associated with particular outcomes, the higher the combination of flexibility and financial or other return that the possession of that specific asset gives to the agent and, consequently, the more desired the outcome in the agent's mind. In other words, the more favourable the expected terms of immediate convertibility of an asset into money the greater its capacity to arrest the attention of the decision-maker. This evaluation, however, is constrained by the degree of potential surprise attached to each of the possible outcomes, for the larger the expected gains, the higher the degree of disbelief associated with its accomplishment in the future and, therefore, the less its capacity to arrest the attention of the decision-maker. Accordingly, these two elements will, simultaneously considered, determine the best outcome (focus gain).

By similar reasoning, the agent develops a focus loss: the worst outcome he can imagine which is still sufficiently likely to command his attention. As Shackle (1988: 5) puts it, '[t]he chooser of action wishes to fix upon the best and the worst imagined outcome of each action that are possible enough; the best that is possible enough to be worth hoping for, and the worst that is too possible to be dismissed'.

Once the agent has defined such a pair of outcomes for each of the assets under consideration, he can compare the pairs among assets and rank the assets in the spectrum of liquidity. For this we need another diagram (Figure 11.4), in which the values of the horizontal axis stand for the focus losses whereas the values of the vertical axis stand for the focus gains. Any combination of a focus loss and a focus gain (that is to say, a pair of expected terms of convertibility) can be represented by a point in such a space. If one links the points which represent situations which are indifferent for a specific agent, i.e. which are 'equally attractive or equally repellent' for an agent 'with his particular temperament, tastes and material endowments', (Shackle 1979: 101) one can form 'gambler indifference curves'; all these curves taken together, by their turn, constitute what Shackle (1979: 101) calls the 'gambler indifference map'.

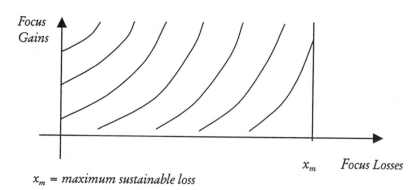

x_m = maximum sustainable loss

Figure 11.4: The gambler indifference map

Note that the map is truncated: for each agent at each moment in time, there exists an outcome which represents the maximum sustainable loss; any larger loss would exceed the minimum of safety the agent needs to avoid bankruptcy. Accordingly, the options giving likely outcomes beyond this barrier are not even considered (Shackle 1961: 164).

In the relevant area of the diagram, then, for any two points, each representing the liquidity attached to a particular asset, having the same ordinate but different abscissas, the one with smaller abscissa is considered as possessing a higher degree of liquidity that the other: it has the same focus gain but a smaller focus loss. Conversely, if two points have the same abscissa but different ordinates, the one with larger ordinate is ranked as the more liquid, for although they both possess the same focus loss, the former is associated with a larger focus gain. Liquidity increases toward the north-west.

With the gambler indifference map we now need something akin to a budget constraint, which Shackle calls a gambler opportunity curve, if we are to proceed from ranking assets in order of their liquidity-benefit to choosing a portfolio of assets with liquidity as a key property. Given the amount of wealth the agent is prepared to hold in realizable form, that is to say, excluding non-marketable assets, we can construct such a curve between the point of complete liquidity (normally money) and maximum focus loss.

The gambler opportunity curve gives the various portfolio combinations which the agent can afford. The gambler indifference map and opportunity curve are put together in Figure 11.5 (Shackle 1961: 164). As in other fields of economic theory, the tangency between the gambler opportunity curve and the gambler indifference map gives the optimal portfolio from the point of view of the agent's expectation of liquidity and return from his wealth.

Ideally, the gambler indifference map and opportunity curve would be portrayed in many dimensions; we have reduced outcomes to their money value but recognize that real use-value is an integral part of the story. Our outcome is still compatible with portfolio diversification, however, as different assets may share the same pair of focus gains and losses, so that a point choice may involve diversification. A multi-dimensional approach would be even more likely to give us portfolio diversification, as the choice would be portrayed as taking place, as in real life, in more than the purely monetary dimension.

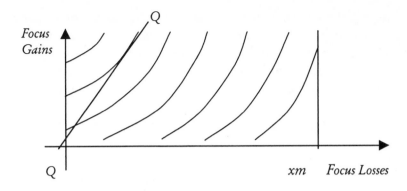

xm = maximum sustainable loss
QQ = Gambler opportunity curve

Figure 11.5: The gambler indifference map and gambler opportunity curve

We point out that in Figure 11.5 we have something truly remarkable: this Figure looks exactly like the Figure in Tobin's famous article, yet it has been derived entirely without reference to probability theory. The main idea was developed by Shackle in 1945, in the context of speculation, but the idea was re-invented, doubtless independently, and has become completely bound up with classical probability in the literature.

We have shown that using Shackle's theory of expectation one can understand how, even in an environment in which liquidity cannot be assessed through the use of probability theory, an agent can rank these assets in a spectrum of liquidity, so that he can subsequently choose those assets which better fulfil his particular needs for liquidity. More importantly, this can be done without substituting an implicit assumption of (at least probabilistic) knowledge for the true uncertainty which he faces.

7 SHACKLE'S THEORY AND PROBABILITY APPROACHES TO LIQUIDITY

We have drawn a sharp contrast between Shackle's theory and probability theory in order to make our case. But it is worth exploring the relation between them in more detail. We have laid several charges against the use of probability theory, and it could be argued that the use of two distinct theories to provide the agents with information to form expectations is neither methodologically nor theoretically acceptable. But it is also important to avoid false or unnecessary oppositions.

It is undeniably the case that in probabilistic expectations there is no unanticipated surprise: all possibilities are assumed known. (From the wider perspective of Shackle that is precisely the trouble with modelling expectations probabilistically.) Therefore anything which can be modelled probabilistically ought to have a distribution which extends no further than the range between x_1 and x_2 of Figure 11.1.

Let us consider Runde's worry about different probabilities which are equally unsurprising, say those attached to outcomes of a throw of a coin and a die. We can represent these probabilities in Figure 11.6 as two rectangular distributions on the Shackle diagram (Figure 11.1). A probability axis is drawn 'over' the potential surprise axis and two horizontal axes are also superimposed. They are adjusted so that in each case, H and T for heads and tails and 1–6 for the outcomes of throwing a die, the probabilities lie entirely between x_1 and x_2. This diagram demonstrates that there is no contradiction between probability and Shackle-elements in these cases. The two approaches are complementary: the gambler knows his focus gain and loss and the probability of each occurring.

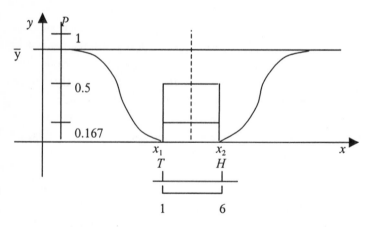

Figure 11.6: Potential surprise and two rectangular probability distributions

By contrast to throws of coins or dice, however, the distribution usually used to illustrate the probability of asset prices is the normal distribution. Since we have argued (and it is common sense) that the past behaviour of prices was one element in the agent's supposed knowledge when he formed his expectations, we must confront the question of the compatibility of a normal distribution with Shackle's apparatus. The difficulty immediately arises that the tails of a normal distribution are asymptotic to the abscissa; see Figure 11.7.

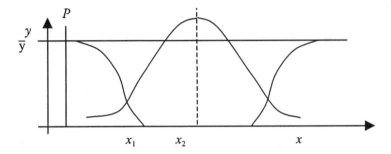

Figure 11.7: Potential surprise and a normal distribution

Let us imagine an asset whose price variation stays within some well-defined bound for a considerable period; say all variation falls within two standard deviations of the mean. The tails can be seen as potentially surprising. Now compare this asset with another whose range of variation is greater. Cannot the rules of stochastic dominance apply? Similarly, if a distribution derived from past experience is skew, is this not information the agent will take into account? We believe that the answer should be yes, but that there are obvious difficulties with combining the two approaches.

Not only does classical probability theory assume that the future will be like the past, but different assets will vary in their stability of behaviour. It can be argued that the prices of those assets called more liquid are generally more stable, whether because they are more subject to regulation (which imposes a certain stability) or because their markets are so large and their use so widespread that a certain degree of continuity is expected. At the opposite extreme of the spectrum of liquidity the markets are often not stable, for an exchange may be 'crucial': a sale may transform its market in a way that makes the use of past records to form expectations concerning the future inappropriate. Thus, although probability theory may be a reasonable technique for a sub-set of markets, it could be useless when another segment is considered. For this segment in which the more illiquid assets are located, it is necessary to use an alternative theory of expectations, in which changes of environment are taken into account (such as Shackle's theory).

Even within the same market there also remains the problem of outlying observations. While one might be able to argue for the use of probability distributions in 'normal circumstances', in, to borrow Leijonhufvud's term (1973), a 'corridor' of unsurprising or normal behaviour, what significance attaches to observations which stray outside that corridor? To explore this, let us return briefly to the foundations of classical probability theory.

Classic Probability Experiments (CPEs) differ fundamentally from the construction of probability distributions from past data. The outcome of a CPE is known *a priori*, as inferred from the properties of the object and the experiment, provided only that enough observations are taken: one knows from first principles that the probability of tails is 0.5. The Experiment is not undertaken to establish that probability; it is undertaken to demonstrate the law of large numbers.

Indeed if a CPE were to go on long enough to damage the object, a drift in the average outcome would disclose the fact that the coin or die was no longer 'true'. This principle is the basis of inventory-theoretic approaches to quality control, in which the parameters, the specification and tolerance limits one can expect, are given by the engineers. A statistically significant departure from these limits indicates, for example, wear and tear in the production machinery. By contrast, there is nothing 'from outside the experiment', akin to engineering specifications, which helps one interpret outlying observations when constructing a probability distribution from past data. There is no objective expectation of either mean or variance to enable one to conclude either that these are simply observations from one of the tails of the distribution or that the parameters of the distribution, and hence, one infers, the generating function, have changed. Therefore the distribution is a most unreliable indicator of future behaviour where there is any possibility of fundamental change.

So there are some markets which are not stable by their nature (thin markets, markets for unique objects) and other markets which may not be stationary over time. If it is (and it may be) legitimate and helpful to use probability theory within the 'corridor' of unsurprising outcomes but unhelpful outside this corridor, it must be faced that there is no guide as to when the boundaries of the corridor have been breached. Nor is there any reliable guide as to which markets are and which are not stable. There is a continuous spectrum of assets. In general the most liquid assets have the most stable markets and the illiquid assets are more subject to the crucial action. But in the middle of these two groups there are the markets of the more or less liquid assets, and about these one cannot say with any degree of certainty if they are or are not stable over time.

It is the existence of this 'grey area' in the spectrum of liquidity that makes the combined use of two distinct theories certainly difficult and perhaps inapplicable. If these two theories were to be used, one would have to define at which point of the spectrum one would give place to the other; in other words, one would have to decide, within the spectrum, which asset possesses a market unstable enough to make the use of probability theory useless when expectations about its behaviour in the future are being formed. But if one is able to point out such an asset, it would mean that the ranking of the assets is already done, which, given the existence of those markets within the grey area, is a contradiction.

Thus, the only way of determining the place of all available assets in the spectrum of liquidity is to adopt a theory capable of ordering the whole range of assets, and not only a particular group, in terms of the liquidity attached to them. And although it is not possible to extend the use of probability theory to form expectations about the changing or less stable markets, Shackle's theory of expectations provides a rationale for forming expectations for the whole set of assets available. The Shackle method is more general, allowing a unified treatment of the whole spectrum of liquidity, for not only are the assets which lie in the extremes ranked, but also those which lie in the grey area.

8 A BRAZILIAN EXPERIENCE

The advantage of the Shackle framework can best be seen when expectations of the future are changing rapidly. The high and increasing inflation in Brazil in the 1980s provides a good example for its application even though we have ruled out inflation in the foregoing discussion.

In response to persistent high inflation, indexed bonds (OTNs) were issued by the Government to help finance its huge deficit. The attractiveness of these bonds lay not only in their being indexed but also that they were refinanced daily in the overnight market and were thus highly liquid. They in fact represented an indexed and interest-bearing quasi-money (Bresser Pereira and Nakano 1991: 43). As a consequence, these OTNs, which represented only 4.2 per cent of GDP in 1980, corresponded to 13.9 per cent in 1989; during the same period, M1 fell from 8.7 per cent to 2.0 per cent of GDP.

This institutional arrangement, however, could not be sustained. Indeed, the Government's falling creditworthiness implied the need for successive rises of interest rates, so that the indexed bonds could maintain their market appeal. However, higher interest rates led to further increases in the budget deficit and diminishing appeal of the OTNs. The unstable financial structure became widely recognized, and this led to the progressive loss of confidence in the capacity of the Government to maintain the liquidity of OTNs. This fear came to a head at the end of 1989 and beginning of 1990, just before a new Government was to take office. At that moment, the expectation of the entrepreneurs (as expressed in several reports, interviews and articles in the press) was that a monetary reform would be implemented, perhaps including a domestic moratorium on the OTNs, in order to restore the fiscal balance of the Government. As a consequence, large amounts of OTNs were sold and the proceeds sent to time deposits or even, in the few days before the change of Government, to current accounts.

According to probability theory, there would be no reason to move from the indexed bond. There was nothing in the past behaviour of the market of that bond which could cause apprehension as to its future behaviour. And even if one acknowledged that the future could prove to be radically different from the past, probability theory would not be capable of incorporating this change of evaluation. These changes, however, can be illustrated in terms of the scheme based on Shackle's theory of expectations, which explicitly incorporates the shifts of evaluations of private agents concerning the operation of specific markets in the future, even if they point to a completely different picture from what has happened in the past.

During the 1980s, the OTN was the asset whose focus gain and focus loss lay more north-westward in the gambler indifference map than any other available asset. However, over the few months before the new government took office the level of potential surprise attached to total loss of wealth held in OTNs fell from high surprise to a real possibility. Simultaneously, the idea that one could lose all one's wealth held in this form commanded more attention: the ascendancy function also shifted. Furthermore, the potential surprise associated with each specific positive outcome was higher than it used to be. The two panels of Figure 11.8 illustrate such shifts.

(a) During the 1980s

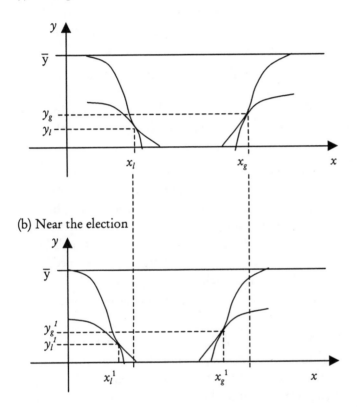

(b) Near the election

Figure 11.8: Perceived liquidity of indexed bonds (OTNs)

9 CONCLUSION

We have suggested in this chapter that while a probabilistic approach to the definition and choice of liquid assets is possible under certain restrictive conditions, Shackle's framework of potential surprise and may be preferable. There are three areas we have identified in which Shackle's approach is superior:

1   As our last example illustrates, the use of Shackle's framework allows for information beyond past market behaviour to be taken into account. Furthermore, it would not rule out a wrong decision, for agents' expectations can be falsified. In particular, it admits the possibility that events which were not even contemplated can come to pass. By contrast, the probability approach implies that all outcomes have been foreseen, extrapolated from past experience. Even if some outcomes are deemed improbable, nothing is considered impossible, or even potentially surprising.

2   In the event, *ex post*, probability theory almost always gives the 'wrong answer', because it can say nothing about individually dated outcomes. Shackle's approach is capable of evaluating the realization values of assets on each date; action is taken on the basis of the assessed best and worst outcomes.

3   Shackle's framework allows for a diversity of liquidity needs, corresponding to expected and unexpected expenditures on different dates, by setting up the neutral outcome on the basis of the expected or intended holding period yield of the asset, which is known only to the agent. Holding periods may vary for different assets; different assets may serve different liquidity needs. In contrast, the probability approach to the portfolio assumes an unspecified unit period. All expected gains and losses refer to that period.

The difficulty with Shackle's approach, of course, is that it is entirely subjectivist. There is little the outsider, such as the economist, can say about liquidity in this framework which can be derived or verified objectively; liquidity is very much in the eye of the beholder.

REFERENCES

Bresser Pereira, L. and Nakano, Y. (1991) 'Hyperinflation and Stabilization in Brazil: the first Collor plan', in Davidson, P. and Kregel, J.A. (eds) *Economic Problems of the 1990s*, Aldershot: Edward Elgar.

Carabelli, A. (1988) *On Keynes's Method*, London: Macmillan.

Carvalho, F. J. Cardim de (1992) *Mr Keynes and the Post Keynesians*, Aldershot: Edward Elgar.

Chick, V. (1973) *The Theory of Monetary Policy*, Oxford: Basil Blackwell.

—— (1983) *Macroeconomics after Keynes*, Cambridge, MA: MIT Press.

Davidson, P. (1982–3) 'Rational expectations: a fallacious foundation for studying crucial decision making processes', *Journal of Post Keynesian Economics* 5: 182–98. Reprinted in Davidson, P. (1991b).

—— (1990) 'Shackle and Keynes vs. rational expectations theory on the role of time, liquidity and financial markets', in Frowen, S. F. (ed) *Unknowledge and Choice in Economics: A Conference in Honour of G. L. S. Shackle*, London: Macmillan. Reprinted in Davidson (1991b).

—— (1991a) 'Is probability theory relevant for uncertainty?: a different perspective', in Davidson, P. (1991b).

—— (1991b) *The Collected Writings of Paul Davidson*, Vol 2: *Inflation, Open Economies and Resources*, (L. Davidson, ed.), London: Macmillan.

Earl, P. E. (1995) 'Liquidity preference, marketability and pricing', in Dow, S. C. and Hillard, J. (eds) *Keynes, Knowledge and Uncertainty*, Aldershot: Edward Elgar.

Hahn, F. H. (1990) 'Liquidity', in Friedman, B. M. and Hahn, F. H. (eds), *Handbook of Monetary Economics*, Amsterdam: North-Holland.

Hicks J. R. (1962) 'Liquidity', *Economic Journal*.72: 787–802. Reprinted as Part I of 'The Foundations of Monetary Theory' in Hicks, J. R. (1982) *Collected Essays on Economic Theory*, Vol. 2: *Money, Interest and Wages*, Oxford: Basil Blackwell.

—— (1976) 'Time in economics', in Tang, A. M., Westfield, F. M. and Worley, J. S. (eds) *Evolution, Welfare and Time in Economics: Essays in Honour of Nicholas Georgescu-Roegen*, Lexington, MA: Lexington Books. Reprinted in Hicks, J.R. (1982) *Collected Essays on Economic Theory*, Vol. 2: *Money, Interest and Wages*, Oxford: Basil Blackwell.

Keynes, J. M. (1930) *The Treatise on Money*, Vol II, London: Macmillan. (reprinted in 1971 as Vol. VI of *The Collected Writings of J M Keynes*, (D. E. Moggridge, ed), London: Macmillan for the Royal Economic Society.

Leijonhufvud, A. (1973) 'Effective demand failures', *Scandinavian Economic Journal*, March. Reprinted as Chapter 6 in Leijonhufvud, A. (1981), *Information and Coordination*, Oxford: Oxford University Press.

Markowitz, H. (1952) 'Portfolio selection', *Journal of Finance* 7: 77–91.

Menger, C. (1871) *Grundsätze der Volkwirtschaftslere*, Vienna: W. Braumüller. Translated as *Principles of Economics* by Dingwall, J. and Hoselitz, B.F., Glencoe, Illinois: The Free Press, 1950.

Mills, T. (1999) *Time Series Techniques for Economists*, Cambridge: Cambridge University Press.

O'Donnell, R.M. (1989) *Keynes: Philosophy, Economics and Politics*, London: Macmillan.

Radcliffe Report (*Report* of the Committee on the Working of the Monetary System) (1959) Cmnd. 837, London: HMSO.

Shackle, G.L.S. (1943) 'The Expectational Dynamics of the Individual', *Economicsa* 10: 99–129. Reprinted in Shackle (1990).

—— (1945) 'An Analysis of Speculative Choice', *Economica* 12: 10–21.

Reprinted in Shackle (1990).

— — (1959) 'Time and thought', *British Journal for the Philosophy of Science 9*, Reprinted in Shackle (1990).

— — (1961) *Decision, Order and Time in Human Affairs*, Cambridge: Cambridge University Press.

— — (1970) *Expectation, Enterprise and Profit*, London: George Allen & Unwin.

— — (1979) *Imagination and the Nature of Choice*, Edinburgh: Edinburgh University Press.

— — (1988) 'The origination of choice', in Frowen S. F. (ed) *Business, Time and Thought: Selected Papers of G. L. S. Shackle*, London: Macmillan.

— — (1990) *Time, Expectations and Uncertainty in Economics*, Ford, J. L. (ed), Aldershot: Edward Elgar.

Tobin, J. (1958) 'Liquidity preference as behaviour toward risk', *Review of Economic Studies* 25: 65–86.

12

THE DEMAND FOR MONEY
IN AN UNCERTAIN WORLD

*Donald W. Katzner**

1 INTRODUCTION

In economics, the traditional perspective from which to explain simultaneous economic behaviour goes under the rubric of general equilibrium analysis. Such an approach is characterized, in part, by the complete elimination of the non-probabilistic uncertainty produced by the realities of human ignorance and historical time. When introducing a demand for money and monetary equilibrium[1] into a model of this sort, economists often take the position that it is first necessary to set out the particular 'indispensable' function, or functions, that money is to perform in that model.[2] Thus one must begin by asking about the purpose to be served by holding money and about the role that money is to play in furthering economic activity. Thereafter, a derivation of the demand for money emanating from the answers to these questions can be given. From such perspectives, a number of specifications of a role for money and a consequent demand for money, some of which are described below, have been proposed. But if one believes, along with Keynes (1937: 216), Shackle (1974: 4, 61, 62), and others, that money is primarily a non-probabilistic 'uncertainty phenomenon',[3] then none of these proposals is satisfactory since they are all embedded in an environment in which non-probabilistic uncertainty, hereafter referred to as just 'uncertainty', is not present.

In a recent development, however, simultaneous economic behaviour has begun to be explored outside of the traditional realm of general equilibrium analysis and, in particular, has been considered in a framework that allows for the uncertainty arising under conditions of ignorance and historical time.[4] That analysis focuses on sequences of decisions and market events that occur across historical time without reference to a general equilibrium. Indeed, a general equilibrium could not exist; nor, in the context of the analysis, would it even make sense to raise the question of its existence. This framework, then, provides an environment in which money as an uncertainty phenomenon amidst simultaneous economic behavior can be studied. The purpose of the present chapter is to show how money might be introduced into such a model and a demand for money derived within it.

The first step is to gain some insight into the problems involved by examining several examples of the ways in which a role for money has been justified and a demand for money derived in the traditional general equilibrium setting. This is the subject-matter of the next section. Section 3 offers a role for money and develops a demand for money that accounts for the uncertainty created by the presence of ignorance and historical time.

Much to what follows, indeed the approach on which it rests, is traceable to G. L. S. Shackle, in whose memory this essay was written. Shackle was a pioneer in his insistence that modern economic analysis has to come to grips with the realities of human ignorance and historical time, and in his pursuit of that goal. His notion of potential surprise and his model of decision-making built upon it are the first analytical constructs specifically designed to deal with economic phenomena in such an environment. Frequent reference is make to his work below.

2 PERSPECTIVES ON MONEY DEMAND

Economists generally agree that there are three main roles for money to play in an economy: Money functions as a standard of value, as a medium of exchange, and as a store of value. To introduce money into a general equilibrium model, then, requires that a place for each of these functions be located within that model.

Now all general equilibrium models contain within their structures a good, called the numéraire, that can be singled out to function as a standard of value. Any good, in fact, can serve that purpose; it is only necessary to employ the normalization that fixes its price at unity. Thus the role of money as a standard of value is always present, at least implicitly, in general equilibrium analysis and need not be considered further. However, with all trades taking place only at equilibrium (as they often do in such models), there is usually no need for a money commodity whose purposes are to facilitate exchange and to carry purchasing power through time. The notion of monetary equilibrium is irrelevant. To be able to speak meaningfully about money as a medium of exchange and store of value therefore requires the presence of trading out of the traditional general equilibrium, or at least some conceptualization of the actual effectuation of the trades envisaged in the general equilibrium. In these latter contexts, money has a role to play and the efficiency with which it plays that role can be analyzed.[5] To the extent that the use of money as a medium of exchange and as a store of value economizes by reducing transactions and opportunity costs in the process of, say, out-of-equilibrium exchange, the purchasing-power value of money (that is, its value as a medium of exchange and store of value) will be positive even if it has no intrinsic value as a commodity.

With money successfully functioning as a medium of exchange, its use in transactions permits the consumer or firm to achieve a higher level of, respectively, utility or profit than would otherwise be the case. Hence there is a demand for money balances for such transactions purposes. Similarly, money performing a successful store-of-value function gives rise to an 'asset' demand for money balances. In this case, money balances are stored to cover a possible lack of coincidence between income receipts and expenditures that cannot be overcome efficiently through the use of futures markets, to cover unforeseen expenditures that might arise in the future, and because of (in light of potential interest rate movements) the possibility of a capital loss on non-monetary assets which might be avoided by holding money balances. (These last three reasons for storing money balances are sometimes referred to as, respectively, the 'transactions', 'precautionary', and 'speculative' motives.) The combined demand for money balances of, say, a consumer, is the sum of that person's transactions and asset demand, and would appear, as suggested implicitly above, to depend on at least his wealth, his total anticipated expenditure, the rate of interest, commodity and non-monetary asset prices, and expectations of future possible changes in those prices. (The non monetary asset prices themselves, of course, depend on the interest rate.) With these ideas in mind, attention now turns to some examples of the way in which the role of money and the demand for money balances have been handled in the literature.

One reason put forward to warrant the holding of money in general equilibrium analysis is simply that people have a preference for doing so.[6] (The rationale for this preference will be considered later on.) That is, money balances enter as an argument in each person's utility function, and individual demands for money arise as the outcome of constrained utility maximization. To illustrate, let $x = (x_1,... ,x_I)$ vary over nonnegative baskets of commodities in a person's commodity space, and let $p = (p_1,... ,p_I)$ represent vectors of respective and positive prices of goods. Take m to denote his nonnegative (nominal) money balances and set the price of money at unity. Then this individual's utility function is often written as

$$v = u(m, x, p), \tag{1}$$

where u is homogeneous of degree zero in m and p for each value of x, and v varies over the range of u. In this approach, money balances are the only asset held by the individual, and the homogeneity suggests the absence of money illusion in his relation to money functioning as a medium of exchange. With $r > 0$ indicating (scalar) rates of interest and $y > 0$ values of the individual's income, his budget constraint is

$$r m + p \cdot x = y,$$

where the dot symbolizes inner product.[7] Sufficient additional assumptions concerning the differentiability, increasingness, concavity, and so on, of u are imposed to make the subsequent derivation of demand functions valid.[8]

From the homogeneity of u, the partial derivative of u with respect to the i th good, namely $u_i(m, x, p)$, is also homogeneous of degree zero in m and p for each x; while that with respect to m, written $u_0(m,x,p)$, is homogeneous of degree minus one in m and p for each x. Hence

$$u_i(m, x, p) = u_i\left[\frac{m}{y}, x, \frac{p}{y}\right], \qquad i = 1,... , I,$$

$$u_0(m, x, p) = \frac{1}{y}u_0\left[\frac{m}{y}, x, \frac{p}{y}\right],$$

where $p/y = (p_1/y,\dots, p_I/y)$. The first-order Lagrangean maximization conditions, together with the budget constraint, are therefore

$$\frac{u_i\left[\dfrac{m}{y}, x, \dfrac{p}{y}\right]}{u_o\left[\dfrac{m}{y}, x, \dfrac{p}{y}\right]} = \frac{p_i l y}{r}, \qquad i = 1,\dots, I,$$

$$r\frac{m}{y} + \frac{p}{y} \cdot x = 1.$$

This is a system of $I + 1$ equations in $I + 1$ unknowns $m/y, x_1,\dots, x_I$. Solving yields the demand functions

$$x_i = \hat{h}^i\left[r, \frac{p}{y}\right], \qquad i = 1,\dots, I,$$

$$\frac{m}{y} = \hat{h}^0\left[r, \frac{p}{y}\right],$$

or

$$x_i = h^i(r, p, y) \qquad i = 1,\dots, I,$$
$$m = y h^o(r, p, y).$$

(2)

Observe that, as in the traditional theory of demand for commodities only, the demand functions for goods, that is, the h^i for $i=1,\dots, I$, are homogeneous of degree zero in all prices and income for each r. However, the demand function for money balances, $y h^o(r, p, y)$, is homogeneous of degree one in all prices and income, again for each value of r. This, as, in part, suggested earlier, is consistent with the old notions of the absence of money illusion and the neutrality of money.

The justification usually provided for including money balances in the utility function, or the reason given to explain why individuals have preferences for them, is that money balances have utility in their functioning as a store of value. Holding an average money balance, says Samuelson,

> yields convenience in permitting the consumer to take advantage of offers of sale, in facilitating exchanges, in bridging the gap between receipt of income and expenditure, etc. The average balance is both used and at the same time not used; it revolves but is not depleted; its just being there to meet contingencies is valuable even if the contingencies do not materialize, *ex post*. Possession of this balance then yields a real service, which can be compared with the direct utilities from the consumption of [ordinary goods].
>
> (Samuelson 1947: 118)

According to Patinkin,

> Were it not for ... [money balances], the lack of synchronization between the inflow and outflow of money in the course of the week would almost certainly force the individual to default on some of the hourly payments he is called upon to make. The security that money... [balances] provide against financial embarrassment of this type is what invests them with utility.
>
> (Patinkin 1956: 63)

Samuelson, however, does qualify his position: 'Given physical amounts of ... [goods] have significance in terms of the want pattern of the consumer, but it is not possible to attach similar significance to a given number of physical units of money... ' (Samuelson 1947: 118). Thus '... as an ultimate *desideratum*, money is no more in the utility function than is ... any... intermediate good. We must, therefore, regard... [equations (1)] as already the result of some behind-the-scenes optimizing and time-averaging' (Samuelson and Sato 1984: 601). But the real problems with this approach are twofold: First, money balances are not the only means for storing value. Non-monetary assets, to the extent that reliance can be placed on their marketability and liquidity, perform a similar function and these, it may be argued, should be in the utility function too so that the consumer can choose an appropriate portfolio for storing value from among competing assets. Second, and more serious, since the irregular timing of expenditures and receipts is, like everything else in a general-equilibrium framework, known in advance (at least probabilistically), and can therefore be overcome (assuming complete markets) through the use of futures markets as described below, a vindication for the existence of a store-of-value role for money balances has not really been supplied, and hence the previously stated justification for placing money balances in the utility function collapses. Thus the approach, as it stands, is not much help in resolving the issues raised in this chapter .

Consider now a typical general-equilibrium model that accounts for the allocation of resources at the present moment and at each of a finite number of successive future moments. Every quantity of every commodity is associated with the date on which it is delivered. There is a single date, that is, the present, at which all trades occur. At that time, goods to be delivered immediately (that is, present goods) are exchanged in present spot markets, and contracts for the purchase and delivery of goods in the future (i.e., future goods) are traded in futures markets. For the moment, transactions costs and uncertainties are assumed away. Consumers and firms optimize by choosing 'lifetime' purchase and sales plans. There are lifetime budget constraints and lifetime profit equations in which future prices are discounted to the present.[9] Once trade takes place, all markets are closed forever. If a market were reopened at some future date nothing would be exchanged in it because there would have been no changes in preferences and technology. In such a world there is no role for money (except, possibly, as a standard of value) and no reason for anyone to hold it. As suggested earlier, since all trades (in both present spot markets and futures markets) are equilibrium trades occurring at the same time, and since everything about the present and future is known with at least probabilistic certainty, the use of money either as a medium of exchange or as a store of value cannot lower costs or raise utilities. However, the next approach to introducing money and a demand for money balances explored here is based on Hicks' (1935: 6) idea that a role for money arises in this model, or a condensed version of it, as soon as certain kinds of frictions or impediments to trade are inserted and, in that case, the introduction of money balances enhances economic efficiency.[10] The general equilibrium that obtains therefore becomes a monetary equilibrium. The frictions and impediments inserted direct attention to the process of trading itself by forcing exchanges to take place out of, or by focusing on the effectuation of the exchanges that occur at, general equilibrium.

For example, Feldman (1973) considers a barter situation, without either futures markets or production, in which he inserts the impediment that all trades occur only on a pairwise basis. Feldman is interested in sequences of pairwise trades (starting at initial endowments), between traders taken two at a time, in which each trade increases the utility of both traders. He shows that, under certain conditions, such sequences converge to 'optimal' situations which cannot be improved upon through further trading. But these situations are optimal with respect to the two-person trading requirement only, and need not be Pareto optimal in general. Feldman also demonstrates that if there were a universally-held good, which he calls money, then general Pareto optimality would be assured. Therefore, by allowing individuals to trade for money as an intermediate step in achieving their final consumption goals, that is, by introducing money as a medium of exchange to be carried from one trade to another, efficiency can generally be increased. Feldman, however, does not derive a demand for money balances in his model.

As a second example of this genre, return to the general-equilibrium model described above, with a full complement of futures markets, but still without production. Suppose, however, that resources are required both to deliver goods and to write contracts for future delivery. Suppose also that, although delivery costs are still incurred, contracts are not written for delivery (and hence the cost of writing those contracts is eliminated) whenever the agreement to purchase (that is, trade) and the delivery of the goods involved occurs on the same date. Thus trading in futures markets would result in higher transactions costs (contract plus delivery costs) than trading in present and future spot markets (only delivery costs). In the face of these transaction-cost frictions, it is clear that, to avoid the higher costs, the use of futures markets in the present would be diminished and, to that extent, markets would reopen and trades would occur at future dates.[11] Furthermore, the single lifetime budget constraint in the original model would be replaced by a sequence of temporary budget constraints ensuring that expenditure equals income at each moment, and utility maximization against those constraints would be repeated correspondingly across time.

Under these conditions, futures markets would be used instead of the cheaper future spot markets when the timing of future receipts and expenditures does not coincide, and when the storage costs of holding the appropriate goods through time until they can be exchanged for the desired commodities is high. However, Starrett (1973) shows that use of the futures markets in this case would result in allocative inefficiency due to the extra resources they require, and that efficiency (that is, Pareto optimality) could be restored by introducing a good, again called money, that has zero transactions and storage costs, that does not enter as an argument in the individual's utility function, and whose purchasing-power value remains constant over time. Rather than go to expensive futures markets, money, functioning as a store of value, would overcome gaps in timing between expenditure and income receipts by carrying purchasing power forward costlessly through time. In this kind of model, money would be used by individuals to balance their budgets, that is, to ensure that expenditures equal receipts, at each date. Those who spend more than they earn would use the money balances they possess or borrow to make up the difference; those who spend less would retain the difference in the form of money balances or lend it out. Thus there is an implicit excess demand for nominal money balances implied in each person's constrained-utility-maximising excess demand for commodities.

One can imagine that this model is generalizable to include production and certain forms of probabilistic uncertainty. But none of these generalizations addresses the fact that money is one among many assets that the individual might hold for storage-of-value purposes. In particular, they provide no answer to the question of why the individual should hold money balances when there are marketable, liquid, non-monetary, income-earning assets available. To deal with such issues requires a conceptualization of money in terms of a portfolio of assets.

There are several ways to treat the demand for money as a demand for an asset in a portfolio. The one described here is founded on the presence of probabilistic uncertainty and is due to Tobin(1958).[12] Suppose there are J assets, with the Jth, say, representing (nominal) money balances.[13] Let j index these assets and write $\beta_j \geq 0, j = 1, \ldots, J,$ and

$$\sum_{j=1}^{J} \beta_j = 1. \tag{3}$$

Denote the nominal rate of return on asset j by γ_j and its per-dollar nominal capital gain or loss due to changes in its price by γ_j. Clearly $r_j \geq 0$, and $\gamma_j \gtrless 0$ according as γ_j reflects, respectively, a gain, neither gain nor loss, and a loss. Moreover, $r_J = 0$ so that $\gamma_J = 0$. Thus the overall return to each dollar of the portfolio is

$$\sum_{j+1}^{J-1} \in_j,$$

where

$$\in_j = \beta_j \left(r_j + \gamma_j \right), \qquad\qquad j = 1,\dots, J\text{-}1. \tag{4}$$

Assume that $(\gamma_1, \dots, \gamma_{J-1})$ is a vector of random variables with zero means and variance-covariance matrix $\left\| \sigma'_{jk} \right\|$. Then $(\in_1, \dots, \in_{J-1})$ is also a vector of random variables. Let its means and variance-covariance matrix be written, respectively, as $\mu = (\mu_1, \dots, \mu_{J-1})$ and $\left\| \sigma_{jk} \right\|$. Then, from (4),

$$\mu_j = \beta_j r_j,$$
$$\sigma_{jk} = \beta_j \beta_k \sigma'_{jk}, \tag{5}$$

where $j, k = 1, \dots J\text{-}1$. It follows that $0 \leq \mu_j$ and

$$0 \leq \sigma_{jk} \leq \sigma'_{jk} \tag{6}$$

$$r_j r_k \sigma_{jk} = \mu_j \mu_k \sigma'_{jk}, \tag{7}$$

for all j and k distinct from J. In addition, the overall expected rate of return on the portfolio as a whole is given by

$$\sum_{j-1}^{J-1} \mu_j = \sum_{j=1}^{J-1} \beta_j r_j,$$

and the risk associated with the portfolio is defined as

$$\left[\sum_{j=1}^{J-1} \sum_{k=1}^{J-1} \sigma_{jk} \right]^{1/2} = \left[\sum_{j=1}^{J-1} \sum_{k=1}^{J-1} \beta_j \beta_k \sigma^{\gamma}_{jk} \right]^{1/2}.$$

Suppose that each specification of μ and $\|\sigma_{jk}\|$ corresponds to a unique, joint probability distribution over vectors $(\varepsilon_1,...,\varepsilon_{J-1})$ in some admissible collection of distributions. Consider an individual with a utility function, $u(\mu,\|\sigma^{\gamma}_{jk}\|)$, representing his preferences among these distributions. Given values for $r_1,...,r_{J-1}$, and $\|\sigma^{\gamma}_{jk}\|$, let this person choose μ and $\|\sigma_{jk}\|$, and hence a probability distribution, so as to maximize his utility subject to constraints (6) and (7).[14] But selection of μ implies, from (3) and (5), the determination of $\beta_1,...,\beta_J$. In particular, as $r_1,...,r_{J-1}$, and $\|\sigma^{\gamma}_{jk}\|$ hypothetically vary, the demand for money balances per portfolio dollar, β_J, is obtained as the function g^J, where

$$\beta_J = g^J(r_1,...,r_{J-1}, \|\sigma^{\gamma}_{jk}\|).$$

Observe that to have a positive demand for money balances (that is, to have $\beta_J > 0$) associated with any particular collection of parameter values $r_1,...,r_{J-1}$, and $\|\sigma^{\gamma}_{jk}\|$ requires that the β_j, for $j \neq J$, determined with respect to these parameter values have the property that

$$\sum_{j=1}^{J-1} \beta_j \neq 1.$$

In any case, the demand for money balances *in toto* thus depends on the total value of the portfolio, and on current rates of return and the variance-covariance matrix associated with capital gains. Clearly, this demand for money balances emerges from speculative motives in conjunction with the store-of-value function of money. But of course it is not, as outlined above, integrated with the non-portfolio decisions of individuals to demand and supply commodities.

There is one further general-equilibrium-type approach to the introduction of money that speaks to the store-of-value function and that is worthy of description here. That approach is based on the overlapping generations model of Samuelson (1958). The presentation below is indebted to Hoover (1988: ch. 6).

Imagine a world in which individuals live for two periods. In the first period they are 'young' and are able to work a fixed number of hours; in the second they are 'old' and cannot. The collection of all persons born in period t is known as generation t, and there is a new generation born every period. There is a single, perishable good that is produced each period and must be completely used up during that period. This good (like, say, sunflower seeds) can either be consumed (eaten) or invested (planted) to increase consumption for the next period. (The per-unit return on that investment is the quantity of sunflower seeds produced for next period per unit of sunflower seeds planted this period.) Clearly, since they do not work, if the old are to survive they have to be able either to invest or carry income earned when they were young through time to their old age for consumption. But with the produced good perishable, the only way to accomplish the latter is to introduce a good, money, that is capable of storing value so that purchasing power can be moved across time. Of course, since investment is possible, there is, at this point, no necessity for individuals to store value by holding money balances.

Suppose further, however, that the young are paid for their work only at the end of the period. Then they are not able to spend their income while they are young and are now forced to carry it over to spend when they are old. To permit this to happen, there is no alternative but to pay them with money that can be stored for consumption in the next period. It is also necessary to give each person an initial endowment of money when young so that he is able consume and not starve in his youth, and to tax him a fixed amount of money when he is old in order to be able to maintain, if desirable, a constant money supply over time. Under these conditions, the overlapping generations model is able to provide a specification of inter-temporal monetary equilibrium.[15]

Mathematically, the overlapping generations model described above can be expressed in terms of each person of generation t maximizing a utility function of the form.[16]

$$v = u^t(x^t_1, x^t_2),$$

subject to constraints

$$\hat{m}^t + w^t\hat{\ell}^t = p^t_1 x^t_1 + p_1{}^t k^t + m^t, \tag{8}$$

$$\hat{m}^t \geq p^t_1 x^t_1 + p^t_1 k^t, \tag{9}$$

$$m^t + \left[1 + r^t\right] p^t_1 k^t = p^t_2 x^t_2 + \hat{\zeta}^t, \tag{10}$$

where, for this person, x^t_1, x^t_2, p^t_1, and p^t_2 represent, respectively, quantities and prices of the perishable good consumed in periods 1 and 2; k^t is the quantity of the perishable good invested in period 1 at rate of return r^t; the parameter $\hat{\ell}^t$ indicates the fixed amount of labor time supplied in period 1 at money wage w^t; the parameters $\hat{m}^t$ and $\hat{\zeta}^t$ are, respectively, the initial endowment and tax of nominal money balances; and $\hat{m}^t$ denotes nominal money balances carried over from period 1 to period 2. Adding (8) to (10) yields the usual budget constraint asserting that, for both periods combined, the individual's income equals his expenditures. Assuming $\hat{m}^t = \hat{\zeta}^t$, this budget constraint is

$$w^t\hat{\ell}^t + r^t p^t_1 k^t = p^t_1 x^t_1 + p^t_1 x^t_2.$$

Inequality (9), known as the finance constraint, says that no matter what their incomes, the young cannot spend more in their youth than the money balance they inherit in their initial endowment. Its purpose is to avoid the indeterminacy that would otherwise arise if the rate of return on capital were so high that the individual does not want to hold sufficient money to cover his period 1 expenditures. Evidently, out of the above maximization the demand for money by an individual of generation t in his youth emerges residually as a function of $p^t_1, p^t_2, w^t, r^t, \hat{\ell}^t, \hat{m}^t \hat{\zeta}^t$. The demand for money so obtained is a demand for money as a store of value. Individuals do not demand money in their old age. Rather, they use all of the money balances they have carried over from their youth to purchase quantities of the consumption good and to pay taxes.

From the models surveyed above it is clear that, in general, money functions as a medium of exchange to increase efficiency in trading. It functions as a store of value to permit the shifting of consumption forward through time and to eliminate the inefficiency that arises from known (or probabilistically known) irregularities in the timing of income receipts and expenditures. In performing its store-of-value function it is one among many assets in a portfolio of assets that stores value over time. Nevertheless, an important aspect of money has been omitted from these analyses because all of them rely on the unrealistic, implicit general-equilibrium assumptions that individuals have prefect knowledge and that time is logical. To say that a person has perfect knowledge means that he knows everything there is to know about the past and the present and that, in addition, he also knows with certainty either the actual outcomes that will arise at appropriate future moments, or at least the complete collection of possibilities together with their probabilities of occurrence at those moments. To take time to be logical is to ignore the factual uniqueness of each moment in history and to permit, merely by restarting an analytical clock, the replication of those historical moments. The end result is to prevent the realities of the (non-probabilistic) uncertainty that arises out of the ignorance in which real decisions are made, and out of the historical uniqueness of actual decision-moments, from permeating the analytical structures of the inquiry undertaken.

This exclusion is especially striking in view of Keynes' argument that it is mostly because of the uncertainty created by the presence of ignorance and historical time that money has any role as a store of value to play at all. According to Keynes,

> ... our desire to hold Money as a store of wealth is a barometer of the degree of our distrust of our own calculations and conventions concerning the future. ... [This] feeling about Money ... takes charge at the moments when the higher, more precarious conventions have weakened. The possession of actual money lulls our disquietude ...
>
> (Keynes 1937: 216)

The role of money as a store of value, then, is to provide 'a refuge from uncertainty.'[17] In particular, the demand for money as a store of value emerges, in part, from ignorance concerning the timing of expenditures and income receipts, since the purposes for which money will be needed, is often unknown and hence uncertain.[18] And money may also be demanded for storage purposes as a consequence of ignorance of future asset prices and the accompanying 'disquietude' associated with the possibility of capital losses on non-monetary assets. The demand for money as a store of value, then, is, in Shackle's words, 'a substitute for knowledge' (Shackle 1972: 216).

The next section adds to the analysis of the roles of money set out above by developing a new model which explains the demand for money in the context of the uncertainty begot from ignorance and historical time. In so doing, it accounts for both medium of exchange and store of value functions. Without commitment to perfect knowledge and logical time, the model focuses, in part, on the Tobin perspective that money is one asset in a portfolio of many assets. Although money balances appear as an argument of the individual's utility function, this inclusion, unlike the previously described Samuelson–Patinkin inclusion, is given a justification that, it is to be hoped, stands up. And, in contrast with the analysis of Starrett and the overlapping generations model discussed above, since money balances provide utility to the individual, the demand for money is explained as the direct outcome of an authentic optimization procedure. The model also incorporates the decision to buy and sell goods simultaneously with the selection of a portfolio that includes money balances.[19]

3 A NON-PROBABILISTIC, HISTORICAL TIME APPROACH

The analytical approach taken below is based on the work of Shackle (1969) and Vickers (1978: pt. 3), (1987: ch. 12). The former proposed and the latter subsequently modified a model of decision-making that applies in situations characterised by the uncertainty that emerges from the presence of ignorance and historical time. Although the combined Shackle-Vickers model has been explored in depth elsewhere,[20] a brief summary is in order here.

In the Shackle-Vickers construction, the decision-maker is faced with a set, called the 'choice set', of well-defined options from which he must choose. For each choice option, he first imagines a collection of as many possible future states of the world or outcomes as he can think of that could emerge as the effects of his decision work themselves out.[21] Each state of the world would, should it arise in the future, combines with each possible decision among choice options to produce a distinct result. Because the presence of ignorance and historical time prevent the decision-maker from knowing what is to come, this collection of imagined future states is necessarily incomplete. There are outcomes, the possibility of which cannot be foreseen in advance. Furthermore, for the same reasons of ignorance and historical time, the decision-maker is unable to determine a probability function defined over the various subsets of the outcomes he imagines. In place of a probability function, however, he is assumed to construct a potential surprise function over those same subsets.[22] Next, using specific evaluations of the outcomes themselves, the decision-maker transforms his potential surprise function into a potential surprise density function defined over all possible outcome-evaluations. Then, maximizing an attractiveness function subject to the potential surprise density function, he obtains a characterization of each choice option that allows its comparison to all other choice options in terms of a decision index. Lastly, the decision-maker selects the choice option that maximizes this decision index. All of the elements of the Shackle-Vickers model — the choice options, the imagined collection of future possible outcomes, the potential surprise function, the attractiveness function, and the decision index — are unique to the moment of historical time at which the decision is made, unique to the decision-maker and, except for the set of choice options and the decision index, unique to a particular choice option.

Turning to the problem at hand, let there be, as before, J financial assets indexed by $j = 1, \ldots J$, and identify the Jth as (nominal) money balances. (Recall that non-monetary assets issued on different dates are different assets.) Although each non-monetary asset j provides a yield in perpetuity, the decision-maker, here taken to be the individual or consumer, plans on holding j for only a predetermined finite number of periods.[23] Suppose the anticipated future rate of return on the entire portfolio is determined by the individual, along with the composition of the portfolio itself. Rather than focusing on the fractions of the total value of the portfolio held in each asset, take portfolios to be defined as vectors $a = (a_1,\dots,a_J)$, where a_j indicates a number of units of asset j. In addition to assets, let the individual also select quantities of goods (including leisure) to consume and represent vectors of excess-demand quantities based on such selections by the symbol x. Thus, since leisure time is included among goods consumed, one of the components of x represents quantities of labor time supplied. In any case, the individual's choice set, X, consists of all nonnegative vectors, (x, a), that satisfy budget and any other constraints under which he operates. Note that the selection of a new portfolio necessarily carries savings or dissavings implications. Moreover, if the individual currently holds portfolio $a^0 = (a^0{}_1,\dots,a^0{}_J)$, and if he chooses to hold portfolio a instead, then his vector of asset excess demands is given by $a - a^0$. In particular, his excess demand for money balances is $a_J - a^0{}_J$.

As in the traditional theory of demand, the parameters of the constraints that define the individual's choice set X, when these constraints are effective, are the variables upon which demand or excess demand quantities are said to depend.[24] Such constraints always include the following: First, assuming for the sake of simplicity that borrowing is not permitted, the dollar amount of the individual's expenditure on commodities and assets cannot exceed his income plus the revenue he would expect to obtain upon the sale of all initial endowments and currently held assets (including money); that is, for all (x, a) in the choice set,

$$p \cdot x + q \cdot (a - a^0) \le (q \cdot a)\psi, \qquad (11)$$

where $p > 0$ is a vector of perceived, current (non-asset) commodity prices, $q = (q_1,\dots,q_J) > 0$ is a vector of perceived, current (not-necessarily-market-equilibrium) asset prices such that $q_J = 1$, and ψ is the anticipated, per-period, rate of return on the portfolio which will be discussed shortly. Inequality (11) includes both income and wealth, and may be thought of as a 'financial resources' constraint. Second, for the choice options (x, a) such that $a_J > 0$, the ratio of expenditure on goods and income-earning assets, e, in (x, a), to the money balances held in the individual's portfolio in (x, a) is less than some anticipated number, v, determined, in part, by his perception of the limit (imposed by his environment) on the 'velocity' with which he is able to spend income receipts and, in part, by his perception of the current rate of interest.[25] This second constraint is written

$$e \leq v a_J \tag{12}$$

and incorporates the idea that a stock of money is held by the individual for the purpose of facilitating a flow of payments or transactions. Although e clearly depends on appropriate components of p, x, q, and $a - a^0$, and although v depends partly on the interest rate, to the extent that (11) and (12) are effective in the selection of (x, a) from X, the excess demands $(x, a - a^0)$ so obtained may still be thought of as dependent on, at least, p, q, e, and v. Further dependence on the initial endowment a^0, and hence wealth, is implicit. The rate of interest in the guise of ψ, comes in indirectly through q and v. These same variables (except for possible future price changes — which enter the present model in the specification of asset rates of return below) were the ones initially suggested as relevant in determining the consumer's demand for money balances at the start of Section 2.

For each (x, a) in X, let ω vary over possible states of the world, as imagined by the individual, that might greet his selection of (x, a).[26] Represent the collection of all such states by Ω. As indicated above, states of the world unknowable to the individual are not contained in Ω. These are combined into a single set and symbolically represented by the null set. Suppose the individual defines a potential surprise function on the subsets (including the null set) of Ω. Both the imagined set Ω and the potential surprise function defined over its subsets depend on the choice option (x, a).[27]

Consider any asset $j \neq J$. Let $t = 0$ denote the present, let y'_j be the income anticipated from holding one unit of this asset for one period, t periods hence (call the period, 'period t'), and take q^t_j to be the asset's anticipated price during that period. The perceived current price of the asset, $q_j = q^0_j$, is assumed to be known and fixed. Define the total anticipated rate of return on asset j in period t as

$$\Psi^t_j = \frac{y^t_j + q_j^{t+1} - q^t_j}{q^t_j},$$

and let t run over all periods, $t = 0, \ldots, T_j$, that the individual plans to hold asset j. To keep matters simple, assume that $Tj = T$, for $j = 1, \ldots, J-1$, and some positive integer T. Clearly, the y_j^t and the q^t_j depend on the state of the world in period t. Hence so do the ψ^t_j. Since the $\psi^t_{j,}$ in turn, determine the per-period average anticipated rate of return on asset j according to the formula

$$\psi_{j_j} = \left[\prod_{t=0}^{T}(1+\psi_j^t) \right]^{\frac{1}{T}} -1,$$

it follows that φ_j, too, depends on these states of the world.[28] It is not necessary, however, to suppose that the individual imagines relations between future states of the world and both the j_j^t and the q_j^t clearly enough to explicitly derive ψ as a function of ω. Rather, it is assumed instead that, without any specification of how, he is able to hypothesize a working condensation or summary of these relations in the form

$$\psi_j = \rho^j(\omega), \qquad j = 1,\dots , J\text{-}1 \qquad (13)$$

linking the average anticipated rate of return on each asset j to future states of the world.

Three things about (13) should be noted. First, ψ_j accounts for both the rates of return r_j and the capital gains γ_j of the Tobin model described in Section 2. Second, the approach abstracts from the way in which future changes in commodity and asset prices might affect the purchasing-power value of money. Third, since φ_j, as indicated above, depends on a future collection of states of the world, one for each period $t = 1,\dots ,T+1$, the state-of-world variable w should really be thought of as a vector $\omega = (\omega^1,\dots , \omega^{T+1})$, where ω_t is the state of the world in period t. However, as subsequent analysis remains substantively the same regardless of whether ω is taken to be a scalar or a vector, little harm will be done if, to keep exposition simple, ω continues to be referred to as a scalar.

Now the value, at currently perceived prices, of any portfolio a of (x,a) in X is $q \cdot a$ or

$$\Gamma(a) = a_J + \sum_{j=1}^{j-1} q_j a_j. \qquad (14)$$

Hence the anticipated, per-period, rate of return on the entire portfolio over all relevant periods can be characterized as

$$\psi = \sum_{j=1}^{J-1} \frac{q_j a_j}{\Gamma(a)} \psi_j, \qquad (15)$$

where each ψ is weighted by the current fraction of the portfolio invested in asset J. Note that under this weighting scheme, the weight assigned to money balances in the portfolio is, from (14),

$$\frac{a_j}{\Gamma(a)} = 1 - \sum_{j=1}^{J-1} \frac{q_j a_j}{\Gamma(a)}.$$

In light of (13), equation (15) defines an anticipated portfolio-rate-of-return function

$$\psi = \xi(a, \omega), \qquad (16)$$

where

$$\xi(a, \omega) = \sum_{j=1}^{J-1} \frac{a_j a_j}{\Gamma(a)} \rho^j(w). \qquad (17)$$

Let Ψ be the collection of all anticipated portfolio rates of return under ξ.

Since the individual is uncertain as to the state of the world that will greet his selection of (x, a), he is also uncertain about what his preferences will be as the effects of his decision work themselves out. To capture this idea suppose the individual has a utility function of the form

$$\upsilon = u(x, \psi, \omega), \qquad (18)$$

defined over the cartesian product $X \times \Psi \times \Omega$, where υ ranges over the collection Γ of all anticipated utility values or outcomes. Thus utility is derived from the consumption of a vector x, the anticipated rate of return, ψ of the entire portfolio, and the state of the world that comes to pass with the realisation of x and ψ. Substitution of (17) into (16), and then the result into (18) yields

$$\upsilon = U(x,a,\omega), \tag{19}$$

where

$$U(x,a,\omega) = u(x, \sum_{j=1}^{J-1} \frac{q_j a_j}{\Gamma(a)} \rho^j(\omega), \omega). \tag{20}$$

Clearly, non-monetary assets have utility because they provide a (non-probabilistically) uncertain income stream. Moreover, money balances a_j now appear as an argument in the utility function. The latter is justified in that money may be said to have utility as a refuge from uncertainty, that is, as a means of calming the fears about the future alluded to by Keynes in the quotation cited near the end of Section 2. In particular, stored money balances avoid the possibility of capital loss on non-monetary assets and are available for covering unknown and unknowable future expenditures.[29] Money also has utility as a medium of exchange since, as shown by Feldman and described in the previous section, it increases utility by permitting purchasing power to be carried from one transaction to another.

Note also that equation (19) suggests substitutability between assets, between goods, and between assets and goods (including leisure). In general, there will be a distinct marginal rate of substitution defined for each pair involving two assets, two goods, or one of each.

Assume that u and the ρ_j have sufficient properties so that for every (x, a) in X, U thought of as a function of ω alone, given (x, a), defines a 1-1 and onto relation between Ω and Y. Then it follows that, for each (x,a) in X, the potential surprise function over subsets of Ω can be translated into a potential surprise density function, $f_{[x,a]}$, over Y such that $f_{[x,a]}(\upsilon)$ is the potential surprise of utility evaluation v.[30]

Utility values are not, of course, the only things over which the individual can construct potential surprise density functions. Any function that he thinks relevant and that maps Ω into values of an economic variable such as, for example, a future price, a future capital gain, or future income will automatically confer the potential surprise of each single-element set (ω), for ω in Ω, on the variable value onto which ω is mapped. However, should such a function not be 1-1, that is, if two values of ω, say, were mapped into the same economic value, then confusion would exist as to the appropriate potential surprise value to assign to that economic value. At any rate, it is certainly possible for the individual to conjure up in his mind an entire system of implicit relations among any subset of variables taken from the combination of the state-of-the-world variable with the economic variables, whose simultaneous solution eliminates the state-of-the-world variable and yields some of the economic variables as functions of the remaining economic variables. To the extent that this is done, the individual would then be able to determine his expectation for the effect of, say, a change in a commodity price on the rate of interest. Conversely, the prior presence of such a system in his mind might, instead, lead to his determination of the initial potential surprise function over states of the world postulated for him above.

Returning to the utility function situation, a hypothetical example in which $\rho^1,\dots,\rho^{J\text{-}1}$ and u are such that U is appropriately 1-1 and onto is obtained by setting.

$$u(x,\psi,\omega) = \lambda(x,\psi), \tag{21}$$

for some function λ that is 1-1 and onto for each x, and

$$\rho^j(\omega) = \theta_j \rho^{J-1}(\omega), \quad j=1,\dots,J\text{-}1, \tag{22}$$

where $\theta_1,\dots,\theta_{J\text{-}2}$ are positive constants, $\theta_{J\text{-}1}=1$, and $p^{J\text{-}1}(\omega)$ is also 1-1 and onto. That is, uncertainty, as it impinges on the state-of-the-world variable, influences utility only as it affects the anticipated rate of return on the portfolio; and the anticipated rate of return on each non-monetary asset moves in its own proportion to the anticipated rate of return on asset J-1. In this case, equations (16) – (22) together imply

$$U(x,a,\omega) = \lambda\left(x,\rho^{J-1}(\omega)\left[\sum_{j=1}^{J-1}\frac{q_j a_j \theta_j}{\Gamma(a)}\right]\right).$$

Since (x, a) and the q_j are fixed, since the θ_j are independent of ω, and since $\lambda(x, \psi)$ and $p_{J-1}(\omega)$ are suitably 1-1 and onto, it follows that U is 1-1 and onto for each (x, a) in X.

Given the potential surprise density function $f_{[x, a]}(\upsilon)$ on Υ, introduce the decision-making individual's attractiveness function for (x, a) and his decision index as described above. Then the Shackle–Vickers apparatus permits the decision index to be expressed as a function of the objects of choice, that is, as a function $D(x, a)$ defined on X.[31] Assume the individual chooses (x, a) so as to maximize $D(x, a)$ over X. The portfolio selected, or course, contains a unique, nonnegative quantity of each asset, and the excess demands for those assets, including money balances, are determined as functions of price, expenditure, and velocity variables as described earlier. Insufficient restrictions have been imposed above on the decision index and the potential surprise, utility, and attractiveness functions to ensure that the demand function for money balances exhibits an absence of money illusion, but there is little harm in adding such restrictions now. Furthermore, if the financial resources constraint (11) holds as an equality, then the choice of x as part of (x,a) fixes (as does the choice of a) the new perceived current dollar value of the entire asset portfolio, a, as $\Gamma(a)$. The question of whether the selected portfolio is diversified, that is, whether it does not lie on one of the coordinate axes of the object-of-choice space, depends on the characteristics of D as built up from the potential surprise function, the function U, and the attractiveness function.

Observe that the traditional approach to portfolio selection which, under certain conditions, is equivalent to the analysis attributed to Tobin in Section 2, is primarily concerned with the spreading of investment over assets whose income streams are not perfectly correlated.[32] It solves this problem by selecting the weights in the individual's portfolio, earlier symbolized as the β_j, so as to minimize the risk (standard deviation) associated with the entire portfolio for a given expected rate of return over the portfolio as a whole. The argument of Section 2 showed, in part, that in this traditional context the structure of the variance-covariance matrix of the returns on the individual non-monetary assets plays a significant role in determining the choice of these weights. In any case, the utility-maximizing portfolio obtained by picking weights to minimize risk for a specified expected rate of return is referred to as optimal. One of the conclusions drawn from this analysis is that, in general, risk is reduced by diversification.

It should be pointed out, however, that the notions of risk and its reduction have no place in the Shackle–Vickers framework in the sense in which those concepts are relevant to probabilistic portfolio analysis. Because the decision event and the decision outcome are seen in the Shackle-Vickers context as unique in (historical) time, because such uniqueness implies that neither the event nor the outcome are replicable, and because knowledge, in general, is so meager, it is not meaningful to speak of means, variances, and other moments of a probability distribution from which outcomes might be drawn. In addition, potential surprise density functions do not possess meaningful parameters like means and variances that are amenable to manipulation and interpretation. Hence it is not even possible to define risk with respect to such parameters, let alone speak of reducing it. Instead, the model proposed here chooses one portfolio and one consumption vector from a set of consumption-portfolio options in much the same spirit (though in a vastly different environment) as the traditional consumer chooses commodities from a budget set.[33] All of the uncertainties and the hazards involved, together with whatever other factors that also influence decisions, are accounted for within the confines of the model. In this way, a full treatment of non-probabilistic uncertainty is provided.

Note that, in particular, as assumption such as (21) from the traditional perspective implies that the returns on all assets are perfectly correlated, and hence that the risk of the portfolio does not vary with a change in weights. Thus all portfolios are associated with the same risk and there is no advantage to diversification. But this conclusion does not apply in the present context because the decision-making individual is not choosing a portfolio to minimize risk. Rather, he selects his portfolio-consumption vector so as to maximize $D(x, a)$ over X.

Moreover, there are special considerations concerning the possible use of futures markets when contemplating the purchase of a commodity that is not needed until a future date. Four options can be identified, each with its own cost. Assume, as in Section 2, that, although there are always delivery costs for goods (as opposed to assets), there are contract costs for goods only when they are not bought and delivered at the same time; that there are contract costs but no delivery costs in the sale or purchase of non-monetary assets; that there are storage costs in holding goods, not portfolio assets, through time; and that (this is partly redundant) there are no delivery, contract, and storage costs associated with money. Then the four options and their costs are as follows:

(i) Buy now and hold the good until it is needed. The costs are for delivery and storage, and the individual runs the risk of a preference or technology change that may alter the time when the commodity is needed (potentially increasing storage costs), and also may, if the commodity has become less desirable, reduce the value of the purchase to him at the time of its use.

(ii) Buy a contract for future delivery in a futures market. In this case there are delivery and contract costs, and the risk of preference, technology, and time of use changes remains. The next (and last) two options have the advantage that the individual purchases the commodity according to preference and technology requirements at (and not before) its time of use).

(iii) Hold money balances and purchase the good in a future spot market. Now the costs are for delivery, along with the interest forgone and the possible forgone capital gains which might have been realized if non-monetary assets had been held in lieu of money.

(iv) Buy non-monetary assets to convert to money at the appropriate time and use that money to purchase the good in a future spot market. Here there are two contract costs (the buying and selling of the non-monetary assets), the delivery cost for the good, and the chances of capital losses on the non-monetary assets.

In choosing among options, the individual must compare the discounted value of his expectation of the future spot price with the present spot price and the present price of futures contracts, and must also compare the anticipated discounted costs of each option.[34] These contemplations are implicit in the model described above in the budget and other constraints that define the choice set X and in the maximizing of $D(x, a)$ over X. Evidently, if the discounted value of the anticipated future spot price, the present spot price, and the present price of futures contracts were all the same, then his selection would be based only on the discounted value of each option's cost.

Regardless, it is clear that, in addition to the selection of portfolios, the model proposed here opens the way for understanding the changes that might occur in portfolios on successive dates. These changes generally arise because, as indicated earlier, all of the elements of the Shackle–Vickers construction (such as the potential surprise function and the decision index) are unique to each moment of historical time. Hence there is no presumption that the demand for any asset, including money (or, for that matter, the demand for any good), will remain constant through time. This provides, in particular, an explanation of the instability of the demand for money over time observed by Keynes (1937: 219) — something that the more standard approaches to the demand for money outlined in Section 2 do not adequately address.

Finally, although the firm, too, can be thought of as holding and demanding money balances for similar reasons, the development of a corresponding analysis for the firm would carry discussion well beyond the scope of the present chapter. Suffice it to say that a Shackle–Vickers model of decision-making in the firm has been constructed elsewhere[35] in which the firm picks a three dimensional choice-option vector, one of whose components is the demand for new capital (durable input). Simultaneously with these decisions, the firm also selects an output to produce, inputs to hire, and an output price to charge. Clearly, by expanding its decision structure, that model could be extended to admit the choice of a portfolio that includes money balances as proposed here.

NOTES

* The author gratefully acknowledges the help of Paul Davidson and Douglas Vickers. A revised version of this chapter has been published as chapter 10 of my *Time, Ignorance, and Uncertainty in Economic Models* (Ann Arbor, MI: University of Michigan Press, 1998), copyright © University of Michigan Press. The original chapter is published here with the permission of the University of Michigan Press.

1 A monetary equilibrium is an equilibrium in which money has a positive purchasing-power value arising from its capacity to function as a medium of exchange and store of value, even though money itself may have no intrinsic value as a commodity.

2 See Hoover (1988: 121).

3 Vickers (1985: 388)

4 Katzner (1995).

5 For example, the presence of, say, bank charges for handling checks, generally causes a decline in the efficiency with which money performs its

medium of exchange function. If, in addition, its purchasing power is declining, money will also function less efficiently as a store of value.

6 See, for example, Patinkin (1956) and Samuelson (1947).

7 If money balances must be borrowed in order to be held, then $r\,m$ reflects the interest cost of holding m. If borrowing is not necessary, either because the individual has a sufficient endowment of money balances to begin with or because he is paid in money balances upon selling his endowment, then $r\,m$ represents forgone interest and y must include the income that would have been earned had the interest not been forgone.

8 The following development follows Samuelson and Sato (1984).

9 This model also presumes unlimited borrowing and lending opportunities at the market rate of interest.

10 See, for example, Starr (1989).

11 This would be true regardless of whether the future is known with certainty or only probabilistically. However, the presence of risk in the latter case means that the costs of using futures markets could be even higher.

12 The presentation here follows that of Katzner (1970: 169–73).

13 Except for money, assets issued on different dates are different assets.

14 It is assumed that u has sufficient properties so that this maximization can always be carried out.

15 In such a model, problems can arise because changing price expectations may generate non-stationary equilibria. This, in turn, may lead to a deterioration in the purchasing-power value of money over time which, if it eventually approaches zero, would destroy the possibility of speaking of a monetary equilibrium in the sense in which that concept has been defined.

16 Again, the utility function is assumed to possess sufficient properties so as to be able to perform the maximization.

17 Vickers (1985: 389).

18 See Shackle (1974: 4, 61, 62). In the context of ignorance and historical time, futures markets are of no use in circumventing this demand for money because neither the future goods that will be needed, nor the timing of their purchase relative to income receipts, is known. However, as indicated below, futures markets may still be employed for other purposes.

19 In this sense, the present analysis is actually more in the tradition of Friedman (1956) who employs a 'portfolio' containing multiple assets (including money), physical goods, and human capital. Recall that the Tobin portfolio, as introduced above, has only multiple assets.

20 Katzner (1989–90, 1989).

21 Shackle (1969: 6–10) argues that decision-makers do not base choices on outcomes that are known but, rather, on imagined possible outcomes. Once the outcome is known, the moment of choice is past and it is too

late to choose.

22 The potential surprise of a subset S is the surprise the individual expects now that he would experience in the future if an element of S were actually to come to pass. That potential surprise functions cannot be derived from probability functions, and vice versa, has been demonstrated by Katzner (1986).

23 The question of the optimal number of periods to keep j is ignored.

24 The parameters of the remainder of the decision structure (such as, for example, the parameters of the utility function introduced below) are, as is typical, suppressed and implicit.

25 A higher rate of interest, say, may induce the individual to hold a larger proportion of liquid assets in non-monetary from, thereby forcing an increase in v.

26 It has been suggested earlier that the choice make by the individual affects the collection of states of the world that he envisages as possible outcomes. This does not mean, however, that the individual is able to conjure up in his mind a formal relation indicating that a particular state of the world might accompany the selection of a particular choice option. From the perspective of the individual, then, ω may be taken to be independent of (x, a).

27 To say that Ω depends on the choice option (x, a) is not to say that an element of Ω depends on that choice option. See note 26.

28 Possible serial correlation in the sequences of values $\psi^{0}_{j}, ..., \psi^{T}_{j}$ is of no consequence for the logic of the present argument.

29 Recall, again, that futures markets cannot necessarily be used to avoid such future expenditures since neither their timing nor the nature of the purchases involved may be known in advance.

30 See Katzner (1987).

31 See, for example, Katzner (1989–90).

32 See, for example, Vickers (1987: 136–47).

33 Because it does not employ the 'gambler's' indifference map, and does not sum the focus gains and focus losses of individual assets to obtain the focus gain and focus loss of the portfolio as a whole, the present model avoids the conclusion implied by Shackle's original analysis that diversification is not rational. See Ozga (1965: 213–16).

34 The discount rate employed in these calculations must be a subjectively determined required rate of return that will, in general, be related to the market rate of interest.

35 See Katzner (1990).

REFERENCES

Feldman, A. M. (1973) 'Bilateral trading processes, pairwise optimality, and Pareto optimality', *Review of Economic Studies* 40: 463–73. Reprinted as ch. 8 of Starr, R. M. (ed.) (1989) *General Equilibrium Models of Monetary Economies: Studies in the Static Foundations of Monetary Theory*, San Diego, CA: Academic Press.

Friedman, M. (1956) 'The quantity theory of money — a restatement', in Friedman, M. (ed) *Studies in the Quantity Theory of Money*, Chicago, IL: University of Chicago Press, 3–21.

Hicks, J. R. (1935) 'A suggestion for simplifying the theory of money', *Economica* n.s. 2: 1–19. Reprinted as ch 2 of Starr, R.M. (ed.) (1989) *General Equilibrium Models of Monetary Economies: Studies in the Stat ic Foundations of Monetary Theory*, San Diego, CA: Academic Press.

Hoover, K. D. (1988) *The New Classical Macroeconomics*, Oxford: Blackwell.

Katzner, D. W. (1970) *Static Demand Theory*, New York: Macmillan.

—— (1986) 'Potential surprise, potential confirmation, and probability', *Journal of Post Keynesian Economics* 9: 58–78.

—— (1987) 'More on the distinction between potential confirmation and probability', *Journal of Post Keynesian Economics* 10: 65–83.

—— (1989) 'The 'comparative statics' of the Shackle–Vickers approach to decision-making in ignorance', in Fomby, T.B. and T.K. Seo (eds) *Studies in the Economics of Uncertainty*, New York: Springer, 21–43.

—— (1989–90) 'The Shackle–Vickers approach to decision-making in ignorance', *Journal of Post Keynesian Economics* 12: 237–59.

—— (1990) 'The Firm Under Conditions of Ignorance and Historical Time', *Journal of Post Keynesian Economics* 13: 125–45.

—— (1995) 'Simultaneous economic behaviour under conditions of ignorance and historical time', in Rima, I. H. (ed.) *Measurement, Quantification, and Economic Analysis*, London: Routledge.

Keynes, J. M. (1937) 'The General Theory of Employment', *Quarterly Journal of Economics* 51: 209–23.

Ozga, S.A. (1965) *Expectations in Economic Theory*, London: Weidenfeld and Nicolson.

Patinkin, D. (1956) *Money Interest and Prices*, Evanston, IL: Row Peterson.

Samuelson, P.A. (1947) *Foundations of Economic Analysis*, Cambridge, MA: Harvard University Press.

—— (1958) 'An exact consumption-loan model of interest with or without the social contrivance of money', *Journal of Political Economy* 66: 467–82.

—— and Sato, R. (1984) 'Unattainability of integrability and definiteness conditions in the general case of demand for money and goods', *American Economic Review* 74: 588–604.

Shackle, G. L. S. (1969) *Decision, Order and Time in Human Affairs*, 2nd edn,

Cambridge: Cambridge University Press.

—— (1972) *Epistemics and Economics*, Cambridge: Cambridge University Press.

—— (1974) *Keynesian Kaledics*, Edinburgh: Edinburgh University Press.

Starr, R.M. (ed.) (1989) *General Equilibrium Models of Monetary Economies: Studies in the Static Foundations of Monetary Theory*, San Diego, CA: Academic Press.

Starrett, D. (1973) 'Inefficiency and the demand for 'money' in a sequence economy', *Review of Economic Studies* 40: 437–48. Reprinted as ch. 17 of Starr, R. M. (ed.) (1989) *General Equilibrium Models of Monetary Economies: Studies in the Static Foundations of Monetary Theory*, San Diego, CA: Academic Press.

Tobin, J. (1958) 'Liquidity preference as behavior towards risk', *Review of Economic Studies* 25: 65–86.

Vickers, D. (1978) *Financial Markets in the Capitalist Process*, Philadelphia, PA: University of Pennsylvania Press.

—— (1985) 'On relational structures and non-equilibrium in economic theory', *Eastern Economic Journal* 11: 384–403.

—— (1987) *Money Capital in the Theory of the Firm*, Cambridge: Cambridge University Press.

13

SHACKLE, IMAGINATION AND THE CAPITAL INVESTMENT DECISION: A MISSING LINK IN MODERN MANAGEMENT ACCOUNTING PRACTICE

*Kenneth C. Cleaver**

1 INTRODUCTION

The failure of the neoclassical economic research community to engage with, explore and respond to the research proposals of George Shackle has led directly to two undesirable consequences. First, the neoclassical economic research community has denied the fundamental challenges posed by the research proposals that Shackle identified and sought to confront; this act of denial is generally justified on the basis of methodological grounds (Earl and Kay 1985). Second, contiguous disciplines that have been strongly influenced by the precepts of the neoclassical economic research community have *inter alia* also failed to actively engage with the Shacklean research proposals. In this chapter I argue that although this second-order failure, with respect to contiguous disciplines, can be explained, it is often less excusable because the methodological rationales for not addressing the Shackle proposals are less apparent or less valid in the context of the contiguous research communities. In order to illustrate the argument I endeavour to relate the experiences of the management accounting research community to the insights offered by the Shackle research proposals with regard to the investment decision process.

2 SHACKLE, THEORY AND THE DECISION MAKER

Shackle consistently argued that his interest was in the interanimation between theory and the practical decision maker: a clear expression is offered in Shackle (1963); another strong indicator of the interest can be found in Shackle (1968). An examination of the bibliography of Shackle (Ford 1994) indicates his abiding theoretical interest in the practical problems of the business decision-making process and although only Shackle (1955) sought to supplement the theoretical interest with an example of empirical survey-based research, Shackle (1983b: 224) argued strongly for 'the need to make case studies, rather than allegedly "general" theories, the vehicle of our thought.' However, the demarcation between Shackle and the neoclassical research community occurs not at the level of the identification of this problem of the decision maker but rather at the level of how to model and then seek to respond to the problem. In a highly stylized form it is plausible to argue that Shackle sought to organize and develop his interest in the problem around two basic research proposals: [1]

Proposal 1

The researcher should seek to examine decision situations from the viewpoint of the individual decision maker. Shackle (1958: 106) observes 'decisions take place in the individual mind. It follows that economics must be concerned with the essence and nature of the moment-in-being of the individual person.'[2]

Proposal 2

The researcher should accept that there is a class of decisions situations which involves uncertainty, and that this class of decisions cannot be reduced to the notion of risk without seriously infringing the strictures of Proposal 1. Shackle (1958: 107) observes '[u]ncertainty is not present when the consequences of the action are actuarially certain.'

Proposal 1 directs attention towards the information available to the decision maker at the time of making the decision. Proposal 1 also embodies another basic premise of the Shackle framework, namely that the researcher should be sensitive to the perception of the decision maker that the decision process represents a point of origination, and that a decision can introduce something 'new' into the skein of things.[3]

Proposal 2 directs attention towards the inevitable lacunae in the information set, given the nature of Proposal 1 and the logical implications of its embodiment of '[t]ime as we experience it...' (Shackle, 1954: 743), namely, that the decision has to be made without reference to the actual consequences of the decision because they could not, logically, exist and therefore could not determine the decision before the decision was taken.

For Shackle the theoretical and practical link between his two research proposals was to be found in the imaginative powers of the decision maker. Shackle recalls that, in his (1942) paper 'A theory of investment decisions',

> Its opening sentence introduced a word which has become the central term of my conception of the business of choice, a business which, as I have become profoundly convinced, is in the first place a work of *imagination*.
>
> (Shackle 1983a: 112)

Crucial to Shackle's commitment to viewing the decision process as a point of origination, with the consequent implication that the individual making the decision believes that they are free-willed, was the idea that the decision maker was 'free' to imagine the possible outcomes stemming from an act of decision; 'free' to choose between those imagined outcomes and in the process 'free' to help 'to make history' (Shackle 1955: 33).

Informed by his two research proposals Shackle (1949) offered a highly original solution to the decision problem. After a brief period of research interest in the Shackle framework, it was confined to the margins of the research agenda of the neoclassical research community, and ultimately it was effectively ignored (Carter 1972, 1993).[4] In the light of this response it is possible to detect a change in Shackle's own research activity: it adopted a firmer orientation towards exploring and expounding an appreciation of the dynamics of the growth of knowledge process. Earl (1993: 247) has observed of this transition that 'Shackle the theoretician on investment decisions and choice under uncertainty in the 1930s, 1940s and 1950s turned into Shackle the philosopher and historian of economic thought in his later career'. In both phases of his academic career Shackle posed many fundamental questions to and of the neoclassical research community. The failure of that community to respond effectively to the research proposals in the first phase left it even more exposed to the critiques of the second phase. The failure to engage with the research proposals in the first phase, however, also had substantial implications for how theory was developed in contiguous disciplines. It is this issue that the current analysis now addresses.

3 MODERN MANAGEMENT ACCOUNTING: THEORY AND PRACTICE

The typical textbook definition of management accounting emphasizes its role in the provision of information to decision makers within an organization, information intended to improve the quality and effectiveness of the decision making process (Drury 1996: 4). Puxty (1993: 4) notes that this mode of definition is 'taken, explicitly or implicitly, by all modern management accounting textbooks' although he notes that uniformity of view with regards to definition and purpose disintegrates away from the world of the textbook. The current analysis wishes to focus on the textbook presentation of the subject and will therefore limit its discussion to what Scapens (1984: 18) has termed *The Conventional Wisdom* of management accounting.

Modern management accounting practice precedes the development of the modern management accounting conventional wisdom by a substantial period. (The process of practice preceding theoretical formalization is not unusual in terms of academic development: see Mill 1836, Cochoy 1998.) The traditional history with regard to the development of management accounting practice tends to emphasize the last quarter of the nineteenth century as being crucial (Garner 1954). Although aspects of management accounting practice had origins in the late eighteenth century (Fleischman, Hoskin and Macve 1995), such earlier developments have often been portrayed as company-specific processes that did not become templates for normal practice at the time of their development (Loft 1995). In terms of the more traditional history the process that gathered pace in the final decades of the nineteenth century had a strong focus on cost allocation; in the UK, where the process initially gathered pace, it is generally argued that the interest was promoted by the experiences of the so-called Great Depression (Saul 1985) and the increased awareness of British manufacturing industry to issues related to a loss of competitiveness. This late nineteenth century focus led to the original title of 'cost accounting'.

In the early twentieth century the stimulus to further change moved across the Atlantic (Loft, 1995). The traditional history stresses how the demands of the emerging and developing industrial structure of the US produced new pressures and objectives for the practice of management; a continued interest with costs was supplemented and augmented by the development of techniques to control the new and rapidly growing organizations: the development of budget systems and the creation of return on investment (ROI) as a single figure performance measure by Du Pont (Loft 1995: 29).[5] The development of a significant role in the elaboration and operation of such management control techniques began to reorientate the practice of the 'cost and works' accountant towards the more generic notion of the management accountant. Like many processes within established systems of order the change was relatively slow and gradual, Miller (1998: 182) notes 'the post-World War II transformation of "cost accounting" into "management accounting".'

These formative periods of development were driven by practical expediency rather than theoretical insight or rigour. Scapens (1984) and Miller (1998) note, for example, that the migration of the 'relevant cost' concept from economic analysis to cost accounting was first mooted in the US by Clark (1923) and espoused in the UK during the late 1930s via the work of Edwards (1937), Coase (1938), Baxter (1938). Buchanan (1973: 12) noted that the impact of this L.S.E. contribution to cost theory should include 'mention of G. L. S. Shackle ... his approach to decision is fully consistent with that developed by the London theorists.' Unfortunately, this synergy between the London theorists and Shackle did not become a major platform for management accounting. Indeed, in commenting on the developments in the 1930s, Parker (1999) argues that they represented a false start to the establishment of an academic management accounting literature. It was not until the development of a larger research community concerned with management accounting, during the 1950s, that the members of that embryonic research community in search of a research framework began to more extensively link the new research agenda to existing research frameworks, alas the links with the work of Shackle were not developed at that time.

In this period of searching for a framework it is uncontroversial to claim that the neoclassical economic research community played a major role in the development of the conventional wisdom of management accounting. The nature and extent of that influence can be immediately perceived in the textbook conventional wisdom of management accounting (Scapens 1984). A clear linkage between the two disciplines, and their respective research communities, is established, and applauded, by Carsberg (1975: 21) when he observes that 'accounting may aptly be regarded as a branch of applied economics'.

The interanimation between management accounting and neoclassical economic theory is usefully perceived from the growth of knowledge tradition. This tradition, derived from initial ideas offered by such authors as Kuhn (1970) and Lakatos (1970), has helped to reshape the perception and analysis of research communities across a wide range of disciplines; it has also directed attention towards the crucial role of the meta-theoretical framework that informs pedagogy and research within a discipline or research community. With regard to management accounting Puxty (1993: 3) notes that it like every other 'subject is governed by its framework.' The neoclassical research community has had a substantial and possibly disproportionate influence on the structure and evolution of the framework of management accounting research and pedagogy. It is not difficult to establish the claim that the framework employed in any act of analysis ultimately constrains the questions that can be asked and, allegedly, solved (Kuhn 1970); Loasby (1971: 868) succinctly notes that a 'paradigm produces intellectual tunnel vision.'

Management accounting has acquired numerous analytical advantages from the process of interanimation with the neoclassical research community, but it is equally true that excessive dominance by the framework has also constrained and limited the management accounting research community, as a source of insight into practice, as a vehicle for research, and as an aid in pedagogy.

A classic example of difficulty arising from the close relationship between the two research communities is the often referenced gap between theory and practice in management accounting (Coates et al. 1983). It can be argued that his gap is largely a product of the dominance of neoclassical economic theory on the conventional wisdom of management accounting (Scapens and Arnold 1986, Scapens 1994). Management accounting textbooks — introductory, intermediate and advanced — are dominated by models of optimal decision making, yet research study after research study of management accounting practice reveal that these models rarely figure in the daily operations of the management accountant.

After the identification of the gap, initial explanations often viewed it as a transitory problem that would erode and ultimately disappear with the passage of time; the newer recruits to the ranks of the management accounting community would be equipped with knowledge of, and ability to employ, the new models and techniques, the older members of the management accounting community would retire, and via this process the new would replace the old. Many of the textbook models had been incorporated since the late 1950s and early 1960s into the education and training process of the management accountant via their inclusion in the syllabuses and examinations of Professional Accounting Institutions. The gap, however, appeared to be persisting stubbornly well beyond an inter-generational transfer effect. Indeed, Scapens (1991: 33) observes that this gradualist, educational transmission process has an underlying theoretical weakness, when examined from foundations of its economic perspective; namely that the forces of competition, assumed as part of the economic perspective, should ensure rapid dissemination of management accounting 'best practice' if it did assist decision makers to maximize their profits. Scapens (1991: 33–4) continued by observing that the continuation of a gap between theory and practice might be explained by one or both of two possibilities:

- the theory simply fails to meet the needs of the decision maker,

- the competitive assumptions of the economic perspective are not valid with regard to the circumstances of management accounting practice.

Scapens concludes his analysis by arguing that explanations of the gap clearly need to question the basis of theory, as well as explore the dynamics of practice.

The current analysis seeks to employ the Shackle research proposals to assist in questioning the basis of the theory. The nature of the gap between theory and practice ranges over a wide range of situations within management accounting; to reduce the task of the current exploration focus will be made on just one area of practice — the capital investment decision process.

4 CASE STUDY: THE CAPITAL INVESTMENT DECISION PROCESS

The typical management accounting textbook treatment of the capital investment decision proceeds *as if* the problem of uncertainty did not exist.[6] This is in part a predictable situation given (a) the aforementioned strong influence of neoclassical economic theory on the initial textbook conventional wisdom of management accounting, and (b) the fact that textbooks are generally designed as vehicles to present techniques of analysis, and the dominant approach to the question of the capital investment decision is nothing if it is not a clear technique of analysis (Puxty 1993).

The management accounting textbook treatment of the capital investment decision is often organized around an explanation and exploration of 'sophisticated' appraisal techniques, but also includes a comparison of 'sophisticated' and 'naive' appraisal techniques: the former represented by discounted cash flow (DCF) approaches — net present value (NPV) and internal rate of return (IRR); the latter by such techniques as the payback period (PB) and accounting rate of return (ARR).

The issue of the capital investment decision has been a subject for sustained and active research within the management accounting research community for over thirty years (Northcott 1998). During that period of time the predominant research instrument has been the questionnaire survey (Sangster 1993; Pike 1996)[7] and the predominant research concern has been what King (1975) classifies as the 'evaluation stage' of the capital investment decision process. King (1975) identifies six stages in the capital investment decision process: triggering, screening, definition, evaluation, transmission, decision, and he offers a sustained critique that the focus of the bulk of the capital investment research literature has been confined to the technical strictures of the evaluation phase, and by implication it has largely ignored the earlier and equally important stages that identify, screen and define projects; and the latter stages during which the members of an organization commit themselves to the project.[8] Since King listed his six stages there has been a tendency in the literature to note a 'seventh' stage which involves 'reviewing capital investment decisions' (Drury 1996: 443–5) via a post-completion audit process. This inclusion reflects changes in practice.[9]

The body of questionnaire survey returns has furnished a wide range of insights into the nature of practice. For example, the aforementioned textbook comparison of 'sophisticated' and 'naive' techniques has often been justified by reference to survey results that establish that 'naive' techniques retain a very strong role in practice, even though — the textbooks typically argue — the 'sophisticated' techniques are far superior.

Pike (1996) reviews a longitudinal study of capital investment appraisal practices encompassing four discrete but related surveys of 100 large UK companies undertaken in the years 1975, 1980, 1986 and 1992. He reports that whereas in the 1975 survey 44 per cent of the sample employed IRR, 32 per cent employed NPV, 51 per cent employed ARR and 73 per cent employed PB, by the 1992 survey these percentages had altered to 81 per cent, 74 per cent, 50 per cent and 94 per cent respectively.

The survey results for 1975 and 1980 strongly supported the idea of a substantial divergence between theory and practice, with the reported utilization of 'sophisticated' appraisal techniques being substantially lower than the level of textbook coverage would lead one to have expected.[10] Pike (1996: 89–90), however, notes that the later survey results indicate a general increase in the use of sophisticated appraisal techniques to a point where the gap between theory and practice, at least for the large firms sampled, is insignificant.

Pike (1996: 90) outlines three main causal factors for this closing of the gap: technical, educational and economic. The technical issues Pike relates to the advent of inexpensive computer hardware and software which allowed NPV and IRR calculations to be completed almost as quickly as calculations for PB. The educational issues Pike relates to the major expansion in management education, with the issue of investment appraisal techniques often a key component in the curriculum. The economic issues Pike relates to the contrasting economic conditions that have emerged and developed over the period of the studies, conditions that have required more refined modelling in order to handle the complexities of inflation and increased competition.

The apparent closing of the gap between theory and practice indicated by questionnaire surveys is, however, less obvious when the results of fieldwork or case studies are reviewed (Northcott 1991, Dugdale and Jones 1995, Miller and O'Leary 1997). Case study research has produced results that indicate:

1 'that investment appraisal calculations are of secondary importance, with "strategic fit" cited as a primary factor in approving investment expenditure' (Dugdale and Jones 1995: 204),

2 'the fact that actual practice, though structured and informed by sophisticated techniques, is not as sophisticated as the documented representation of the decision process would suggest' (Cleaver 1998).

Such results have tended to disturb management accounting researchers committed to the neoclassical framework, and they have sought various modes of reconciliation. In reviewing the use of DCF techniques in the United States, particularly with reference to the appraisal of investment in advanced manufacturing technology (AMT), Kaplan and Atkinson (1998) seek to counter the argument that sophisticated techniques are too limited in scope to be effectively employed in appraising investments in AMT. They argue that company-based research indicates that the flaws that do exist occur due to errors in application rather than in the underlying theory of DCF appraisal. This mode of reconciliation returns analysis to the aforementioned failings in the educational transmission process, and envisages that a solution can be achieved via the elimination of these errors. This line of reconciliation will be returned to in the final section of the current analysis.

Pike (1996) summarizes another recurrent finding of the various studies, namely that over the period 1975–1992 the sampled firms have shown an increasing tendency to employ multiple techniques in the appraisal process, with over one-third of the sample — the largest group of the sample — employing all four techniques at the time of the 1992 survey, compared to only 11 per cent adopting this practice in 1975.

Pike (1996: 84) notes that this 'movement towards a 'more the merrier' approach to evaluation may be due to the ease of calculation with the aid of computers, but, equally, it may reflect the need to explore the many faceted aspects of investment performance', while Sangster (1993: 322) comments that the 'use of more than one criterion is indicative of caution. Prudence would suggest that the more methods used in the appraisal process, the better, because the possibility of an inappropriate decision being taken is reduced as the number of checks implemented is increased.'[11]

Northcott (1991: 230) argues that the accumulation of capital budgeting survey results 'illustrates how a field of enquiry can become implicitly rooted in a particular "world view" — in this instance the pervasive view of economic "rationality".' The final section of the current analysis seeks to provide a Shackle Prospect to challenge the dominant view of economic rationality on aspects of the existing survey results and suggests future directions for further case study research.

5 A PROSPECT BASED ON THE SHACKLE RESEARCH PROPOSALS

The capital investment decision assumes great importance within the Shackle framework, a fact made abundantly clear in the following observation that links the significance of the investment decision to the methodological requirements of his research proposal 1:

> The question of how the business man's mind works and what materials it works with in approaching a decision whether or not a particular investment proposal is worth while or not is one of the most fascinating, to my mind, in the whole of economics.
>
> (Shackle 1955: 37)

The first and most obvious impact of restoring Shackle to the textbook treatment of the capital investment decision would be the reinstatement of the distinction between risk and uncertainty, a distinction which in the typical textbook treatment may be noted but is then effectively ignored.

A good example of such a mode of textbook treatment is offered by Drury when, after drawing attention to and briefly discussing the distinction between risk and uncertainty, he observes:

> Most business decisions can be classified in the uncertainty category, but the distinction between risk and uncertainty is of little importance in our analysis and we shall use the terms

interchangeably.

(Drury 1996: 348)

Clearly, Shackle's two research proposals make such a universal and cavalier treatment of the distinction unacceptable. Shackle was prepared to acknowledge that under certain circumstances decision makers may effectively adopt the Drury solution and represent a particular decision in terms of a risk formulation.[12] It is a great shame, however, that the standard textbook treatment is not prepared to make the reciprocal gesture and accept that some decision situations cannot easily be represented in terms of a risk analysis without seriously compromising the validity or usefulness of the model of the decision process.

It is not uncommon to find attempts to buttress the typical textbook approach in terms of the adoption of an implicit subjective probability stance; this line of defence is clearly not a valid or acceptable response from a Shackle prospect, for although the response can be argued to represent a potential 'solution' to the second Shackle research proposal it runs foul of the first Shackle research proposal. This difficulty is particularly acute if evidence of management accounting practice is again referred to; Drury Braund, Osborne: and Tayles (1993: 73), in a survey of 300 UK manufacturing companies identify that 49 per cent of the 288 respondents never use statistical probability analysis to estimate payoffs from alternatives, 25 per cent rarely use such techniques, 20 per cent sometimes use them, and only 6 per cent often use such techniques. Clearly these results help to undermine theoretical attempts to justify the conversion of uncertainty into risk via the use of objective or subjective probability estimates as an effective solution, as such activities are not reflected in day-to-day practice.

Directly related to the restoration of a distinction between risk and uncertainty would be the need to reassess the interpretation of certain features of practice as revealed in the questionnaire survey reports on capital investment decision making. Ho and Pike (1991: 228) observe: 'these surveys indicate an increasing use of risk analysis techniques, but a predilection for simple risk-adjustment methods.' For example, Pike (1996) reports that in 1992 a sample of 98 companies revealed that the three leading techniques, used with varying degrees of frequency, were:[13]

- use of sensitivity analysis (88 per cent of respondents)

- raise required rate of return (65 per cent of respondents)

- shorten payback period (60 per cent of respondents)

The high prevalence of sensitivity analysis can in part be seen to reflect the impact of information technology:[14] the widespread availability of computer hardware and increasingly sophisticated software packages has made the exploration of the impact of possible changes in key variables relatively easy and cheap to produce. Drury (1996: 435) notes that the sensitivity 'approach requires that the NPVs are calculated under alternative assumptions to determine how sensitive they are to changing conditions.' Sensitivity analysis, therefore, produces additional information for the decision maker with regard to critical variables, and their possible impact on the NPV of the project under review. An extension of the employment of sensitivity analysis is to engage in scenario analysis, when the analyst no longer engages in partial equilibrium analysis, but attempts to explore the implications of multi-factor variation on the analysis of the proposed project; this can assist the decision maker in terms of 'best/worst case analysis' (Pike 1996: 85).

The linkage between scenario analysis and the implementation of the ideas of Shackle has already been well documented (Jefferson 1983, Loasby, 1990). With regard to the possibility of exploring the future via the power of the computer, an essential aspect in the increased popularity of sensitivity analysis, Shackle made the following pertinent observation:

> The computer has immensely increased the speed at which the process of examination of the true nature and implications of what has been conceived can be carried through, *so far as that examination can go*. Logic can be applied to problems of cost and revenue, of minimizing the one and maximizing the other, so long as those problems are formulated *as if* we knew all that we need to know. The paradox of business, in its modern evolution, is the conflict between our assumption that we know enough for our logic to bite on, and our *essential*, prime dependence on achieving *novelty*, the novelty which by its nature and meaning in some degree discredits what had passed for knowledge.
>
> (Shackle 1970: 155, emphasis in original)

It is clear that for Shackle the possibilities offered by the computer can be seen to be a powerful supplement to the decision maker's analytical techniques, but it can only assist in helping the individual's imagination to explore the problem of uncertainty, it can not, and never could, resolve it. As Shackle notes,

> The new techniques, the new tools of the computer revolution, are new and more powerful means of doing what we have always had to do: feel for the edges of the possible, elect those plans of action which leave, so far as we can judge, *disaster* outside that edge, while leaving a generous, a satisfying success inside it. We cannot tell, now more than yesterday, what *will* happen. We can hope only to judge, with some presumption of skill and a fair basis of experience, what *can* happen, at best and at worst, if we do this or if we do that.
>
> (Shackle (1963: 7, emphasis in original)

The other popular 'risk-adjustment' methods identified in questionnaire studies can be given a Shackle perspective, but for Shackle (1970: 77) increasing the required rate of return and shortening the payback period should be construed as techniques in 'the *management of uncertainty*' not in the adjustment for risk. Ford (1994: 301) notes that this line of analysis has its roots in the earliest macroeconomic interests underlying Shackle (1938) but that it increasingly focused upon the microeconomics of the investment decision. The transition from macroeconomic to microeconomic was achieved via a series of papers written in the 1940s and the resulting arguments were synthesized in Shackle (1961: ch. XXVI; 1970: ch. 4).

Underpinning his line of analysis was the idea of the time horizon, which Shackle (1961: 223) took 'to mean the most distant future date with which, in some particular matter, the decision-maker concerns himself.' Shackle (1961: 224) argues that the 'concept of horizon is inextricably bound up with that of uncertainty' that a decision maker who imposes a time horizon is seeking to place restrictions on the uncertainty of the situation, the restrictions are essential for as Shackle (1961: 224) observes: '[w]hen the decision-maker is free to suppose that any act can have any consequence without restriction, there is no basis of choice of act. The boundedness of uncertainty is essential to the possibility of decision.' Thus, for Shackle, the imposition of a time horizon by a decision maker is a technique tackling the problem of uncertainty, and the decision to increase the discount rate employed in an application of the NPV approach, or the decision to shorten the required payback period in the PB approach, represent a manifestation of the decision to adopt a time horizon to the problem of uncertainty. Shackle notes:

> It appears, then, that several superficially diverse ideas are essentially one and the same. To reject any investment, as some businessmen say they do, unless it holds out to them some hope of 'paying for itself in three years' (or even in two years), that is, of yielding in the first two or three years of its life net earnings equal in total to the purchase price of the investment, is in effect to ignore all possibilities of positive net earnings beyond those early years; to ignore those remoter earning is in effect to impose a horizon cutting off the vista of expectations at a certain distance from the viewpoint; the reason for such cutting off is that given time enough, anything can happen; that 'time enough' is, at most, only these first few years ahead of the viewpoint; and that when anything can happen as a sequel to each and every available present action, there is no basis of choice between them; finally, to allow for the rapidly increasing uncertainty and unreality of suppositions about remoter dates by applying a high percentage per annum as a 'risk discount' is again, in effect, to ignore all but the nearest years' possibilities of earning: the wheel has come full circle, the whole argument in all its forms is simply that uncertainty cuts off from relevance all those years whose discounted earnings would be noticeably altered by a shift, such as could occur within a space of a few months, between two ordinary levels of the interest rate.
>
> (Shackle 1961: 237)

Drury et al. (1993: 45) report that the 'average payback period is 3.13 years for investments in advanced manufacturing technologies (AMTs) and 2.83 years for non-AMT projects. The most frequently used payback period is three years for both types of investments.' If establishing a payback period of approximately three years is a device to 'manage uncertainty', as Shackle argues, it appears to be a device that has had a sustained grip on capital investment decision practice for many decades.

Returning to the previously noted attempt by Kaplan and Atkinson (1998) to support the utilization of DCF techniques in the appraisal of AMT, they advance the following argument and related points:

> Our study of the actual practices used by firms in applying discounting procedures to proposed capital investments reveals many flaws; but these are flaws in application, not in the underlying theory. Therefore, if students wish to apply DCF procedures in practice, they need to understand these flaws and how to overcome them. The flaws occur when managers

> 1 Require payback over arbitrarily short time periods
> 2 Use excessively high discount rates
> 3 Adjust inappropriately for risk
> 4 Compare new investments with unrealistic status quo alternatives
> 5 Emphasize incremental rather than global opportunities
> 6 Fail to recognize all the costs of the new investment

> 7 Ignore important benefits from the new investment..
> (Kaplan and Atkinson (1998: 594–5)

From a Shackle prospect the first three points can be related to the issue of the time horizon. As observed above the restoration of the distinction between risk and uncertainty can cast a new light onto the rationale behind the current management accounting practice. Rather than being viewed as flaws in application, practice can be presented, and reviewed, as a set of devices for coping with the inevitable problem of uncertainty, for engaging in 'the *management of uncertainty*' (Shackle 1970: 77). With reference to point 1, Kaplan and Atkinson (1998: 595) note that opting for shortened time horizons may reflect, among other things, 'managerial distrust of the estimates of future cash flow savings' but they then argue that such an adjustment is ad hoc and not related to 'the economics of discounted cash flow analysis' but from a Shackle prospect the adoption of a shortened time horizon may well reflect a distrust of cash flow estimates, based on the nature of the human condition rather than as some ad hoc adjustment to the neoclassical framework. With regard to points 2 and 3, Kaplan and Atkinson (1998: 595) observe '[p]erhaps the major pitfall to the successful application of

DCF occurs when companies use discount rates in excess of 20 per cent and 25 per cent to evaluate proposed new investments' and they note the substantial literature that exists with regard to determining the appropriate opportunity cost of invested funds, but they again do not address directly the question of 'managerial distrust of the estimates of future cash flow savings' and the implication of that distrust that could underpin the decision to opt for high discount rates. Kaplan and Atkinson (1998: 598) do note the possibility that managers could employ scenario analysis to explore the possible outcomes from an investment after applying sophisticated appraisal techniques to all future cash-flows. This invocation of scenario analysis to buttress the application of DCF techniques has a distinct Shacklean feel; however, Kaplan and Atkinson advance their argument on the basis of a far more optimistic analysis than the previously noted Shackle view with regard to the possible contribution of computing technology, and the related adoption of simulation techniques, in helping to resolve decision-making issues involving uncertainty.[15] It is, of course, an empirical issue which view of the impact of computer technology has most affected practice in the subsequent years, a research issue that management accounting could throw significant light upon.

An examination of Points 4 to 7 would also be usefully informed by adopting a Shackle prospect. The analysis offered by Kaplan and Atkinson appears to identify a clear failure of imagination on the part of the information collector and analyst: a failure to establish an acceptable 'imagining' of the impact of the investment project. Such failure arises because of incomplete exploration, within the imagination, of the decision situation. Imagination, although a key component in the Shackle framework, is hardly, if ever, noted in the standard textbook analysis of management accounting. Incorporation of imagination into a system of analysis, however, cannot be conceived simply as a mechanical addendum, the formal introduction of imagination into any system of analysis poses many issues with regard to the nature of that analysis (Earl, 1983; 1984). It is not an accident that the neoclassical research framework has generally averted its attention from the multiple issues posed by allowing a substantial role for the imaginative powers of the decision maker. Invoking the idea of imagination returns any analysis to the philosophical problem, as Shackle (1958: 26) noted, 'whether men's conduct is pre-determined or whether it is fashioned by their free will': are Kaplan and Atkinson discussing a failure to 'accurately imagine' a pre-determined and objective future; or are they discussing a limited human ability to explore in the imagination *all* the possible futures that exist before the decision is made?

A focus on the role of the imagination in the capital investment decision would also offer new insight into the aforementioned increase in the utilization of a post-completion audit. If the substance of investment appraisal is in the power of the imagination then it is necessary for an organization to invoke some form of control mechanism. Shackle (1958) starkly summarizes the problem by contrasting the creation of daydreams and expectations.[16] In a business context the post-completion audit becomes an organizational mechanism seeking to ensure that capital investment decisions reflect realistic expectations and not daydreams.

Finally, adopting a Shackle prospect would assist the management accounting research community re-examine and re-evaluate the previously noted gap between theory and practice not only in the area of capital investment decisions but more generally. For example, the attempt by academics, and picked up by textbook writers, to extend simple deterministic models into probabilistic models and the general lack of impact of such attempts have had on practice acquires a new dynamic from a Shackle prospect with its emphasis on issues of uncertainty.[17] In broad methodological terms the neoclassical economic research community has typically attempted to provide solutions to questions that although they are both interesting and significant are not necessarily the most pressing issues for the management accountant or the management accounting researcher (Scapens and Arnold 1986). The level of appropriate application of the research community's approach is a good example: the neoclassical approach typically focuses its analytical endeavours on market or industry tendencies; the management accountant and, accordingly, the management accounting researcher will have a more direct interest in the individual enterprise or division (Scapens and Arnold 1986). Shackle's first research proposal is far more appropriate for a research community concerned with the individual enterprise or division of an enterprise.

Were they to commence from the basis of Shackle's two research proposals, management accounting researchers, engaging in detailed case studies into the decision-making processes within firms, would begin to view observed practice from a Shacklean perspective; the resulting analysis could then contribute to the process of evaluating the usefulness of the Shackle (1949/52) framework for approaching the practical problems of decision making under conditions of uncertainty.

NOTES

* I would like to thank Peter Earl and Sandy Guthrie for many helpful comments in preparing this chapter.
1 Identification of the factors that influenced the formulation of Shackle's research proposals is beyond the scope of the current analysis. It was in part a product of the career path followed by Shackle (Harcourt 1990), within that path one significant factor was Shackle's involvement with the Oxford Economists' Research Group (Shackle 1955, Lee 1981).
2 Lachmann (1990) examined Shackle's contribution to the development of subjectivist thought; while Littlechild (1979) queried the ultimate impact of Shackle's approach on the subjectivist programme.
3 Shackle (1958: 21) 'I do not pretend that introspection is bound to yield truth, but our habits of thought and speech treat decision as a point at which in some real sense a new strand enters the pattern of events.'
4 Hillebrandt (1985) and Earl (1995) represent rare examples of contemporary textbooks that offer a serious introduction to and treatment of the Shackle framework.
5 The events propelling these developments were key components that fashioned the ideas of Chandler (1962, 1977) and influenced the work of Williamson (1975, 1985); as Loft (1995: 29) notes 'use of management accounting to control the transaction costs was of crucial importance to the firms.'
6 Northcott (1992: 111) provides a summary of the textbook conventional wisdom and notes that: 'There is little provision in the CI [Capital Investment] literature for dealing with uncertainty.'
7 Pike (1996: 80) lists the major capital budgeting surveys in the UK since 1966.
8 For a discussion of the decision cycle see Loasby (1976) and Earl (1995).
9 Pike (1996: 85) reports that in 1975 only 33 per cent of a sample of 100 companies required post-completion audits, by 1992 the figure had increased to 72 per cent.
10 Similar survey results for the USA indicated substantially higher utilization rates of 'sophisticated' appraisal techniques (Klammer and Walker, 1984).
11 Shackle (1966: 275) notes that '[t]he business men are not 'unscientific', they are cautious.'
12 For example: 'A mass of our daily acts, it is true, are aimed only at

immediate and routine results whose character and effect upon us, nearly enough for all practical purposes, we know for certain.' Shackle (1966: 160), while Shackle (1958: 36) notes 'We can admit that for practical purposes a set of action-schemes, reasonably defined, can seem to the person concerned to be such as will present itself again.'

13 The ranking of techniques is not stable across studies; for example Drury, et al. (1993) report results from a sample of 240 respondents in the UK Manufacturing sector which identifies payback reduction as the most popular (85 per cent); sensitivity analysis (82 per cent); use of conservative cash flow forecasts (80 per cent); alteration of discount rate (66 per cent). Clearly variations can reflect differences in the sample, changes in practice if the samples are temporally differentiated, and variations in the questions posed.

14 Pike (1996: 86) reports that use of sensitivity analysis in 1975 had been only 28 per cent. Sangster (1993: 310) notes that it was not until 1979 that the first commercial electronic spreadsheet was introduced.

15 Kay (1993: 344) observes: 'The technological optimism of the 1960s — the belief that management was a process which could one day be defined with sufficient precision to be entrusted to a computer — has now sharply diminished.'

16 Shackle (1958: 15) notes: 'The individual can create situations and events in imagination. If he is content to leave these unrelated to the world of external experience, to the way the world of nature and of human nature works, and to the specific character of the moment-in-being, they are mere fantasies or daydreams... But he may instead set conscious limits to the scope of these acts of imagination, by constraining them into some supposed congruity or consistency with the permanent and inherent nature of things and with the specific character of the moment-in-being within which his act of imagination takes place...They can then be called *expectations*.'

17 Scapens (1991: ch. 5) offers an illustration with reference to the attempt to introduce aspects of uncertainty within the basic cost-volume-profit (CVP) model.

REFERENCES

Baxter, W. T. (1938) 'A note on the allocation of oncosts between departments', *Accountant* 5: 633–6.

Buchanan, J. M. (1973) 'Introduction: L.S.E. cost theory in retrospect', in Buchanan, J. M. and Thirlby, G. F. (eds) *L.S.E. Essays on Cost*, London: L.S.E./Weidenfeld and Nicolson.

Carsberg, B. (1975) *Economics of Business Decisions*, Harmondsworth: Penguin.

Carter, C. F. (1972) 'On degrees Shackle: or, the making of business decisions', in Carter, C. F. and Ford, J. L. (eds) *Uncertainty and Expectations in Economics: Essays in Honour of G. L. S. Shackle*, Oxford, Basil Blackwell.

—— (1993) 'George Shackle and Uncertainty: A Revolution Still Awaited', *Review of Political Economy* 5: 127–37.

Chandler, A. D. (1962) *Strategy and Structure*, Cambridge, MA: MIT Press.

—— (1977) *The Visible Hand: The Management Revolution in American Business*, Cambridge, MA: Harvard University Press.

Clark, J. M. (1923) *Studies in the Economics of Overhead Costs*, Chicago, IL: University of Chicago Press.

Cleaver, K. C. (1998) 'Accounting for time: an initial exploration of the impact of adopting a subjectivist view of time in management accounting', Paper presented at the British Accounting Association Annual Conference, Manchester.

Coase, R. H. (1938) 'Business Organization and the Accountant', *Accountant*, 1 October to 17 December, reprinted in Buchanan, J. M. and Thirlby, G. F. (eds) *L.S.E. Essays on Cost*, London, Weidenfeld and Nicolson.

Coates, J. B., Smith, J. E. and Stacey, R. J. (1983) 'Results of a preliminary survey into the structure of divisionalized companies, divisionalized performance appraisal and the associated role of management accounting', in Cooper, D., Scapens, R. and Arnold, J. (eds) *Management Accounting Research and Practice*, London: ICMA.

Cochoy, F. (1998) 'Another discipline for the market economy: marketing as a performative knowledge and know-how for capitalism', in Callon, M. (ed.) *The Laws of the Markets*, Oxford: Blackwell.

Drury, C. (1996) *Management and Cost Accounting*, 4th edn, London: ITP.

——, Braund, S., Osborne, P. and Tayles, M. (1993) *A Survey of Management Accounting Practices in UK Manufacturing Companies*, Chartered Association of Certified Accountants Research Report Number 32.

Dugdale, D. and Jones, T. C. (1995) 'Financial justification of advanced manufacturing technology', in Ashton, D., Hopper, T. and Scapens, R. W. (eds) *Issues in Management Accounting*, Hemel Hempstead: Prentice-Hall.

Earl, P. E. (1983) *The Economic Imagination: Towards a Behavioural Analysis of Choice*, Brighton: Wheatsheaf.

—— (1984) *The Corporate Imagination: How Big Companies Make Mistakes*, Brighton: Wheatsheaf.

—— (1993) 'The economics of G. L. S. Shackle in retrospect and prospect', *Review of Political Economy* 5: 245–61.

—— (1995) *Microeconomics for Business and Marketing*, Aldershot, Edward Elgar.

—— and Kay, N. M (1985) 'How economists can accept Shackle's critique of economic doctrines without arguing themselves out of their jobs', *Journal of Economic Studies* 12: 34–48.

319

Edwards, R. S. (1937) 'The rationale of cost accounting', in Plant, A. (ed.) *Some Modern Business Problems*, London: Longman.

Fleishman, R. K., Hoskin, K. W. and Macve, R. H. (1995) 'The Boulton and Watt case: the crux of alternative approaches to accounting history?', *Accounting and Business Research* 25: 162–76.

Ford, J. L. (1994) *G .L. S. Shackle: The Dissenting Economist's Economist*, Aldershot: Edward Elgar.

Garner, S. P. (1954) *Evolution of Cost Accounting to 1925*, Tuscaloosa, AL: University of Alabama Press.

Harcourt, G. C. (1990) 'Introduction: Notes on an Economic Querist — G. L. S. Shackle', in Frowen, S. F. (ed.) *Unknowledge and Choice in Economics*, London and Basingstoke: Macmillan.

Hillebrandt, P. M. (1985) *Economic Theory and the Construction Industry*, 2nd edn, London: Macmillan.

Ho, S. S. M. and Pike, R. H. (1991) 'Risk analysis in capital budgeting contexts: simple or sophisticated?', *Accounting and Business Research* 21: 227–38.

Jefferson, M. (1983) 'Economic uncertainty and business decision-making', in Wiseman, J. (ed.) *Beyond Positive Economics*, London: Macmillan.

Kaplan, R.S. and Atkinson, A.A. (1998) *Advanced Management Accounting*, 3rd edn, Upper Saddle River, NJ: Prentice-Hall.

Kay, J. A. (1993) *Foundations of Corporate Success*, Oxford: Oxford University Press.

King, P. (1975) 'Is the emphasis of capital budgeting theory misplaced?', *Journal of Business Finance and Accounting* 2: 69–82.

Klammer, T.P. and Walker, M.C. (1984) 'The continuing increase in the use of sophisticated capital budgeting techniques', *California Management Review* 27: 137-51.

Kuhn, T. S. (1970) *The Structure of Scientific Revolutions*, 2nd edn, Chicago, IL, University of Chicago Press.

Lachmann, L. M. (1990) 'G. L. S. Shackle's place in the history of Subjectivist thought', in Frowen, S. F. (ed), *Unknowledge and Choice in Economics*, Basingstoke, Macmillan.

Lakatos, I. (1970) 'Falsification and the Methodology of Scientific Research Programmes' in Lakatos, I. and Musgrave, A. (eds) *Criticism and the Growth of Knowledge*, Cambridge: Cambridge University Press.

Lee, F. S. (1981) 'The Oxford challenge to Marshallian supply and demand: the history of the Oxford Economists' Research Group', *Oxford Economic Papers* 33: 339–51.

Littlechild, S. C. (1979) 'Comment: radical subjectivism or radical subversion?' in Rizzo, M. J. (ed.) *Time, Uncertainty, and Disequilibrium*. Lexington: Lexington Books.

Loasby, B.J. (1971) 'Hypothesis and paradigm in the theory of the firm',

Economic Journal 81: 863–85.

—— (1976) *Choice, complexity and ignorance*, Cambridge: Cambridge University Press.

—— (1990) 'The Use of Scenarios in Business Planning', in Frowen, S. F. (ed.) *Unknowledge and Choice in Economics*, London and Basingstoke: Macmillan.

Loft, A. (1995) 'The history of management accounting: relevance found', in Ashton, D., Hopper, T. and Scapens, R. W. (eds) *Issues in Management Accounting*, Hemel Hempstead: Prentice-Hall.

Mill, J. S. (1836) 'On the definition of political economy; and the method of investigation proper to it', *London and Westminster Review*, October, reprinted in Robson, J. M. (ed.) (1967) *John Stuart Mill Collected Works*, IV, Toronto: University of Toronto Press.

Miller, P. (1998) 'The margins of accounting', in Callon, M. (ed.) *The Laws of the Markets*, Oxford: Blackwell.

—— and O'Leary, T. (1997) 'Capital budgeting practices and complementarity relations in the transition to modern manufacture: a field-based analysis', *Journal of Accounting Research* 35: 257–71.

Northcott, D. (1991) 'Rationality and Decision Making in Capital Budgeting', *British Accounting Review* 23: 219–33.

—— (1992) *Capital Investment Decision-Making*, London, Academic Press.

—— (1998) 'Studies of capital investment practice: a comparison of approaches and a suggested way forward', paper presented at the British Accounting Association Annual Conference, Manchester.

Parker, R. H. (1999) 'Searching the British accounting literature 1179-1998', *British Accounting Review* 31: 15–30.

Pike, R. (1996) 'A longitudinal survey on capital budgeting practices', *Journal of Business Finance and Accounting* 23: 79–92.

Puxty, A. G. (1993) *The Social and Organizational Context of Management Accounting*, London, Academic Press.

Sangster, A. (1993) 'Capital Investment Appraisal Techniques: A Survey of Current Usage', *Journal of Business Finance and Accounting* 20: 307–32.

Saul, S. B. (1985) *The Myth of the Great Depression, 1873–1896*, 2nd edn, London: Macmillan.

Scapens, R. W. (1984) 'Management Accounting — A Survey Paper', in Scapens, R. W., Otley, D. T., and Lister, R. J. *Management Accounting, Organizational Theory and Capital Budgeting*, London: Macmillan.

—— (1991) *Management Accounting: A Review of Recent Developments*, 2nd edn, London: Macmillan.

—— (1994) 'Never mind the gap: towards an institutional perspective on management accounting practice', *Management Accounting Research* 5: 301–21.

—— and Arnold, J. (1986) 'Economics and management accounting research', in Bromwich, M. and Hopwood, A. G. (eds) *Research and Current Issues in Management Accounting*, London, Pitman.

Shackle, G. L. S. (1938) *Expectations, Investment and Income*, Oxford: Oxford University Press.

—— (1942) 'A Theory of investment decisions' *Oxford Economic Papers* 6: 77–94.

—— (1949) *Expectation in Economics*, (2nd edn 1952), Cambridge: Cambridge University Press.

—— (1954) 'The complex nature of time as a concept in economics', *Economia Internazionale* 7: 743–57.

—— (1955) 'Business men on business decisions', *Scottish Journal of Political Economy* 2: 32–46.

—— (1958) *Time in Economics*, Amsterdam: North-Holland.

—— (1961) *Decision, Order and Time in Human Affairs*, (2nd edn 1969), Cambridge: Cambridge University Press.

—— (1963) 'Theory and the business man', *Scientific Business* 1: 5–11.

—— (1966) *The Nature of Economic Thought: Selected Papers 1955-1964*, Cambridge: Cambridge University Press.

—— (ed.) (1968) *On the Nature of Business Success*, Liverpool: Liverpool University Press.

—— (1970) *Expectation, Enterprise and Profit: The Theory of the Firm*, London: George Allen & Unwin.

—— (1983a) 'A student's pilgrimage', *Banco Nazionale del Lavoro Quarterly Review* 145: 108–16.

—— (1983b) 'Review of: Hutchinson, T.W., *The Politics and Philosophy of Economics*', *Economic Journal* 93: 223–4.

Williamson, O.E. (1975) *Markets and Hierarchies: Analysis and Antitrust Implications*, New York: Free Press.

—— (1985) *The Economic Institutions of Capitalism*, New York: Free Press.

14

DISREPUTABLE ADVENTURES: THE SHACKLE PAPERS AT CAMBRIDGE

*Stephen C. Littlechild**

I should have wished to write a poem, but not
being a poet, I have had to be content with a sort
of New Arabian Nights of disreputable adventures
in an intellectual shadow-world.
> (G.L.S. Shackle, letter to Professor Denis O'Brien,
> 9 July 1974)

1 INTRODUCTION

The basis of the Arabian Nights was a collection of romantic tales from
Persia. When the Mogul emperors arrived in India they brought Persian
civilisation with them. They also built elegant and imposing
mausoleums in Persian style to honour their families and preserve their
memory. 'They created a culture which, in buildings such as the Taj
Mahal, stamped its image on India for ever.'[1] Some consider the Taj
Mahal the most beautiful building in the world.

This collection of books and correspondence at Cambridge
University documents George Shackle's romantic or disreputable
adventures in the world of economics: it is his mausoleum. He was
fond of using metaphors, and I hope he would not be displeased with
this allusion. The mausoleum is built entirely of materials he crafted or
selected, and assembled to his own painstakingly detailed design. It
appears to contain almost everything that he ever wrote on scholarly
matters or that anybody wrote to or about him on these matters before
he died. The project was largely implemented during his lifetime, with

six deposits from 1965 to 1987. His widow Catherine made further deposits after his death, bringing the work to a fine and faithful conclusion. Miss Cann, the present custodian, has provided an extensive listing of the contents and their location.

What the monument needs now is professional evaluation. Mrs Shackle and Professor Frowen have kindly invited me to survey the papers. I have not had time to do this comprehensively, nor do I have the knowledge necessary to put the papers in their full economic and historic context. Instead, I have tried to illustrate the kind of material available, in the hope that others will wish to visit and appraise. I am sure that more qualified scholars will find it worthwhile to explore this material in more depth.

I have dipped into only a few of the boxes in the collection but they whet the appetite. After a brief summary of the available material, I have used illustrations and excerpts to indicate the origin and nature of the correspondence and the marginal notes on books and articles, and what they show of Shackle's views on economics, economists and more general themes.

2 OVERVIEW OF THE MATERIAL

The Shackle papers are catalogued as Add. MS 7669 in Cambridge University Library. Miss Cann in the Manuscripts Department there has devoted several months to preparing a most extensive, lucid and helpful paper listing out the contents of the collection. A slightly shortened version of this paper follows the present chapter to conclude this volume. The next few paragraphs draw on her paper.

The core of the Shackle papers are 'The Sybilline Books', the title given by Shackle to the collection of books, articles and letters put together by him as representing the core of his work. This comprises 3 books by Shackle and 5 chapters by him in books edited by others, 6 books containing material on Shackle's themes, 8 articles on Shackle's work, 3 manuscripts by him, and 6 letters to him, together with 3 photographs added by Mrs Shackle and 8 successive bibliographies and lists of his work.[2]

But these are the contents of only the first box in the collection. In total there are 30 boxes, now grouped into eight sections or categories. Section 1 (boxes 2 to 7) contains some 15 books by Shackle together with the original hand-written manuscripts, subsequent revisions and related papers. Section 2 (boxes 8 to 9) contains the same for 29 out of 43 chapters that he contributed to books, section 3 (box 10) ditto for 38 out of 73 articles, and sections 4 to 6 (box 11) ditto for 10 out of 16 review articles and 8 out of a dozen shorter articles or notes. Section 7 (boxes 12 and 13) contains some 60 unpublished and unidentified manuscripts, typically invited lectures and seminar papers.[3] Section 8 (boxes 14 to 17) is called Miscellaneous: boxes 14 and 15 include book illustrations, a table of work in progress, reports on manuscripts to editors and publishers, papers for degree examinations including questions on Shackle's theories, honorary degree citations, correspondence with his publisher on books he might write, and pamphlets on the theme of 'expectation in economics'; boxes 16 and 17 contain about a dozen books by other authors and two dozen journals, with annotations by Shackle. Section 9 (boxes 18 to 28) comprises Shackle's correspondence. Two boxes were added later: box 29 contains lectures for Queen's University Belfast 1969–1971 (classified into section 8) and box 30 contains miscellaneous material deposited in 1995 (classified into section 7).

In addition to the items listed in Miss Cann's paper on Add MS 7669 there are two small supplementary collections:

- Add. 8816: letters between Shackle and Stephen Frowen 1951–1992, and miscellaneous papers, presented by S. F. Frowen 1989, 1990, 1999.[4]

- Add. 8817: letters between Shackle and Henry Boettinger 1967–1989, presented by H. Boettinger 1989.

A very few of the items in the Shackle collection, mainly personal references, are not presently available for inspection. There are also certain items not in the collection at Cambridge. Mrs Shackle gave Shackle's annotated copy of J. M. Keynes' *General Theory Of Employment, Interest And Money* to Professor Frowen and his annotated copy of James Meade's *The Rate of Interest in a Progressive State* to Professor Ford; they may keep these until their death, when the books are to be restored to the collection in Cambridge. Photocopies of these two sets of annotations are being placed in the collection. Shackle's correspondence with Lord Cherwell 1940–1945 is held at Nuffield College Library, Oxford. The Department of Special Collections and Archives, Sydney Jones Library, University of Liverpool, contains many boxes of Shackle Papers, mainly MS and typed drafts for articles and books, with associated correspondence, together with a collection of offprints and annotated copies of his books, covering the period 1949–1969. It also has microfilms of some of Shackle's general correspondence from this period (reference D.29), the originals of which are in the Cambridge collection. My impression is that the printed material in the Liverpool collection is broadly duplicated in the Cambridge collection, but not all the manuscripts and drafts are, and there are different annotated books, as discussed below. Shackle's periodicals were transferred to the University of Strathclyde. The remainder of his library, comprising about 200 books and a similar number of papers by other authors, was disposed of to Mr Graham Meadows, who has printed a very helpful annotated catalogue of them.[5]

3 OVERVIEW OF THE CORRESPONDENCE

As Miss Cann's paper explains, Shackle divided his correspondence into two main categories: the first he called 'ee letters', that is, letters on *Expectation in Economics* and its sequels, 'which has been my predominant field of interest'. The second category is 'letters diverse', that is, 'all other letters which I have specially valued'.

There are 872 'ee letters' from the period 1949–1977, 1160 'letters diverse' from 1938–1982 and 348 letters of general correspondence from 1982–1987. All these are letters to Shackle, arranged in 12 chronological series. A few of the 'ee letters' have responses from Shackle, and there is a whole box of responses to the general correspondence. In addition there are three boxes of correspondence files from 1977–1992, arranged alphabetically to 90 correspondents, containing a mixture of outgoing and incoming letters. In total, there seem to be over 2500 incoming letters and Miss Cann's index of the correspondence includes over 650 correspondents. There is a further box of correspondence with Cambridge University Press and two boxes of miscellaneous correspondence.[6]

Shackle organized his early correspondence in meticulous detail, as he explained in a covering note.

Letters are arranged in four size classes: large, medium, small and folded.

These classes are arranged in that order from below.

Within each size-class, each writer's letters are grouped, and the groups are arranged in order of the dates of their earliest letters, from below.

Within each group, the letters are arranged in date order from below, or in case of conspicuous differences in size, in size order with biggest letter lowest.

[9/1][7]

Miss Cann has subsequently organized the material on a slightly different basis, to make it more accessible to researchers.

The first deposit of books and papers took place in 1965, when Shackle was about 62, some four years short of retirement.[8] However, the above specification for the organization of his correspondence was first drafted on 5 April 1952, when he was still only 48, some six months after he had been appointed to his chair at Liverpool. He was evidently thinking and planning well ahead.

Why did Shackle so methodically preserve this correspondence for posterity?

I fear all this sounds terribly pretentious, but I have been privileged to correspond with very remarkable men and women, and their letters will be interesting to whomever addressed. I must care for those written to me.

[9/4: letter to Henry Boettinger, 12 May 1973]

Who were these remarkable people with whom Shackle corresponded, particularly before 1952? He kept a dozen letters from 1938 to 1948, including from J. M. Keynes, R. F. Harrod and D. H. Robertson. There are three dozen 'ee letters' from 1949 to 1951, including from L. R. Klein, H. S. Houthakker, R. S. Sayers, F. Modigliani, W. J. Baumol, H. G. Johnson, M. H. Dobb and M. Allais. Letters diverse were also received in 1951 from E. A. G. Robinson, E. H. Phelps-Brown, R. F. Kahn and J. Marschak. This is quite a distinguished list of economists.

The very first letter in the collection, dated 30 April 1938, was from J. M. Keynes, commenting on the copy of *Expectations, Investment and*

Income that Shackle had sent him. This was the revised version of Shackle's Ph.D. thesis, written on Keynes. Since Shackle's views on Keynes have been published at length, but Keynes' views on Shackle are hitherto unknown, it is of interest to read Keynes' letter, which has been reprinted in full as an appendix to this chapter.

Shackle was acutely sensitive to views expressed about his work, and on a few occasions he recorded even conversation with painstaking precision.

on the conception of focus-values:

'... your scheme | would remain as a very elegant method of | showing the effect of different influences... '

[R. F. Harrod said this to me on 4:V:42; words enclosed thus | | are verbatim: the rest gives the sense of the context]

[9/12]

The letters Shackle received would of course have been incomplete without the outgoing ones. But one also has the impression of a systematic plan by Shackle to present the entire and imposing body of work, by himself and others, associated with his own original line of thinking. This included documenting the extent and rate of adoption of this thinking by others, as well as by himself. Shackle's thinking was incorporated not only in his published work: in some respects it may have been reflected earlier or with less inhibition in his letters, annotations and other unpublished work.

4 NATURE OF THE CORRESPONDENCE

The letters from Shackle are generally in his own hand, in his distinctive careful and large-formed handwriting, and in pencil.[9] More precisely, they appear to be the drafts of his replies, which he then copied out in order to send, carefully noting on the draft where he made revisions, typically minor, to the text. This was evidently a time-consuming and thoughtful process, which Shackle took very seriously. His early letters, most of which do not seem to have survived, must have been secondary to his prolific writing of books and articles. But by 1974, when he had just turned 70, and after a spell in hospital the previous year, he says rather disparagingly that he is devoting much or most of his time to correspondence.

> I am doing very little but write letters, and these make it perhaps too easy for me to think I have an idea when in truth, concealed from me through not having to work the thing out in thoroughgoing depth, I have only a phrase or two.
>
> [9/4: letter to Henry Boettinger, 12 January 1974]

Correspondence occupied him even on Christmas Day:

> I have not given up trying to work, though I seem to spend most of my time writing letters. I still get a considerable correspondence, which has to be answered with exactness, and also in longhand.
>
> [9/4: letter to Miss (Rosalind) Glover (later Tigwell),
> 25 December 1974]

In fact, this 'very little' but writing letters amounted to a couple of books and some 40 articles, book reviews and invited Forewords after 1974.[10] There is no doubt that Shackle still had ideas, but 'a phrase or two' in a letter was an effective way of planting the seeds of these ideas in the minds of others.

Shackle said that it was not his normal practice to initiate a correspondence.

> I hope you will forgive a letter from an unknown correspondent. It has been my almost invariable rule to wait until I receive a letter from someone, and not to thrust one on them. But I found so much in your book with which I am wholly in tune.
>
> [9/4: letter to Professor Nicholas Rescher, 30 July 1974][11]

In such cases he often took the opportunity to point out similarities in his own writings, and possible differences of view on particular aspects, as well as praising those aspects he found especially interesting, novel or thought-provoking.

In contrast, Shackle appears to have been very liberal in distributing complimentary copies of his books or reprints of his articles, sometimes without evidence of preceding correspondence. This often led to letters of thanks, and sometimes to further correspondence.

A frequent source of correspondence was letters from those who had read his work without having previously received copies. Some, while admiring much of what he had to say, found aspects of it unconvincing. This was especially true, for example, of the focus gain and loss concepts in his early work on expectations. Unfortunately Shackle's responses are generally not preserved here, but it seems that that he would reassert his argument, sometimes conceding a small part of it. His critics typically accepted some but not all of his points — see, for example, the early letters from Graaff, Baumol and Houthakker [9/1]. I suspect that the essence of Shackle's counter-arguments is to be found in his published writings.[12]

Shackle was invariably generous. Even papers purporting to identify limitations of his work had admirable features. For example, to one reviewer he wrote

In reading you I have learnt many truths which hardly another reviewer of my book has perceived; certainly not one has come anywhere near taking such pains to instruct me in precise, clear and invincible terms.

[9/4: letter to Professor Denis O'Brien, 9 July 1974]

He once wrote to me: 'I think your paper is unmatched, amongst the comments which have been written on my work, for what I must call a surgical beauty' [9/4: letter to Professor Stephen Littlechild, n.d. (28 May 1973)].

Even the deferring of a detailed response is done with charm and novelty:

Your discussion of *neutral outcome* is brilliantly ingenious. The considerations about the gambler indifference map, to which it leads, will require me to spend many days of thought, and since such subtle questions are best left to turn themselves over at leisure, occupying the real workshop of one's mind while trivial daily tasks are being done in the front office, and then suddenly presenting themselves in a new aspect, it may be some time

330

before I can respond in any adequate way to your rich gamut of questions and proposals.

    [9/4: letter to Professor Stephen Littlechild, 21 February 1973]

Some correspondents were enthusiastic admirers, and several submitted work of their own, written in what they perceived as a similar spirit. One even wrote from Borneo: 'I like your book [*Expectation in Economics*] very much, and it held my attention through hundreds of miles of jungle, despite the competition for my attention from crocodiles, alligators, pythons, baboons, orang-utangs etc.' [9/1/66: letter from Benjamin Higgins, signed 'Monetary and Fiscal Expert', 27 May 1953].

Shackle's responses to all these admirers were invariable warm. Often he spoke of the satisfaction their letters brought him: a computer word-count might identify 'intense happiness' as a frequent single phrase. He was clearly gratified to find others of like mind when his own position was such a lonely one. In addition, his own letters were typically extremely encouraging and flattering; invariably they were expressed with elegance and imagination.

> Your letter gave me an extraordinary pleasure. Amongst several hundred letters that I have received on this subject since my *Expectation in Economics* came out in 1947, yours is one of the three or four most important and interesting; its luminous cogency is a sheer delight.
>
>   [9/1/170a: letter to Gerald Gould, 31 January 1957]

> It is said that life is made worthwhile by isolated moments of intense happiness. I owe to you the experience of such a moment. Yesterday I read in the *Revue d'Economie Politique* your article on my book. If there were no other reward for my work of the last twenty-two years, this would be all-sufficient.
>
>   [9/1/220a: letter to Henri Guitton, 18 March 1959]

> For almost the first time, someone has really understood what I am trying to say.
>
>   [9/1/255a: letter to Guy Devillebichot, 14 October 1960]

Of all those who have written to me about my book, or have discussed it in print, you alone have perfectly understood me. When I read your account of my own ideas, I gain fresh insight into them.

[9/1/320b: letter to Guy Devillebichot, 20 January 1963]

No author could possibly deny himself a few moments of uninhibited pride and glowing pleasure when finding such an honour accorded him as a review by yourself [of *Epistemics and Economics*]. But much more enviable still is to see his work examined in a light of brilliant and searching clarity, which few beside you could supply.

[9/4: letter to Professor Denis O'Brien, 9 July 1974]

Typically the welcoming words to those who sent copies of their own writings were only the opening sentences: there would follow suggestions for further work, perhaps in the most promising or interesting areas, or perhaps identifying areas or arguments that Shackle felt obscure or unsound. All recipients must have felt encouraged and often inspired to continue their work, and several wrote to say so. Henry Boettinger wrote, 'I can say I have never received a letter which meant more to me' [9/1/461: 10 August 1967].

5 REVISION·AND PRECISION

I have not examined the manuscripts of Shackle's own books in any detail, but a casual glance suggests that, in the main, his books were typically revised only once, and then only in some parts. There is a presumably first draft then a fair copy, all in longhand, all neatly packaged, and that's it. Thus his terse comment covering the manuscript to *Epistemics and Economics*: 'Begun December 69. Finished October 71. Manuscript manu propia' [1/12/1].

Perhaps this particular book was exceptional, as a later letter explained:

To confess the truth, the book itself is something of a mystery to me. For one thing, I can say with essential truth that it seemed to 'write itself'. I have no clear understanding of how it

332

got itself on paper (with vast amounts of re-copying in long-hand as the only effective and searching method of revision) in 22 months, while I was engaged in fortnightly forages to Queens [University, Belfast] to give two lectures or so each time. One of the consolations of old age is that one can let oneself go, can be heretical in unlimited degree, without hazarding one's chances of promotion or risking the sack.

> [9/4: letter to Professor Denis O'Brien, 9 July 1974]

It was after this passage that Shackle made the observation about his disreputable adventures quoted at the beginning of this chapter.

Shackle advised one correspondent to work without excessive revision, and provided an intriguing justification.

[W]hat I want to urge you most strongly is, don't cut out passages because they don't, on a superficial view, seem to fit with other passages. One can pay too much attention to consistency.

A mountain does not look the same when you see it from different sides, but these sides are not *inconsistent* with each other.... .

... You have such an immensely rich reading and experience to draw on, the thing is to get *as much* of it in your book as you can, not keep trying to pare things down. The famous books are all mysterious, complex, puzzling, inconsistent, rich, endlessly arguable and commentable.

> [9/1/376a: letter to Burton Kierstead, 1 December 1965]

Consistent with this, he defended Keynes against the criticism that 'the logic of the work is "sloppy" because Keynes was anxious to reach his audience as soon as possible': 'How could anyone think of a book so obviously written by intense questioning and inventive process as 'sloppy'?' [8/118: annotation on Leijonhufvud (1968: 17)].

Shackle nevertheless took considerable pains to express himself accurately and concisely, and typically requested editors not to suggest changes: '... if you find my review too long, may I ask you simply to reject it, rather than require any shortening or alteration' [9/12: letter to Dr John Maloney, 27 January 1986].

He explained his thinking as follows.

The subject-matter I have tried to discuss is subtle and elusive to an extreme degree. I have for many years made a sustained and unremitting effort to attain the exact expression of my ideas. My theme is regarded by most scholars who have given any attention to it as a heresy and a subversion of received ideas. I cannot feel that a copy editor's 'stylistic improvements' could be other than destructive. My words and expressions in the article are weighed and chosen with the best thought that I can give.... If you yourself find any sentence of my manuscript obscure, I must accept that I have failed. But I believe if you read the manuscript you will find in my sentences a stringent effort to be concise, lucid and efficient.

[9/12: letter to Professor Israel Kirzner, 16 May 1985]

Shackle was similarly very particular about the titles of his books. Professor Frowen has said that he transferred *Imagination and the Nature of Choice* (1979) to Edinburgh University Press because Cambridge University Press had been unwilling to accept the title.[13] In 1988 there was a tense and lengthy debate to persuade Macmillan's editor to use the phrase *Business, Time and Thought* as a title for his selected papers.

6 ANNOTATIONS OF BOOKS AND ARTICLES

Shackle annotated the books and articles in which he was particularly interested — in the early days, those that he was appraising for his research and, later, those of particular relevance to his theme or that he was invited to review. [14] The annotations are of particular value to students of his work for at least three reasons. First, these are not the hastily scribbled and often-indecipherable comments and !!?? symbols that one often sees (and makes oneself): in contrast, they are carefully considered, grammatical and clearly written, with longer comments written on a separate sheet and pasted in. Second, they are often dated, so that a diligent scholar might trace the development of Shackle's thought. Third, being primarily for private use, they are often expressed in more direct language than Shackle might employ in a published book or article or even a letter.

The use of dating is rather remarkable, and goes beyond the annotations. Ford (1994: 13–14) has remarked on this and Shackle (1967: 224–5) himself has given an illustration but some further description may be of interest. Shackle would note the date and place where he finished each reading of a book or article, and the nature of that reading. It is apparent that he worked extremely carefully and methodically through each step of an argument. To take an example at random, consider Hayek's (1934) article 'On the relation between Investment and Output'. Shackle's pencil notes at the end say 'First reading 23/VI/34. Second, not definitive, reading 5/X/34. Fresh reading 13/4/35' [8/138]. But it is clear that each reading was not completed at one sitting. On the first reading, for example, he got from page 207 to page 211 on 15 June then to page 215 on 20 June before completing the 25-page article on 23 June. On his second reading he got to page 209 on 6 September, to page 213 on 10 September in a 'second reading from beginning of article', then to page 221 on 13 September, before finishing this 'not definitive' reading on 5 October.

Other examples show even more detail and repeated reading. For example, Knight's (1934) article on "Capital, time and the interest rate' has on page 271 'First reading (omitting footnote on p. 267) 17/VIII/34' and on page 278 'First reading including fn. 29/VIII/34' [8/127]. At the end of Hicks's (1935) article 'A suggestion for simplifying the theory of money',) Shackle's notes are as follows:

First reading 4/3/35
Fresh reading 2:10:35
Second fresh reading 3:10:35
Definitive reading of whole article completed in one day 3:10:35
Third fresh reading 4:2:37
Fourth reading 25:12:65.

[8/128]

In the early years, Shackle's comments seem mainly to focus on identifying ambiguities or crucial steps in arguments. His comments are firm but remarkably courteous for a private annotation. For example, 'While Prof. Hayek uses these two definitions as equivalent, it would seem that only the latter is correct.' [8/138: Hayek's 1934 article cited above]. At times he seems to restrain himself. At the end of Lionel Robbins' (1938) article on "Live and dead issues in the methodology of economics' he writes on 13.8.38 (the date unusually in ink), 'This article is very badly spelt' [8/134]. I am not sure what this means.

Shackle's rereading of some of the classics often provokes him to comment. As always, the reading is spread over time and we can trace his progress. For example, in 1977 and 1978 he was re-reading (he must surely have read it when it first appeared) Hayek's (1941/1976) *Pure Theory of Capital*. He completed Chapter I on 21 December 1977. Hayek's footnote on page 20, criticizing the use of general short-term equilibrium in then-recent monetary analysis, is deemed 'acute and persuasive'. He got to page 25 by 23 December, took a break on Christmas Day, and got to page 31 on Boxing Day. On 29 December he found that 'The contortions of pp. 60–64 are both unsatisfactory and needless'. He continued to page 72 on 30 December. The next day, New Years Eve, was fairly intensive, taking him to page 79 with half a dozen marginal comments in those half a dozen pages, plus a more lengthy comment taped into the book.

Occasionally, Shackle even notes the time he finished reading, and this provides some further evidence of his reading habits. He got to page 124 of Nicholas Rescher's (1973) book *Conceptual Idealism* at 6.30 am on 22 July 1974. This was after a series of marginal notes on Chapter VII, beginning on page 119. Given his deliberate rate of progress, he must have started very early in the morning. He evidently found the book satisfactory. On page 126 he writes 'I can virtually agree with nearly all of this, and have largely said it long ago' [8/121].

These insights into Shackle's reading habits provide some defence to a criticism made by some otherwise sympathetic commentators. Peter Earl has complained that

> A ... frustrating feature of Shackle's papers is their old-fashioned style of scholarship, in particular their seemingly homespun origins and consequent failure to include the kinds of bibliographical back-up that nowadays one normally takes for granted and which referees of journals usually insist upon. This cannot have helped advance his key themes. It leads his readers to fail to realize the extent of his implicit overlap with, for example, the work of Herbert Simon and George Richardson and to become puzzled, like Lachmann,[15] about Shackle's own philosophical roots.
>
> (Earl 1993: 247)

Denis O'Brien's (1974) review of *Epistemics and Economics* evidently levelled a similar charge. Shackle responded to O'Brien as follows.

> I accept the justice of your remarks about the absence of some names, of high importance, from my book. Yet I could not have written the book as it stands if I had tried to survey the field rather than drive single-mindedly to a goal.... My excuses for failure to name individuals are two. First, that I was wholly intent on painting my own picture rather than recalling my visits to the great galeries.[16] Secondly, that I had tried to salute a few of them in *Years of High Theory* whose purpose was thus somewhat different from this gallop over the downs after my harness had been removed.
>
> [9/4: letter to Professor Denis O'Brien, 9 July 1974]

Consideration of Shackle's working style suggests a further explanation: he simply did not have time to read, in the depth necessary to appraise and comment adequately, all the literature that some of his critics considered relevant or related. A further quotation below reveals that he had not read most of the work of Popper for example. And if more scholars can do literature reviews than original thinking, should economists complain about specialization and the division of labour?

7 KEYNES, HICKS AND HAYEK

One of the instructive pleasures of reading the letters and annotations is to see Shackle's less inhibited comments on some of the great economists of the day. Three illustrations must suffice here.

Keynes, whom in many respects Shackle admired greatly, attracted some critical remarks, particularly in later years. In a 1965 manuscript comment on Bertil Ohlin's (1937) article 'Alternative theories of the rate of interest: rejoinder', Shackle says 'Ohlin's theory is an ex ante liquidity preference theory. I have no quarrel with it. Keynes in so far as he differs (much less than he thinks) is wrong.' [8/145] In the margin of Keynes's (1930/1971) *Pure Theory of Money* Shackle comments on page 161 'clear and sound', and on page 165 'A wonderful book, full of insight and thus of foresight, applicable forty years on (1972).' A new reading got him to the same place on 23 May 1984. By 12 June 1984 he had reached page 202, and comments 'All that this farrago (pp. 199-202) says is... .' Keynes's treatment of equilibrium was especially problematic for Shackle: 'Keynes has a habit of writing out an identity and calling it an equilibrium'; 'One might as well talk of the length of a thing in inches being out of equilibrium with its length in centimetres.' These comments are on page 202. Then on the next page he wrote: 'All this is fantasy.' And by page 230, 'So after all this rigmarole we are back to Wicksell.' 8/117a]. Shackle inserted a paper note between pages 124 and 125 of J.C. Gilbert's (1982) book *Keynes's Impact on Monetary Economics* near a marginal note dated 4.40 pm 17.2.89. It reads: 'What Keynes lacked was a grasp (or even an awareness) of the ex ante – ex post distinction, the distinction between what can be seen *after the event* and what was imagined before it, which was expected' [8/110].

Shackle (1967: 83) wrote highly of Hicks, describing him as 'the great technologist'. But Hicks's (1950) *Contribution to the Theory of the Trade Cycle* got its share of manuscript comment. On page viii Hicks writes that '... demand as a whole and output as a whole can ordinarily be taken to be one and the same thing ... so long as price movements keep supply and demand of commodities in balance with one another'. Shackle comments 'So long, in other words, as we can get away with the swindle of working a theory of disequilibrium in terms of an equilibrium theory'[8/114: probably 1963 or 1964].

Shackle's view of Hayek and his work was always coloured by his appreciation of Hayek's generosity as his former PhD supervisor. Nonetheless he commented more freely in later correspondence. For example, in response to a review of his *Epistemics and Economics*, he writes that one chapter

> tries to present the Austrian theory [of capital], and to make sense of it. But I cannot find the Austrian theory usable, I can only admire it as a work of art. (Yes, one day, someone will provide an exegesis of Hayek's *Prices and Production* which will show that intense enigma to be a brilliant jewel.)
>
> [9/4: letter to Professor Denis O'Brien, 9 July 1974]

Two years later O'Brien invited Shackle to write a paper on Hayek's work. In replying, Shackle recalled the early debates involving Hayek, Knight and Keynes which caused me to embark on the forty-five year voyage which you are inviting me to prolong.... The intellectual intensities, excitements and anxieties of those years 1935–36 were strangely renewed this April, when (by some complex skein of events) I was Hayek's companion on his tour of universities and banks in Barcelona, Valencia and Madrid, where we gave talks on our respective themes and my admiration for Hayek was further deepened and my realisation reinforced of his profoundly generous nature.

> [9/4: letter to Professor Denis O'Brien, 25 July 1976]

Shackle notes that he is familiar with Hayek's work on monetary, trade cycle and capital theory, but not with his work on 'law, liberty and constitutions', and that Hayek's economic and constitutional thoughts are intimately related.

I think you will understand my difficulty. Hayek's life-work has been the construction of a theory of freedom in which an essential reliance is placed on the market economy. Money, in this system, is looked on as a dangerous intoxicant leading to disorderly and destructive behaviour, an unavoidable ingredient of life which needs to be kept under strict or very precisely designed control. At one time he digressed from the concern with neutral money and the individual-choice economy to examine capital theory with an intensity which, I think, did not result in the elegant, incisive tool he desired. A man of strange brilliance, a figure with a permanent and most distinguished place in the history of thought.

> [9/4: letter to Professor Denis O'Brien, 25 July 1976]

A further two years later, in the conclusion to his review, Shackle wrote:

Hayek as economist has perhaps been eclipsed by Hayek the apostle of freedom. On any reckoning he must be accorded by friend or foe his unquestioned place amongst the giants.

> [2/28/1 at pp. 55–6:
> typescript 'Hayek as economist', dated 9 June 1978]

I once asked Shackle in conversation about his views on Hayek. He would not easily be drawn, remarking again how conscious he was of Hayek's generosity as supervisor in allowing him to switch topics to study the work of Keynes. But he did make one remark that has always stuck with me. 'Hayek opened a window and showed us a beautiful vista. Then he shut it.'

8 OXFORD AND CAMBRIDGE ... AND BIRMINGHAM

Not all the Shackle letters concern matters of great moment, but they are invariably interesting. In some of his later letters Shackle reminisced about the two universities of his youth.

> The Oxford Centre filled me with envy and nostalgia. Of course I saw it at a peak of vitality — your presence was making it crackle with electric fire — but I had a very strong sense of its practical, real, assured and relaxed effectiveness. The sense of companionable effort, each man on his own line but these lines forming a skein visible as whole to all of them — it is the same as I felt at the Oxford University Institute of Statistics in 1937–39. I was a full-time paid Research Assistant, but mainly occupied in bashing a hand-operated Munro calculator. This soul-destroyer's only merit was the noise it made when doing division, which was like a cavalry charge in fiction, and expressed the operator's occasional feelings well.
>
> [9/4: letter to Henry Boettinger, 12 January 1974]

> Oxford casts a spell on one. My own feelings about Oxford v. Cambridge are difficult to spell out and analyse. My loyalty in the last resort is to Cambridge. My father took his degree there as a Wrangler (i.e. first class honours) in the Mathematical Tripos *101 years ago*! (I know this sounds impossible. But so does the fact that the first Duke of Wellington, born in 1769, was still alive when my father was born.) I was born in Cambridge, went to school there for 10 years and had my home there or nearby for 27 years. But in spite of this Oxford gives me the feeling that I had a second and separate existence there (I did in fact get a D.Phil. there). When I am in Cambridge I feel a driving urge and

conscience to be doing something useful, but in Oxford I can relax.

[9/4: letter to Henry Boettinger, n.d.(spring 1975?)]

The correspondence also reveals inadvertent snapshots of other universities. Some of the letters, even on minor administrative matters, are of interest as shedding light on academic conditions of the day. Here is a series from Terence Gorman in 1956 that may still cause a few rueful smiles in Birmingham:

11 Feb: I have got a little note on potential surprise which I would rather like to send you sometime. I hope to have it typed out within the next week or two.

30 May: Here is the note I promised you so long ago... I feel ashamed to send it to you in its present condition, but the Faculty Office is so busy at the moment that it might be weeks before its turn came up.

7 June: I have just been looking through the retyped paper on coincidences — I had quite forgotten what a shocking mess it is in. How very kind of you it was to offer to have it retyped in Liverpool. I would be most grateful if you would do so.

[9/1/156-9]

9 SUBJECTIVISM AND IMAGINATION

Of wider potential interest are Shackle's comments on economics. His views are well known, and there are probably no great surprises here. It is nonetheless appealing to see the ideas expressed with a freshness or succinctness that provides variety to the expositions in his books and articles. In particular, Shackle refers frequently to his focus on subjectivism and the central role of imagination. The following is an early and striking illustration.

It seems to me that in all orthodox work up to the present, the treatment of uncertainty is quite analogous to the treatment that would be given of the effect of a lowering of the quality of some quite definite and precisely known commodity being sold in an ordinary market. If a particular box of oranges are rather over-ripe, they will be cheaper, but they are still oranges. The future flow of income from an asset is treated as something quite definite, but a little 'lowered in quality' by 'uncertainty'. One might feel tempted to say that what the buyer of an asset is really getting is a 'bundle of possibilities'. But even this phrase suggests something objective: there is again a suggestion that objectively meaningful frequency-ratios might be attached to the possibilities, and then we should be right back, as you say, at certainty-equivalents. The frequency-ratio approach, in whatever way it is applied, necessarily assumes away all true uncertainty. For my part I should say that what the buyer of an asset is really getting is the right or freedom to indulge his imagination in pictures of what he may get out of the asset. The whole thing is subjective, and doubly subjective, because there is subjective evaluation of something which is imagined rather than measured.

[9/1/28a: letter to Jacob A Stockfisch, 14 October 1951]

One letter concerned rational expectations. It began:

'Rational expectations' remains for me a sort of monster living in a cave. I have never ventured into the cave to see what he is like, but I am always uneasily aware that he may come out and eat me.

[9/12: letter to Sir Bryan Hopkin, 20 August 1980]

Shackle found a staunch and consistent ally in Ludwig Lachmann, with whom he had corresponded over many years. It seems that Lachmann persuaded Shackle of the importance of institutions. As late as the mid-1980s Shackle was able to write

I am a little puzzled in these days by what seems to be an attempt to get round the difficulties posed for analysis by uncertainty, 'volatility' of expectations, and the manifest impossibility of co-ordinating plans which are the continuously evolving products of thought, by discussing side-issues: property rights, institutions, and other distractions.

'Institutions' do not seem to me to affect the basic scheme of things, except perhaps by gathering individuals into gangs, so that they march together without a visible road map, instead of going each on his own. The mistake is to think that economic affairs can be reduced to a 'system', a 'model', a machine.

[9/12: letter to Professor Ludwig M. Lachmann, n.d.. (c. 1985?)]

But by 1987 Shackle's view had changed.

You have rightly reproved me in the past for not grasping the nature and dominant role of institutions, but I think I have gained that insight. Institutions are the contours which constrain and direct the stream of affairs, helping indispensably to make the plans of individuals mutually coherent and, indeed, realizable.

[SB/24a: letter to Ludwig M. Lachmann, 9 August 1987]

The letter continues with a familiar theme.

The prejudice against introspection, which prevailed fifty years ago, always seemed to me absurd and the very opposite of the economist's proper attitude. How can we interpret the aims and efforts of others except by trying to understand our own?

In the past economists have tried to make economic theory a rigid logical structure bound in a mechanical view of the nature of action, or rather, as you insist, *re-action*.

As you know, I would give imagination the precedence over all other capacities of the economic action-taker. This of course implies an utter rejection of mechanical objective theories of action.

Some of the criticisms of Shackle's work strike him as misplaced. For example, in his letter to O'Brien after the latter's review of his *Epistemics and Economics*, he refers to an earlier (otherwise welcome) review by Professor Kenneth Boulding.

Boulding charges me with nihilism, and, what shakes me more, you yourself allow an echo of this to be heard. It is extreme *subjectivism* with which I should be (and have been) charged. The world is a world of thought, and each man can think his own, if he can hear himself think above the cataract of impressions

[9/4: letter to Professor Denis O'Brien, 9 July 1974]

Shackle does not understand why others cannot see the importance of subjectivism and the imagination, and the consistently wrong direction taken by conventional economic theory. He warms to Loasby's similar concern.

> Your enterprise has been to show where economic theory has been led in its enthralment to the ideals of all-encompassing consistency of reason. Art, I think, is the producing, by means which are subject to explicit constraints, effects in the recipient's thought and feeling. (Constraints: e.g. limitation of the painter to a flat surface or the bas-relief sculptor to one effective viewpoint, and so on.) General Equilibrium is an art form in this sense. Its rules unfit it for illuminating the Human Affairs, except in showing what all-pervading consistency would consist in, namely, something wholly alien to our condition and experience. Then, you have explained and examined in detail some of the kinds of responses to that condition which experience has evolved. The resulting contrast between economic 'pure theory' and management science must surely astound anyone who comes upon it without preparation. I have been astounded for many years (forty?) at people's *failure* to be astounded.
>
> [9/4: letter to Professor Brian Loasby, 24 April 1975]

10 PSYCHOLOGY

Not surprisingly, these views made Shackle an early advocate of a greater role for psychology in economics.

> My own feeling is that, in order to make progress in investment-theory, economics must now begin to make excursions across the frontier of psychology, and must try to analyse the reasons for preferring one kind of asset to another.
>
> [9/1/28a: letter to Jacob A Stockfisch, 14 October 1951]

He evidently mixed with psychologists, and in one book listed half a dozen valued friends and correspondents from this discipline.[17] Eminent psychologists also sought him out. A colleague from the Department of Psychology informed him that '[W]e are having Professor [Jerome] Bruner of Harvard University to give a talk ... on "'Strategies in Thinking".... Professor Bruner is ... a great admirer of your work and is particularly anxious to meet you during his visit to Liverpool' [9/1/145: letter from Professor L. S. Hearnshaw 31 October 1955]. Shackle had Bruner's (1986) book *Actual Minds, Possible Worlds* read to him in 1987.[18]

Shackle's work was highly regarded by John Cohen, Professor of Psychology at the University of Manchester who, according to a covering note from Shackle's friend Professor Charles Carter, 'seems to be about as odd as most psychologists' [9/1/165: letter of 13 October 1956]. Cohen wrote to him,

> You have fashioned a bridge between economics and psychology.... You have established a combined discipline in which the fundamental concepts belong to both sciences. You are the only economist I have come across who has made his subject meaningful to a psychologist by bringing it to life.' [
> 9/1/276: letter of 29 June 1961].

Shackle had four of Cohen's books in his library, one of which discussed Shackle's ideas in terms of Psychological Probability.[19]

Shackle's view on psychology evidently led him to comment on faculty organization within the university. A former colleague from the University of Leeds wrote to him, 'You are led to resist separation [of disciplines] for practically the same reasons as I am encouraging it. I believe that the Social Sciences ... would enhance each other if they were grouped together.... If I could get Econs, Soc. Sc., Psychology together I think we might do something new (and enable others to do likewise)' [9/1/105: letter from L. S. Johnson, 21 May 1954]. Shackle's original letter does not seem to be in the collection at Cambridge, but a later letter recalls the situation:

> At the university where I taught, economics was, until a few years before the end of my time, one of that group of subjects known there as the Faculty of Arts.... Then came a movement

to make economics, sociology, and psychology, with one or two others, a Faculty on their own. I was, I think, the sole opponent of this move. Is there perhaps a case for treating economics as an aspect of history?

[9/12: letter to Professor Irving Kristol, 8 November 1980]

An earlier sentence in the same letter indicates the thinking that led Shackle to argue for keeping economics as part of the Arts faculty: 'How can a theory [in economics] serve us, which utterly excludes those very powers of original thought and imagination, the poet's and musician's inspiration, which most of all make the human entity distinct?'

Shackle's relationship with the philosopher Sir Karl Popper seems to have introduced him to a surgeon with an interest in psychology. In 1957 Shackle sent Popper a copy of his *Uncertainty and Business Decisions*. On Guy Fawkes' Day Popper sent back a little firecracker saying that 'Although I cannot say that I have really read it yet (having received it only this morning) ... I have some serious criticisms to make.' He concludes, 'I do not think that these objections apply to your own theory.' [9/1/184: letter from K. R. Popper, 5 November 1957]. This last phrase is rather odd, given the general tenor of the letter, unless Popper is referring to objections to his own theory against Shackle. It seems that Popper then sent Shackle several offprints of his papers. Shackle's library contained four papers by Popper from the 1960s but they may well have remained unread because they have none of Shackle's manuscript notes or sidelining.[20] There seems to have been no further correspondence until Popper sent Shackle a paper that for some reason he did read, and enjoyed not so much for its content as for its 'supremely beautiful conjunction of art and thought'. Shackle comments that '"Of clouds and clocks" is unapproached by any other philosophical discourse I have ever read in the beauty of its exposition' [8/113: letter to Sir Karl Popper n.d., found in Shackle's copy of J. R. Hicks' *Value and Capital*].

There is apparently no response from Popper. In 1974 Shackle remarked rather wistfully (in a passage subsequently crossed out, presumably for omission from the final letter)

I heard Popper giving what I think was his first formal lecture at LSE in the middle 1930s. But since then I have sometimes felt that he has little wish to allow me entry into his academy... .
[9/4: letter to Professor Denis O'Brien, 9 July 1974]

As a result of the barter economy operating in Aldeburgh, Shackle was re-introduced to Popper's work, and to the work of an eminent surgeon. Referring to a copy of a paper that I had sent him, he wrote

I have given one to my doctor, who has lent me a copy of the book by Karl Popper and John Eccles called *The Self and Its Brain*. Before this I had read only one thing by Popper, his article 'Clouds and Clocks' of which he sent me an off-print. Now I find what he says in this book profoundly congenial.'
[letter to Professor Stephen Littlechild, 3 July 1978][21]

A couple of years later Shackle was writing about *The Human Mystery*, a book by Sir John Eccles that he liked [9/12: letter to Monsieur Beaugrand, 11 December 1980?] He had also acquired another book co-authored by Eccles, so it seems that the psychology as well as the philosophy appealed to him. In 1987 Catherine read to him Popper's *The Open Universe, an Argument for Indeterminism*.[22]

I think Shackle would have been sympathetic to the recent argument of the eminent Harvard biologist Edward Wilson that

the [economic] theorists have unnecessarily handicapped themselves by closing off their theory from serious biology and psychology... they have carried parsimony [and generality] too far. The result of such stringency is a body of theory that is internally consistent but little else.... To advance much further, ... [economists] and other social scientists will have to cross the boundary between the social and natural sciences and trade with the biologists and psychologist they find on the other side ... and take seriously the biological and psychological foundations of human nature.

(Wilson 1998: 223–6)

Wilson's aim and book title — *Consilience, The Unity of Knowledge* — would have particularly attracted Shackle, whose own aim was expressed succinctly in his reference, in replying to a letter from another medical surgeon, to 'the unity and singleness of the task of understanding human beings in their nature and history' [9/1/324b: letter to Douglas Lang Stevenson, 2 May 1963].

11 MATHEMATICS

Shackle took an interest in the sciences and was especially keen on mathematics. His father taught mathematics and coached Keynes for his scholarship to Eton (Ford 1994: 4). Shackle (1983: 108) said, 'As a child I had at first only one playmate, my father, a mathematician. Thus early I breathed a little mathematical ozone.' But school provided little opportunity in this direction.

> The Perse School was devoted mainly to languages, both classical and modern, and no hint of higher mathematics came my way until I discovered that magic field for myself in grown-up life (I left school at seventeen). My father was a Wrangler in the Cambridge Mathematical Tripos, but I was born in his 52nd year and did not get the electric current that I might have had from him if he had been a younger man when I was eleven or twelve.
>
> [9/13/29a: letter to Revd. Dick Hare, 5 May 1991]

Several references in Shackle's letters suggest the influence that his father had on him.

> I have an interest in [the neutrino] through having heard about it from the lips of Max Born himself, in a lecture at King's College, London, half-a-lifetime ago (say, 1935). When I was a schoolboy, my father tried to take me to hear a lecture at Cambridge, in 1917, by Eddington, about Einstein's General Theory of Relativity. Fate took a hand and we could not get in. It was, of course, packed out. I think if I had heard it I might have been hooked on physics. But anyway, there were many barren years to go before I could get hooked on anything.
>
> [9/4: letter to Mr H. M. (Henry) Boettinger, 15 July 1974]

He did of course get hooked on something, namely subjectivism in economics, and seemed keen to establish a connection with possible analogies in mathematics.

> I am most excited and delighted with your quotations from Sir William Rowan Hamilton. He has been for me a mysterious figure ever since, as a child, I heard from my father the story that Hamilton had the inspiration of a non-commutative algebra, whose expression he called quaternions, while out walking with his wife, and that as he was standing that moment on a bridge, he wrote the expression there and then on the parapet of the bridge itself. I have never followed up his work, and the fascinating passages you quote are something new to me. In modern algebra books his work seems to be dismissed in a summary and disdainful manner. I suppose this is because the notion of non-commutative expressions has been subsumed in more general algebras, but having read your quotations, I see that there is far more in his vision than I had ever imagined. I believe that mathematicians treat the notion of 'successor' as a primitive or indefinable. Hamilton seems to have pointed to the experience of time as the basis of our intuition of succession. Your quotations make me wonder how many of the mysteries that remain, despite all efforts, in getting at an intuitive as distinct from a merely logical meaning in even such all-pervasive notions as those of 'limiting process' itself, might be solved along his lines.
>
> [9/4: letter to Dr Edgar Taschdjian, 7 March 1975]

Catherine Shackle conjectures that George would probably have read mathematics at Cambridge University if he had gone straight from school, and that maths was one of his subjects in the three prep schools where he taught after working as a bank clerk.[23] Ford (1994: 4 and footnote 4, page 4) says that he was an able mathematician and had thought (but not overly long!) of following in his father's footsteps, and that he would almost certainly have read for a degree in Latin or in the Romance languages.

Shackle's various books and articles show that he was comfortable with the differential calculus used in economics research in the 1930s and with Leontief's input-output matrices. But how much mathematics did Shackle himself have? His library contained a number of standard mathematical textbooks.[24] He had a particularly strong interest in algebra. There are extensive manuscript comments and insertions in A. Adrian Albert's (1941) *Introduction to Algebraic Theories*. The invoice from Heffer's bookshop in Cambridge is still preserved at the back of the book, showing purchase on 9 January 1943, and the dates of his comments range from early 1943 to spring 1946, with at least three readings of the book, in 1943, 1944 and 1945. His comments include working out problems, sometimes providing alternative and perhaps more elegant explanations and even on occasion taking issue with the author. This is all explained on a page taped into the back of the book.

> I discovered the existence of this book on 9th January 1943, by finding it on Heffer's shelves, and immediately bought it. The discovery was a great thrill. I had tried to read Albert's *Modern Higher Algebra*, but had been put off by the use in Chapter 1 and 2 of that book (which deal with the subject-matter of Chapter 6 of this book) of German gothic capitals, which I could neither name to myself nor distinguish between, and which therefore made it impossible to follow an exacting argument. I was convinced that Albert was the finest exponent of this subject, and here was a compact book by him presenting in full rigor the core of the subject, yet within my powers. I began to read the book as far as the end of section 2 of Ch. 5, but without any serious attempt to do the exercises. In the summer of 1944 (June–July) I read Ch. 5 from its beginning to about the end of Section 4. On July 3rd 1945, I began a real attempt to master the book. At every point where I discovered the solution of some difficulty, or felt that I could gain by expressing an argument in my own words, I interleaved the book. I did large parts of the exercises, and was deeply impressed with the absolute necessity of actually handling concrete examples in order to master and really penetrate its arguments. An example performed throws a brilliant spotlight on the real meaning and working of matrix algebra. By 9th January 1946 I had worked through the book thus as far as the end of Section 4 of Chapter 5. I begin to feel that I know what this subject is about, and how it works. I propose now, concurrently with finishing the parts of the book not yet read, to turn to Birkhoff and MacLane: *A Survey of*

Modern Algebra, much of which I have already read once, and work through it in the same way as I have this. I am fascinated by this subject. One day I shall strike out from it some new ideas for my own subject. G.L.S.S. 10:1:46

Whether Shackle did move on to Birkhoff and MacLane is unknown: that book is not in the Cambridge collection or in Meadows *Working Library*. The annotations in his copy of W L Ferrar's (1945) *Higher Algebra for Schools* [8/109] show that in 1946 he was assiduously studying this book, chapter by chapter, and conscientiously recording his daily progress.[25] This seems odd. The Preface to Albert's *Introduction* says that the manuscript has been used for third and fourth year undergraduate and beginning graduate students. Birkhoff and MacLane would be graduate level. In contrast, Ferrar's *Higher Algebra* was self-evidently aimed at schools. It seems that at this point Shackle turned to writing his own textbook for children, rather than striking out some new ideas for his own subject. Perhaps this is not surprising: he was nearly 40 when he acquired his copy of Albert's book, which is late for anyone to take up serious mathematics.

In 1952 he published an introductory textbook entitled *Mathematics at the Fireside*. It must have been written while he was at the Cabinet Office. It is said to have been written for his children, and perhaps it reflected what went on in his own childhood. Certainly his father was in his mind.

[My father] never wrote anything for publication. Many years after his death in 1934, I wrote the book he should have written: I called it *Mathematics at the Fireside*. I think my father would have been pleased.
[9/13/29a: letter to Revd. Dick Hare, n.d. (spring) 1991]

This was not the original title. The Memorandum of Agreement signed on 16 November 1948 was for *Mathematics in Dialogue* 1/3/4/1]. The publishers were evidently not convinced: 'I hope you are thinking about possible alternative titles. We are. Our latest candidate for consideration is Mathematics with Father!' [1/3/4/7: letter from F. H. Kendon of University Press, Cambridge, 9 August 1950]. Three months later Kendon wrote to say that they needed 'a title which conveys more of what the book really is than your present title' [1/3/4/8]. He offered

14 suggestions including The Mathematical Family, and Mathematics on Holiday. Shackle held out for a long time, then evidently accepted the need to change. But the eventual title was not one of those on the publisher's list.

Shackle had evidently mastered the material he read, probably more thoroughly and with greater flair and enthusiasm than even the better mathematics students. The allusions in his correspondence indicate a mathematical intuition beyond the merely mechanical. His later letters make rather wistful reference to his interest in mathematics: 'The enclosure in your letter fascinates me, as number theory always has done. Is mathematics, at its very remotest frontiers, both logic *and* fiction?' [9/4: letter to Henry Boettinger n.d. (spring 1975?)].

Could Shackle have made more use of mathematics? What techniques would have been relevant? A few correspondents had drawn his attention to the theory of games, but he had reservations.

> Theory of Games has so immense a fertility that I cannot doubt it would provide illustrations of many of my themes. My basic feeling about Theory of Games is that it assumes (no matter with how much intervening complexity) that each player's knowledge is fundamentally complete. How else could there be a calculus of strategy? And, if so, where is there room for the supreme battle-winning ploy, *surprise*.
>
> [9/4: letter to Sidney Weintraub, 17 September 1977]

He had similar reservations about 'fuzzy set theory', commenting (1982: 228) that 'this great arabesque of brilliant endeavour has still the same essential purpose: to eliminate the true un-knowledge which gives us imaginative freedom.' However, he was rather tickled by a claim put to him by two French mathematicians, writing that, '[A]ccording to these chaps, the "axiomatique" of fuzzy sets resembles that of potential surprise proposed in my *Expectation in Economics* in 1949' [9/12: letter to Professor Stephen Littlechild, 5 December 1983].

In the same letter he reports that he had been invited to take part in the equivalent of a viva for a French doctorate on this topic:

> My question to last week's candidate was whether she thought fuzzy-set theory could help to graduate the interval between

'perfect-possibility' and 'absolute non-possibility', both of these bounds being of course subjective.

He does not tell us the answer she gave, but he wrote a preface to her published thesis.[26] He went on to use fuzzy set theory as part of his case for introducing a Section for Mathematics into the British Academy.

> In 1965 a Frenchman, L. A. Zadeh, invented a line of thought which enables matters that are essentially imprecise and uncertain to be handled with rigorous reasoning. This field, known in French as the theory of 'les sous-ensembles flous' (fuzzy sets) has shown an extreme vitality (thousands of articles) since Zadeh's origination of it, but has been rejected by some of the most mathematically-oriented economists. This is a question not for mathematicians only but, most essentially and centrally, for epistemologists. Ought there not to be, somewhere, a niche for *Mathematical Epistemics*?
>
> [9/12: letter to P.W.H. Brown Esq.
> (Secretary to the British Academy), 19 January 1984]

Perhaps, if Shackle had had a better opportunity to master higher mathematics at an earlier and more receptive age, he himself would have been able to represent some of his ideas more formally and (to the increasingly quantified profession) more persuasively. For example, he referred to topology in the context of economic theories (see next section below). I once put to Shackle that it might be possible to use mathematics to illustrate the kaleidic process, or at least some aspects of it, but that there seemed no possibility of using such models for detailed predictions. He replied that this

> makes explicit the heart of our trouble at this moment about the future of economic theory. The question is: how can mathematical originality... be used in a field where the making of history (the kaleidic, partly uncaused, making of history) is the business which goes on. I *acutely feel* this dilemma. We need a *poetics of mathematics*. We need to invent a new suggestive notation. It could show how things could go in any one of many or infinitely many rival ways, following some one inceptive

course of action, yet show how this numerical infinity is bounded in diversity.

[9/12: letter to Professor Stephen Littlechild, 11 September 1981]

Catastrophe theory, albeit unfortunately named, or general systems theory as suggested by Jason Potts in his chapter in this volume, might have appealed as means of analyzing his kaleidic economy. These techniques were developed too late to be of practical assistance to him. But I suspect that his inherent skills lay predominantly in imagination, understanding and exposition, rather than in mathematical origination or manipulation.

12 POETRY AND ECONOMICS

Shackle's correspondence with Henry Boettinger, especially, contains wistful references to poetry as well as to mathematics.

The poet tells more truth than the historian, so said the Greeks of antiquity. Poetry is theory, for it embodies *general* truth. But fiction is poetry, for it is a work of the originative gift, the imagination supreme amongst all human faculties.

[9/4: letter to Henry Boettinger, n.d.(spring 1975?)]

Poetry leads him on to other concepts.

I have been a theoretician, because that was the nearest I could get to being a poet. A theory is a poem, at any rate literally, a *thing made*, a work of art. The Greeks, you will tell me, believed that the poet told more truth than the historian. I have long thought that truth was too elusive and remote to be the real goal. The goal for the theoretician is beauty. The theoretician *in excelsis*, the mathematician, is all for beauty (elegance of proof and result). My wife has a book of crochet patterns, one of which is called 'A supple trellis'. It is a shawl of very fine, gossamer wool, with structure and coherence, yet with no rigidity, its mathematics are topological. Such is economic theory. It must stretch and twist, but must not tear (the invariants of topology are these). But this book I speak of is full of shawls, of all colours, designs, conformations and structures (stitches). We need that too. Find the one that fits the scene, is the only way.

Another analogy I like is, that the bricks of the universe can be permanent and unchanging (the laws of Nature), yet the buildings that they can form can be of limitless variety, always extending the infinite reach of novelty.

But I wonder whether economics should not, instead, be done by *history*, as many have thought. I have a feeling that those historians delude themselves, who think that they could, with enough documents, enough 'original sources', get down to bedrock, ultimate, unassailable truth. I don't believe it. The real *original* sources are the fleeting thoughts of individuals, that not even they could recall. Writing seems to me like sub-atomic physics. How do we know what there is beyond the electron and the neutrino?

[9/4: letter to Henry Boettinger, 15 July 1974]

According to Professor Frowen,[27] in his later years (late 1980s and early 1990s) Shackle frequently returned to the subject of poetry in his correspondence with his niece Hilary Clapham and his friend The Revd Dick Hare and also himself (Frowen). In Shackle's mind, economics was increasingly and inextricably linked with poetry and mathematics, and with science generally, as means of understanding and representing the physical world and human affairs. The concept of beauty was also all-pervasive.[28]

13 POLICY

Shackle almost never strayed into policy issues. Some years ago I tried to find even one micro-economic prescription for public policy, and the strongest I could find was the faint suggestion that government intervention could be problematic insofar as it was an additional source of uncertainty for the businessman.

But he was conscious of the need to provide some kind of guidance.

The question put to us 'extreme subjectivists' ... seems to be: If you deprive teachers of economics of the constructions which exhibit business as a rational process giving to every participant the best results he can get by free exchange with other equally free people, what do you offer us as explanations and policies instead of the picture of universal ideal rationality?

... I think we have to persuade them to think of economics as a *taxonomy, a catalogue raisonnnee* of the kinds of situations that can arise and the kinds of upshot which each can produce. Such a classificatory scheme would plainly not be more than illustrative and suggestive. It might give administrators some hint of what to be prepared for in the immediate short term and allow them to devise and re-direct what the Shell planners would call a 'resilient' policy. After all, I suppose all evidence and all theory, short of pure axiomatic abstraction, are essentially suggestive. Why should we not write this into the 'subjectivist manifesto'?

[9/12: letter to Professor Stephen Littlechild, n.d. (18 October 1981)]

An arresting remark appears in one of his letters to Henry Boettinger, who was a director of the large US telephone company AT&T, at that time the subject of Court action regarding divestment.

I read with amazement and incredulity of the move to divide up AT&T. It seems to me like putting an army or a fleet under several independent commanders in order that they might compete in attacking the enemy.

[9/4: letter to Henry Boettinger, n.d. (spring 1975?)]

I can only say (as former electricity regulator, who propounded restructuring in that industry) that I read this passage with equal amazement and incredulity. A fascinating analogy, but who did Shackle think the enemy were? Telephone customers? I hope that a few minutes reconsideration would have convinced him of the merits of facilitating competition and the exercise of entrepreneurial imagination in all the utility industries.

Fortunately, rereading the work of Hayek redeemed him, at least in my eyes.

> An economist as such will rest his case for freedom on its superior economic efficiency. Hayek is immensely more than an economist and ... has examined the indispensable foundations of freedom itself in its essence. Compared with the ultimate nature and meaning of freedom for the free and for the unfree, economic efficiency is perhaps a lamp of minor brilliance. Even the notion of economic efficiency is itself elusive and hard to define. But more arresting than that question is the argument, surely invincible at the first impact, that authoritarian control of business is a huge and all-encompassing waste of the original powers of the human mind. Every instance of an individual's having a practical improvement of his own invention which he is *not allowed* to put into practice is the destruction of possibilities, the closing of some vista which might lead beyond any horizon. Even this is a lesser aspect of a far greater whole. To be free is breath itself. But would life be a keen invigorating air if it did not release the poet's splendour of words and the painter's tide of colour, and encourage the mathematician's web of gossamer entailment and even the business man's enterprise and ambition?
>
> [2/28/1 at pp.55-56: typescript
> 'Hayek as economist', dated 9 June 1978][29]

14 LAST YEARS

Shackle was at Liverpool for some 18 years. He records with pride and precision a remark made about him:

> 'He is the ablest man on the staff of Liverpool University.' Mr Verney (lately of Department of Political Theory) said this about me to Mr Shone, who told me of it on the train on Wed 3 January [19]62.[30] Mr Shone told me that he, himself, had referred to me, in speaking to Mr Verney, as 'a quiet little man whom I have to say "Good morning" to three times before he thinks I'm all right to speak to'. Mr Shone, after quoting

Verney's remarks to me, said 'That will cheer you up on a dull morning'.

[9/12]

When he indicated his intention to retire from Liverpool University, the president of the Commerce and Economics Society wrote to Shackle 'on behalf of a large number of students in the Economics department who have expressed their deep regret at your proposed departure.... Many of these students ... were eagerly awaiting ... the seminars and tutorials that you made so stimulating' [9/7/644: letter from Ross M. MacMillan, 21 May 1969].[31] Not surprisingly, Shackle was touched by this tribute.

> A warm and powerful bond, in my own feelings, has united me to the members of all my classes in each of these many years, it is they who have inspired me and enabled me to put into the work everything I have. Without them, without their spiritual glow and vitality, I should have lost half the motive and purpose of effort. No one can do his best, or do a good job as a teacher or as a scholar, whose feelings do not catch fire when he stands in front of his class....
>
> I should like to try to explain ... why I felt it necessary to retire at this time. The reason that matters, is that I felt I had not the strength left to go on doing this work as it should be done. I have become rather used up. I have the feeling also that what I teach is no longer in fashion, and does not meet the practical needs of the members of my classes. I have no doubt that at sixty six a man should go.
>
> [9/7/644a: letter to Ross M. MacMillan, 29 May 1969]

Fortunately Shackle still had the strength to write: no less than three books and three articles between 1970 and 1973, followed by the two books and 40 items thereafter, as noted above. But by 1987 he was encountering an additional problem.

> I am hampered by the deterioration of my eyesight, which now means that I cannot read, and I fear my writing is nearly illegible. Thanks to my wife I can still work. She continues to copy out what I have scribbled and she reads to me with such

zest and insight that I get far more than I should if I could read things for myself.

> [letter to Professor Stephen Littlechild, 8 July 1987][32]

He persevered, but in January 1991 he wrote 'It used to be a pleasure for me to write. I mean the actual performance of the movement of the pen, but my hand has become stiff and my writing barely legible' [9/13/29a: letter to Revd Dick Hare 5 January 1991]. In February 1991 he wrote to Professor Austin Robinson

> My wife has just finished reading aloud to me your article in the current E.J. on the economics of the next century; it is hard to find words of praise to do justice to this marvellous article.
>
> [9/13/65]

This seems to be the last professional letter written in his own (now very shaky) hand. (There are a few subsequent handwritten letters to his friend Revd Dick Hare.) In March he was barely able to draft notes for his review of Professor Sir John Hicks' *A Market Theory of Money*, which was subsequently written up by Catherine. On 4 April his letter to John Pheby had to be written out by Catherine, but he was able to sign it. This was the practice for almost all his subsequent letters.

In August 1991 Shackle went into Ipswich hospital for one night to have a test for anaemia. While there he fell and broke his hip, and was hospitalized for the next three months.[33] On 5 October he dictated from his hospital bed a letter to Professor R. B. de Urquia: 'Your kindness is inspiring and my heart is lifted by it to ignore the trifling temporary disabilities that I am at present suffering from' [9/13/58].

He continued to work.

> One would think that a period of this kind would be a golden opportunity to get some creative thought down on paper. I do find it possible to do such transmission because of the marvellous help of all my kind friends.... There are various plans in the air which I am extremely anxious to realize and I hope that I shall be in a position and condition to do so while there is yet time.
>
> [9/13/29a: letter to Revd. Dick Hare, 20 October 1991]

By mid-November Shackle was back home and executing one of these plans.

> It is said that the three essentials of happiness are something to do, someone to love, and something to hope for. I have all three. Something to do is provided by the desire to put my thoughts on paper.... I am in the middle of writing a piece which explains the fascination of economics as owed to its combination of mathematical ideas and insight into human thought. It is not a subject which lends itself to expression in poetry but to my mind prose can be poetic. I have always believed what seems to me obvious that form and content are one. I should be ashamed of writing anything to which I had not given the most powerful and beautiful expression that I am capable of.
>
> [9/13/29a: letter to Revd. Dick Hare, 13 November 1991]

On 22 November Shackle dictated a letter to Philip Arestis, who had written concerning the forthcoming *Biographical Dictionary of Dissenting Economists*, to which Shackle had contributed (Arestis and Sawyer 1992: 505–10). Even at this stage of his declining health Shackle's message was an encouraging, considered, substantial (two pages) and radical one.

> There can be no standing still at a fixed frontier of our discipline. Imaginative and bold thought will always have urgent calls for their exercise, not only to deal with new developments in the course of history itself but also to shed the light of new thought on the course of past events and continue the gaining of insight into the foundations of our subject.
>
> [9/13/2]

On 3 December he dictated and signed a reply to Syed Ahmad who had sent a copy of his (1991) book *Capital in Economic Theory: Neoclassical, Cambridge and Chaos*. This evoked in Shackle a remarkably vigorous response considering the physical state that he must have been in.

The subject is one of great intricacy. I am very much in sympathy with your views and I agree entirely with you in thinking that the idea of 'rational expectations' is a nonsense. How can expectations be rational when we know nothing of what the morrow may bring. The forming of expectations, moreover, is influenced by the whole experience of the person who forms them of which others can know little or nothing. The influences that go to form expectations must be a chief source of the advance of ideas.

[9/13/19]

Bravely, Shackle promised more: 'I shall still owe you a further letter when I have been able to acquaint myself properly with the contents of your book and study them without haste.' He also wrote to Stephen Frowen that day, saying that he hoped 'to go on working at our subject for some time yet' (Frowen 1993: 266).

But it was not to be. He suffered a relapse with a kidney failure, and entered a nursing home. George Shackle died on 3 March 1992, exactly three months after dictating those last letters. On the headstone of his grave is the essence of 'a prayer that came into my mind a while back and that I have had in my pocket book ever since' [9/13/29a: letter to Revd Dick Hare, 14 June 1991 and enclosure dated October 1990]:

'Oh Lord I beseech thee, illumine my mind and shape my thought to beauty.'

15 CONCLUDING COMMENT

It is fitting that what seem to be George Shackle's last letters should contain such a firm reaffirmation of the theme to which he had devoted the whole of his scholarly life, and a determination to take it forward. It was a remarkably consistent theme, and this collection of books and papers shows how single-minded he was in pursuing and disseminating it. He may have described his life in terms of disreputable adventures in an intellectual shadow-world, but his theme is one that will increasingly commend itself in future, as economics develops and integrates with the other social and biological sciences. George's own writings have always been acclaimed for their beauty. They will increasingly be appreciated and respected as a distinguished, imaginative and original contribution to the scientific understanding of human affairs. A visit to the Shackle collection at Cambridge will bring pleasure and insight to scholars of all persuasions.

APPENDIX: LETTER FROM KEYNES TO SHACKLE (CAMBRIDGE UNIVERSITY LIBRARY Add MS 7669 9/5/1)

TELEPHONE: RIPE 26   TILTON,
STATION: LEWES   FIRLE, LEWES

G. L. S. Shackle Esq.,   April 30, 1938
97 Woodstock Road,
Oxford

Dear Mr Shackle,

I have to thank you sincerely for sending me a copy of your book which, of course, has interested me very much. I quite agree with you that the next step is to try 'to build up a chain of situations growing one out of another representing a process in time'. The difficulty is, of course, that this stage of the argument does not readily lend itself to a priori generalisation. There are too many possible varieties of situation, and one can certainly make no progress except with a much fuller statistical background than one generally possesses at present.

In my chapter on the Trade Cycle, and also to a certain extent when I deal with the Multiplier, I did try to move a few steps in this direction. But, in the main, I was, as you say, [mainly][34] concerned with the preliminary task of establishing the conditions of short-period equilibrium.

I think that your distinction between the 'improvement-phase' and the 'testing-phase' is a very useful one. I also agree as to the delayed effect of the multiplier through its being imperfectly foreseen. This is, however, part of the general thesis that to a very great extent business decisions are approached by a process of trial and error based on the latest realised results, not much modified except by reference to the prospective orders already in hand. I do not think that as yet (whatever may come to be the fact in the future) business men can make any serious attempt at all to foresee the future six months or a year ahead in the way in which we are trying to foresee it.

I like your clear and reliable logic which marks the book all through. There is indeed only one passage which I find rather perplexing, namely, the second paragraph on page 112, where I am far from clear, at a first reading, what you are driving at.

Yours very truly,

[signed] J M Keynes

NOTES

* I am pleased to acknowledge the invitation and encouragement from Mrs C. Shackle and Professor S. F. Frowen to carry out this work; helpful conversations with and information from Professor J. L. Ford, Professor R. E. Backhouse and Mr G. Meadows; assistance from Mr Adrian R. Allan, University Archivist, Liverpool; and financial support towards research expenses from the University of Birmingham School of Business. I am particularly indebted to Miss Kathleen Cann in the Manuscripts Department of Cambridge University Library for her valuable assistance in accessing the Shackle papers, checking the references and following up queries, and generally making possible the preparation of this paper within the deadlines of publication.

1 Crofton (ed.) (1993: .236).

2 For extensive published bibliographies of Shackle's publications, see Frowen (ed.) (1990: 197–209) and Ford (1994: 490-503). Such Harvard-system referencing to these sources is in keeping with the rest of this volume. Shackle preferred to write his references in full each time, claiming that "'op.cit." is a wretched waste of the reader's attentive power'.

3 Some of the apparently unpublished papers may have been subsequently published, albeit not contained in the extant lists of publications, including those in the collection. For example, the note 'Professor Kirzner on entrepreneurship' (22 May 1978, first given at a conference in Birmingham on 1 June 1978) containing the memorable question 'Were Dante, Michaelangelo, Shakespeare, Newton and Beethoven merely alert?' was subsequently published in the *Austrian Economics Newsletter* and reprinted in Littlechild (ed.) (1990).

4 The letters in this collection are due to be published in Frowen (ed.) (2000). I have therefore refrained from quoting from these letters here.

5 *Books, Pamphlets and Offprinted Articles from the Working Library of Professor G. .L. S. Shackle*, privately printed, Introductory Note dated 16 July 1997 (henceforth Meadows 1997). Scholars wishing to access this collection should contact Mr Meadows at Avenue General Leman 75, B-1040 Brussels.

6 Unfortunately the correspondence does not seem to be entirely complete. I have found examples of letters to and from Shackle that do not seem to be included in the collection.

7 References in square brackets are to items in Add MS 7669 at Cambridge University Library. Miss Cann's paper gives details of the box numbers in which they can be found.

8 A brief outline of the main milestones in Shackle's professional life may be of assistance in appreciating the significance of his letters or comments at different times. He was born 14 July 1903; worked in a bank and in teaching from 1920; was research scholar at L.S.E. from 1935; at Oxford University Institute of Statistics from 1937; first marriage 1939; at Cabinet Office (Statistical Branch then Economics Section) from 1939; Reader at Leeds University 1950; Professor at Liverpool University 1951 until retirement in 1969; lectured in Belfast 1969-71; widowed 1978; second marriage 1979; died 3 March 1992 aged 88. A more extensive outline is provided in the Introduction to this volume.

9 '[H]e wrote all of his manuscripts in pencil, so that he could easily erase unwanted material, and present his secretary with a clean, easy-to-read, text.' (Ford 1994: 13). According to Harcourt (1990: xvii) 'Shackle's mother said of him that he practised the three Rs – reading, writing and rubbing out.'

10 See the lists of publications in Frowen (ed.) (1990) and Ford (1994).

11 See section 6 below for Shackle's view on this book.

12 See, for example, his (1961/1969) *Decision, Order and Time in Human Affairs* and the explanation in his Preface there.

13 Personal communication 21 May 1999.

14 About half a dozen of the items in Meadows (1997) catalogue are said to have marginal notes by Shackle whereas all the items in the Cambridge collection seem to have them; no doubt the latter items were selected with this in mind. The Shackle Papers at Liverpool contain 11 books by other authors, all of which have annotations by Shackle.

15 Earl's reference is to Lachmann (1990: 2).

16 He originally added 'of Europe and the world'. Perhaps that is why (being a romance linguist) he subconsciously wrote the French spelling 'galeries' rather than 'galleries'.

17 *Decision, Order and Time*, p. xiii.

18 As noted in Meadows (1997: 49).

19 See Meadows (1997: 57–8).

20 See Meadows (1997: 165–6).

21 The draft of this letter does not appear to be in the Shackle collection at Cambridge.

22 See Meadows (1997: 65 (Eccles),104 (Popper)).

23 Personal communication, 24 March 1999.

24 Meadows (1997) lists Albert (1946), Allen (1950), Almon (1967) and Courant (1936/1937); also Singh (1959) (with sidelinings and notes by Shackle).

25 The phrase D.W.B. was frequently used, which seems to indicate an exercise completed.

26 See Meadows (1997: 4, 21–4).

27 Personal communication, 3 June 1999.

28 Shackle's grandfather on his father's side was curator of paintings at the Fitzwilliam Museum in Cambridge, and his uncle (his father's only brother) was an architect and painter. The curator's father was a smallholder in Norfolk and when the curator died of consumption at an early age his two sons were taken back to the farm. Source: Mrs C. Shackle, personal communication, 28 June 1999.

29 Subsequently published as a chapter 'F. A. Hayek' in O'Brien and Presley (eds) (1981).

30 A second version of this note records that the train was the '10.23 from W K' [West Kirby, west of Liverpool, where Shackle then lived].

31 Ford (1994: 9–10) has also testified to the stimulation that he derived from Shackle's teaching.

32 The draft of this letter does not appear to be in the Shackle collection at Cambridge.

33 Mrs C. Shackle, personal communication, 29 June 1999.

34 In the original letter, 'mainly' is typed here but Keynes deleted it.

REFERENCES

Albert, A. A. (1941) *Introduction to Algebraic Theories*, Chicago, IL: University of Chicago Press (2nd impression 1942).

—— (1946) *College Algebra*, New York: Mcgraw-Hill Book Company.

Allen, R. G. D. (1950) *Mathematical Analysis for Economists*, London: Macmillan.

Almon, C. (1967) *Matrix Methods in Economics*, Reading, MA: Addison-Wesley Publishing Co.

Ahmad, S. (1991) *Capital in Economic Theory: Neoclassical, Cambridge and Chaos*, Aldershot: Edward Elgar.

Arestis, P. and Sawyer, M. (eds) (1992) *Biographical Dictionary of Dissenting Economists*, Aldershot: Edward Elgar.

Bruner, J. (1986) *Actual Minds, Possible Worlds*, Cambridge, MA: Harvard University Press.

Courant, R. (1936.1937) *Differential and Integral Calculus*, London: Bladine and Son Ltd, vol. I 1937, vol. II 1936.

Crofton, I. (ed.) (1993) *The Guinness Concise Encyclopedia*, Enfield: Guinness Publishing Ltd.

Earl, P. E. (1993) 'The economics of G L S Shackle in retrospect and prospect', *Review of Political Economy*, 5: 245–61.

Eccles, J. (1979) *The Human Mystery*, Berlin: Springer International.

Ferrar, W. L. (1945) *Higher Algebra for Schools*, Oxford: Clarendon Press.

Ford, J. L. (1994) *G.L.S. Shackle: The Dissenting Economist's Economist*, Aldershot: Edward Elgar.

Frowen, S. F. (ed.) (1990) *Unknowledge and Choice in Economics*, London: Macmillan.

—— (1993) 'In memoriam: G. L. S. Shackle, 1903–1992', *Review of Political Economy*, 5: 263–6.

—— (ed.) (2000) *Economists in Discussion — The Correspondence between G.L.S. Shackle and S.F. Frowen*, London: Macmillan, New York: St Martin's Press (forthcoming).

Gilbert, J. C. (1982) *Keynes's Impact on Monetary Economics*, London: Butterworths

Harcourt, G. C. (1990) 'Introduction: notes on an economic querist – G.L.S. Shackle', in Frowen, S.F. (ed.) *Unknowledge and Choice in Economics*, London: Macmillan.

Hayek, F. A. (1934) 'On the relation between Investment and Output', *Economic Journal* 44: 207–31

—— (1941) *The Pure Theory of Capital*, London: Routledge & Kegan Paul, (reprinted 1976).

Hicks, J. R. (1935) 'A suggestion for simplifying the theory of money', *Economica* 2 (new series): 1–19.

—— (1939) *Value and Capital*, Oxford: Oxford University Press.

—— (1950) *A Contribution to the Theory of the Trade Cycle*, Oxford: Clarendon Press (reprinted 1961).

—— (1989) *A Market Theory of Money*, Oxford: Oxford University Press.

Keynes, J. M. (1930) *A Treatise on Money 1 The Pure Theory of Money*, London: Macmillan. Reprinted in *The Collected Writings of John Maynard Keynes*, vol.V, New York, St Martins' Press for the Royal Economic Society.

Knight, F. H. (1934) 'Capital, time and the interest rate', *Economica*, August: 257–86.

Lachmann, L. M. (1990) 'G. L. S. Shackle's Place in the History of Subjectivist Thought, in Frowen, S.F. (ed.) *Unknowledge and Choice in Economics*, London: Macmillan.

Leijonhufvud, A. (1968) *On Keynesian Economics and the Economics of Keynes*, New York, London and Toronto: Oxford University Press.

Littlechild, S. C. (ed.) (1990) *Austrian Economics*, 3 vols, Aldershot: Edward Elgar.

Meadows, G. (1997) *Books, Pamphlets and Offprinted Articles from the Working Library of Professor G. L. S. Shackle*, Brussels: privately printed.

O'Brien, D. P. (1974) 'The development of economics', *Scottish Journal of Political Economy* 21: 187–99.

Ohlin, B. (1937) 'Alternative theories of the rate of interest: rejoinder', *Economic Journal* 47: 423–7.

Popper, K. R. (1982) *The Open Universe, an Argument for Indeterminism*, London: Hutchinson.

—— and Eccles, J. (1977) *The Self and Its Brain*, Berlin: Springer International.

Rescher, N. (1973) *Conceptual Idealism*, Oxford: Basil Blackwell.

Robbins, L. (1938) 'Live and dead issues in the methodology of economics', *Economica,* August: 342–52)

Shackle, G. L. S. (1938) *Expectations, Investment and Income*, Oxford: Oxford University Press.

—— (1952) *Mathematics at the Fireside*, Cambridge: Cambridge University Press.

—— (1961) *Decision, Order and Time in Human Affairs*, Cambridge: Cambridge University Press (2nd edn 1969).

—— (1967) *The Years of High Theory*, Cambridge: Cambridge University Press.

—— (1981) 'F. A. Hayek' , in O'Brien, D. P. and Presley, J. R. (eds) *Pioneers of Modern Economics in Britain,* London: Macmillan.

—— (1982) 'Means and meaning in economic theory', *Scottish Journal of Political Economy* 29: 223–34; reprinted in Shackle (1988).

—— (1983) 'A student's pilgrimage', *Banco Nacionale del Lavoro Quarterly Review*, no. 145: 108–16; reprinted in Shackle (1988).

—— (1988) *Business, Time and Thought: Collected Essays, 1964–1988*, edited by S. F. Frowen, London: Macmillan, London.

——, Carter, C. F. and Meredith, G. P. (eds) (1954) *Uncertainty and Business Decisions*, Liverpool: Liverpool University Press (2nd edn 1957).

Singh, J. (1959) *Mathematical Ideas, Their Nature and Use*, London:Hutchinson.

Wilson, E. O. (1998) *Consilience, The Unity of Knowledge*, London: Little, Brown & Company.

15

CATALOGUE OF THE
SHACKLE PAPERS

Kathleen Cann

THE PAPERS

George Shackle's papers are held in Cambridge University Library (CUL) and catalogued as Add. MS 7669. Professor Shackle began depositing his papers in CUL in 1965, and made further deposits in 1966, 1973, 1978, 1982 and 1987. A final deposit was made by Mrs Shackle in 1992 and 1995. The papers fall into two main divisions: writings (published and unpublished) (sections 1–7 of list) and correspondence (section 9). There is an introductory section (SB) of material put together by Shackle, and a miscellaneous section (8) of, for example, items of biographical interest, and articles by other people.

Writings

For each of Shackle's works there may be any or all of :

- preliminary jottings and drafts
- longhand fair copy of final text
- correspondence with the publisher
- final printed text
- reviews, articles mentioning the work..

They have been arranged by category (books, articles, reviews and so on) and chronologically within each section, following the bibliography in S.F. Frowen (ed) *Unknowledge and Choice in Economics: Proceedings of a Conference in Honour of G.L.S. Shackle* (London: Macmillan, 1990). There is a final section (7) for unpublished or unidentified works.

Correspondence

This consists mainly of letters to Shackle from other academic economists, from the publishers of his books, and from editors of journals. There are some copies of his replies, either interfiled, or in separate series. Shackle himself selected and arranged the letters, and had the earlier ones microfilmed before depositing them at Cambridge. He numbered and listed them in eleven chronological series, beginning in 1949 (the year of publication of *Expectation in Economics*) and extending to 1982. There are a few letters for the years 1938–1948, and a final series of letters c.1978–1992, deposited by Mrs Shackle and arranged alphabetically by name of writer. Further details and an index of correspondents conclude this catalogue.

SB 'THE SYBILLINE BOOKS' (box 1)

The title given by GLSS to a collection of books, articles and letters put together by him, as representing the core of his work (deposited 1992):

SB/1   List of 'Sybilline Books' and explanatory memorandum beginning 'The main theme of my scholarly effort has been the nature of the psychic business of decision' and continuing with twelve propositions making up 'the elements of my theme' (notebook).

SB/2   Draft lists and description of 'Sybilline Books' (notebook).

Books by Shackle or with a contribution by him

SB/3   *Expectation in Economics*, Cambridge 1949.

SB/4   *Time in Economics*, Amsterdam 1957.

SB/5   *Imagination and the Nature of Choice*, Edinburgh 1979 (with quotation from Dante's *Purgatorio* Canto XVII, invocation of imagination, loosely inserted).

SB/6   *Uncertainty and Business Decisions*, 2nd edn, edited by. C. F. Carter, G. P. Meredith, and G. L. S. Shackle, Liverpool 1957.

SB/7   *Time, Uncertainty, and Disequilibrium*, edited by M. J. Rizzo, Lexington 1979 (Chapter 2: 'Imagination, formalism, and choice' by GLSS).

SB/8   *Beyond Positive Economics?*, edited by J. Wiseman, London 1983 (Chapter 2 'The bounds of unknowledge' by GLSS).

SB/9   *Esperance Mathematique de l'Utilité Floue*, by B. Mathieu-Nicot, Dijon 1985 (Preface by GLSS).

SB/10   *Subjectivism, Intelligibility and Economic Understanding*, edited by. I. M. Kirzner, New York 1986 (Chapter 20: 'The origination of choice' by GLSS).

Books on Shackle's themes

SB/11   *Applications of Inductive Logic* (Proceedings of a Conference ... 1978), edited by. L. J. Cohen and M. Hesse, Oxford 1980.

SB/12   *Logic and Philosophy* (Symposium ... 1978), edited by G. H. von Wright, The Hague 1980.

SB/13   *Method, Process, and Austrian Economics*, edited by I. M. Kirzner, Lexington 1982.

SB/14   *The Market as an Economic Process*, by L.M. Lachmann, Oxford 1986.

SB/15   *Uncertainty and Expectations in Economics*. Essays in Honour of G. L. S. Shackle, edited by C. F. Carter and J. L. Ford, Oxford 1972.

SB/16   *Great Economists since Keynes*, by M. Blaug, Brighton 1985 (biographical dictionary with entry on GLSS).

Journals and articles

SB/17   *The University of Liverpool Recorder* no. 78 October 1978 (oration at award of Honorary Degree of Doctor of Social Science to GLSS).

SB/18   'An interview with G. L. S.Shackle', by R. Ebeling, in *Austrian Economics Newsletter* vol. 4 no. 1 Spring 1983.

SB/19   *Journal of Economic Studies* vol. 13 no. 5 1986 'Essays in reappraisal', edited by F. H. Stephen: includes 'Decision making under uncertainty: in defence of Shackle' by F. H. Stephen, and 'Decision' by GLSS.

SB/20   'Elasticities of surprise in the concept of policy', by GLSS for *Contemporary Issues in Money and Banking* edited by P. Arestis (1988) (marked proof).

SB/21 Review of *Imagination and the Nature of Choice*, by James Buchanan, in *Austrian Economics Newsletter* vol .3 no. 1 Summer 1980.

SB/22 'From radical subjectivism to radical subversion: a comment on G. L. S. Shackle's 'Imagination, Formalism and Choice'', by S. C. Littlechild, *University of Birmingham Discussion Paper Series A*, no. 215 (May 1978), and revised ed. 'Radical subjectivism or radical subversion?', no. 219 (September 1978).

SB/23 'The domain of subjective economics: between predictive science and moral philosophy', by James Buchanan, *Virginia Polytechnic working paper* (1981).

SB/24 'Austrian economics as a hermeneutic approach', by L. M. Lachmann (typescript, n.d..) with letter of acknowledgement from GLSS 8 August 1987 (refers to it as 'your chapter').

Manuscripts

SB/25 'The *imagined, deemed possible* as the basis of choice of action. The nature of *focus outcomes*' (15 paragraphs setting out steps in arguments developed in GLSS's books) (MS and typescript).

SB/26 'Suggestion: the neglected factor' (MS, n.d..)

SB/27 'Insight and the creative potential of mind' (MS, 29 December 1987).

Letters

SB/28 (1) Dr P. Hennipman, Amsterdam, 13 September 1984 (with GLSS reply).

(2) Prof. Rafael Rubio de Urquía, Madrid, 29 October 1984 (2 letters).

(3) Dr Charles W. Suckling, Maidenhead, 5 May 1987.

(4) Ross M. MacMillan, Liverpool University, 21 May 1969 (with reply).

(5) Dr Albert Arouh, Athens, 5 May 1987.

(6) J. A. Smyth, Chicago, 11 February 1970.

Photographs (added by Mrs Shackle)

SB/29 (1) and (2) Cambridge 1949 (2 different photos).

(3) Aldeburgh c.1980.

Bibliographies and lists

SB/30 (1) Bibliography of GLSS's work (typescript, up to 1964).
(2) Ditto (typescript, 31 pp.) up to 1984.
(3) Bibliography of works on theme of 'expectation in economics' (MS, chronological list up to 1960).
(4) Ditto divided into 'books' and 'articles' up to 1964.
(5) Summary of material sent to CUL in 1965.
(6) List of material sent in 1966.
(7) Ditto 1978.
(8) Ditto 1982.

1 BOOKS (boxes 2–7)

(Entries in brackets refer to items not represented in the collection.)

1/1   *Expectations, Investment and Income*, OUP 1938, 2nd edn 1968.(box 2)

     1/1/1 Printed book, 1st edn
     1/1/2 Printed book, 2nd edn
     1/1/3 Reviews and articles on 1st edn (8 items, with list)
     1/1/4 Reviews of 2nd edn (env)
     1/1/5 Handwritten text of prefatory essay for 2nd edn

1/2   *Expectation in Economics*, CUP 1949, 2nd edn 1952.   (box 2)

     (SB/3 Printed book, 1st edn)
     1/2/1 Printed book, 2nd edn
     1/2/2 Handwritten original text
     1/2/3 Corrections and new preface for 2nd edn (MS, env)
     1/2/4 Reviews of 1st edn (box, with list)
     1/2/5 'Translations of articles and review articles' (env)
     1/2/6 Handwritten index

1/3   *Mathematics at the Fireside*, CUP 1952.   (box 2)

     1/3/1 Printed book

1/3/2 Handwritten original text
1/3/3 Proof of drawing for frontispiece by J. Hookham
1/3/4 Contract November 1948 and correspondence 1949–1952 with CUP
1/3/5 Letters about the book (nos 1–34) 1951-1958 with list
1/3/6 Reviews (env and 3 loose items)

1/4 *Uncertainty in Economics and other reflections,*
CUP 1955, 1968.   (box 3)

1/4/1 Printed book, 1st edn
1/4/2 Printed book, reprint, CUP Library Edition
1/4/3 Material for 1st edn: correspondence with CUP etc. on planning and progress of book 1953–1955 (including contract 6 November 1953), proofs of blocks, drawings, advertisements in journals (env)
1/4/4 Author's note for reprint (in env. with 1/4/3)
1/4/5 Reviews of 1st edn (18 items, with list) and of reprint (box)

1/5 *Time in Economics,* Amsterdam 1958
(F. De Vries Lectures).   (box 3)

(SB/4 Printed book)
1/5/1 Handwritten original text
1/5/2 Reviews (2 envs with lists, probably some duplication)

1/6 *Economics for Pleasure,* CUP 1959, 2nd edn 1968.   (box 3)

1/6/1 Printed book, 1st edn
1/6/2 Printed book, 2nd edn
1/6/3 Handwritten original text (with title 'Economics in words')
1/6/4 Handwritten text of new chapters 9 and 27 for 2nd edn
1/6/5 Reviews of 1st edition (2 envs, one with list)
1/6/6 Reviews of 2nd edition (box)

1/7   *Decision, Order and Time in Human Affairs*, CUP 1961,
       2nd edn 1969.   (box 4)

    1/7/1 Printed book, 1st edn
    1/7/2 Printed book, 2nd edn
    1/7/3 Corresp. with CUP 1956–1961 inc. contract May 1960
           (env)
    1/7/4 Notes, drafts, trial passages, progress reports 1957–1961
           (8 notebooks, gatherings and loose pages) including:
           'Decision and Value' (17 July 1957) 57 pp. (loose)
           'Time in Economics' (Luncheon talk 16 October 1957)
           (notebook)
           'Decision and Order: scheme of writing' 1958
           (notebook)
           'Decision in face of uncertainty: some criticisms and
           extensions of a theory' 15 April 1958 (lecture?)
           (typescript)
           'Expectation and decision' (lecture at Tilburg 22 April
           1958, typescript)
    1/7/5 Handwritten final copy, including diagrams (box)
    1/7/6 Handwritten index (6 exercise books)
    1/7/7 Drawings, tracings and proofs of blocks (3 packets and
           1 file)
    1/7/8 Reviews (box and 1 journal, list of reviews of 1st edn)
    1/7/9 Handwritten text of Appendix for 2nd edn
    1/7/10 Preface for French edn 1967

1/8   *A Scheme of Economic Theory*, CUP 1965.   (box 5)

    1/8/1 Printed book
    1/8/2 Handwritten drafts of preface, chapters 1 and 7,
    diagrams
    1/8/3 Handwritten original text
    1/8/4 Reviews, with list (env)

1/9   *The Nature of Economic Thought. Selected Papers 1955–1964*,
       CUP 1966.   (box 5)

    1/9/1 Printed book

1/9/2 Handwritten drafts of (1) preface, (2) The unity of European economic thought (reprint of 2/12), (3) Scale, risk and profit

1/9/3 Reviews, with list (env)

1/10 *The Years of High Theory*, CUP 1967.   (box 5)

1/10/1 Printed book
1/10/2 Handwritten original text
1/10/3 Photographs of GLSS's drawings for blocks
1/10/4 Reviews (env)

1/11 *Expectation, Enterprise and Profit*, Allen and Unwin 1970.(box 6)

1/11/1 Printed book
1/11/2 Handwritten original text
1/11/3 Review in TLS
1/11/4 Correspondence with publisher and others, and contract 1968
1/11/5 Drawings, corrections, MS index
1/11/6 Notes, drafts and discarded pages (box)

1/12 *Epistemics and Economics*, CUP 1972.   (box 6)

1/12/1 Handwritten original text
1/12/2 Reviews (env)
1/12/3 Drafts, progress sheets etc.

1/13 *An Economic Querist*, CUP 1973.   (box 7)

1/13/1 Printed book
1/13/2 Handwritten original text
1/13/3 Handwritten preface to Spanish edn 1977
1/13/4 Reviews (env)

1/14 *Keynesian Kaleidics*, Edinburgh University Press 1974.   (box 7)

1/14/1 Handwritten original text
1/14/2 Handwritten index (4 notebooks)

1/15   *Imagination and the Nature of Choice*, Edinburgh U.P. 1979.(box 7)

(SB/5 Printed book)

1/15/2 'Notes and drafts for Imagination and the Nature of Choice and for "Imagination formalism and choiceæ" et cetera.'

1/15/3 Handwritten text (4 vols) with preface (loose) dated May 1974)

1/15/4 Chapter headings, notes etc., (13 small notebooks)

1/15/5 First draft (44 small notebooks)

1/15/6 Reviews (3 items, loose)

1/15/7 Drafts, notes, and discarded pages

(1/16   *Business, Time and Thought. Selected papers of G.L.S. Shackle*, ed.ited by S.F. Frowen, Macmillan 1988.)

1/17-30 *Translations of Shackle's books:*   (loose on shelf)

Mathematics at the Fireside: French 1967

Economics for Pleasure: Spanish 1962, Portuguese 1964, Dutch 1964, French 1965, Italian 1966, Czech 1969, German 1974 (2nd edn)

Decision, Order and Time: Spanish 1966

A Scheme of Economic Theory: Portuguese 1969

The Nature of Economic Thought: Spanish 1969

Epistemics and Economics: Spanish 1976

An Economic Querist: Spanish 1977

Expectation, Enterprise and Profit: Spanish 1976

2 CHAPTERS CONTRIBUTED TO BOOKS (Boxes 8–9)

(Entries in brackets refer to items not represented in the collection.)

Box 8

(2/1   'Capital, theory of' in *Chambers Encyclopaedia*, new edn 1950)

2/2   Foreword to English translation of *Value, Capital and Rent*, by Knut Wicksell, London 1954, New York 1970.

2/2/1   Printed book

2/2/2 Handwritten original text

2/3 Chapter 'Expectation in economics' and concluding comment on Part One in *Uncertainty and Business Decisions*, ed. C. F. Carter, G. P. Meredith, G. L. S. Shackle, Liverpool 1957.

2/3/1   Printed book

2/3/2   Handwritten texts of Foreword, 'Expectation ...', final comment

2/3/3 Reviews (box)

2/4 Chapter 'The nature of the bargaining process' in *The Theory of Wage Determination*, edited by. J. T. Dunlop, London 1957.

2/4/1   Printed book

2/4/2   Handwritten text

2/5 Chapter 'Expectation and liquidity' in *Expectations, Uncertainty and Business Behavior*, edited by M. J. Bowman, New York 1958 (Conference 1955).

2/5/1   Printed book

2/5/2   Preliminary text (typescript)

2/6 Foreword and final English text of *The Theory of General Static Equilibrium* (Elementi di economia razionale), by Eraldo Fossati, Oxford 1957.

2/6/1   Printed book

2/6/2   Handwritten text

2/7 Foreword and chapters 'The liberal tradition in economics', The role of the economist as official adviser', 'Bank rate and the modernisation of industry' in *Economic Issues*, edited by S. F. Frowen and H. C. Hillmann, London 1957 (articles from *The Bankers' Magazine*).

2/7/1   Printed book

2/7/2   Handwritten text of foreword

Box 9

2/8 Chapters 'What is economics?', 'What is a theory?', 'The toolbox of the economist', in *A New Prospect of Economics*, edited by G.L.S. Shackle, Liverpool 1958.

2/8/1   Printed book

2/9 Chapter 'Time, nature and decision' in *Money, Growth and Methodology*, ed.ited by H. Hegeland, Lund 1961.

2/9/1   Printed book

2/9/2   Handwritten text

2/10   Introduction 'Keynes i charakter spraw ludzkich' ('Keynes and the nature of human affairs', translation of article 3/45) in *Wstep do teorii economicznej Johna Maynarda Keynesa*, London 1961, also two chapters, translations of 'The nature of the business cycle' 1938 (from book 1/1) and 'Twenty years on ...' 1951 (article 3/21).
       2/10/1   Printed book
       2/10/2   Handwritten text (English) of introduction

2/11   'Capital, theory of' new article written 1961 for revised edn of *Chambers' Encyclopaedia*
       2/11/1   Handwritten text, and letters from publisher

2/12   Chapter 'The unity of European economic thought' in *Le collettività locali e la costruzione dell'unità europea*, Milan 1963 (reprinted in 1/9)
       2/12/1   Summary and letter from editor

2/13   Chapter 'The interest elasticity of investment' in *The Theory of Interest Rates*, edited by F. H. Hahn and F. P. R. Brechling, London 1965.
       2/13/1   Handwritten text

2/14   Survey article 'Recent theories concerning the nature and role of interest' in *Surveys of Economic Theory* vol I, New York 1965 (reprinted in 1/9).
       2/14/1   Printed book (for MS and correpondence, see 3/45)

2/15   Article 'Economic expectations' in *International Encyclopedia of the Social Sciences*, edited by D. L. Sills, London 1968.
       2/15/1   Handwritten text
       2/15/2   Offprint

2/16   Foreword to *Theories of the Bargaining Process*, by A. Coddington, London 1968.
       2/16/1   Handwritten text

2/17   Preface and chapter 'Policy, poetry and success' in *On the Nature of Business success*. Ten papers delivered to the British Association for the Advancement of Science, edited by G. L. S. Shackle, Liverpool 1968. ('Policy ...' was GLSS's Presidential address to Section F (Economics) 1 September 1966).
       2/17/1   Printed book (for MS, see 3/55)
       2/17/2   Reviews

(2/18   Introduction and chapter 'Policy, poetry and success' in *Essays in Modern Economic Development*, edited by R. L. Smyth, London 1969.)

(2/19   Chapter 'Theory and the business man' in *Studies in Accounting for Management Decision*, ed. A.M. Bourn, London 1969.)

(2/20   Chapter 'Discussion paper on Robert Clower: theoretical foundations of monetary policy' in *Monetary Theory and Monetary Policy in the 1970s*, edited by G. Clayton, J. C. Gilbert, R. Sedgwick, Oxford 1971.)

(2/21   Chapter 'Marginalism: the harvest' in *The Marginal Revolution in Economics*, edited by R. D. Collison Black, A. W. Coats, C. D. W. Goodwin, Durham North Carolina 1973; for MS, see 3/58).

2/22   Chapter 'Decision: the human predicament' in *The Information Revolution*, edited by D. M. Lamberton, Philadelphia 1974.

    2/22/1   Handwritten text (see also article 3/60)

2/23   Chapter 'News from Sweden' in *Population, Factor Movements and Economic Development. Essays in honour of Brinley Thomas*, edited by H. Richards, Cardiff 1976 (reprinted in 1/16).

    2/23/1   Handwritten text

    2/23/2   Typescript

2/24   Chapter 'Time and Choice: Keynes Lecture in Economics 1976' in *Proceedings of the British Academy*, vol LXII 1976, London 1977.

    2/24/1   Preliminary notes

    2/24/2   Handwritten text

    2/24/3   Offprint

2/25   Chapter 'New tracks for economic theory, 1926-1939' in *Modern Economic Thought*, edited by S. Weintraub, Oxford 1977 (reprinted in 1/16).

    2/25/1   Handwritten text, dated 22 Nov 1975

2/26   Chapter 'Time, choice and uncertainty' in *Making Sense of Time* (Vol I of *Timing Space and Spacing Time*), edited by T. Carlstein, D. Parkes, N. Thrift, London 1978.

    2/26/1 Handwritten texts (draft and fair copy, with title 'Time, choice and history')

    2/26/2   Correspondence with editors 1974-5

2/27   Chapter 'Imagination, formalism and choice' in *Time, Uncertainty and Disequilibrium*, edited by M. J. Rizzo, Lexington, MA 1979.
        SB/7 Printed book (for MS, see 3/61)

2/28   Chapter 'F. A.Hayek' in *Pioneers of Modern Economics in Britain*, edited by D. P. O'Brien, J. R. Presley, London 1981.
        2/28/1   Typescript 'Hayek as economist', dated 9 Jun 1978

(2/29   Chapter 'Letter to the author: a comment' in *Subjectivist Economics*, by A. H. Shand, Pica Press 1981.)

2/30   Chapter 'Cantillon far ahead of his time' in *Homenáje a Lucas Beltrán*, Madrid 1982.
        2/30/1   Typescript (1980)

(2/31   Foreword to *The Entrepreneur*, by R.F. Hébert and A.N. Link, New York 1982.)

2/32   Chapter 'The Bounds of Unknowledge' in *Beyond Positive Economics*, edited by J. Wiseman, London 1983. Originally lecture to Section F of BAAS (reprinted in 1/16)
        2/32/1   Partial draft
        2/32/2   Handwritten fair copy

(2/33   Foreword to *The Economic Imagination*, by P. E. Earl, Brighton 1983.)

(2/34   Chapter 'Shackle on Harrod' in *Contemporary Economists in Perspective*, edited by H. W. Spiegel and W. J. Samuels, Greenwich, CT 1984. Is this 7/20 'Harrod as economist', 1981?)

(2/35   Chapter 'To cope with time' in *Firms, Organization and Labour*: Approaches to the Economics of Work Organization, edited by F. H. Stephen, London 1984.)

(2/36   Foreword to *The Capitalist Alternative*: An Introduction to Neo-Austrian Economics, by A. H. Shand, Brighton 1984.)

2/37   Chapter 'Keynes the meeting-point of history and thought' in *Les Écrits de Keynes*, by F. Poulon and others, Paris 1985 (repr. in 1/16)
        2/37/1   Handwritten text 3 Mar 1984

(2/38   Chapter 'The origination of choice' in *Subjectivism, Intelligibilty and Economic Understanding*: Essays in Honour of Ludwig M. Lachmann, edited by I. M. Kirzner, London 1986. Is this 7/28?)

2/39   Foreword to *The Economics of Alfred Marshall*, by D. Reisman, London 1986.
        2/39/1   Handwritten text

(2/40   Chapter 'Treatise, theory and time' in *La Herencia de Keynes*, edited by R. Rubio de Urquía, Madrid 1988.)

(2/41   Chapter 'Method in economic theory'. In book 1/16)

2/42   Foreword and chapter 'Elasticities of surprise in the concept of policy' in *Contemporary Issues in Money and Banking*: Essays in Honour of Stephen Frowen, edited by P. Arestis, London 1988. 2/42/1   Handwritten text 1987 with title 'The signals of surprise'

(2/43   Chapter 'What did the *General Theory* do?' in *New Directions in Post Keynesian Economics*, edited by J. Pheby, Aldershot 1989.) 2/43/1   MS drafts 1987 (6 notebooks)

3 ARTICLES (boxes 10-11)

(Entries in brackets refer to items not represented in the collection.)

(3/1   'Some notes on monetary theories of the trade cycle', *Review of Economic Studies*, vol 1 no. 1 Oct 1933)

(3/2   'The breakdown of the boom: a possible mechanism', *Economica* (New Series) vol 3 no. 12 Nov 1936)

(3/3   'Dynamics of the crisis: a suggestion', *Review of Economic Studies* vol 4 no. 11 Feb 1937)

(3/4   'The multiplier in closed and open systems', *Oxford Economic Papers* no. 2 May 1939)

(3/5   'Expectations and employment', *Economic Journal* vol 49 no. 195 Sep 1939)

(3/6   'The nature of the inducement to invest', *Review of Economic Studies* vol 8 no. 22 Oct 1940)

(3/7   'A reply to Professor Hart', *Review of Economic Studies* vol 8 no. 22 Oct 1940)

(3/8   'A means of promoting investment', *Economic Journal* vol 51 nos 202, 203, Jun, Sep 1941)

(3/9   'A theory of investment decisions', *Oxford Economic Papers* no. 6 Apr 1942)

(3/10   'The expectational dynamics of the individual', *Economica* (New Series) vol.10 no. 38, May 1943)

(3/11   'Myrdal's analysis of monetary equilibrium', *Oxford Economic Papers* no. 7, Mar 1945) (reprinted in 1/4)

(3/12   'An analysis of speculative choice', *Economica* (New Series) vol
        12 no. 45, Feb 1945)

(3/13   'Interest-rates and the pace of investment', *Economic Journal* vol
        56 no. 221, Mar 1946) (reprinted in 1/4)

(3/14   'The deflative or inflative tendency of Government receipts and
        disbursements', *Oxford Economic Papers* no. 8 Nov 1947)
        (reprinted in 1/4)

(3/15   'The nature of interest rates', *Oxford Economic Papers* (New
        Series) vol 1 no. 1 Jan 1949) (reprinted in 1/4)

(3/16   'Some theoretical aspects of payment by results', *Economica
        Internazionale* vol 2 no. 4, Nov 1949)

(3/17   Part III of a symposium on Expectation in Economics,
        Economica (New Series) vol 16 no. 64, Nov 1949) (reprinted in
        1/4)

3/18   'A non-additive measure of uncertainty', *Review of Economic
        Studies* vol 17 no. 42, 1949-1950 (reprinted in 1/4)
        3/18/1   Handwritten text

3/19   'Probability and uncertainty', *Metroeconomica* vol 1 no. 3, Dec
        1949 (reprinted in 1/4)
        3/19/1   Handwritten text

3/20   'Three versions of the f-surface: some notes for a comparison',
        Review of Economic Studies vol 18 no. 46 1950–1951 (reprinted
        in 1/4)
        3/20/1   Handwritten text

3/21   'Twenty years on: a survey of the theory of the multiplier',
        Economic Journal vol 61 no. 242, Jun 1951 (reprinted in 1/4)
        3/21/1   Handwritten text
        3/21/2   Offprint of German version: 'Zwanzig Jahre danach
                 ...' from Wilhelm Weber, *Konjunktur-und
                 Beschäftigungstheorie* (and see correspondence 1950–
                 1951 in box 27)

3/22   'The nature and role of profit', *Metroeconomica* vol 3 no. 3 Dec
        1951 (reprinted in 1/4)
        3/22/1   Handwritten text

(3/23   'Interest-rates as an instrument of economic policy', *Liverpool
        Trade Review* vol 50 no. 12, Dec 1951)

3/24   'On the meaning and measure of uncertainty, Part I',
        Metroeconomica vol 4 no. 3, Dec 1952 (reprinted in 1/4)
        3/24/1   Handwritten text

3/25   'Economics and sincerity', *Oxford Economic Papers* (New Series) vol 5 no. 1, Mar 1953 (reprinted in 1/4)
      3/25/1   Handwritten text
      3/25/2   Printed extract 'Reflections on Econometrics', *Economic Digest*, June 1953

3/26   'A chart of economic theory', *Metroeconomica* vol 5 no. 1, Apr 1953 (reprinted in 1/4)
      3/26/1   Handwritten text, with title 'An ordering of economic theory'

3/27   'The logic of surprise', *Economica* (New Series) vol 20 no. 78, May 1953 (reprinted in 1/4)
      3/27/1   Handwritten text, with title 'Counter-expected and unexpected events and the logic of surprise'

3/28   'What makes an economist?', Liverpool University Press 1953 (reprinted in 1/4)
      3/28/1   Handwritten text

3/29   'On the meaning and measure of uncertainty, Part II', *Metroeconomica* vol 5 no. 3, Dec 1953 (reprinted in 1/4)
      3/29/1   Handwritten text

3/30   'The economist's view of profit', *The Company Accountant* N.S. 26, Jun 1953 (reprinted in 1/4)
      3/30/1   Handwritten text

3/31   'Bank rate and the modernisation of industry', *The Bankers' Magazine* vol 177 no. 1323, Jun 1954
      3/31/1   Handwritten text

3/32   'The complex nature of time as a concept in economics', *Economica Internazionale* vol 7 no. 4, Nov 1954
      3/32/1   Handwritten text, dated Apr-May 1954

3/33   'Business men on business decisions', *Scottish Journal of Political Economy* vol 2 no. 1, Feb 1955 (reprinted in 1/9)
      3/33/1   Handwritten text, with title 'Business decisions'
      3/33/2   Offprint
      3/33/3   Completed questionnaires used in survey
      3/33/4   Answers to same questions, given at conference at St Andrews, with covering letter of Alec Cairncross, June 1955

(3/34   'Expectation, income and profit', *Economisk Tidskrift* vol 57 no. 4, Dec 1955)

(3/35 'Expectation and cardinality', *Economic Journal* vol 66 no. 262, Jun 1966. Handwritten text at 7/3, lectures in Sweden 1955 no.4

3/36 'The nature of inflation', *The Company Accountant* N.S. 41, 1955 (reprinted in 1/9)
    3/36/1   Handwritten text

(3/37 'Marshallian and Paretian stems', *Metroeconomica* vol 8, no. 3 Dec 1956)

(3/38 'Some reflections and a further note on "Odds, possibility and plausibility in Shackle's theory of decision" by Gerald Gould', *Economic Journal* vol 67 no.268, Dec 1957)

3/39 'The economist's model of man', *Occupational Psychology* vol 32 no. 3, Jul 1958 (reprinted in 1/9)
    3/39/1   Handwritten text

(3/40 'Decisions in face of uncertainty: some criticisms and extensions of a theory', *De Economist* no. 10 Oct 1958)

3/41 'Time and thought', *British Journal for the Philosophy of Science* vol 9 no. 36, 1959
    3/41/1   Handwritten text, subtitled 'Lecture for Toronto, 23 Jan 1958'

(3/42 'Business and uncertainty', *The Bankers' Magazine* vol 189 no. 1392, Mar 1960) (reprinted in 1/9)

(3/43 'Incertezza e profitti', *Mercurio* vol 4 no. 2, Feb 1961)

3/44 'Recent theories concerning the nature and role of interest', *Economic Journal* vol 71 no. 282, Jun 1961 (reprinted in 1/9)
    3/44/1   Handwritten text
    3/44/2   Typescript used by printer
    3/44/3   Notebook with preliminary notes and drafts
    3/44/4   Correspondence with editors of Economic Journal (inc. Roy Harrod) 1958-1961
    3/44/5   Letters to GLSS requesting offprints 1961–2

(3/45 'Keynes and the nature of human affairs', *Weltwirtschaftliches Archiv* vol 87 no. 1, 1961) (reprinted in 1/9, MS and Polish text 2/10)

3/46 'The ruin of economy', *Kyklos* vol 14 no. 4, 1961
    3/46/1   Handwritten text

(3/47 'Décision et incertitude', *Futuribles* (Bulletin SEDEIS) no 813, supplement no. 26, 1 Mar 1962)

3/48 'L'eclissi della 'Grande Teoria'', *Mercurio* vol 5 no. 10, Oct 1962
    3/48/1   Printed text (journal)

(3/49 'Descrizione dello stato di incertezza', *La Scuola in Azione* vol 21 no. 1, 17 Sep 1962)

(3/50 'I tre significanti del tempo nella trattazione ecomonica marshalliana', *Rivista Internazionale di Scienze Economiche e Commerciali* vol 10 no. 1, Jan 1963)

(3/51 'Theory and the business man', *Scientific Business* vol 1 no. 1, May 1963) (reprinted in 1/16)

3/52 'L'équilibre: étude de sa signification et de ses limites', *Cahiers de l'Institut de Science Economique Appliquée: Les cahiers Franco-Italiens* (Série BA) no. 2, Feb 1963
    3/52/1   Handwritten English text, with title 'Tools of thought in economics, Chapter 1: Equilibrium' and note by GLSS that this became the draft original of 'L'équilibre ...'

3/53 'General thought-schemes and the economist', *Woolwich Economic Papers* no.2, Mar 1963
    3/53/1   Handwritten text
    3/53/2   Printed text (leaflet)

3/54 'The hedgehog and the fox', *The Indian Journal of Economics* vol 44 no. 175, Apr 1964 (reprinted in 1/9)
    3/54/1   Handwritten text, dated 2 Feb 1964, with original title 'A scheme of economic theory' and note that it is also a 'Paper for Durham'

3/55 'Policy, poetry and success', *The Advancement of Science* vol 23 no. 111, Sep 1966 (Presidential Address to Section F (Economics) of British Association for the Advancement of Science, 1 Sep 1966)
    3/55/1   Handwritten draft 30 Mar 1966, with title 'Decision theory'
    3/55/2   Handwritten text of new opening to lecture (3 pp.)
    3/55/3   Preprint from *The Advancement of Science*

3/56 'Policy, poetry and success', *The Economic Journal*, vol 76 no. 304, Dec 1966
    3/56/1   Offprint
    3/56/2   Handwritten text of abstract, and letter from editor

3/57   'On the nature of profit', *Woolwich Economic Papers* no. 13, Jul 1967 (reprinted in 1/16) (The Finlay Lecture, University College, Dublin, 24 May 1967)

       3/57/1   Outline of theme of lecture

       3/57/2   First draft, with note by GLSS that this was discarded and a new lecture written on different lines.

       3/57/3   Handwritten text of final lecture

       3/57/4   Printed text (leaflet)

3/58   'Marginalism: the harvest', *History of Political Economy* vol 4 no. 2, 1972 (reprinted in 2/21 and 1/16)

       3/58/1   Handwritten text, dated 1 May 1971

       3/58/2   Offprint

3/59   'Keynes and today's establishment in economic theory: a view', *Journal of Economic Literature* vol 11, Jun 1973

       3/59/1   Italian translation, offprint from *Rivista di Politica Economica* May 1974

3/60   'Decision: the human predicament', *The Annals of the American Academy of Political and Social Science* vol 412, Mar 1974 (also in book 2/22)

       3/60/1   Offprint

3/61   'Imagination, formalism and choice', *Teorema* vol 6 nos 3–4, 1978 (for drafts, see 1/15/2)

       3/61/1   Handwritten text (paper read to Department of Logic and Philosophy of Science, University of Valencia, 27 Apr 1976)

       3/61/2   Offprint of English text

       3/61/3   *Teorema* vol VII/3-4 1977 (1978) with Spanish text

3/62   'Evolutions of thought in economics', *Banca Nazionale del Lavoro Quarterly Review* no.132, Mar 1980

       3/62/1   Offprint

3/63   'Imagination, unknowledge and choice', *Greek Economic Review* vol 2 no.2, Aug 1980 ('Paper for B.A.A.S. York 1981')

       3/63/1   Photocopy of handwritten text

       3/63/2   Offprint

3/64   'Sir John Hicks's `IS–LM: an explanation': a comment', *Journal of Post-Keynesian Economics* vol 4 no. 3, Spring 1982 (reprinted in 1/16)

       3/63/1   Handwritten text, dated 1980

       3/63/2   Offprint

(3/65 'Means and meaning in economic theory', *Scottish Journal of Political Economy* vol 29 no. 3, Spring 1982) (reprinted in 1/16)

(3/66 'Comment', *Journal of Post-Keynesian Economics* vol 5 no. 2, 1982)

3/67 'Nature, notion et notation de l'incertitude', (paper in English read at conference Dec 1982 at Paris II University)
3/67/1 Rough notes
3/67/2 Fair copy 15 Dec 1982

(3/68 'The romantic mountain and the classic lake: Alan Coddington's Keynesian Economics, *Journal of Post-Keynesian Economics* vol 6 no. 2, Winter 1983-4) (reprinted in 1/16)

3/69 'Levels of simplicity in Keynes' theory of money and employment', *The South African Journal of Economics* vol 51 no. 3, 1983 (repr. in 1/16)
3/69/1 Handwritten text

3/70 'A student's pilgrimage', *Banca Nazionale del Lavoro, Quarterly Review* no. 145, Jun 1983 (reprinted in 1/16)
3/70/1 Draft in pencil
3/70/2 Handwritten final text

(3/71 'Comment on: Randall Bausor's "Toward a historically dynamic economics" and Malcolm Rutherford's "Rational expectations and Keynesian uncertainty", *Journal of Post-Keynesian Economics* vol 6 no. 3, Spring 1984)

3/72 'Economics and the educator's art', *Varta* - Indian Institute of Economic Research (contributed 1986)
Manuscript with correspondence at 9/13/34 below, corresp. with Indian Institute

(3/73 'Decision', *Journal of Economic Studies* vol 13 no. 5, 1986. Copy filed at SB/19.

4 REVIEW ARTICLES (box 11)

(Entries in brackets refer to items not represented in the collection.)

(4/1 'The new economics', *The Cambridge Review* vol 70 no. 1704 Dec 1948) (review of *The New Economics*, edited by S. Harris)

4/2 'Measuring industry's output', *Accounting Research* vol 1 no. 2, Jul 1949 (review of *The Measurement of Production Movements* by C. F. Carter, W. B. Reddaway, J. R. N. Stone)

  4/2/1 Offprint

(4/3 'Automatic control for economic systems', *Nature* vol 174 no. 4427, Sep 1954) (review of *The Mechanisms of Economic Systems*, by A. Tustin)

4/4 'Professor Kierstead's theory of profits', *Economic Journal* vol 64, no. 253, Mar 1954 (review of *An Essay in the Theory of Profits and Income Distribution*, by B. S. Kierstead)

  4/4/1 Handwritten text

4/5 'The liberal tradition in economics', *The Bankers' Magazine* vol 178 no. 1329, Dec 1954 (Review of *The Economist in the Twentieth Century*, by L. Robbins)

  4/5/1 Offprint

4/6 'The role of the economist as official adviser', *The Bankers' Magazine* vol 181 no. 1345, Apr 1956 (review of *The Role of the Economist as Official Adviser*, by W. A. Jöhr and H. W. Singer)

  4/6/1 Galley proof

4/7 'The life of Knut Wicksell', *The Bankers' Magazine* vol 187 no. 1380, Mar 1959 (review of *The Life of Knut Wicksell* by T. Gardlund)

  4/7/1 Galley proof

(4/8 'The stages of economic growth', *Political Studies* vol 10 no. 1, Feb 1962) (review of *The Stages of Economic Growth* by W. W. Rostow) (reprinted in 1/9)

(4/9 'Battles long ago', *Weltwirtschaftliches Archiv* vol 89 no. 1, 1962) (review of *Essays on Value and Distribution. Essays on Economic Stability and Growth* by N. Kaldor) (reprinted in 1/9)

(4/10 'Values and intentions', *Kyklos* vol 15 no. 4, 1962) (review of *Values and Intentions* by J. N. Findlay) (reprinted in 1/9)

4/11 'On Hicks's Causality in Economics', *Greek Economic Review* vol 1 no. 2, Dec 1979 (review of *Causality in Economics* by J. R. Hicks)

  4/11/1 Offprint

(4/12 'Decisions, process and the market', *Journal of Economic Studies* vol 10 no. 3, 1983) (review of *Method, Process and Austrian Economics*, edited by I. M. Kirzner)

4/13   'Controlling industrial economies', *Kyklos* vol 38 no. 1, 1985) (review of *Controlling Industrial Economies*, edited by S. F. Frowen (repr. in 1/16)

      4/13/1   Handwritten text

4/14   'Markets, entrepreneurs and liberty', *Newsletter* of History of Economic Thought Study Group, no. 36, Spring 1986 (review of *Markets, Entrepreneurs and Liberty* by W. D. Reekie)

      4/14/1   Handwritten text, Jan 1986

      4/14/2   Drafts (3 notepads)

4/15   'Richard Cantillon: entrepreneur and economist', *Journal of Economic Studies* vol 14 no. 3, 1987 (review of *Richard Cantillon: Entrepreneur and Economist* by A. E. Murphy)

      4/15/1   Handwritten text Jun 1987

4/16   'Anna Carabelli on Keynes's method', *Journal of Economic Studies* vol 16 no. 1, 1989 (review of *On Keynes's Method* by A. Carabelli)

      4/16/1   Handwritten text

5 REVIEWS (Box 11)

Manuscripts and printed reviews (cuttings, galley proofs, and so on) of items listed in Shackle's bibliography, and additional unlisted items (2 boxes).

6 SHORT ARTICLES OR NOTES (Box 11)

(Entries in brackets refer to items not represented in the collection.)

6/1   'A comment on Mr J. D. Sargan's paper', *Yorkshire Bulletin of Economic and Social Research* vol 5, no.1, Feb 1953

      6/1/1   Handwritten text

      6/1/2   Offprint

(6/2   A note included in the report of the colloquium on 'The theory of risk in econometrics', Paris May 1952, *Colloques Internationaux du Centre National de la Recherche Scientifique* vol 40, 1953)

(6/3   'Interest rates and inflation', *Liverpool Daily Post, Annual Banking, Insurance and Commercial Review*, Jan 1956)

6/4   'Some reflections on Mr Gould's article', *Economic Journal* vol 67, no. 268, Dec 1957

      6/4/1   Handwritten text

6/5   'Comments on "Wahrscheinlichkeitstheorie ..." by Dr Gerhard Merk, and "Kritische Betrachtungen ..." by ...H. G. Krusselberg', *Weltwirtschaftliches Archiv* vol 82 no. 2, 1959

      6/5/1   Handwritten text dated 13 Mar 1959

6/6   'Stephen Frowen, editor of The Bankers' Magazine 1955–1960', *The Bankers' Magazine* vol 189, no. 1393, Apr 1960

      6/6/1   Handwritten text

6/7   'The nature of business', *Scientific Business*, pilot issue Mar 1963

      6/7/1   Handwritten text

(6/8   'A comment on Mrs V. Mukerji's papers ...' *Journal of the Gokhale Institute of Politics and Economics* vol 7 no. 4, Dec 1965)

6/9   'Eraldo Fossati 1902–1962', *Econometrica* vol 33 no. 3, Jul 1965

      6/9/1   Handwritten draft

      6/9/2   Offprint

(6/10   A note on A. Coddington's 'Deficient Foresight ...', 1982 [in?])

6/11   Comment on R. Bausor's Time and the Structure of Economic Analysis, 1982 (published as 3/66)

      6/11/1   Handwritten text, 20 Sep 1982

(6/12   'Suggestion: the neglected factor', *Wirtschaftspolitische Blätter* (special issue on F. A. Hayek's 90th birthday) 1989)

7 UNPUBLISHED AND UNIDENTIFIED MANUSCRIPTS (boxes 12–13, 30)

(Probably some of these were published, but were not identified during cataloguing.)

7/1   'Borrowed capital ratio and scale of investment', Leeds c.1950. Handwritten drafts and typescripts.

7/2   'A note on the private choice of a language' MS, 9 Jun 1951, 2pp.

7/3   Four lectures given in Sweden 1955:

      1.   Expectation and uncertainty

      2.   Expectation and liquidity

      3.   Expectation, income and profit

	4.	Expectation and cardinality (in *Economic Journal*, see 3/35)

7/4 'Decision making', MS for seminar, University of Manchester, Department of Government, 8 Feb 1957

7/5 'Expectation: some difficulties', MS, Nov–Dec 1957

7/6 Lecture beginning 'The scheme of thought I have outlined in the preceding lecture ... ' MS, May 1958

7/7 'Business and uncertainty' MS marked 'Harrogate', 11 May 1959

7/8 'Business and uncertainty' (different text, also marked 'Interest rates and uncertainty'), MS, 29 May 1960

7/9 'Scale, risk and profit: a curious appendix', typescript 31 Jul 1961 with note that it is addition to paper given at meeting of Econometric Society, Paris 1961.

7/10 L. Sheynin: 'Wages and the productivity of labour'. (GLSS edited this for publication). Typescript and letters from Sheynin in Moscow re alterations, 1964–5, also published article in *Economic Journal* vol LXXV no. 298, June 1965. Further correspondence with Sheynin in series 9/7 below.

7/11 'Decision theory' (synopsis of a paper for a seminar in Liverpool University, School of Business Management), MS, 13 Apr 1966

7/12 'The nature of economics' MS, 4 Mar 1967

7/13 'Economic theory since the Victorians', MS, 12 Nov 1967

7/14 'The bounds of money' (paper for conference on money, Sheffield), MS and typescript 9 Sep 1970

7/15 'The scope and method of political economy', MS and typescript 26 Jan 1974

7/16 'The Nobel Laureates in Economics', MS and typescript 14 Oct 1974 ('A note invited by the journal *Science*, Washington DC, USA')

7/17 'Is there a logic of uncertainty?' MS Aug 1976 ('15 minute paper for Professor Littlechild's seminar, Birmingham ... MS retained in case of need to compare printed copy' 26 Feb 1978), also typescript

7/18 'Professor Kirzner on entrepreneurship', MS, 22 May 1978 (for Prof. Littlechild's seminar at Birmingham Jun 1978)

7/19 'Opportunity-cost and the concept of focus-outcomes', MS and typescript 22 Oct 1978

7/20 'Harrod as economist', MS and typescript 30 Mar 1981 (is this 2/34 'Shackle on Harrod'?)

7/21 'The unquiet market', typescript, 5 Apr 1981

7/22 Notes for lectures:
  (a) lectures on Keynes at conference at Middlesex Polytechnic in May 1983
  (b) lecture 'Subjectivism' at European University Institute June 1983

7/23 'Decision as a first cause', MS, Mar 1986 ('new chapter for *Expectations in Economics*')

7/24 '*Event* conceived as a tool in decision', MS, 1986 (2 notebooks, and envelope with handwritten drafts and typescript)

7/25 'What did the *General Theory* do?' MS drafts 1987 (6 notebooks; transferred to 2/43/1)

7/26 'Word-efficiency and the economist', MS, Jul 1990 (2 notebooks)

7/27 'Formal systems and the process of history', MS drafts n.d. (4 notebooks)

7/28 'The origination of choice' and 'The *essentially vague* in economic conceptions' (two drafts of same paper n.d., is this 2/38?)

7/29 'Business decisions', MS, n.d.

7/30 'Expectation and decision', MS, n.d.

7/31 'Plan, profit and surprise', MS, n.d.

7/32 'Chapter: Uncertainty', MS fair copy, n.d.

7/33 'Method in economic theory', MS, n.d.

7/34 article beginning with p. 2: 'The century which followed the Napoleonic War ...' MS, 1979 (is this 'Evolutions of thought in economics', *Banca Nazionale di Lavoro* vol 132 1980?)

7/35–60 Rough drafts, notes, incomplete or discarded papers (Numbered arbitrarily and not listed):
  35–57 separate notebooks
  58–60 bundles of loose pages etc.

7/– Miscellaneous drafts, jottings, unpublished articles etc., deposited 1995 (box 30)

8 MISCELLANEOUS (boxes 14–17, 29)

8/1   Book illustrations: 'photographs of the ψ-surface model, diagrams of Decision, Order and Time, and like material ... 19 April 1967' (box file)

8/2   A table of work in progress, June 1961, and list of books planned 1967/8

8/3   Reports on MSS for editors and publishers 1963–66 (envelope)

8/4   University Bookshop, Liverpool University: list of books written by staff members 1969.

8/5   Papers for degree examinations in Economics, of several Universities, which include questions on Shackle's theories, 1950s.

8/6   Notes or article: 'The need for a means, other than frequency-ratio probability, for measuring or describing uncertainty'. (MS with envelope cover postmarked Nov 1950.)

8/7   'Economics involving time. 3rd year lecture no. 3, 19 Oct 1962'.

8/8   'Scheme for course on Decision, Pittsburgh, winter trimester 1967'.

8/9   The New University of Ulster: Congregation for the conferment of degrees 4-5 July 1974 (Hon. Doctorate for GLSS) (printed booklet)

8/10   Citation for presentation of Honorary Degree to GLSS by University of Birmingham (typescript), with covering letter from Registrar W. R. G. Lewis 14 July 1978.

8/11   Biographical article: 'Notes on an Economic Querist: G. L. S. Shackle', by G. C. Harcourt, in *Journal of Post Keynesian Economics*, Fall 1981, vol IV no. 1.

8/12   Correspondence with C. A. Furth 1961
8/12/1–6 Letters to and from C. A. Furth of Messr Allen & Unwin Ltd, Jan-Apr 1961, about possible books that Shackle might write; includes synopses by GLSS of several projected books, and comments on the marketability of these by CAF.

8/13   *Metroeconomica* vol XI, Fasc.I-II, Apr–Aug 1959, 'A symposium on Shackle's theory of decision'.

8/14–55 Miscellaneous pamphlets (mostly by others).

8/56–104 Pamphlets collected by GLSS on theme of 'expectation in economics' and listed by him (see SB 30/3), formerly in six box files (five bundles with lists, one without list).

8/105–150 Books and journals by other authors, with annotations by GLSS. Presented by Mrs C. Shackle through Prof. S. F. Frowen Feb 1993, with lists. No access, except by permission of Prof. Frowen).

8/– Lectures for Queen's University, Belfast 1969-1971 (box 29)

9 CORRESPONDENCE (boxes 18-28)

Shackle divided his correspondence into two main categories: the first he called 'ee letters', that is, letters on *Expectation in Economics* and its sequels, 'which has been my predominant field of interest' (memo 1965, SB/30/5). These form three series of incoming letters 1949-1977 (9/1–3), and a series of outgoing letters 1973–1977 (9/4).

The second category is 'letters diverse' that is, 'all other letters which I have specially valued'. Of these there are two main series 1951–1982 (9/7–8) and two separate and smaller series, containing some earlier letters (9/5–6) (all incoming).

Letters for the years 1982–1985 (plus some earlier material) are listed in three separate and overlapping sequences (9/9–11), the distinction between them being unclear — possibly one may be further 'ee letters'. There are also copies of outgoing letters c.1980–1987 (9/12), with a 1983 note by GLSS that he had hoped to put these in 'some systematic arrangement, but this undertaking now seems too much for me' (his eyesight was failing).

The final series of letters (9/13) was deposited after Shackle's death, and consists of files of incoming and outgoing letters, arranged alphabetically by name of writer.

The incoming letters are numbered chronologically within each series (for 9/13 the files are numbered), and each series has its own list. Where outgoing letters are interfiled, they are numbered as appendages (a, b etc.) to the letters to which they relate. The two sequences of outgoing letters are not numbered or listed.

'ee' letters 1949–1977

9/1	1949–1967	(letters 1–463)	with list	(box 18)
9/2	1967–1973	(letters 1–135)	with list	(box 19)
9/3	1973–1977	(letters 1–274)	with list	(box 19)
9/4	1973–1977	(outgoing letters, not numbered or listed)		(box 19)

Letters diverse 1938–1982

9/5	1938–1948	(letters 1–12)	with list	(box 20)
9/6	1949–1954	(letters 2–79)	with list	(box 20)
9/7	1951–1970	(letters 1–726)	with list	(box 20)
9/8	1971–1982	(letters 1–344)	with list	(box 21)

General correspondence 1982–1987

9/9	1982–1985	(letters 1–177)	with list	(box 21)
9/10	1982–1983	(letters 1–158)	with list	(box 21)
9/11	1978–1984	(letters 1–13)	with list	(box 21)
9/12	1980–1987	(outgoing letters, not numbered or listed)		(box 22)

Correspondence files c.1977–1992

9/13	c.1977–1992	(files 1–33 A–H)	with list	(box 23)
		(files 34–62 I–P)	with list	(box 24)
		(files 63-90 R–W)	with list	(box 25)

Correspondence with Cambridge University Press
1965-1973 (box 26)

Miscellaneous correspondence

(not listed), includes small box of corresp. about article 'Twenty Years on' (3/21) (boxes 27–28)

INDEX OF CORRESPONDENTS

This is a cumulative index to the letters to Shackle in series 1–13. The references are to the series, not to the individual letter; thus it is necessary to go from the reference '9/7' to the list of letters for series 7, which is filed with the letters. There may be one or many letters from the named person in any series.

Arrow, Prof Kenneth J.	Stanford Univ., CA/	
	Harvard Univ.	9/1, 2, 6
Arthur, Doreen	Liverpool Univ. (Admin.)	9/7
Ash, Peter	Temple, London	9/7
Aubrey, Henry G.	New York,	
	Federal Reserve Bank	9/1
Auspitz, Dr Josiah L.	New York, Sabre	
	Foundation	9/13
Austin, Prof R. G.	Liverpool Univ.	9/7
Avison, David	Leicester Univ.	9/7
Baba, Masao	Kyoto, Japan	9/7
Babcock, Henry A.	Los Angeles, CA	9/6
Bagiotti, Tullio	Milan, *Rivista Internazionale*	9/7
Baker, Martin	Cambridge University Press	9/9
Banca Nazionale Del Lavoro	(Periodical) See Also Ceriani	9/8
Barker, J R	Dundee Univ., (Library)	9/7
Barnes, Sarah (Mrs W.)	Liverpool	9/7
Barnes, Winston H. F.	Liverpool Univ.	
	(Vice-Chancellor)	9/7
Barry, Richard	Mallow , Eire	9/7
Bartley, William	Freiburg Im Breisgau	9/9
Baumol, William J.	Princeton Univ.	9/1, 7
Bausor, Randall	Amherst, Univ. Of Mass./	
	Cambridge	9/9, 13
Beaugrand, Philippe	Paris / Togo	9/9, 10
Bedwell, Dr W. L.	Billingham, Co. Durham	9/1
Beltran, Lucas	Madrid	9/3, 8, 9,
		10, 13
Bier, Willem	Washington, International	
	Monetary Fund	9/9
Black, R. D. Collison	Belfast, Queen's Univ.	9/2, 3, 7, 8,
		9
Blandy, Richard	Adelaide, S. Australia	9/1, 7, 8
Blatt, John	Jerusalem/Kensington, NSW	9/9, 13
Blaug, Prof Mark	London Univ. Institute of	
	Education	9/9, 10
Boettinger, Henry	New York (A.T.& T.)/	9/1, 2, 3, 7,
	Cornwall	8, 10, 13
Böhm, Prof Stephan	Graz Univ., Austria	9/9, 13

	Univ.	9/8, 10, 13
Burchnall, H. H.	Liverpool Univ., Registrar	9/3, 7, 8
Burns, Prof Arthur L.	Princeton Univ.	9/1
Burns, Tom	Edinburgh Univ.	9/1
Butchart, J. D.	Monash Univ. (Registrar)	9/8
Butt, David Bensusan	Cabinet Office/Canberra	9/1, 3
Buxton, Richenda	Cambridge University Press	9/9
Byrne, J. J.	Dublin, Trinity College	9/7
Cadman, David	Reading Univ.	9/8, 10
Cairncross, Sir Alec	Glasgow Univ.	9/7
Cambridge University Library		
	(Photography Dept)	9/10
Caro, Gaspare De	Rome, *Enciclopedia Italiana*	9/8
Carr, J. L.	Reading Univ.	9/1
Cartea, M. J.	Reading Univ. / Chicago	9/3
Carter, Sir Charles	Camb/Belfast/Manchester/	9/1, 2, 6, 7,
	Lancaster	8, 9, 13
Carvalho, Fernando	Piscataway, NJ	9/13
Ceriani, Luigi	Rome, Banca Nazionale Del	
	Lavoro	9/8, 9, 10
Chambers, R. J.	Sydney Univ.	9/3
Champernowne, David	*The Economic Journal*	9/2, 3, 8
Chand, Mahesh	Allahabad	9/8, 11
Chase, Richard X.	Univ. of Vermont	9/3
Chick, Victoria	University College, London	9/3, 9, 10,
		13
Church, Barbara	Secretary to B. Kierstead	9/1, 7
Cleaver, Dr K.	Liverpool University	9/13
Coats, Prof A. W. (Bob)	Nottingham Univ./Duke	
	University, Durham, NC	9/9, 10
Coddington, Alan	Queen Mary College, London	9/2, 3, 7, 8,
		13
Cohen, John	Manchester Univ.	9/1, 2, 7
Cohen, Ruth	Cambridge, Newnham College	9/7
Collard, Prof David	Bath Univ.	9/9
Cordy, John K.	Oxford University Press	9/3
Corry, Bernard	London, Queen Mary College	9/7
Courakis, A. S. ('Tony')	Oxford, Institute of Econ./	
	Brasenose College	9/3, 8

Drever, James	Dundee Univ. (Principal)	9/7
Dubois, Prof Didier	Toulouse (article and GLSS to)	9/13
Dumbell, Stanley	Liverpool Univ. (Registrar)	9/7
Duncan, David C.	London, Inst. of Industrial Psychology	9/1
Duncan, Prof G. A.	Dublin, Trinity College (Bursar)	9/7
Dunlop, W. R.	London	9/1, 6, 7
Earl, Peter	Stirling/Tasmania Univs	9/8, 10, 13
Eason, E. K.	Blackrock, Co. Dublin	9/6
Eastham, Kenneth	World Association for Advancement of Science	9/7
Eatwell, John	Cambridge, *Contributions to Political Economy*	9/9
Ebeling, Richard	New York	9/8
Eccleshare, Colin F.	Cambridge University Press	9/1, 6, 8
Edwards, Prof Richard	Amherst, Univ. of Massachussetts	9/9
Egerton, R. Ansell	Belfast, Queen's Univ./ London	9/1, 7, 8
Eleftheriou, T.	Athens (and see J. Ford)	9/7
Elliott, Keith	Liverpool	9/7
Eltis, Walter	Oxford, Exeter College	9/10
Emblem, L. F.	Cairo/Mombasa/Addis Ababa	9/1, 7
Epton, S. R.	Whitby, South Wirral	9/8
Evans, E. V.	London School of Economics	9/6
Fagan, Elmer D	Stanford Univ., CA	9/7
Fair, Frank	Huntsville, Texas, Sam Houston Univ.	9/8
Fairhurst, D. W.	Liverpool Univ. (Student)	9/7
Farebrother, R. W.	Manchester Univ.	9/8
Fareed, Prof Q. M.	Karachi Univ.	9/7
Farmiloe, T. M.	Macmillan (Publishers)	9/2, 9, 10, 11
Farrar, Kathleen R.	Manchester, Brit. Soc. for History of Science	9/1
Favereau, Olivier	Université Du Maine, France	9/9

Hetherington, Carrie	Oxford Publishing Services	9/8
Hey, John	York Univ. (UK)	9/8
Heyn-Johnson, Carsten	Aalborg Univ., Denmark	9/9
Hicks, Sir John R.	Blockley, Glos	9/8, 13
Hicks, Lady Ursula	(Obituary, with Sir J.Hicks)	9/13
Higgins, Benjamin	Djakarta, National Planning Bureau	9/1
Hillebrandt, Patricia	London, University College	9/1, 2, 3
Hillmann, H. C.	Leeds Univ.	9/7
Hirshleifer, Jack	Santa Monica/Los Angeles, CA	9/1, 3
Hitch, Charles J.	Malibu, CA	9/1
Hockley, G. C.	Cardiff, University College	9/3
Hodgkiss, A. G.	Liverpool Univ.	9/7
Hodgson, Geoffrey	Birmingham/Uppsala	9/13
Hooker, John J.	Washington, Catholic Univ of America	9/7
Hopkin, Brian	Aberthin, Cowbridge, Glam.	9/3, 8
Hotson, Prof J. H.	Waterloo University, Canada	9/3
Hoult, C. B.	Nathan, Brisbane, Griffith Univ.	9/8
Houthakker, H. S.	Cambridge, Dept of Applied Economics	9/1
Howkins, John	Keele Univ.	9/7
Hugh-Jones, Prof E. M.	Keele Univ.	9/1, 7
Hunter, Prof L. C.	Glasgow Univ.	9/8
Hurley, Neil P.	Drongen, Belgium	9/1, 7
Hurt, Ambrosine	London School of Economics	9/9
Ikeda, Sanford	New York, *Austrian Economics Newsletter*	9/10
Indian Institute of Economic Research, Allahabad		9/8, 13
Ingamells, W. J.	Liverpool, Lloyds Bank	9/1, 7
Isbister, John	Santa Cruz, Univ. of California	9/3
Isles, K. S.	Belfast, Queen's Univ.	9/6
Ivens, Michael	London, Aims of Industry	9/10
Jaffé, William	Toronto, York Univ.	9/2, 3, 8
Jain, Prof P. C.	Allahabad Univ.	9/2, 8

Kermode, Graham	Liverpool (Student)	9/7
Keynes, John Maynard	Tilton And Bloomsbury	9/5
Khamei, Prof Anvar	Kinshasa, Université Lovanium	9/2
Khan, Prof Shakoor	Bhopal, India, Saifia College	9/7
Kibbe, Prof Matthew	George Mason Univ., VA	9/13
Kidd, Franklin	Cambridge	9/7
Killoch, M. G.	Usa (A.T.& T.), to H. Boettinger	9/3
Kingsford, Anthony L.	Cambridge University Press	9/1
Kinsman, K.	Cardiff, University of Wales	9/6
Kirzner, Prof Israel	New York Univ.	9/9, 13
Klein, Lawrence R.	Newport, RI/Univ. of Michigan	9/1, 7
Köhler, Walter	Freiburg Im Breisgau	9/1, 7
Kojima, Kiyoshi	Bramhope, nr Leeds	9/1, 7
Kontos, Donna	Pittsburgh Univ. (Admin)	9/7
Kornai, János	Budapest, Hungarian Academy of Sciences	9/3
Körner, Prof Stephan	Bristol	9/1
Koslowski, Dr Peter	Munich	9/9
Kravis, Irving B.	Philadelphia, Univ. of Pennsylvania	9/7
Kregel, Prof J. A.	Groningen, Netherlands	9/3, 8, 9, 10, 11, 13
Krelle, Prof W.	St Gallen/Bonn Univ.	9/1
Krishnaswamy, K. S.	London (of N. R. Mohalla, Mysore)	9/6
Kristol, Irving	New York, Editor *The Public Interest*	9/8
Kristy, James E.	Buena Park, CA	9/8
Krüsselberg, Hans-Günter	Cologne/Marburg (Lahn) Univs	9/1, 2, 7
Kubinski, Z. M.	Leeds/Achimota, Gold Coast	9/6
Kuper, Dr Jessica	Leiden, Social Sciences Encyclopedia	9/10
Kushwaha, Prof D.S.	Allahabad, Indian Inst of Economic Research	9/9
Kvergic, G. (Mrs)	Gerald Duckworth & Co.	

Macfie, A.L.	Milngavie, near Glasgow	9/1, 7
Mackenzie, W. J. M.	Manchester Univ.	9/1
Macmillan & Co.	London (Publishers)	9/13
Macmillan & Co.	Canada	9/2
Macmillan, Ross	Liverpool Univ. Student	Sb/28, 9/2, 7, 8
Maeyer, E. A. De	Brussels, Editor Who's Who in Europe	9/7
Maggi, Prof Raffaello	Bologna Univ.	9/1, 7
Makower, Helen	London School of Economics	9/2, 6
Malach, V. W.	Royal Military Coll. of Canada	9/1, 7
Malmgren, Harald B	Oxford, Nuffield College	9/1, 7
Maroth, Frederick	Eugene, Oregon Univ.	9/7
Mars, John	Manchester Univ.	9/1, 6, 7
Marschak, J.	Chicago	9/7
Massé, P.	Paris, French National Electricity	9/7
Mathieu-Nicot, Bernadette	Dijon Univ.	9/9, 10
Matthews, Robert	Kingston Polytechnic	9/8
Mayer, Jacques	Paris, Institute of Applied Economics	9/6
Mays, W.	Manchester Univ.	9/1
Mcavinchey, Ian D.	Belfast	9/7
Mccubbins, Ronald Wayne	Blacksburg, Virginia Polytechnic Inst.	9/7
Mcdowell, Moore	Dublin, University College	9/2
McGregor, Peter	Glasgow, Strathclyde Univ.	9/9
Mcguigan, John	Philadelphia, Univ. of Pennsylvania Press	9/8
Mclelland, Prof W. G.	Manchester Business School	9/1
Mcmanus, Maurice	Univ. Of Minnesota	9/1
Mcnutt, Paddy	Galway, Univ. College	9/9
Meade, James E.	London School of Economics	9/7
Meenan, James	Dublin, University College	9/3, 7
Mehta, Prof J. K.	Allahabad Univ.	9/1, 2, 3, 7, 8
Meier, G. M.	Stanford Univ., CA	9/7
Melhuish, George	Bristol	9/1

Newsom, Christopher	London, Longmans Green & Co	9/7
Nicholson, Michael B.	Manchester Univ/Univ Coll, Lond	9/1, 7
Niehans, Prof Jürg	Erlenbach	9/1
Niekirk, Paul	London, Longmans Green & Co	9/7
O'Brien, Conor Cruise	Dublin	9/9
O'Brien, Prof Denis P.	Durham Univ/Queen's Univ Belfast	9/3, 7, 8, 9, 10, 13
O'Brien, George	Dublin	9/7
O'Connor, D. J.	Keele, Univ. Coll of N. Staffs	9/6
O'Kane, John Gerard	Liverpool University Press	9/1, 2, 7, 13
Ohlin, Bertil	Stockholm	9/3
Ollmann, Peter	Hamburg	9/7
Ortiz, Sutti	Cleveland, OH	9/3
Ostraat, Inger	Oslo	9/6
Oxlade, P. C.	Woolwich Polytechnic	9/7
Ozga, S. A.	London School of Economics	9/1, 7
Page, Richard C.	Canterbury, Kent University	9/3
Palander, Prof Tord	Uppsala	9/7
Palomba, Giuseppe	Naples, Academia Nazionale Dei Lincei	9/3
Paris–X (University)	(Seminar, GLSS paper for)	9/13
Parkes, Don	Newcastle Univ., NSW	9/3
Patinkin, Don	Jerusalem	9/13
Peacock, Prof Alan T.	York Univ. / London	9/2, 7
Peck, Olwen	'Woodlands'	9/9
Pen, Prof Jan	's-Gravenhage/Groningen	9/1, 7
Pengelly, Kenneth	Goudhurst, Bethany School (Head)	9/7
Pereira Da Silva, A.	Sao Paulo, Brazil	9/13
Perkins, G. S.	London, Lloyds Bank	9/7
Perlman, Mark	Pittsburgh, PA, Univ.	9/1, 2, 3, 7, 8, 9, 10, 11, 13
Perrin, J. R.	Nottingham/Lancaster Univs	9/7
Peters, Alan	London, Shell Centre	9/10
Petit, Michel	Paris	9/2

Steel, Robert W	Liverpool Univ.	9/7
Steiner, Hillel	Manchester Univ.	9/8
Stephen, Frank	Glasgow, Univ. of Strathclyde	9/8, 9, 10, 13
Stevenson, D. Lang	Ilford / Redbridge, Essex	9/1, 8
Stevenson, R. C.	Liverpool Univ.	9/7
Stockfisch, Jacob A.	Kansas City/Los Angeles/ Wisconsin	9/1, 7
Strain, Michael	Worcester	9/8, 9
Strathclyde University	Glasgow (Hon D.Litt for GLSS)	9/13
Streeten, Paul	Oxford/Univ. of Wisconsin	9/1
Streissler, Dr E	Vienna, Univ.	9/1
Stubbings, B. J. W.	Liverpool, Ministry of Education	9/7
Studart, Rogerio	London	9/13
Sugden, Robert	Newcastle upon Tyne Univ.	9/10
Supian, B. H. A.	York (of Kuala Lumpur)	9/8
Supper, Dr Meinhard	Vienna (Hayek's 90th Birthday)	9/13
Sutherland, Alvern H.	Washington, Federal Reserve System	9/7
Svennilson, Ingvar	Stockholm Univ.	9/7
Swanson, Dr Earl	Ames, Iowa State College (GLSS to)	9/13
Sypher, Wylie	Auburndale, MA	9/1
Szasz, André	Amsterdam	9/7
Tanzer, William	Wellington, New Zealand	9/1
Tarullo, Ronald	Pittsburgh Univ., PA	9/7
Taschdjian, Dr Edgar	New York	9/3, 13
Tempest, Norton	Liverpool Univ.	9/7
Tennant, Brian S.	Bromley, Kent	9/7
Thewis, Patricia E.	Leeds	9/6
Thirlby, G. F.	London School of Economics	9/6
Thirlwall, Prof A. P. (Tony)	Canterbury, Univ. of Kent	9/2, 8
Thomas, D. R. (Roy)	Cardiff, Univ. College	9/7
Thomas, J. J.	London School of Economics, Economica	9/7

NAME INDEX

419

SUBJECT INDEX

SUBJECT INDEX